The
Families
Who
Made
Rome

ANTHONY MAJANLAHTI

The Families Who Made Rome

A HISTORY AND A GUIDE

CHATTO & WINDUS
LONDON

For Madeleine
and in memory of Nicholas Boas

Published by Chatto & Windus 2005

2 4 6 8 6 10 9 7 5 3 1

Copyright © Anthony Majanlahti 2005

Anthony Majanlahti has asserted his right under the Copyright, Designs
and Patents Act, 1988 to be identified as the author of this work

First published in Great Britain in 2005 by Chatto & Windus
Random House, 20 Vauxhall Bridge Road, London SW1V 2SA

Random House Australia (Pty) Limited
20 Alfred Street, Milsons Point, Sydney, New South Wales 2061, Australia

Random House New Zealand Limited
18 Poland Road, Glenfield, Auckland 10, New Zealand

Random House (Pty) Limited
Endulini, 5A Jubilee Road, Parktown 2193, South Africa

The Random House Group Limited Reg. No. 954009
www.randomhouse.co.uk

A CIP catalogue record for this book is available from the British Library

ISBN 0 7011 7687 3

Papers used by Random House are natural, recyclable products made
from wood grown in sustainable forests; the manufacturing processes conform
to the environmental regulations of the country of origin

Printed and bound in Great Britain by William Clowes Ltd, Beccles, Suffolk

Contents

List of Maps and Plans

Foreword

I first visited Italy in 1959 on vacation from Cambridge, the start of a continuing love affair with that country. I saw Rome briefly then, and can still remember the astonishing impact of entering the city by the piazza del Popolo, the traditional route for pilgrims from the north. After I fell in love with Rome and began to get to know it properly I came to think that it is by far the most fascinating and beautiful city in the world; there is some merit in the eighteenth-century view that nobody can be considered properly educated who has not been to Rome, at least in his or her imagination.

It occurred to me a few years ago that, among the many books I'd read about Rome, what was missing was one which painted a picture of the great families, such as the Colonna, Barberini, Chigi, and others, whose names and crests visitors come across all the time. I started thinking about writing such a book when I retired, but then one evening, dining in the courtyard of the British School at Rome, I found myself sitting next to Anthony Majanlahti, a scholar researching the archives of the English College. I quickly realized that he had an extraordinary passion for Rome and already knew almost everything I wanted to research. For the last couple of years my wife Elisabeth and I have assisted him to write this book. We have enjoyed many walks round Rome with him and spent many hours discussing what should be included and what had sadly to be left out. I hope it will come to be seen as an essential book for the traveller to Rome making a physical or mental journey to this ancient city.

J.R.S. Boas
London, February, 2005

Acknowledgements

When I fell into conversation at dinner with an English couple one summer evening in 2001 at the British School at Rome, I never imagined it would result in a three-year project. Bob and Elisabeth Boas and I found we shared a mutual interest in the history of Roman families, and the following day they generously offered their support if I would write a book on the subject.

In writing this book, I crossed paths with people who taught me things I didn't know and corrected me when I was wrong, which was often. Foremost is the brilliant Helen Langdon, whose friendship and deep knowledge of Roman art history were alike essential to me. Xavier Salomon carefully read through different drafts of the manuscript. Mark Lewis, S.J., assisted me with the history of the Jesuits. The friendly staff of the Biblioteca Casanatense were instrumental in obtaining the illustrations. I've also been lucky in my editor, Jenny Uglow, whose sharp critical eye has made this book immeasurably better, and whose kindness has seen me through many a difficulty.

This project was, in large part, made possible by the assistance of the British School at Rome and its director, Andrew Wallace-Hadrill. Through the School I met my closest collaborator, Cathy Hawley, whose elegant maps are such a feature of this book. Academically I owe a debt to the late Richard Krautheimer for his work on Alexander VII, Carolyn Vallone for what she taught me about women's patronage of art, Eamon Duffy for his history of the popes, Robert Coates-Stephens for his knowledge of Roman archaeology, John Varriano for his books on literary Rome and Baroque architecture, Robert Brentano for casting light on the medieval Colonna, Patricia Waddy and J. Beldon Scott for their work on Roman palaces, and Joseph Connors, whose work on urban design in seventeenth-century Rome was, more than any other single source, the inspiration of much of what follows.

Many of my friends have, over the past three years, been subjected to impromptu lectures and occasional research tours: thanks to the knowledgeable and enthusiastic Gregory Bailey in particular, and to Gail, Jennifer, Paul, Piero, Rachel, Sophie, and my online friends at worldcrossing.com. For personal support I could not have done without Tom Desmond, who provided a voice of love and reason through thick and thin. Thanks too to the Wallace-Hadrills, Jo, Andrew, Sophie, and Michael, who have been a second family to me. My parents, my sister Tina and her husband Duncan, as well as my friends Francesco and Alex in Toronto, have encouraged and supported me in every way. In the best tradition of Roman nepotism, this book is dedicated to my niece Madeleine.

My deepest thanks go to Bob Boas. His was the idea that germinated into this book, and it only did so through his kind encouragement and generous financial support, including the use of his family's beautiful apartment in central Rome for the duration of the writing process. Bob, my closest reader, has edited and error-checked the text from start to finish. He and his wife Elisabeth gave me not only the opportunity of a lifetime, but also their affection and friendship. I join with them in the hope that this book will give visitors and readers a fresh look at the fascinating palimpsest that is Rome, and the families who made and remade it in their own image.

Anthony Majanlahti
Rome, October 2004

Perhaps one should say that there are two historical Romes: one, the plasticine city that classical scholars re-created, or created, particularly in the nineteenth century, a city of vast colonnades, perfect arches, perfect hexameters, stretching into that unbearable dullness that provoked orgy, murder, and satire; the other, the broken city, the foundation for new things to be broken in their turn – with the lovers in each house among these ruins dreaming in part the dreams of their predecessors, all hopelessly interwoven, like their houses, with their own.

Robert Brentano, *Rome before Avignon*

Introduction: the broken city

I am sitting at a tiny round table outside a caffè in piazza Navona. It is early May, just as the warm weather has begun, and my cappuccino is steaming in front of me as I have a look around. I try to concentrate on the place, with difficulty looking past the strolling Romans, the tourists, the pilgrims with their yellow kerchiefs and the usual array of Navona life: vendors, mimes and musicians. The lengthy oblong of the piazza is measured out in blocks of colour – blue, ochre, yellow, white – and across its width, behind the spray from the huge Fountain of the Four Rivers with its obelisk, a white church with dome and twin bell towers rears up, flanked to right and left by buildings in a similar grey-blue. To the left is a huge noble residence and to the right is its partial reflection, another residence, less grand. Though the piazza is built on the foundations of an ancient stadium and was the site of an important market in the Middle Ages, almost everything I'm looking at now is linked in one way or another to a noble family of the seventeenth century – one of the families who made Rome. I try to step back mentally to the piazza Navona of the Middle Ages, to picture it without the stamp of the family that ordered its redevelopment: no palace, no great church, no central fountain, just grim fortress-like buildings, low houses and ruins, mud and straw. It is hard to imagine and I take refuge in a sip of coffee.

We tend to think of Rome's history as a continuity, but this diminishes the alterations of time. There was no predestined path from ancient Rome to the city we see today: modern Rome is only the great-great-great-grandchild, at best, of its ancient predecessor. The city was continually inhabited, true. But its post-classical population was a fraction of its ancient peak and its memories of greatness were vague.

By the year 1300 the ancient city of colonnades and arches lay shattered and buried in the mud left by the Tiber floods, and a quite different city had taken its place. It would appear almost unrecognisable to our eyes. Indeed, 'city' might be the wrong word for the collection of settlements scattered around the great churches. The majority of Romans lived by the riverside towards the Vatican, all within the ancient walls which contained fewer houses than uninhabited land given over to pasturage and vineyards. Poor, crumbling, depopulated, the medieval town huddled into the lowlands of the Tiber bend where at least water was plentiful. It had two notable physical elements: towers and ruins.

In this engraving by Etienne Dupérac, the great Torre delle Milizie (background) looms over the ruins of the temple of Antoninus and Faustina in the Forum.

Like broken bones, memorials of the ancient world poked up through the mud, well beyond repair, incomprehensible fragments of a lost urban anatomy. Much was forgotten, even the name of the Roman Forum, which became the *Campo Vaccino*, the Cow Field, and the Capitol, the heart of the ancient state cults, was known as *Monte Caprino* (Goat Hill). Large chunks of the ancient city obtruded even into the built-up medieval centre, around the great church of Santa Maria Rotonda, the Pantheon. The ruined sub-structures of the imperial palaces clambering up the Palatine hill were used as storage and as pens for livestock. Out of nearly every new building, particularly buildings of note, poked pieces of old cornice and entablature; old monumental inscriptions were used as tomb slabs; marbles too small to build with became veneers for church floors.

The towers of medieval Rome must have made an equally strong impression. They were thicker on the ground than their surviving examples suggest; the poet Joachim du Bellay, writing in the sixteenth century, called Rome a city *'couronnée de tours'* (crowned with towers). Those that still survive stand as powerful testimony to the dominant social force of medieval life: the local nobility, the barons of Rome. A maze of streets, some running along the course of ancient ones, wove between the towers, the houses of artisans, the fortress-like monasteries and the mansions of clerics. This was the landscape of Rome in 1300.

Four centuries later it resembled the magnificent capital we know today – and the people who built it were the great noble Roman families. This book follows their story and lets us see how the old town gradually transformed, expanded and transformed again as different families rose and fell in power, spending their huge wealth on palaces and churches, streets and piazze. Extravagant characters, wild ambitions and sudden tragedies are built into the map of Rome; the theatrical quality of Roman history is reflected in the theatrical design of the city, explicitly remade as it was, again and again, to tell a story. The buildings of piazza Navona are trying to tell us something. To understand what they are saying, though, we need to confront the history of the city.

The most vital fact, which set Rome apart from any other, was that this was the province of the pope. Noble families vied to get their members made cardinal, a member of the papal electoral college and then pope, because once they reached that office they had access to almost limitless funds and influence. For 400 years successive popes showered wealth and lands upon their relatives, exalting them from sometimes humble origins to become dukes and princes, who clung on to their power long after their pope had vanished for ever. These nobles expressed their pride, their interests, their ambitions and their piety in the buildings and artwork they commissioned.

Such commissions cost a great deal of money. Though land was at the base of most noble fortunes and banking created the wealth of others, key positions at the papal court were even more lucrative. Members of the court could be immensely rich and, since many of the figures in the chapters that follow had positions in the papal administration, a look at the 'pope's men' might be helpful.

To begin with, the pope was bishop of Rome. He appointed a vicar or substitute to administer his local diocese. As a tribute to his Roman power base, his cardinals were each traditionally given a Roman church as their *titulus* or titular church (reflecting an old tradition that the bishop of Rome was elected by a council of Roman parish priests). These titular churches were natural focuses of building efforts by different cardinals. Until the sixteenth-century Council of Trent forbade the practice, cardinals (and, indeed, other prelates) generally held numerous bishoprics and arch-bishoprics as well as wealthy abbacies. Members of this cardinalate class could function as diplomats and administrators, but they were, first and foremost, princes of the Church.

The papal bureaucracy was mainly priestly, though there were a few secular posts, the principal one being that of captain-general of the Roman Church, the head of the pontifical army. The castellan of the pontifical fortress, the Castel Sant' Angelo, was generally a layman, and so were the small cadre of church lawyers, consistorial advocates. However, the great administrative positions, which brought the largest income and the greatest power, were reserved for priests. The most important of these was the *cardinal nipote* (cardinal nephew), virtually a secretary of state; as the title indicates, the office was reserved for a papal relative. His role varied with each pope, but could be vital, especially in foreign affairs and the government of the Papal States.

Other positions were almost as important. The *camerlengo* (chamberlain) controlled the *Camera Apostolica* (Treasury) and was in charge of financial policy and taxation and he appointed almost all his subordinates except the *tesoriere* (treasurer) himself, a papal appointee. The Chancery, where papal decrees or bulls were written up and legal disputes settled, was under the control of the *vice-cancelliere* (vice-chancellor). Below the vice-chancellor, a position appointed for life, was the *datario* (papal datary), one of the hardest-working officers, whose job was nominally to put the dates on papal bulls. In fact, he was in charge of the scriptors, the writers of bulls and the abbreviators, who summarised the bulls for the general record, as well as the *protonotario apostolico* (chief legal clerk). A papal judiciary existed, to judge court cases from all over Christendom. The last department was the penitentiary, headed by the *gran penitenziario* (grand penitentiary). This was responsible for ecclesiastical punishments like excommunications, and reconciliations following penance. In addition, the three great churches of St Peter's, San Giovanni in Laterano and Santa Maria Maggiore all had *archipreti* (archpriests) who performed various liturgical functions, often in the pope's stead. Rome itself was ruled by a governor, appointed by the pope, and the ordinary municipal government was left to the chief city officials, the *conservatori*, generally nobles.

Until 1870 the pope also ruled the Papal States, which stretched diagonally across central Italy. He governed in one of two ways, either directly, through governors or legates, or with noble intermediaries who ruled territories as hereditary *signori* (lords), on his behalf. Occasionally, the pope would unseat a family from its hereditary signory and impose a governor on it. At other times he would insert his own family into a territory as rulers. These experiments met with uneven success, as we shall see.

The wealth that these positions generated is hard for us to grasp in modern terms, all the more so because the currency changed in value and denomination over the centuries. From the late fifteenth century until 1530, the principal papal coinage was the ducat, the 'gold ducat of the Chamber', equivalent to its predecessor, the gold florin. In 1530, Clement VII de' Medici introduced a new coin, the gold scudo. The ducat, the florin and the scudo were all more or less equivalent in value. But what does that mean? A typical annual wage should provide a context: a schoolteacher or parson might make 25 ducats annually in the early sixteenth century: by contrast, Don Camillo Pamphilj in the 1650s gave 60,000 scudi for the construction of Sant' Andrea al Quirinale – equal to two years' tax income for an entire city in the Papal States.

Century by century, Roman families changed the urban map. Fourteenth-century barons needed their towers and fortresses for security, especially as the papacy had moved its seat to Avignon in 1309 and did not return until 1378, after which a rival pope set up court in Avignon, opening the Great Schism. The following period was one of the harshest since the fall of the ancient empire: the economy, fragile and dependent on the pope, collapsed in his absence, while wars ravaged the Roman countryside and the city itself. Food supplies were scarce and public order was a remote dream.

Medieval barons like the Cenci, Santacroce, Orsini and Colonna had their way unopposed in the pope's absence; as a fourteenth-century chronicler wrote:

> everywhere lust, everywhere evil, no justice, no law; there was no longer any escape; the man who was strongest with the sword was the most in the right. A person's only hope was to defend himself with the help of his relatives and friends; every day groups of armed men were formed.

Catholic Christendom only reunited in 1417, with a Roman noble, Martin V Colonna, as pope. The restored papacy of the fifteenth century was dead set against the power of the old barons. The two popes of the della Rovere family both strove against the disorder implicit in baronial rule. They provided a role model for future papal families, as they were the first to succeed in carving out a hereditary sovereign domain for themselves from the Papal States, against the background of the Italian Wars (1494–1559). The Farnese of the sixteenth century were the next family to follow their example.

The great families of the seventeenth century, the Borghese, Barberini, Pamphilj and Chigi, focused their attention on splendour rather than sovereignty: instead of conquering and ruling their own territory, their ambitions lay in Rome itself and in its surrounding *campagna*. (Because the history is so complex and the succession of popes can be baffling, this book includes a very short chronology to set the context.) All this time the different families were changing the face of the city, patronising architects and artists, adopting new styles, from Renaissance to Baroque, Rococo to

Neoclassical and giving commissions to the greatest artists – Michelangelo, Raphael, Bernini. Though they could be callous and venal, the Roman nobility were also capable of acts of sincere faith, and to dismiss or ignore that would be to miss a big part of the picture.

The opening chapter describes three walks based on families in a single area of the city, which bring to life certain aspects of the urban landscape and introduce the social world of the Roman aristocracy in the fourteenth century. The Cenci, Santacroce and Mattei families expressed on a smaller scale the same ambitions and desires that motivated their great successors.

This book guides you through the city, but it is written for the armchair traveller as well. Each chapter has two sections. The first tells the history of one family, with its notable characters described in detail. The second is an itinerary of sites related to that family. In general the itineraries do not offer a particular route between monuments, preferring to focus on sites of specific relation to the family in question rather than suggesting a walking tour of a neighbourhood, though sometimes within the itinerary a walking tour may be included. We will sometimes make several visits to the same site, as it returns in the story of successive families. There are surprises in store. Some of the main hubs of power, like piazza San Pietro, are obvious, but few would expect the hidden piazza Santi Apostoli, for example, to play host to so many men of power.

Looking at the map of Rome in this way reveals an alternative history, the story of an urban aristocracy, a patriciate and its effect on the city that it ruled. Rome's apparently confusing street plan is, suddenly, rational and comprehensible: if we can learn its language, we will start to read it as a map not just of streets but of ambitions and dreams, envy and hatred, pride and love. All these emotions are built into the streets and buildings of the city, elaborated in the history of the families who made Rome.

▌ Looking at the city

Giovan Battista Nolli's map of 1748 shows the warren of roads and alleys in the centre of Rome. The street superimposed in bold is the via Papalis, the main papal procession route between the two poles of San Pietro and San Giovanni in Laterano. It was a major focus of urban redesign in the early modern period. Today its main section (passing below piazza Navona) has been replaced by the nineteenth-century corso Vittorio Emanuele II.

> *Rome,* the Queen of Cities, vaunted herself of two myriads of inhabitants; now that all-Commanding Country is possessed by petty Princes, *Rome* a small village in respect.
>
> Robert Burton, *The Anatomy of Melancholy,* 1621

When we look at the Rome of today, we need to remind ourselves that it is hugely different from that of the Rome of the seventeenth century, let alone the fourteenth. We have to train our eyes to filter out the high buildings of later periods if we are to gain a sense of how the city appeared in the past. Not only that, but we also have to imagine a city with only some streets paved, in brick or even wood. We must forget about water pipes bringing drinkable water into the houses and remember that fountains in Rome served a far more important purpose than decoration: the provision of water to the people. We must abandon the idea of cars and street lamps and sewers.

We also have to ignore one of the most characteristic features of Rome, the *palazzo d'affitto*, the apartment building, which sprang up in the late seventeenth and early eighteenth centuries when the population was rising. Previously, noble palaces and workmen's two-storey workshop-dwellings had made up Rome's fifteenth- and sixteenth-century streetscape. The new apartment buildings raised the street profile of the city: for the first time, artisans and merchants could live in buildings as tall as those of the rich. What we see today is a higher and much more uniform streetscape.

Another aspect of Roman city blocks is how frequently they express architectural ambition on the part of different property owners. An owner would construct part of a larger building, then would gradually purchase the site next to it, demolish the house that stood there and enlarge his own. This process was frequently interrupted by lack of funds, an intransigent neighbour, or the death of the ambitious proprietor, with the result that Rome is a city of half-built houses: the key to identifying them is the distinctive serrated edge that can often be seen running up the side of a building. One example is palazzo Mattei di Paganica in piazza dell' Enciclopedia Italiana. The palace looms over a fifteenth-century house next door; its rough unfinished divide, left so the new part of the façade could be butted into the old one, resembles nothing so much as a set of teeth, preparing to devour its neighbour. The art historian Joseph Connors, regarding this aspect of Roman streets, refers to the 'fundamental unneighbourliness' of the city's buildings. These greedy, expansionist façades with their jagged edges also play their part in giving Rome its appearance of a broken city.

One way of thinking about

The jagged edge of palazzo Mattei di Paganica. Behind the sign for the Enciclopedia Italiana lurk the menacing teeth of an advancing façade, closing in on the smaller building.

Rome is in terms of its different subdivisions. In the Middle Ages, Rome was divided into different administrative regions or *rioni*, successors of the regions of the city decreed by Augustus in the first century BC. The first *rione* was called Monti (hills) and covered the higher land within the walls, perhaps a third of the whole area. Since population determined the boundaries of *rioni*, we can see once again that the medieval inhabitants had largely abandoned the area of the ancient centre in order to concentrate on the Tiber bend. There were thirteen *rioni*. Most of the population was huddled into the *rioni* of Ponte, Parione, Regola, Sant'Angelo (where the Jewish ghetto stood), San Eustachio, Pigna and Campitelli, all within the Tiber bend and close to the river bank. Less populous were the *rioni* of Colonna, Campo Marzio and Trevi, which ranged around the eastern flank, while Ripa to the far south and Trastevere on the other side of the river were both bustling mercantile districts. The Borgo in front of St Peter's was added as a fourteenth *rione* later in Rome's history, but for most of the period under consideration it was a separate papal settlement.

Within these subdivisions, however, lurked smaller and more meaningful designations of places. Notably, and unlike many other cities in the medieval period, the parish division was relatively insignificant and, indeed, parish size could expand and contract in response to the increase or decline in numbers of parishioners. Romans of the Middle Ages and later saw their town less in terms of parishes, and of *rioni*, than of neighbourhoods, dominated by local nobles who often gave their name to the area, even in legal documents.

Local authority, as represented by noble families, was commonly expressed in physical terms, as an island (*isola*), a stretch of land (*contrada*), or a hill (*monte*). Three brief walking tours of one area, within the *rioni* Sant'Angelo and Regola, will show how these areas could cluster together and function, displaying a number of standard features.

ITINERARY

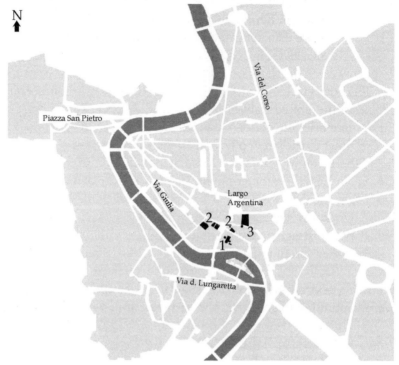

N

Via del Corso

Piazza San Pietro

Via Giulia

Largo
Argentina

2 2 3

1

Via d. Lungaretta

Key: 1. The *monte* of the Cenci   2. The *contrada* of the Santacroce
3. The *isola* of the Mattei

▌ The *monte* of the Cenci
Start: piazza Cenci, off via Arenula

In this visit and the next two, we will be looking primarily at the traces of medieval nobles and the ways in which noble families retained their traditional physical centres long after the Middle Ages were a memory.

A popular poem recalls the emotion generated in the Roman people by their medieval barons. It was dread:

> *Orsin, Colonna, Cenci e Frangipani*
> *Riscuoton oggi e pagano domani.*
> *Più assai che peste, papa, ed Imperiali,*
> *Più a Roma sono assai crudeli e fatali,*
> *Più assai che fame, Galli, e Aragonesi,*
> *Savelli, Orsini, Cenci, e Colonnesi.*

(Orsini, Colonna, Cenci and Frangipani,
They collect today but pay tomorrow.
More than plague, pope and supporters of the Empire,
More, at Rome, are cruel enough and deadly,
More than hunger, the French and the Aragonese,
Savelli, Orsini, Cenci, and Colonna.)

The busy via Arenula, the product of urban redesign after Rome became capital of the united Italy in 1870, is close to the beginning and the end of these three brief introductions to noble families in their urban context. It is a newcomer to the street plan and as it is not really possible to imagine it not being there, ignoring it for the time being would be best. However, **piazza Cenci**, in which we begin, is decidedly older. The Cenci family claimed descent, probably wrongly, from one Marcus Cincius, a Roman whose name we know because he sponsored a law, the *lex Cincia de donis et muneribus*, relating to taxes. The family's confirmed appearance in history began rather later. Pope John X (914–28) was a Cenci; in the eleventh century, Paolo and Bernardo Cenci took part in the First Crusade. The following century saw three cardinals of the family, showing that the Cenci were continuing to engage in the struggle for power in the papal court that

Family building clusters
near the Tiber island,
from the 1748 Nolli map

Key:
1 The *monte* of the Cenci
  I   palazzetto Cenci
  II palazzo Cenci-
      Bolognetti
  III San Tommaso ai
      Cenci

2 The *contrada* of the Santacroce
  I   palazzo Santacroce
  II Santa Maria in Publicolis
  III palazzo Santacroce Pasolini
  IV palazzo del Monte di Pietà
      (ex-palazzo Santacroce)

3 The *isola* of the Mattei
  I   piazza Mattei and the fontana delle Tartarughe
  II palazzo di Giacomo Mattei
  III palazzo Mattei di Giove
  IV palazzo Mattei Caetani
  V palazzo Mattei Paganica

was in large part one for control of Rome. A Cardinal Cenci in 1106 had his family towers here demolished by Pope Calixtus II, because the pope did not consider him a loyal supporter. Indeed, the Cenci, like their more successful peers the Colonna, had the reputation of being generally anti-papal, a tricky but potentially remunerative position. The papacy was sporadically weak and reliant on the military support of the king of France or of the Holy Roman Emperor, and when one or the other of these monarchs fell out with the pope, they offered handsome rewards to Roman nobles who made trouble for the pontiff. Furthermore, the pope's authority in Rome was regularly contested by the nobility; papal absolutism was not a foregone conclusion.

The Cenci were among the bloodiest and most fractious of Rome's medieval barons. One Cenci who was excommunicated by Gregory VII in 1075 kidnapped the pope from the altar of Santa Maria Maggiore, where he was saying Mass, and held him prisoner for a few days in the Cenci fortress in another part of Rome, before the Roman populace rose up to free him. Gregory then went calmly back to Santa Maria Maggiore and completed the service without comment. Another family member, Pietro Cenci, organised a conspiracy against Boniface IX in the fourteenth century.

Standing in piazza Cenci, we see a large palace with a slightly off-kilter eighteenth-century entrance way wedged between two older parts of the building. To our left, too, another palace rises, joined to the first by an arch across the street. This is a cluster of Cenci buildings. The streets around, though their names were formally established only later, reflect their dominance of this neighbourhood: via Monte de' Cenci, via Beatrice Cenci, via dell' arco de' Cenci, piazza Cenci and piazza Monte de' Cenci. Even the nineteenth-century embankment road, the Lungotevere, is named for the family. If the front gates of the palace are open, we may go up the steps and enter; to our right is a large early nineteenth-century vestibule, with a massive staircase and an ancient imperial bust. This room is a testament to the constant reworking of this palace and, by extension, all Roman palaces.

Back outside, our route takes us towards the river, where we turn up the unexpected steep hill of **Monte Cenci**. As the narrow street winds upwards, we pass various remnants of ancient building materials in the walls on both sides, a common feature of Roman buildings. What is this strange hill, rising like a goosebump on the skin of the city? It seems clear that the structures of Monte Cenci are built, like those of Monte Giordano, on the ruins of some ancient building or set of buildings. Archaeological soundings, linked with the surviving fragments of the ancient *Forma Urbis* (a detailed map of the ancient city, commissioned in the late first or early second century AD), have suggested that the hill may be made up of the ruins of various ancient structures, including a warehouse or apartment house and a temple, that of Castor and Pollux, the Gemini or Heavenly Twins. The two statues of these deities that flank the top of the ramp to the Campidoglio were reconstructed from their fragments, found here in the late sixteenth century.

At the top, the street opens into a small piazza, piazza Monte de' Cenci. A restaurant, Piperno, is on the right, while directly in front is a small church, San Tommaso ai Cenci. To our left is the upper entrance of the Cenci palace block, decorated with a broken Gorgon mask of ancient provenance. This entrance commands a view down the street opposite and originally looked directly into the Jewish ghetto, through piazza Giudea, which lay at the bottom of the hill: the ghetto buildings were levelled in the nineteenth century. The wall at right angles to the one with the Gorgon mask reveals a series of successive reworkings: from a fourteenth- or early fifteenth-century tower, it developed into a sixteenth- and seventeenth-century extension to the floor levels of the newer Cenci palace next to it. Thus the original window apertures, small and rectangular, were blocked up, the floors were shifted and new windows were opened. The small white rectangle below one of the upper-floor windows is the obsolete window frame of the original building.

A white plaque on the façade of the church records its completion by Francesco, son of Cristoforo Cenci, in 1575. Cristoforo had been a churchman and Francesco a legitimised son, but the latter remains the family's most famous historical bastard in quite another sense. Francesco was heir to the multiplying Cenci estates, which included a thriving bank business, but squandered his wealth. He married a noblewoman of a neighbouring family, Ersilia Santacroce, and they had twelve children. Several of these died in childhood, but Francesco was a tyrant to them all, one daughter even fleeing to the pope to beg him to marry her to someone in order to get away from her violent father. Ersilia died; Francesco remarried another noblewoman, Lucrezia Petroni, and they lived unhappily here together with Francesco's surviving children Francesco, Giacomo, Cristoforo, Rocco, Beatrice and Bernardo. Francesco, allied with the Colonna family, then obtained the Colonna fief of Petrella Salto, with its castle, to which he transferred his family. His daughter Beatrice (1577–99), who wanted to marry a Colonna retainer, was imprisoned there with her siblings and stepmother. Among the family servants it was whispered that the lord Cenci regularly raped his beautiful young daughter. Francesco's oppressed family decided to take drastic action.

On the night of 9 September 1598, two assassins and some of Beatrice's brothers caught Francesco by surprise in a tower room of the castle, cut his throat and threw his corpse off the balcony, which they damaged to make

'Beatrice Cenci', by 'Guido Reni'. Both subject and author are disputed. Widely diffused in copies, this image caught the Romantic imagination: Shelley, in the preface to *The Cenci* (1819), saw 'a simplicity and dignity' in the portrait which he found 'inexpressibly pathetic'.

the death look accidental – hard, as his head was nearly severed from his body. A blackmail attempt on the part of the hired assassins led to a denunciation of the Cenci brothers and they were put to the torture. During the subsequent trial, in which Francesco's brutality was made famous, sympathy spread for Beatrice and her brothers. However, the pope, Clement VIII Aldobrandini (1592–1605), took the view that parricide must be punished by death: Beatrice, all but one of her brothers, and their stepmother Lucrezia were executed. Even the man Beatrice wanted to marry was killed, though there was little evidence of his involvement. The youngest Cenci son, Bernardo, was forced to watch his siblings die at the piazza di Ponte. Popular sentiment blamed the pope for an 'unjust justice' and, indeed, there was something questionable about the way the Cenci estates were put up for auction secretly and bought for a song by Cardinal Pietro Aldobrandini, the pope's nephew. The family heredity, much diminished, continued through Bernardo and the family survives today, though no longer in its old fortress here. The Cenci merged, through marriage, with the Bolognetti, another rich Roman family.

San Tommaso ai Cenci (St Thomas at the Cenci) was first noted in the twelfth century as 'San Thomas *in capite molarum*' (St Thomas at the head of the mills), a name which referred to the old watermills which floated in the Tiber at this point. With the building of the Tiber embankments in the late nineteenth century, the city was permanently divorced from its river and it is hard to imagine the vital economic importance it had in the life of Rome. The watermills were a principal industry of this region, on the edge between the *rioni* of Sant'Angelo and Regola, and this Cenci hill offered them protection. The church was associated with the Cenci family, although they were not exclusively buried here, as one might have imagined, but also in Santa Cecilia in Trastevere and in the big church of the

Cenci's zone, Sant'Angelo in Pescheria. Beatrice herself is buried by the high altar of San Pietro in Montorio, a church on a peak of the Janiculan hill whose retaining wall was built with money left for the purpose in her will. The church of San Tommaso ai Cenci is rarely open (the side entrance is used; there are guided tours every second Sunday of the month at 10.30 a.m.), but inside it is a good example of late sixteenth-century mannerist decoration, with an altarpiece in the first chapel on the left by Girolamo Siciolante da Sermoneta, one of the better artists of the period. Set into the façade is an ancient Roman tombstone, of one Marcus Cincius Theophilus, inserted there by Francesco Cenci to give antiquity to his family name.

Following the side of the church and turning to the left, we leave the summit of the Monte de' Cenci and enter the **piazza delle Cinque Scole** (piazza of the Five Schools), a name which refers to the former presence of Talmudic *yeshivas* here. This is the edge of the Jewish ghetto, a repeatedly rebuilt part of the city. Before the main core of the ghetto was demolished in 1888, this façade of palazzo Cenci overlooked piazza Giudea. In line with the palace's portal on the piazza, the nearby **great fountain of the ghetto** was reconstructed in 1930, after the demolition and rearrangement of piazza Giudea. The marble fountain is one of a number made by Giacomo della Porta (1533–1602) during the first widespread phase of fountain building, after the construction of a new aqueduct under Sixtus V Peretti (1585–90). This is, however, the second fountain intended to bring water to the suffering Jews of the ghetto: the first, designed by della Porta in 1581, was requisitioned by the powerful Mattei family and now stands not far from here, in piazza Mattei. The fountain in piazza delle Cinque Scole was its replacement, after a delay of over ten years: for three centuries, this was the only fresh water source for the Jews of Rome. Subject to various restrictions in the kind of trades they could undertake, they worked in the business of reselling old furniture and clothes: the Italian word for 'rags' is *cenci*.

If we turn along via Santa Maria del Pianto, we pass an entrance to the left into a restaurant called Al Pompiere, on the *piano nobile* (noble floor) of the palace. Here you can lunch, under the blackened ceiling frescoes of the main reception rooms. Further along, turn left round the corner of the Cenci building to see the **Arco de' Cenci**, a fifteenth-century house which preserves the right of way underneath it by means of a huge arched passage. Go through the arch and look at the thick wooden beams of the ceiling, which are still doing their job after more than five centuries. This brings us back to the piazza de' Cenci. The final building, the **palazzetto Cenci**, is the large sixteenth-century construction to the right, attached to the Monte de' Cenci by the arch. This elegant building dates from barely twenty years before the catastrophe of Francesco's murder and its atmospheric courtyard is framed on two sides by a colonnade, while on a third it is interrupted by the pre-existing structure of the house of the Arco de' Cenci. The Cenci heraldic emblem, the crescent moon, decorates the corners of arches and even appears in a painting of the Madonna above the main staircase.

The Cenci complex illustrates a number of typical features of Roman nobles and their residences. First, the complex is set above the other buildings of the neighbourhood: this would have been even more striking before the eighteenth- and nineteenth-century building boom. Second, the family had a church under its patronage, San Tommaso, where their tombs were usually placed, although they also sponsored other churches and chapels elsewhere in Rome. Third, as time passed, the family sought to express their dominance of the neighbourhood in explicit architectural terms. The palazzetto Cenci, too, shows the expansionist inclinations of Roman families, whose secondary branches, while preferring to be near their relatives, still liked to make an ostentatious display of wealth and power by constructing a new palace for themselves. Finally, the Roman tomb slab decorating the façade of San Tommaso and the crescent moons of the Cenci in the arches and cornices of the Cenci palaces show the taste for self-advertisement so common among the Roman aristocracy.

2   The *contrada* of the Santacroce
Start: via di Santa Maria del Pianto 43

Families did not always distinguish themselves geographically by allying themselves with a convenient landmark, like the Monte Cenci. With the Santacroce family a different sort of landholding is evident, stretching across a larger geographical area and with breaks in territorial continuity. Theirs is a *contrada*, a neighbourhood, not a hill.

The Santacroce, whose name means Holy Cross, were a violent medieval baronial family not unlike the Cenci. Their *contrada* crossed the boundaries of three *rioni* and their violence was part of the larger picture of aristocratic infighting that we will see in the story of the Colonna family, which met with increasing resistance from the popes as the Middle Ages gave way to the Renaissance. The Santacroce were allied with the powerful Orsini family, one of whose main palaces stands nearby in the Campo de' Fiori, and the two families intermarried: in return for Santacroce support, the Orsini gave them valuable fiefs outside Rome.

They have a peculiarly blood-soaked history. In 1480 Prospero

Santacroce stabbed a fellow nobleman, Pietro Margani, at the gate to the Margani tower in piazza Margana near the foot of the Capitoline hill. To forestall a feud and to make an example to other nobles who might otherwise think the law did not apply to them, Sixtus IV della Rovere (1472–84) razed the Santacroce fortress on this site. The area remained desolate for twenty years, until Alexander VI Borgia (1492–1503) granted Antonio Santacroce the right to rebuild his palace, as long as he respected the existing street plan and created a linear façade. Santacroce rebuilt accordingly, completing the work in 1501, and the building we are now standing in front of is the result.

Palazzo Santacroce is something of an oddity because, though it has many decorative characteristics of Renaissance buildings, it has the overall character of a medieval fortress, pointing to the intention of the builder, who must have regretted the loss of the previous building. The corner of the palace, which now juts out commandingly into the street, originally had no such prominence. Instead, the builders achieved visual authority in two ways: first, by constructing a tower on the corner; second, by decorating the ground-floor façade with unusual 'diamond-point' stonework that was guaranteed to catch the eye with its arresting play of light and shade. Higher up on the corner, a crest of the Santacroce in carved stone proclaimed the family's presence. Like many noble palaces, this was a multi-use building, with shops on the ground floor rented out to tenants, and the upper floors alone reserved for the use of the family and household.

From here we turn right, up via in Publicolis. The street, too, owes its name to the family, as they claimed descent from the ancient Roman *gens* (clan) Valeria Publicola, one of whose number, Publius Valerius Publicola, took part in ousting the ancient Tarquin kings from Rome in 510 BC and later became consul. The entire right-hand side of the street is taken up with the palace, whose *portone* is inscribed with the name ANTONIUS DE SANTACRUCE. The diamond-point decoration of

The corner tower of palazzo Santacroce. No self-respecting noble residence at the end of the fifteenth century could do without a tower, the ultimate status symbol.

the tower façade is visually striking from this vantage as well: it was an unusual style, deriving from a Spanish model, and other buildings nearby have followed its example, including the early twentieth-century palazzo on the via Arenula that houses the Ministry of Grace and Justice.

Following the façade, we find ourselves in piazza Costaguti, named for another family whose palace overlooks the far end of the space. Round the corner, high up under the eaves of what looks like another building, we can see the traces of a painted decoration on a late fifteenth-century loggia, now glassed in: the decoration includes painted crosses, a clear reference to the Santacroce family which, from the rough 'teeth' of the building next to it, might at one time have been facing demolition. From the piazza, looking back towards via in Publicolis, we can see our next destination, the small family church of **Santa Maria in Publicolis**.

This church is of great antiquity, though one would be hard pressed to detect that from its exterior: the whole building, in fact, is a Baroque replacement of its Renaissance predecessor. Its antecedents date back to as early as the eighth century, when this region of Rome was on the edge of the inhabited area and buildings were beginning to branch out towards the Vatican from the Capitoline hill. A bull of Pope Urban III (1185–7) records the church as 'Santa Maria *in publico*' and the Santacroce family took over its patronage in the following century, perhaps adapting the legend of their family origins to reflect the name of their church. The architect of the final version of the church was Giovan Antonio de' Rossi (1619–95), who served as a family architect. The façade is simple, but graceful, a minor Baroque success. Next to it on the right is the priest's house, now apartments. The church is rarely open (Sunday mornings, irregularly), but if it is, step inside. It is an utterly Santacroce monument, with family floor tombs of fifteenth- and sixteenth-century date, and more grandiose seventeenth- and eighteenth-century wall tombs, the most impressive by Giovanni Battista Maini (1690–1752), whose style indicates the coming shift from Baroque gesture to Neoclassical gravity and seriousness.

From here, walk a few steps to the upper end of the street and turn left on to via dei Falegnami. A block beyond is the via Arenula, whose name derives from the medieval Latin word for sandbank, *arenula*: this was the old name of the *rione* that is now called Regola. The sandbank has vanished under the Tiber embankment, but for most of Rome's history a sandy beach stretched up the right-hand shore of the river. The via Arenula cuts across the Santacroce *contrada* and the next family building we will visit is on the other side, **palazzo Santacroce Pasolini**. At the end of the sixteenth century the head of a secondary branch of the Santacroce family, Onofrio, decided to demolish a number of houses he owned here, in order to build himself a new palace. He commissioned plans from the best-known architect of the period, Carlo Maderno (1556–1629), but these came to nothing and he himself fell victim to Clement VIII Aldobrandini's efforts to curtail aristocratic violence. Onofrio's brother Paolo had murdered their mother, Costanza, and Onofrio was convicted of having incited the murder: Costanza had refused to name them her heirs. Both brothers were decapitated. It was the third in a series of such convictions and executions: the first involved the Massimo family, in which Eufrosina, the second wife of Lelio Massimo, the head of the family, was murdered by her stepson. The second was the famous case of Francesco Cenci. Together, they cast a different light upon the pope's execution of the Cenci: there was clearly a problem with nobles taking the law into their own hands.

After the death of the brothers the property was the subject of a long and exhausting lawsuit by various indirect heirs. After over twenty-five years of legal limbo, the site of the palace passed into the hands of Valerio Santacroce, who commissioned Francesco Peparelli (d. 1641) to build the palace between 1630 and 1640. Peparelli, one of the lesser lights of Maderno's studio, could be expected to carry out a design that would not be entirely different from that of his late master. The palace has three decorated façades, but the fourth faces on to a narrow alley. Valerio's successor, Cardinal Marcello Santacroce, decided to extend the palace across the alley, for which task he hired Giovan Antonio de' Rossi (1616–95). De' Rossi built a bridge across it, creating a sort of hanging garden accessible from the *piano nobile*. On the ground floor of the building that he designed on the other side of the alley, also a Santacroce property and destined for use as stables and servants' quarters, he created a long perspective in axis with the two *portoni* of the main palace, culminating in a huge monumental fountain. This arrangement is remarkably sophisticated and demonstrates vividly the way that noble families, increasingly deprived of the ability to express their domination through overt displays of violence, showed their local authority in visual terms, by stretching sightlines across piazze, courtyards and alleys.

The nineteenth-century writer Augustus Hare tells sensational stories about this palace:

> This is one of the few haunted houses in Rome: it is said that by night two statues of Santa Croce cardinals descend from their pedestals and rattle their marble trains about its long galleries. In recent alterations for the sake of making a lift, an *oubliette* was discovered, lined with sharp-pointed instruments, and at the bottom lay a mass of skeletons, one of them in armour, with a dagger driven through the helmet and far into the skull. A figure, fully dressed, but mummified, was also found walled up in a niche.

According to Hare, the palace contained secret passages, through which, at some point in the nineteenth century, a prisoner who had escaped from the Castel Sant'Angelo had wandered from the river bank. His case was considered by the princess Santacroce of the time. She decided his sentence was unjust and had him conveyed to a safe place outside Rome in her own carriage. This lurid history hardly seems to match the elegant palace, but Hare, an inveterate teller of ghost stories, might have been embellishing the kernel of a real Roman tale.

With the extinction of the family, the palace went through various owners before the counts Pasolini dall'Onda bought it in 1904. Now it houses the Istituto Latino-Americano. The palace and its surroundings have been greatly restructured over the centuries. In the nineteenth century a *portone* was inserted in seventeenth-century style on the façade across from the church of San Carlo ai Catinari, on an axis with the westernmost door in the church façade. In fact, this is now the principal entrance to the palace and the brilliant early planning of the main axis is almost invisible. The fountain in piazza Cairoli, however, shows the modern town planners' sensitivity, as it acts as one of the two end points of the axis, though it was only set there at the end of the nineteenth century. Viewed as part of the larger piazza, it makes no sense in its current position, but it should be seen as the centre of a ghostly piazza of much smaller size.

The final building of the Santacroce family is now entirely un-recognisable as such. Leaving piazza Cairoli by via degli Specchi, we proceed two blocks – not neglecting to take a couple of steps down the alley on our right to look at the end of the great axis with its wall fountain – and find ourselves in piazza del Monte di Pietà. The vast **palazzo del Monte di Pietà**, which rises up on our left, occupying one whole side of the piazza, was originally built as a Santacroce family palace in the mid sixteenth century. The heirs of Cardinal Prospero Santacroce sold it in 1591, three years after it had been restructured by Ottaviano Nonni, called Il Mascherino (1524–1606), a skilled architect whose work prefigured the classical trend of the Baroque. In 1603 the new owners sold it to the papal pawnbrokers, the Monte di Pietà, an institution set up in direct competition with Jewish moneylenders; the Romans quickly came to call it the Monte d'Impietà for its outrageous interest rates. Interestingly, the Santacroce stable of architects, including Peparelli and de' Rossi, found work altering the palazzo for its new use. Today it is a branch office of the Bank of Rome, but it still functions as a pawnbroker's shop. It has a lovely late Baroque chapel, if you have the courage to enter and ask to see it.

With the Santacroce, further qualities of the Roman nobility become apparent. First, as we have already seen with the Cenci, branches of the same family tended to like to live close to each other, initially for mutual protection, and then for prestige, because a multiplicity of family palaces in a single area had the effect of impressing residents and passers-by with the power, wealth and authority of the family. Second, as time passed, this expression of authority by way of architecture became more and more sophisticated. Third, families tended to use the same set of artists and architects to work on their commissions, which means that quite often the name of an architect of a particular structure will say something about who was paying for the construction. All these details are part of the 'vocabulary' of the city, which can be very instructive in understanding why and how it came to be as we see it today.

3 The *isola* of the Mattei
Start: piazza Mattei 17

In the beautiful piazza Mattei, with the Fountain of the Turtles playing, it is still possible to sense the wealth and power of this now vanished family. The building that lines the northern edge of the piazza is the oldest of the Mattei palaces to be built on the site, but attached to it are three others owned by them. Together they form a unity, which was known even in the Middle Ages as the *isola* (island) of the Mattei.

The Mattei had a long and complex genealogy. They may, in fact, have sprung from the even older family of the Papareschi of Trastevere, which produced a pope, Innocent II (1130–43). The Papareschi, in their turn, took over the Trasteverean territory of the great ancient family of the Anicii. There is little evidence to ascribe such antique origins to the Mattei. Their first palace, or rather house, still stands in piazza in Piscinula in southern Trastevere. However, towards around 1400 one branch of the family acquired the property in *rione* Sant'Angelo. The two branches had two separate titles: the Mattei of Trastevere were dukes of Paganica, while the Mattei who took up residence in *rione* Sant'Angelo became the marquesses and then the dukes of Giove.

The Trastevere house of the Mattei was sacked by Sixtus IV in 1484, as punishment for their alliance with the Colonna family, who had set themselves against the pope. In the mid sixteenth century the Mattei of Trastevere had to give up their residence, under unusual circumstances. Three Mattei brothers living there, Marcantonio, Curzio and Alessandro, were famous for their quarrelsome natures. Marcantonio fell at the hands of an assassin sent by his cousin Pietro and Alessandro then killed the assassin in revenge. Peace seemed to return among the surviving brothers and in fact Gerolamo, Alessandro's son, was soon betrothed to Curzio's daughter Olimpia (after having obtained the necessary papal dispensations), though Curzio made trouble by refusing to pay a dowry. The wedding, in 1555, was a bloodbath: accounts differ, but it seems that Curzio's son Vincenzo quarrelled with the groom, Gerolamo, and killed him, wounding the bride in the process. One of Gerolamo's men killed Curzio in retribution, and Alessandro killed his nephew Vincenzo and ended by slaughtering Curzio's killer as well and throwing his body into the Tiber. All Rome was scandalised by this massacre and Alessandro, the sole surviving brother, was forced to flee to avoid papal justice.

In contrast, the Sant'Angelo branch of the family was thriving. Their estates outside Rome, which had been augmented through their alliance with the Colonna, formed part of the vital supply network that kept the city fed with grain and the Mattei did not scorn commerce, building up a fortune from the operation of a family bank, whose funds were secured by their estates. In addition, the Sant'Angelo Mattei profited vastly by being granted the concession to run the gates of the newly walled Jewish ghetto created by Paul IV Carafa (1555–9) and to charge a fee to anyone going in or out. The ghetto was now a controlled area rather than merely a Jewish district. As life got harder for the Jews, it got easier for the Mattei.

The Mattei property here occupied the site of one of ancient Rome's public theatres, the Theatre of Balbus, whose curve of seats rose under the palace. The stage and stone backdrop stretched across the entire length of the block, along the edge of the Mattei *isola* traced by the street today called via Michelangelo Caetani. Indeed, the palace in front of us has a strange floor plan that in part reuses the ancient *cunei* (wedges), segments of the half-circle upon which the theatre's seats were laid. This is the **palazzo di Giacomo Mattei**, the oldest of the present Mattei palaces here. Giacomo Mattei was described as living here in the Rome 1527 census of inhabitants, along with his sons Pietro Antonio and Ciriaco. The building was almost entirely reconstructed at the order of a second Giacomo, Pietro Antonio's son, in the mid sixteenth century. The architect was a Florentine, Nanni di Baccio Bigio (d. 1568), and the façade resembles buildings of the same period in Florence. Nanni often worked with the celebrated Sangallo family of architects, and designed the great villa on the Pincian hill now called the villa Medici (one of his pupils was Ottaviano Nonni, Il Mascherino, who constructed today's palazzo del Monte di Pietà for the Santacroce). Nanni di Baccio Bigio was probably also the architect of two of the other Mattei palaces in the *isola*, palazzo Caetani and palazzo Mattei di Paganica. The palace of Giacomo Mattei has two courtyards and two separate *portoni*. Both courtyards served as movie sets for the director Sergio Leone in the 1960s, when they stood in for Mexican haciendas in spaghetti Westerns.

The **Fontana delle Tartarughe** (Fountain of the Turtles) is a creation of the great architect and fountain designer Giacomo della Porta. He was responsible only for the series of basins, however: the four languid youths who are helping four turtles into the upper basin were added by the Florentine sculptor Taddeo Landini (1550–96), the Florentine connection perhaps indicating the hand of Nanni di Baccio Bigio in the commission. A story commonly

The Fontana delle Tartarughe in a nineteenth-century print. Perhaps Rome's most beloved fountain, its lightness and charm mask a darker history.

told about the fountain is revealing about Mattei power. A Mattei duke was gambling with his future father-in-law and losing. He lost everything except the palace of Giacomo Mattei. At this point his prospective father-in-law told him that the marriage was off: his daughter was not to be married to a penniless gambler. The Mattei duke made one last, desperate bet. He bet his palace, against the hand of the girl and all the rest that he had already lost, that he could assemble a fountain in the piazza outside in the course of a few hours. The other noble assented, because it was a ridiculous claim. What he didn't know was that the pipes had already been laid and the pavement reset, and the fountain was in a service courtyard waiting to be assembled. The Mattei duke invited his adversary to supper and, when it was over, flung open the window of his dining room to show the fountain playing in the piazza. 'See what a Mattei can do, even penniless!' he said, and the other man was forced to give back all that he had won from the duke and also grant his daughter's hand anew. The story has a bitter ending: the young bride was said to have been very unhappy and ordered that the window from which her ruin had first been seen should be bricked up. A wider tragedy, however, was that the fountain had originally been commissioned for the ghetto, to provide fresh water to the Jews; as we have seen, they had a thirsty ten-year wait.

This palace was built before the Mattei made their banking fortune and got the commission to keep the gates of the ghetto. Next door, however, the

palazzo Mattei di Giove vividly manifests the family fortune as it rocketed skywards. We will leave piazza Mattei by the via dei Funari, named after the rope makers who were recorded in this district as early as the second half of the fourteenth century. A look upwards will show the difference in size between the relatively modest palace of Giacomo Mattei and the vast dimensions of its attached neighbour.

To depict palazzo Mattei di Giove, the eighteenth-century engraver Giuseppe Vasi had to dispense with the buildings on the other side of the street. This image shows the building's prominent *altana* or summer dining-room, an open-air loggia on top of the palace – the sixteenth-century successor to the tower as a marker of noble prestige.

Palazzo Mattei di Giove is the last of the Mattei palaces to be built (1598–1618) and is perhaps the greatest masterpiece of Carlo Maderno's secular architecture. Maderno, whom we have encountered with the Santacroce, was most famous for his completion of the basilica of St Peter's, for which he designed the façade (as we will see in the Borghese itinerary). The faces of this palace are, by contrast, rather austere. An inscription above the door proclaims the name of the builder, Asdrubale Mattei, the newly minted Marquess of Giove: this was a title he was able to buy with his new wealth and it was soon upgraded to the level of a dukedom. The great *portone* conducts us into an entrance corridor and the exterior austerity suddenly gives way to one of Rome's most beautiful courtyards.

In order to proclaim his taste and wealth, Asdrubale Mattei collected ancient sculpture, as did many of his predecessors and contemporaries. The

Mattei collection is now extraordinary as being among the only ones still *in situ*. It survived because of its incorporation in the structure of the building itself: the courtyard, loggia and staircase were constructed with the sculpture collection in mind, and in many cases the works are simply impossible to take off the walls. The courtyard proclaims the family's taste and also its connections: a marriage alliance between the Mattei and the Gonzaga, rulers of Mantua, made the Mattei distant relations of the Habsburg Holy Roman Emperors, and the decoration of the loggia refers to it with outsize portrait busts of Habsburg emperors on the balustrade. Inside, the state rooms are lavishly decorated with scenes from the Old Testament. The choice of subject matter was a compromise between Asdrubale and his Gonzaga wife: he could make the courtyard as pagan as he pleased, as long as the interior was unimpeachably orthodox and biblical. The palace now houses the Institute for American Studies and the great reception rooms have been converted into a library, not generally accessible to casual visitors. Inside, the ceilings are frescoed by different artists, notably two stars of the young Baroque style: Pietro da Cortona (1596–1669), whose first major work this was, and Giovanni Lanfranco (1582–1647). Asdrubale was a patron of art and his collection, now dispersed, was one of Rome's greatest.

Palazzo Mattei di Giove makes up for its inability to dominate its neighbourhood in terms of imposing views from outside by having not one but two sightlines inside. The first, and in fact the main, axis is from the entrance to the right of the courtyard, which culminates in the first landing of the staircase and a large antique vase in a niche. The staircase itself is also designed so that every viewpoint had a focus, going up or going down: end walls contain statues in niches, or windows, or ancient sculptural relief work, like the front of a great hunt sarcophagus, visible on the first landing as one is descending the stairs. The secondary axis is the one along which we have entered from the great *portone*: it has been given greater prominence than Maderno intended by the opening of the central arch in the wall opposite the entrance. Originally you reached the second courtyard through openings in the side arches, which have now been closed.

Through the arch into the second courtyard, which was once a garden with a grotto and fountain, there is a further display of Mattei antiquities on the large wall to our right. If you leave through the service gateway in that wall and turn left, you enter via Michelangelo Caetani. The third Mattei palace in the *isola* has its main entrance on the via delle Botteghe Oscure, round the corner. It was the home of Ciriaco, brother of Asdrubale Mattei. When Ciriaco was in residence, his household or *famiglia* included, for a time, the painter Michelangelo Merisi (1571–1610), called Caravaggio after his village near Milan. Caravaggio painted a number of works for Ciriaco and Asdrubale, which have now been scattered. It was not unusual for noble households to include painters or other artists, as part of a train of servants and courtiers whose purpose was to enlarge the glory of the patron. But this palace, thought to be the work of the Florentine architect Bartolomeo Ammanati (1511–92) or the aforementioned Nanni di Baccio Bigio, quickly passed out of the hands of the Mattei family: Gerolamo, first Duke of Giove and the son of Asdrubale, sold it in the second half of the seventeenth century and in 1776 it became **palazzo Caetani**, the city palace of an old family of medieval potentates whose territory extended across southern Lazio. The Roman noblewoman Vittoria Colonna, who married the heir to the Caetani duchy of Sermoneta in 1901, lived in palazzo Caetani in the early twentieth century. Her autobiography is explicit about its disadvantages:

> I have always hated Palazzo Caetani with its gloom. It is sad to think of the countless marriages in Italy that have turned out badly and unhappily owing to the old-fashioned custom of young wives having to live with their parents-in-law . . . Palazzo Caetani is in itself rather a fine building . . . but spoilt by an extra storey built above its cornice by a practical but inartistic Caetani. Its darkness and melancholy are overwhelming. On the first floor, the so-called *piano nobile*, where my parents-in-law lived, the electric light was in constant use at luncheon during the winter, and in several of the drawing-rooms it was necessary literally to grope one's way in the perpetual gloom.
>
> I remember the evening I arrived at Palazzo Caetani for the first time after my honeymoon in Frascati. Dusk was falling, dinner-time approaching, and there was no sign of life anywhere in my part of the house. I sat in the bedroom that had been allotted to me; my husband had been given one on another floor and so far off that I never really learned the quickest way to his room as there were several staircases and innumerable passages. My dear old English nurse, Sizy, sat near me. She was very ruffled at having left beautiful Palazzo Colonna with all its luxuries and comforts, and not at all disposed to make the best of things. Finally when it got quite dark, I suggested: 'Suppose we rang the bell and asked the housemaid for some hot water?'
>
> 'There is no bell, there is no housemaid, there is no hot water in this house,' was Sizy's gloomy retort; and the funny part of it was that it was absolutely true . . .

This discomfort was typical of Roman palaces, which were built for grandeur rather than ease. The duchess did, however, note that the polished marble floors of the palace were excellent for roller skating, which was a craze at the time. The Caetani family died out in the 1960s and the palace is now home to an embassy, as well as the headquarters of the Fondazione Caetani, which administers the various properties of the extinct family. It is safe to assume that there is at least hot water there now.

The final Mattei palace, **palazzo Mattei di Paganica**, is round the next corner to the left. As we continue along the via delle Botteghe Oscure, we will see a wall shrine at the corner, with an inscription. Wall shrines are very common features of the Roman landscape. They offer passers-by the opportunity to pray at a revered image and they also reflect the desire of their patrons to draw attention to the building they are attached to. The buildings on this corner are not all part of the palace, but include a couple of older houses, which were once intended for demolition, as the threatening raw edge of the palazzo Mattei di Paganica still shows.

This was the home of the Mattei dukes of Paganica, descendants of the Pietro Mattei who had his cousin Marcantonio murdered in the 1550s. Pietro commissioned the palace in 1541 from the family architect Nanni di Baccio Bigio. The Paganica branch of the family died out in the eighteenth century and the palace passed to the Giove branch, who sold it to the Istituto della Enciclopedia Italiana, the current proprietors, in 1928. Occasionally there are conferences and exhibitions here, which permit a brief visit to the courtyard and some of the ground-floor rooms. Like the palace of Giacomo Mattei, this is built on the ruins of the *cavea* of the Theatre of Balbus, and its odd floor plan and irregular courtyard are due to the presence of pre-existing ancient walls incorporated into the current structure.

The family property was not restricted entirely to their *isola*, of course. The Mattei owned a vineyard on the Palatine and the villa Celimontana on the Celian hill, now a public park. Their principal family chapels, too, were not contiguous to their palace block: one is in the great church of Rome's civic life, Santa Maria in Aracoeli on the Capitoline hill, and the other is the jewel of Santa Maria della Consolazione on the Tiber side of the Forum.

Some typical aspects of the Roman nobility appear in the history and monuments of the Mattei. They show the by now familiar attachment to living close together, though in separate palaces. Like their peers, the Cenci and the Santacroce, their violent behaviour continued throughout the sixteenth century, but by the end of the century the family had in Asdrubale Mattei and his brother Ciriaco two great collectors and patrons. Though the Mattei art collections have been scattered, some of Asdrubale's sculpture collection survives to give the visitor a sense of his taste, and of the quality and range of the works the family owned. The presence of artists in a palace of this kind is attested to by Caravaggio, who lived in palazzo Mattei Caetani for some time.

These three brief walks reveal different aspects of the Roman aristocracy and their effect on the streetscape. In our more detailed looks at the monuments, churches and palaces of a few select families, some of the themes that have appeared here will recur, elaborated in different ways. The Cenci, Santacroce and Mattei were circumscribed by financial and legal constraints, whereas the great families of sixteenth- and seventeenth-century Rome had almost unlimited power and wealth during the reign of their family pope. Even the baronial Colonna, with their fifteenth-century pope, succeeded in placing a distinct stamp on a larger part of Rome than did any of the families we have met so far.

2 The Colonna

No other patrician family has enjoyed so long a prominence as the Colonna. From the thirteenth to the nineteenth centuries almost no important event took place in Rome that did not involve them in some way. The great medieval Colonna rivalry with the Orsini has passed into legend; their famous opposition to the papacy and allegiance with the imperial faction in the Middle Ages are commonplaces of medieval Roman history. As a result of their antiquity, the Colonna have served as a sort of measuring stick for other Roman families. A sign of whether a newer family had arrived at the top was how quickly a marriage could be arranged with an appropriate Colonna. They sit at the centre of a genealogical web that includes all the other families in this book.

The family established itself in Rome by the end of the twelfth century, but a certain fog hovers over their origins. Some authorities assert their descent from the family of the counts of Tusculum, though the only basis for this is the geographical proximity of the power bases of the two families. The column which forms the family emblem was said to represent that of Trajan, which rises not far from the family palace, and this was also claimed as the origin of the name. Later centuries gave the Colonna a ridiculous ancient pedigree, claiming descent from Julius Caesar and thus from the goddess Venus herself, a rich inheritance indeed for a family which contained many cardinals and a pope. But the history of the Colonna shows their great aptitude for covering all bases.

The first Colonna of whom we have any sure record is *Petrus de Columna* (1078–1108), whose patronymic derives not from a physical column, but from the principality of Colonna in the Alban hills not far from the city. This was his property, though the family rapidly expanded its holdings into the strategic town of Palestrina, which was soon to be the principal seat of the clan. Pope Paschal II, in 1101, despite having married his niece to Petrus, seized the property of this country baron, as punishment for his 'lawless depredations', but his successors were forced to return it.

THE RISE TO POWER

The Colonna moved from these origins outside Rome to authority within the city through advancement within the church. The first cardinal of the family was *Giovanni the Elder* (d. 1209), whom Pope Celestine III created cardinal of the church of Santa Prisca in 1192; this Cardinal Giovanni was also the first in the family's long line of passionate devotees of St Francis. He helped to establish the Rule of the saint's new order and sponsored the construction of a great hospital for the poor in the southern coastal town of Amalfi.

In 1212 a second Colonna was elevated to the cardinalate. *Giovanni the Younger* (d. 1244) was the certain founder of the family's fortunes; he was one of the most important and well-travelled of the curia's diplomats, and in 1217 was sent to the East as papal legate to Jerusalem and Constantinople. He returned in 1222 with a relic that connected conveniently with the family name: the Holy Column, at which Christ was supposed to have been flagellated. His diplomatic career ended in 1240–1 in circumstances that were to prove prophetic for the family's political position over the following centuries.

In the thirteenth century the principal conflict in Italy was between pope and emperor. The conflict derived from competing claims of superiority in the sphere of worldly authority: the emperor claimed dominance over the secular world, as the ancient Roman emperors did; the popes asserted that, since it was by their hands that emperors were crowned, they were the supreme authority. This idea has its most magnificent expression in Innocent III's 1202 decree *Venerabilem*, which asserted that the emperor could be deposed by the pope and that the pope had the right to intervene in disputed imperial elections (for the emperor was elected by the princes of Germany). Supporters of the emperor in Italy were known as Ghibellines and the adherents of the pope were called Guelfs. The battle between Guelf and Ghibelline consumed many Italian communes in the thirteenth century and beyond, and the conflict set the scene for the struggle in Rome between the generally Guelf Orsini and the generally Ghibelline Colonna.

Cardinal Giovanni the Younger, a practised court diplomat, was placed in the middle of the ongoing tussle between the pope, Gregory IX (1227–41), and the emperor, the brilliant and unstable Frederick II of Hohenstaufen. Failing to reconcile these two powerful figures, the cardinal finally threw in his lot with the emperor in 1240, which provoked swift reprisals from the pope. The chronicler Matthew Paris in 1244 blamed him for the diplomatic failure, describing the cardinal as 'a vessel filled with pride and insolence; who, as he was the most illustrious and powerful in secular possessions of all the cardinals, was the most efficacious author and fosterer of discord between the emperor and the pope'.

The Colonna had already helped themselves to a large territory within the walls of Rome. Their property extended from the porta del Popolo, the great northern city gate that admitted the via Flaminia into Rome, all the way to the markets of Trajan near the Roman Forum. They possessed great fortresses: the mausoleum of Augustus, which dominated the northern part of the city, the Ripetta; a fortification on the *Mons Acceptoris*, an artificial mound near the Column of Marcus Aurelius which today is Montecitorio, the site of the Parliament building;

Cardinal Giovanni the Younger. His alliance with the Holy Roman Emperor Frederick II established the Colonna as opponents to the pope.

and the greatest of them all, the Colonna stronghold in piazza Santi Apostoli. This enormous swathe of land, which they either owned or dominated militarily, was in large part uninhabited, though the trickling course of the Aqua Virgo (in Italian the Acqua Vergine), the one ancient aqueduct that continued to function throughout the Middle Ages, passed through Colonna property and fed a small *borgo* (settlement) in the depopulated area within the walls. This was the heritage of the Colonna in Rome: vineyards, farms and half-abandoned monasteries.

COLONNA VERSUS ORSINI

Papal reprisals for the Colonna defection in 1240 were harsh and at the head of the pope's forces was the Orsini family. Slightly more established than the Colonna, the Orsini wanted to maintain their power against the new rival family from the Alban Hills; the family head, Matteo Rosso Orsini, led an attack against the Colonna stronghold at the mausoleum of Augustus and razed it. The other Colonna fortresses were similarly reduced, though they were soon rebuilt. No new Colonna cardinal was created until 1278 and during this period the family reconsolidated their position. The two brothers of Cardinal Giovanni the Younger, *Oddone* (d. before 1252) and *Giordano Colonna* (d. after 1188), founded the two main dynastic branches of the family, those of **Gallicano** and **Palestrina**; Giordano was the eldest and his was the dominant branch in the Middle Ages, the Colonna of Palestrina. A third branch resulted from the next generation, that of **Riofreddo**, and a fourth branch also split off from the Palestrina branch, taking the name of **Genazzano** from its principal seat.

The return of the Colonna to the cardinalate was brought about by a surprising peacemaker, the Orsini pope, Nicholas III, who as part of his policy of pacification raised *Giacomo di Giordano* (d. 1318), of the line of Palestrina, to the purple in 1278. Giacomo was, however, half an Orsini himself, the product of a clever marriage alliance. The two families of Orsini and Colonna began, at this time, to intermarry, although this seldom prevented their traditional rivalry for more than a generation. Giacomo's brother *Giovanni* (d. 1293) held the office of senator of the city repeatedly after 1279. Cardinal Giacomo was joined in the cardinalate by his nephew *Pietro* (d. 1326), Giovanni's son, in 1288, appointed by a pope from a family allied with the Colonna, Honorius IV Savelli. These two cardinals were the first to sponsor major public works: Giacomo's contribution was the great apse mosaics in Santa Maria Maggiore, masterpieces of the Roman mosaicist Jacopo Torriti, while Pietro founded the great hospital church of San Giacomo in Augusta, close to his family's fortress in the Mausoleum of Augustus.

Clerical members of the family attended the most prestigious universities, such as that of Bologna. Expressions of this cultivated aspect of the family were, among other things, the large law library assembled by Cardinal Pietro and the biography written by the senator Giovanni of his saintly sister *Margherita*. Prior to her early death in 1280 – she was beatified in 1847 – Margherita founded a community of nuns in a fortress near Palestrina and her Franciscan devotion itself became a family tradition. Her brother, Cardinal Giacomo, wrote the Rule for the order founded by Margherita, which, in 1285, found a new home in the abandoned Benedictine monastery of San Silvestro in Capite, which was conveniently situated in the middle of Colonna-dominated Rome.

A second community of Franciscan nuns was founded by Giacomo, the convent of San Lorenzo in Panisperna, not far from the Santi Apostoli centre of Colonna power. Over the following centuries it became one of the most exclusive institutions in Rome, whose purpose was comfortably to house unmarried female members of Roman noble families. Both Cardinals Colonna encouraged the more radical Franciscan wing, whose emphasis on poverty and a rejection of the temporal in favour of the spiritual was soon to bring them into direct conflict with the papacy.

CRISIS AND RETRENCHMENT: THE LATE MIDDLE AGES

Family struggles eroded the unity of the Colonna clan, even during the troubled reign of Boniface VIII Caetani (1294–1303), when the family needed the most cohesion. Open conflict with the pope broke out in May 1297 when Stefano Colonna (c. 1265–c. 1349), along with his brothers *Agapito* (c. 1260–1302) and *Giacomo*, known as *Sciarra* (1270–1329), stole a considerable sum of treasure destined for the papal coffers. The enraged pope demanded in response that both Colonna cardinals declare once and for all whether or not they admitted the legitimacy of his election; Boniface, as cardinal, had induced his predecessor, the saintly hermit Celestine V, to abdicate, a legally questionable act that threw his own election into doubt.

Though the Colonna returned the pope's money, Boniface's insistence on submission grew more and more demanding and after a few days the Colonna replied with the so-called Manifesto of Lunghezza, a resounding rejection of the pope's legitimacy. In December 1297, Boniface declared a 'crusade' against the Colonna, whom he had already excommunicated the previous May. (Excommunications of the clan were so frequent that among the Romans it was said that the annual bull *In Coena Domini* was issued principally for that purpose.) The pope's troops destroyed the Colonna stronghold of Palestrina and imprisoned members of the family at Tivoli: nothing remained but flight and the family scattered across Europe. Even the ruins of the Temple of Fortune at Palestrina, on which the Colonna fortress stood, were destroyed by Boniface's army, which was headed by a Colonna of the Riofreddo branch – another example of the family's internal conflicts.

The Colonna quickly reassembled at the court of the French king, Philippe IV le Bel,

Sciarra ('Sarra') Colonna in a sixteenth-century engraving. The dealer of the famous 'schiaffo d'Anagni', the 'slap of Anagni', helped to bring the medieval papacy to its lowest ebb of power.

who rejected the pope's claims to temporal supremacy and was thus the exiled clan's natural ally. In autumn 1303 Philippe sent an army into the Papal States with the aid of the Colonna exiles and inflicted the most spectacular humiliation ever to be experienced by the medieval papacy: led by Sciarra Colonna, the French expedition marched into the pope's birthplace of Anagni and captured him in his family palace, when Sciarra slapped him smartly across the face. Though the people of Anagni rescued the pope after three harrowing days in captivity, the damage was done: never again could he exercise the control over temporal affairs in Europe that a pope had in the days of Innocent III, a century before. The Colonna had chosen the winning side yet again.

By 1306, three years after Boniface's death – he did not long survive his humiliation at Anagni – the Colonna were restored to their properties. Further struggles between Guelf and Ghibelline continued through the early fourteenth century. The Colonna, led particularly by the ultra-Ghibelline Sciarra Colonna, contributed greatly to the violence of life in Rome. Early in that century family groups began to form into larger alliances, as the Colonna joined with the Savelli and other clans against a similar faction headed by the Orsini. Even when fighting, both factions pursued the same goals, which were to erode or use papal authority in their own favour.

In 1309, fed up with the constant violence in Rome and under pressure from the French king and his cardinals, the French pope, Clement V, moved the Curia to Avignon. So many Colonna then moved to Avignon that we may begin to speak of an 'Avignonese' or Provençal branch of the family. Colonna intellectuals abounded at the court of Avignon over the next half-century, and the family gained an academic and literary distinction that raised it far above the other families of Rome. They also gained cultural importance by their support of the greatest of the early humanists, Francesco Petrarca or Petrarch (1304–74). The poet expressed his gratitude, especially towards the aged Stefano Colonna, the family head, to whom he grew particularly close, in his letters and in the dedications to some of his sonnets. This client relationship did not, however, prevent Petrarch in 1347 from distancing himself from his patrons under the influence of the fiery tribune Cola di Rienzo, who dreamed of a renewed power and glory for the Roman people against the strength of the nobility.

While the cultural life of Avignon prospered throughout the fourteenth century, Rome was devolving into greater chaos without the stabilising influence of the papacy. The Roman nobility increased their attacks on each other and the desperate Roman people came to see Cola di Rienzo as their defender against them. The Colonna sustained a devastating defeat in the battle of Porta San Lorenzo in November 1347, at the hands of Cola's followers ('it is better to die than to bend one's neck under the yoke of such a peasant,' exclaimed a Colonna upon receiving news of his family losses in the battle). At Cardinal Giovanni's death in 1348, his friend Petrarch wrote the sonnet 'Rotta è l'alta Colonna' ('Broken is the tall column').

This was the period of the plague, the Black Death, in Rome and marked perhaps the lowest ebb of the city's fortunes since the fall of the ancient empire. In 1350 the new head of the house, *Stefanello Colonna* (d. *c.*1366), avenged himself on Cola di Rienzo for the deaths of his relatives by provoking a popular reaction, which resulted in Rienzo's death. Two years later, in 1352, Stefanello was elevated to the rank of senator. However, the decades of the 1360s and 1370s were hard ones for the family, lacking as it did a skilled head to navigate the rocky shoals of politics. The situation was difficult. This was the era of the Great Schism, with one pope in Rome and the other at Avignon; a council summoned at Pisa in 1409 to resolve the schism only added a third pope to the others. Without the family's usual representation in the Curia, Stefanello's sons, *Niccolò* (d. 1410) and *Giovanni Colonna* (d. 1413), became soldiers of fortune under the banner of King Ladislas of Naples against the Pisan pope, John XXIII, but John bought back their services with the feudal holdings of Civita Latina, Genazzano and Frascati. Niccolò and Giovanni did not, however, live to see the dawn of the most splendid days of their family's power.

POPE MARTIN V (1417–31)

Though previously other branches, those of Palestrina and Provence, had dominated the Colonna clan, it was a member of the hitherto obscure Genazzano branch of the family who was raised to the papal throne on the feast of St Martin in 1417, when the Council of Constance chose *Oddone Colonna* (1368–1431) as pope under the name of Martin V, ending the Great Schism which had witnessed two papal successions warring against each other from Rome and Avignon. This pope finally returned the united Holy See to its place in Rome in 1419. He found the city depopulated and moribund, and immediately began to put it in order. At Rome, Martin V took pains to revive the urban fabric of the exhausted city: he lived at the old guest house at the Vatican, abandoning the ruinous papal residence at the Lateran, and sought to re-establish the basic necessities of life in Rome. Most notable among his decrees was one which urged cardinals and patricians to invest, for the good of their souls, in founding or maintaining family chapels in Roman churches; this began a small ecclesiastical building boom that gathered pace through that century and those following.

The Colonna pope brought his family a rich windfall of titles, estates and benefices. They also profited from their friendship with the Queen of Naples, Giovanna II, who withdrew her troops from Rome to enable the pope to return. Through her favour the pope's brother, *Giordano Colonna* (d. 1424), became Duke of Amalfi and Venosa in 1419 and also Prince of Salerno, making him the most titled nobleman of southern Italy. The pope's nephews also received more than adequate recompense: *Prospero* (d. 1463) received the cardinal's hat and held a commanding position in the Curia for decades. *Antonio* (*c.* 1400–72) and *Odoardo Colonna* (*c.* 1400–85) became lords of Paliano, Serrone, Nettuno and Marsi. Martin V also obtained excellent marriages for his family with members of the most powerful noble dynasties of the peninsula.

The Colonna family pope in an engraving after a portrait by a follower of Pisanello. Martin V resided both at the Vatican and at the Colonna fortress, expressing his dual role as pontiff and clan leader.

THE COLONNA IN THE FIFTEENTH AND SIXTEENTH CENTURIES

Martin V died in February 1431 and, predictably, a reaction against his family rapidly followed. His successor, Eugenius IV Condulmer (1431–47), demanded the immediate return of the papal treasury, which had been transferred to the Colonna family palace, and of many of the estates distributed by his predecessor. In the violent conflict that followed, Palestrina, the home of the old dominant branch of the dynasty, was razed to the ground by the fierce Cardinal Vitelleschi.

With the death of Eugenius the family returned to their usual position of influence over the Curia: in various conclaves Cardinal Prospero Colonna came close to winning the tiara. This prince of the Church, appreciated by his contemporaries for his well-stocked library, was closely linked with Enea Silvio Piccolomini, to whom in 1458 he gave the winning vote for election as Pope Pius II. Yet the Colonna once again engaged in bloody conflict with the pope near the end of the next pontificate, of Sixtus IV della Rovere, whose persecution of the family culminated in the beheading of the .papal protonotary, *Lorenzo Oddone Colonna*, in the Castel Sant'Angelo in 1484, and the imprisonment of the family cardinal, *Giovanni* (1457–1508). Popes of this period all had to engage with Colonna power in one way or another, either allying themselves with the family or with their enemies, the ever present Orsini. Beginning particularly with the Borgia pope, Alexander VI (1492–1503), the popes tried to free themselves of this necessity, with increasing attacks on Colonna and Orsini properties and privileges, the profits of which necessarily went to the popes' own families.

When the Colonna's most important soldier, *Fabrizio I* of Paliano (1460–1520), set himself against Alexander VI, the anger of the Borgia pope resulted in the confiscation of Colonna lands and their redistribution among the pope's own family. Fabrizio had previously sold his services to Pope Innocent VIII Cibò, then to the king of Naples, then to his rival Charles VIII of France and finally to Spain, which conquered the kingdom of Naples in 1504. In the service of the Spanish king Ferdinand, the Colonna won glory and were rewarded with estates. They were also given the dignity of Great Constables (*Grandi Conestabili*), with the annual ritual duty of conveying the *chinea*, the white horse of tribute, from the viceroy of Naples to the pope, in recognition of the pope's feudal overlordship of the kingdom; the Colonna performed this duty until 1788.

Cardinal *Pompeo Colonna* (1479–1532), of the Paliano branch, continued to fight the papacy (the *Catholic Encyclopaedia* of 1911 quaintly observed that 'the sword was more congenial to him than the breviary'). He led a rebellion against his former ally, Julius II della Rovere, in 1511, along with the Orsini. A new *Pax Romana* between Orsini and Colonna made life easier in Rome for a few years, but in 1526, in the reign of Clement VII de' Medici, the Colonna led a bloody attack on Rome that amounted almost to a sack. Cardinal Pompeo himself looted the Vatican palace and when the pope, from the safety of the Castel Sant'Angelo, excommunicated him, Pompeo retaliated with a call for a general Church council. The following year the Colonna sided with the troops of the Holy Roman Emperor Charles V, which sacked Rome thoroughly, for close to a year, after breaching the walls on the night of 6 May 1527.

At the same time the Colonna were once again producing cultured and educated family members, which they had not done since the distant days in Avignon. The poetess *Vittoria Colonna* (1492–1547) was a close friend and spiritual companion of Michelangelo Buonarroti. Vittoria Colonna was part of a circle of thinkers who sought to renovate the Catholic church with a more interior focus of faith, away from outward ritual and towards sincere charity and deep feeling. Her unhappy marriage to the Marchese of Pescara, the great captain of the Holy Roman Emperor in Italy, ended early with his death in 1525 and she dedicated herself thereafter to her faith; after her death, she and her circle were accused of being involved in a Lutheran-like heretical movement.

MARCANTONIO II COLONNA (1537–85)

Vittoria's brother *Ascanio I Colonna* (*c.* 1498–1557) continued to fight the inherited battle against the papacy. Paul III Farnese sequestered Colonna properties and they were not returned until his death. Ascanio's son, *Marcantonio II Colonna* (1537–85) at first continued the old struggle, with a bitter conflict with Paul IV Carafa (1555–9), but after more loss of property the family were sufficiently subdued to submit to papal authority with the Peace of Cave in 1557. Marcantonio's dealings with the papacy then improved greatly with the election of Pius V Ghislieri (1566–72) and his friendly rapport with the pontiff, as well as his peacemaking marriage to an

Orsini, turned his career into one of faithful service to the pope, who in return elevated Paliano to the dignity of a principate in 1569.

Marcantonio Colonna represents the final degree of familial glory for the Colonna; even more than Martin V, the family pope, he is the emblematic family member. This is due entirely to his success as a naval commander at the battle of Lepanto, which merits further explanation.

From the fall of Constantinople in 1453, Christian Europe had been constricted by the crescent of Ottoman Turk power that edged the eastern Mediterranean. The Ottomans, a traditional enemy of the West since the Middle Ages, offered a serious naval threat to the Catholic powers of the Mediterranean basin, particularly

Marcantonio II Colonna, victor of Lepanto. His loyalty to Pius V was richly rewarded and marked the arrival of a permanent peace between the Colonna and the papacy.

through the use of pirates who made merchant traffic along the coasts of Spain and Italy increasingly dangerous. Venice, whose maritime interests made it the natural head of opposition to Ottoman expansion, suffered a terrible invasion of its territory of Friuli in 1499, which it repelled with great difficulty; in 1538 the republic was defeated in a battle at Prevesa and in 1571 it sustained the worst blow of all, the loss of Cyprus, whose lucrative sugar plantations made it the object of Ottoman desire. Suddenly the nightmare of Turkish dominance over the Adriatic was a reality and to combat the peril Pius V hastily arranged a Holy League, made up of Venetian, Spanish and papal fleets. The League was placed under the supreme command of the king of Spain's son, Don Juan of Austria, but the papal fleet had Marcantonio Colonna as its commander; it engaged the enemy on 7 October 1571 off the coast of Greece at Lepanto and destroyed the Ottoman fleet.

The impact of this victory on Catholic Europe was extraordinary. Up to that battle the Ottomans had appeared as invincible terrors, but Lepanto shattered the myth of Turkish invulnerability. The themes of Christ triumphing over Islam, and of the special intervention of the Virgin of the Rosary whose feast day occurred on the day of battle, were stressed in most depictions of the event, which also gave Marcantonio Colonna the pre-eminent role as commander. News of the victory reached Rome on the night of 21 October, two weeks after the battle, and Pius V celebrated a great Te Deum, with magnificent pomp and minted coinage to commemorate the event. Marcantonio Colonna was formally received on 4 December, when he began a triumphal procession at Marino on the coast, a Colonna family fief, and processed up alongside the Tiber before entering the city at the porta Capena, where he was greeted by the principal magistrates. His triumph, which consciously emulated those of the ancient emperors, made a huge impression on spectators. A large body of Turkish captives formed the core of his procession and captured banners and standards lined the streets of Rome, which were specially decorated with temporary triumphal arches and paintings of notable episodes and figures from the battle. The procession reached the Capitoline hill, then went on to the papal palace, where Pius V greeted Colonna rapturously, even to the extent of kissing his feet, an unheard-of honour. The results of the battle were, however, disappointing. Cyprus was never recaptured and Venice abandoned the Holy League after only two years, preferring instead to maintain a policy of prudence regarding the Turks, their most important eastern trade partners.

THE COLONNA SUCCESSION

All this glory somewhat disguised the fact that the Colonna were undergoing an increasingly serious financial crisis. The family, as befitted a leading house of Rome, lived far beyond their means. This prompted the sale, bit by bit, of the territory that had been accrued with so much bloodshed and opportunism. Marcantonio poured his coffers into the construction and elaboration of the family palace at Genazzano; *Pompeo Colonna* (d. 1584) and his son *Marzio* (d. c.1601) both overspent at Zagarolo, which obliged Marzio's son *Pierfrancesco Colonna* (d. 1633) to sell the central properties of the clan in 1614. In that year Montefortino and Olevano went to the Borghese family; eight years after that Zagarolo, Gallicano and Colonna itself passed into the hands of the powerful new family of the Ludovisi, relatives of the then pope, Gregory XV; this last sale brought the Colonna a million ducats, which gave them a chance to check the free-fall of their fortunes, but not in time to prevent the cession of the old ancestral seat of Palestrina to the family of Urban VIII Barberini in 1630. The new work begun on their property at Carbognano was a meagre consolation. The Colonna of Zagarolo died out in 1661 with the death of the last male heir and the remaining properties of the branch were absorbed by the Paliano branch.

The Colonna of Paliano, through careful management of their remaining wealth, managed to make an impressive economic recovery in the eighteenth century, despite maintaining a small private army to keep their territory safe from the banditry of the Roman countryside. Even in the leaner years of the seventeenth century the Paliano branch of the family had managed to generate a few spicy personalities. Cardinal *Girolamo Colonna* (1604–66) ordered the construction of the imposing Galleria Colonna and his nephew, *Lorenzo Onofrio Colonna* (1637–89), transformed the family residence in piazza Santi Apostoli into a magnificent late Baroque palace; Lorenzo Onofrio drew attention not only for his patronage of grand architectural work but also for his marriage to Maria Mancini, the niece of Cardinal Mazarin and former lover of the French king, Louis XIV. She was of a family of Colonna retainers – her grandfather had been the palace's butler – and her own family's rise was meteoric. The Mancini family lived close to the papal palace on the Quirinal, on the other side of the Colonna gardens in what is now Palazzo Pallavicini Rospigliosi. It was to that palace, then out of Rome entirely, that Maria Mancini fled when her marriage to Lorenzo Onofrio Colonna finally collapsed in 1672; he blamed her irrational jealousy and violent temper, but her departure probably owed as much to his endless philandering.

Giulio Cesare Colonna (1702–87) of the Sciarra-Carbognano branch managed to regain the old family seat of Palestrina by marrying the last Barberini heiress: this marriage, in fact, was the basis of the current Barberini family. At the end of the eighteenth century the Paliano branch of the family possessed ninety-seven estates, twenty-seven in the Papal States and the rest in the kingdom of Naples and Sicily, and was at the top of a feudal pyramid that included 150,000 vassals. The pope, in 1816, forced the family to renounce its feudal rights over its vassals in church territories. The palazzo Colonna at piazza Santi Apostoli, with its great Galleria, remained an inalienable property of the family and the Colonna of Paliano live there even now. Two Colonna princes, *Prospero* and *Pietro Colonna* (1858–1937 and 1891–1939 respectively), held the position of mayor of Rome and the head of the family, until the reforms of Paul VI in 1970, had the privilege of assisting, along with the head of the Orsini, in the enthronement of the pope.

Today the Colonna retain their position at the apex of the Roman aristocracy. While their rivals, the Orsini, have faded into insignificance, the Colonna still live in their grandiose palace in the heart of their old district, where they continue the tradition they set in the seventeenth century of opening their art collection to the public once a week.

COLONNA ITINERARY

Very few of the Colonna's many medieval building works have survived; some of their foundations bear no trace of their original patrons and others show very little. This is, therefore, an itinerary of secrets: the treasures of the Colonna palace are accessible only one morning a week and retracing the steps of the Colonna rise to power, the family's political and religious affiliations, and their marriage alliances is in large part as much an act of the imagination as it is a physical walk.

Though the family did not undertake significant street building or the rearrangement of their local neighbourhood, as did the Farnese, the Colonna's large area of territorial influence is still visible, stretching as it once did from the hospital of San Giacomo degl' Incurabili on the via del Corso all the way to Trajan's Markets. In a sense, the Colonna did not need to impose their own family stamp on part of Rome: they *were* Rome.

▌ Chapel of the Holy Column, Santa Prassede
Entrance from via di Santa Prassede or via di San Martino ai Monti.
Open 9–12, 16.30–18.30

Colonna sites in and around Santa Maria Maggiore, from the Nolli map of 1748

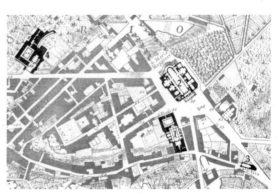

Key:
1 Santa Prassede, with the chapel of the Holy Column
2 Santa Maria Maggiore: apse and façade mosaics
3 San Vito
4 S. Lorenzo in Panisperna

In 1222 Cardinal Giovanni Colonna the Younger, the intelligent nephew of the first Colonna cardinal, returned from his mission as legate to the Latin eastern kingdoms. Constantinople had fallen to the Fourth Crusade in 1204; the old capital of the Greek Empire was in the hands of a noble family of Flanders, which had been installed as the new imperial house. The forced reunion of the Greek Orthodox and Catholic Churches that resulted required a good deal of careful attention and Cardinal Giovanni was the pope's envoy to Constantinople and Jerusalem. The king of Jerusalem gave him one of the most important relics of Christendom: the Holy Column, purporting to be the one at which Christ was flagellated.

Cardinal Colonna had been given as his *titulus* or cardinalate church the old basilica of Santa Prassede in 1212, so the Holy Column was duly brought there for veneration. For many centuries it was kept in the sacristy of the church and only shown to pilgrims on great feast days. In 1699 it was moved to its present position and a niche in the ninth-century chapel of St Zeno was cut away to make a doorway into the new chapel. The reliquary in which the Column stands was made in 1898 of bronze, designed by the artist Duilio Cambellotti, prominent as a designer of ceramics, posters, medals and stained glass. It is a strangely art nouveau setting for such a fundamentally medieval relic.

The short column, which once bore a metal loop at the top to which Christ's hands were allegedly tied, looks very much like part of a balustrade. Its current neglected location and the inevitable questions of authenticity that hover over such relics have tended to diminish the importance of the Holy Column. But until the Second Vatican Council reduced the importance of relics in the 1960s, Santa Prassede was one of the most significant relic churches in the city.

Representations of the real appearance of the Holy Column occur from time to time in other Roman monuments. It can be seen, in company with other emblems of Christ's Passion, in a relief in the Chigi chapel in Santa Maria della Pace. It also makes another appearance in effigy, in a much more prominent place: one of the angels on the bridge to the Castel Sant'Angelo, carved by one of Bernini's followers, Antonio Raggi (1624–86), is carrying Cardinal Colonna's Holy Column, looking for all the world like a chess player about to put an opponent into checkmate with an enormous rook.

2 Apse mosaics, Santa Maria Maggiore
Entrance from piazza Santa Maria Maggiore. Open 9–19

To enter the great basilica of Santa Maria Maggiore at noon is to be confronted with the full splendour of the thirteenth century and with the apex of Colonna artistic patronage during the Middle Ages. Even sceptical Protestant viewers will share the opinion of Ferdinand Gregorovius, the nineteenth-century historian of medieval Rome:

> The mosaic fills the building with a solemn golden splendour that is more
> than earthly. When illumined by the sunlight falling through the purple
> curtains [which no longer remain, though the effect is unchanged], it
> reminds us of that glowing heaven, bathed in whose glories Dante saw

Santi Bernard, Francis, Dominic and Bonaventura. Then the spell of the work seizes us with its radiance like the music of some majestic anthem.

The church itself was decorated, in the first instance, to commemorate the decision of the Council of Edessa (AD 431) to affirm the Virgin Mary as *Theotokos*, the mother of the divine as well as the human Christ. New decoration on this theme was required, however, when Pope Nicholas IV Maschi (1288–92) demolished the old apse of the basilica and constructed a larger one. The pope, a Colonna ally who had grown up in the service of the family, was interested in restoring sites of papal glory and in this effort he had the support of Cardinal Colonna, his *éminence grise*. The former Girolamo Maschi was of humble birth: he rose, as Sixtus IV would in the fifteenth century, through the ranks of the Franciscan order, becoming its general, before receiving the cardinal's hat in 1278. He was widely perceived to be a tool of the Colonna and a satire depicted him as encased entirely in a column, with only a mitred head sticking out of the top.

Cardinal Giacomo Colonna represented the joint power of Orsini and Colonna, as his mother was an Orsini; Giacomo had received his elevation at the hands of his uncle, the Orsini pope, Nicholas III (1277–80), who had also made Girolamo Maschi a cardinal. Giacomo was connected, too, with the Franciscan order, which was much patronised by the Colonna; there is a chance that his uncle, Nicholas III, as a child had actually met St Francis. We see, in the interventions in this church, the close spiritual, familial and clientage ties between pope, Orsini and Colonna that existed in the last decades of the thirteenth century.

In the apse mosaics of Santa Maria Maggiore, St Francis stands furthest out from the holy throne of Jesus and Mary, but in the venerated company of Peter and Paul, the two uniquely Roman saints. Jacopo Torriti, the artist who created the mosaics, was himself a Franciscan. Torriti had already completed his other mosaic work in the apse of San Giovanni in Laterano (though the present apse mosaic there was almost completely remade when Leo XIII barbarously demolished and rebuilt the apse at the end of the nineteenth century). It is only at Santa Maria Maggiore that we can see the original splendour of Torriti's achievement.

The Byzantine style of the mosaic has often been used as an example of the 'decadence' of Roman art in the thirteenth century, but in fact Torriti had a difficult task, uniting elements from the previous mosaic of the fifth century with the requirements of his own day. Torriti's colossal figures of Christ and the Virgin dominated the basilica until the eighteenth century, when Ferdinando Fuga's huge *baldacchino* was built, obscuring the mosaics and changing the focus from apse to altar.

To signify the dominion of heaven, Christ and his mother are seated on a Byzantine *kathisma* (double throne), like an emperor and empress. The blue aureole surrounding the holy couple represents the heavens and the sky behind the figures is a star-scattered lapis blue; the sun and moon both hang unpretentiously beneath the two pairs of holy feet. Christ, expressing the doctrine of the Council of Edessa, which must also have been represented in the original mosaic, is in the act of crowning his mother. Surrounding the aureole is a host of angels, all with the fluttering multicoloured wings that are such a feature of Roman religious art of the thirteenth century. Above the aureole a pleated veil represents the empyrean, the highest level of heaven, and in the upper field of the apse an elaborate vegetal decoration springs from two trunks at the far edges of the mosaic, two trees of life that have their roots in the four rivers that spring from the centre of the lower edge. By the banks of this quadruple stream, beautifully observed details of nature and country life are represented and on either side, kneeling on the upper banks, are the portraits of the two patrons: to the left is Pope Nicholas IV and to the right is Cardinal Giacomo Colonna himself, mitred and robed as a bishop, with a pious expression on his clean-shaven face.

The lower register of the apse is decorated with five scenes from the life of the Virgin, demarcated by the interruptions of three Gothic arched windows. In the left-hand section are the Annunciation and the Nativity, in the right-hand section the Offering of the Three Kings and the Presentation at the Temple, and in the long central section is the Death (or Dormition) of the Virgin. The central panel is the most remarkable, due to its profusion of figures and to the presence of Christ in the centre, holding the soul of his mother as if it were a baby itself, bringing the cycle of divine birth, death and rebirth to a close. At the side of the Virgin's bed, and practically invisible from the ground, are three small figures, representing the three orders of the Franciscans: two men, one tonsured and the other with hair intact, and one woman, all wear the habit of St Francis.

The mosaic was completed in 1295, three years after the death of Nicholas IV, but before the accession of Boniface VIII, whose war against the Colonna would have interrupted the work. Despite Boniface's interdict upon the clan, and the 'crusade' he called against the Colonna, Cardinal Giacomo's nephew Pietro, the son of the senator Giovanni and a cardinal himself, sponsored the mosaic decoration of the façade of the basilica, which is still visible despite its concealment behind Fuga's elegant eighteenth-century cladding (a guided tour, giving access to the upper porch, and a closer look at the façade mosaics can be obtained upon request in the gift shop). Made for the jubilee of 1300 by the mosaicist Filippo Rusuti, the central window is surmounted on both sides by the crest of the Colonna. The work is made up of two bands, the upper certainly by Rusuti, who put his signature at the bottom of the central aureole, and the lower mostly by pupils, in which the influence of Giotto has been detected. In the upper band the central focus, as in the apse, is on an aureole, this one containing a Christ in Benediction, surrounded by the Virgin and Saints. In the lower band are episodes from the legendary founding of the church: the Roman patrician Giovanni, in the fifth century, had a dream of the Virgin, who ordered him to build a church on the area which she, miraculously, would cover with snow the next day, 5 August, on the Esquiline hill. This legend, in fact, forms part of the mythology of another Roman family, the Patrizi, who claim descent from the patrician Giovanni and whose family tombs stand in the basilica.

Another, much later, manifestation of Colonna presence is a relief-work panel on the tomb of Pope Pius V Ghislieri, in the Sistine Chapel off the right-hand aisle near the altar, a huge and sumptuous domed chapel built as a funerary monument for and by Pope Sixtus V Peretti (1585–90) and to honour Sixtus's patron, Pius V, who was later canonised. Sixtus, a stern, even despotic ruler, succeeded in pacifying the ongoing conflict between Orsini and Colonna by marrying his nephews to an Orsini and a Colonna. Sixtus established the heads of both families as assistants at the papal throne. The tomb of Pius V, mirroring that of Sixtus V across the floor of the chapel, contains five scenes of episodes in the pope's life; the left-hand relief, by the minor sculptor Nicolò Pippi (d. c.1601), depicts the defeat of the Turks at Lepanto, with Marcantonio Colonna, the commander of the papal fleet, kneeling before the pope. Sixtus V, in 1574 while still cardinal, also commissioned the tomb of the medieval Colonna client-pope Nicholas IV Maschi; it stands to the left of the main entrance.

3 San Silvestro in Capite, Colonna chapel
Entrance from piazza San Silvestro or via del Gambero. Open daily 9–12, 16–19

This quiet church, whose front courtyard insulates it from the bustle of the busy piazza in front, shows little trace of its medieval appearance. This is, in fact, characteristic of Colonna monuments, which generally were kept *au courant* and were redecorated in the style of successive periods; this makes imagining the erstwhile appearance rather difficult.

The original church was built during the pontificate of Stephen II (752–7) and by his successor and brother, Paul I, who completed it and dedicated it to the pope-saints Silvester and Stephen I, over the ruins of the Temple of the Invincible Sun (*Sol Invictus*), a military cult endorsed by the Emperor Aurelian in the third century AD, so it had a long history as a sacred site. Though the brother popes partly constructed the church over their own house, they also used the site of the temple to make a point about Christianity triumphant over its rival faiths; in addition Christianity commandeered the great feast day of the Invincible Sun, 25 December, as Christmas. The church was called a series of different names, *cata Pauli* after the house of Paul I, *inter duos hortos*, between two gardens, in honour of the vast tracts of arable space that surrounded it, and finally *in Capite*, referring to its great relic, the severed head of St John the Baptist.

In 1285 the property was given by the Savelli pope, Honorius IV, to Margherita Colonna's small informal community of female followers of St Francis. The procurer of this rich monastery for such a young community – Margherita had died only five years before – was, tellingly, Cardinal Colonna himself, the dead girl's brother. The Colonna family had a stake in keeping Margherita's memory alive. It was to their advantage to have a saintly figure in their pedigree, certainly; but the sincerity of the Colonna affection for Franciscan forms of faith was equally important. Margherita's brother Giovanni wrote her biography and both brothers, Giovanni and Cardinal Giacomo, extended their protection over the little community she left behind.

Franciscan faith had struck medieval society with the force of a thunderbolt. Francis, born of a wealthy merchant in Assisi in about 1182, renounced his worldly goods and went to live in the wilderness, attracting followers who were transported by the passion of his sermons and the shining, romantic example of his rejection of the world of the senses for that of the spirit. This renunciation, which amounted to a scathing critique of the Church, prompted emulators all over the Italian peninsula and further abroad: it was a genuine popular movement, which electrified the otherwise somewhat indifferent spirituality of the high Middle Ages. The Church strove to contain it: Francis was canonised rapidly after his death and even before then his Rule, creating a monastic order for his followers, had been accepted by Innocent III.

Francis and his great female follower Clare both struggled to resist the forces of gift-giving traditional society and tried to keep the poverty of their orders complete, not to be tied to property owning but to rely, instead, on charity. In this, however, they were thoroughly defeated after their deaths. Clare, in particular, was keenly aware of the spiritual dangers of communal wealth; she had seen the old religious orders of the Cistercians and

Benedictines slump under the weight of property, concerning themselves increasingly with managing their wealth and aggrandising their houses. Once, when a cardinal offered to absolve her from her vow of poverty if it were standing in the way of her establishing a religious order, she replied, 'Holy Father, absolve me from my sins if you will, but I wish not to be absolved from following Jesus Christ.'

In 1253 Clare obtained papal approval for her own Rule, which embraced absolute poverty. However, after her death a subsequent pope divided the order in two, with one Rule for the followers of Clare, the Claress Rule, which was slightly stricter, and the Minoress Rule, which was more comfortable. The Claresses and Minoresses were made to accept property, to live enclosed in convents and to wear conventional habits. Thus the Church tamed the Franciscan female orders, as it had, to varying degrees, the male orders. It was in this spiritual setting that the followers of Margherita Colonna came to Rome from their place in the open hills around Palestrina. The history of Margherita's community reflects, in miniature, this compromised history of Franciscanism. When Margherita's body was brought down from the hills into the church, the bells in the bell tower were said to have rung spontaneously; these bells, ringing in celebration, were also tolling the knell of Margherita's own intentions for her community.

Honorius IV Savelli accepted Margherita's followers into the order of Minoresses, ordered six friars to serve them (for they were an enclosed order, unable to beg for alms on their own behalf) and gave them the rich monastery of San Silvestro in Capite. This was a subtle gesture for, as the monastery lay deep in Colonna-controlled land, not very far from the Colonna fortress in the Mausoleum of Augustus, it was likely to receive a good deal of protection and support from the family. The house was, in fact, very soon richly endowed by Colonna bequests.

This remained a principal Colonna house for centuries: in 1347, three grief-stricken Colonna widows retreated there with the corpses of their husbands, killed in the family struggle against the populist Cola di Rienzo. In 1417 the comfortable nunnery housed not only two Colonna women, Maria and Egidia, but also other aristocratic ladies, from the houses of Orsini, Annibaldi, Anguillara and Caffarelli. The poetess Vittoria Colonna died here in 1547. Clearly the monastery of San Silvestro in Capite offered a not unpleasant alternative to marriage for Roman noblewomen. By the eighteenth century the nunnery's kitchens were using 10,000 eggs a month in the creation of pastries.

Not much remains of the thirteenth-century church. The basic plan is the same, with the forecourt in front of the main entrance still full of ancient sculptural fragments, and some floor tombs of medieval nuns and abbesses have been set into the façade. The long inscription in the porch contains the word *columpna* several times over: this does not, however, refer to the Colonna family, but to the charges made to pilgrims wishing to climb the stairs within the Column of Marcus Aurelius in the nearby piazza Colonna. The cornice over the entrance, too, dates from the thirteenth century and the original bell tower still houses the bells that rang of their own accord to welcome Margherita's remains.

The current building, however, spans the seventeenth century, the church itself dating from 1598–1601 and the façade from 1703. The **interior** is a somewhat decayed but still sumptuous showpiece of the late Baroque. It is striking, given the Franciscan and Colonna history of the church, how little either Francis or the Colonna family, or indeed Margherita, appear in the decoration of the church, a signal of the decay in the connection between the original Colonna patrons. The **Colonna chapel** lies closest to the high altar in the right-hand transept of the church. It contains four very old crests, two of which display the Colonna column alone, and two others which contain the column paired with the Orsini rose and stripes: this is the crest of Margherita and Giacomo, and must be of thirteenth-century date. A later Colonna, Lucrezia Tomacelli Colonna (d. 1622; her portraits can be seen in the Galleria Colonna and her tomb stands in the family chapel in San Giovanni in Laterano), had the chapel redecorated in 1601, by which time, it seems, memories of Margherita were too faint to influence the altarpiece, by Baccio Ciarpi (1574–1654), sporting a banal iconography of Virgin and Child with Saints. Another chapel, the **chapel of St Francis**, also has Colonna crests on the side walls, two familiar crests with columns in relief against a red mosaic ground. Before leaving the church, by all means examine the skull of 'John the Baptist', conserved in a chapel forming a side entrance.

Though Margherita Colonna was beatified in 1847, she had been venerated as a saint in Colonna territories for many centuries; it is strange, therefore, to find no memorial to her. When her convent was dissolved at the end of the nineteenth century, during the suppression of the religious orders that gave offices in Rome to the ministries of the new Italian state, the last of Margherita's nuns may have taken her body with them when they left. The more one thinks about this, the more peculiar it seems for the Colonna to have let their family saint be neglected. The only place where she seems to be commemorated is, unexpectedly, in the Princess Cornelia Costanza apartment in palazzo Barberini.

4 Torre Colonna

Via Quattro Novembre, angle with via delle Tre Cannelle. No admission

On the tightly curving modern street called the via IV Novembre that joins via Nazionale with piazza Venezia, among modern buildings like the Waldensian church and the Pace Elvezia Hotel, rises a curious and unprepossessing brick structure of greater antiquity than that of its neighbours. It is, in fact, an old fortified outbuilding of the Colonna family and it dates from the twelfth century, when it was built by a predecessor of Colonna power here, whose heirs ceded it to the Colonna in the thirteenth century. It originally had three floors (whose windows can be seen on the side of the tower facing via delle Tre Cannelle; the six windows facing on to via IV Novembre are modern) and a crenellated cornice, now missing.

In its heyday this building was a significant monument in the neighbourhood, overshadowed only by the huge Torre delle Milizie not far away. The **Torre Colonna** is today the only trace visible of the broad defensive network that the Colonna installed round their family stronghold. It is decorated with fragments of ancient carving, just above door level, and atop the display is a heraldic Colonna column, somewhat hard to identify due to the grime of a century of car exhaust. Another Colonna emblem also appears here, an original piece of ancient sculpture: the Siren, an image taken up by Marcantonio II Colonna with the motto 'She Despises the Storms'. The ruthless slicing of new streets through the old urban fabric in the late nineteenth century created the via IV Novembre from two narrower streets, one of which was called vicolo dei Colonnesi (Colonna Alley). Now the Colonna tower is curiously exposed and anonymous, isolated on the wrong side of the busy road from the massive bulk of the Colonna palace.

It is hard today to imagine the wilderness of this part of Rome in the thirteenth century. The street that is now called via IV Novembre, in its brief straight stretch between its two turns, more or less follows the traces of a street called the via Biberatica, a name it bore from ancient times, when it was part of the market complex built by the Emperor Trajan not long after the year AD 100: it was Drinks Street ('drink' in Latin is *biber*), where beverages could be purchased. If you walk up to where the street turns towards the via Nazionale and look over the fence there, you can see the ancient street, excavated in the 1920s and 1930s under Mussolini's orders, set well below current ground level but still following more or less the same course and faced on either side by surprisingly modern-looking shopfronts. The *contrada Biberatica* (Biberatica district) was an area of small houses, dirt paths and kitchen gardens, all unquestionably Colonna territory. The road ran along the fortified flank of the old Colonna fortress. Today, as via della Pilotta, it still defines the edge of the Colonna palace, and it is faced on both sides by Colonna property; it is still *colonnese*. The striking feature of the via della Pilotta remains the group of four bridges that join the palazzo Colonna with the family's private gardens on the other side of the street, on the slope of the Quirinal hill.

5 Palazzo Colonna and its Galleria

Entrance from piazza Santi Apostoli 66. No admission without prior appointment (see below)

I THE PALACE
AND ITS DEVELOPMENT

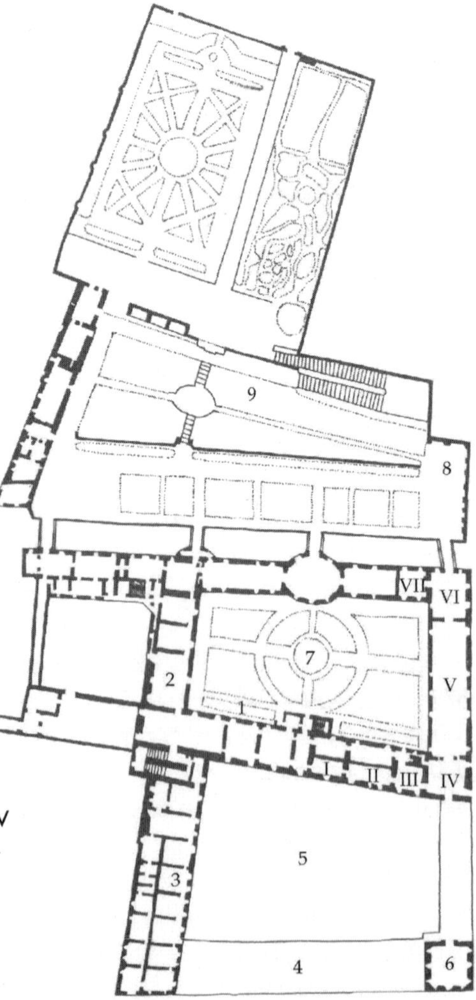

The palazzo Colonna and villa Colonna

Key:
1 site of medieval/Renaissance Colonna fortress
2 palazzina della Rovere
3 wing running alongside basilica of SS. Apostoli (formerly part of Riario-della Rovere palace)
4 stable wing
5 stable courtyard
6 coffee house
7 main courtyard
8 monument to Marcantonio II Colonna
9 villa Colonna

Galleria Colonna
I   Room of the Primitives
II   Throne room
III   Room of the Apotheosis of Martin V
IV   Room of the Landscapes
V   Great Gallery
VI   Room of the Column
VII   Vestibule

The massive block that comprises palazzo Colonna, the basilica of the Santi Apostoli and the Franciscan house called the 'palazzo dei Santi Apostoli' attached to the basilica have gone through many alterations over the years. Though they form one block, we may see the two buildings as two separate complexes, one an ecclesiastical agglomeration of cardinalate palace and basilica, the other an accumulation of fortified houses belonging to a baronial family. These two complexes were in competition, one struggling to build over the other; it is a mark of Colonna skill and patience that the baronial family won out over the cardinalate palace, swallowing half of it along with most of its garden and a little garden pavilion which is now incorporated into the vast bulk of the Colonna palace. The cardinalate palace was driven back behind the dividing line created by the basilica.

In its original condition the Colonna stronghold most likely resembled a typical fortress of the type of palazzo Anguillara, at the beginning of the viale Trastevere on the other side of the river: a tower formed one corner, with a large courtyard enclosed by a strongly fortified wall containing various outbuildings and stables. The body of the fortress, as with that of the modern palace, stretched north–south across the middle of the block, more or less halfway between the piazza Santi Apostoli and the via della Pilotta, and the massive area in front was an enclosed forecourt. The southern part of the building was apparently known as the palace of the elm (palazzo dell'Olmo). To the north the Colonna palace stretches northwards behind the apse of the basilica of Santi Apostoli, where it meets the former palace of Giuliano della Rovere, the future Pope Julius II, a Colonna ally.

None of the medieval constructions survives to give us a sense of their layout: the successive destructions by Boniface VIII and Sixtus IV, and rebuilding in the seventeenth and eighteenth centuries, made sure of that. The palace that Martin V Colonna, of the Genazzano branch, took over from the old dominant Palestrina branch in 1419 has completely vanished. However, late fifteenth century sections still exist and documents can allow us to reconstruct the complex. To begin with, much of the building flanking the basilica was linked to the church, rather than the palace: the building on the basilica's south side was originally a palace built for the basilica's titular cardinal, John Bessarion (1403–72), a refugee from the fall of Constantinople to the Turks in 1453 who was of great learning and famous for his holiness. It was said that he could have been elected pope, if only he had agreed to shave his beard, which was that of a Greek monk.

His successor in the *titulus*, and the cardinalate palace, was Pietro Riario, the rapacious young nephew of Sixtus IV della Rovere, a Colonna enemy. Riario's palace was soon to be linked, across the front of the basilica via a

One of the Colonna palaces in the early sixteenth century, by Etienne Dupérac. The medieval fortress gave way to a palace with a modest portico. Higher up the Quirinal hill, the remains of the temple of Serapis stood in the Colonna gardens, until it was demolished and recycled in the early seventeenth century.

new double loggia which still stands today, with another wing (today's Franciscan monastery, which we will visit in the della Rovere itinerary) built to the north of the basilica by Giuliano della Rovere as his principal seat during his long stint as cardinal. The same man, an industrious builder, extended his property behind the basilica to form a garden, in the middle of which he constructed a pavilion, the palazzina della Rovere. The Colonna alliance with Giuliano della Rovere resulted in a gift: in 1508, Julius II gave the south wing of his palace, and much of the garden along with its palazzina, in perpetual lease to a Colonna prince who had married his niece. Clement VII de' Medici (1523–34) once attended a banquet in the palace where he assisted in tossing small birds and delicacies to the crowd in the piazza below, who were taking part in races to catch pigs for prizes distributed by the Colonna, while members of the family showered cold water on them from the upper windows.

Massive rebuilding took place in the second half of the sixteenth century, when Cardinal Carlo Borromeo (1538–84) rented the palazzina and spent 10,500 scudi on redecorations and renovations, money which was later counted as part of the dowry of Anna Borromeo, the cardinal's sister, who married Marcantonio II's eldest son, Fabrizio. At the same time the northeast corner of the block, previously part of the gardens of Giuliano della Rovere's palace, was built over, with a structure that today houses the Pontifical Biblical Institute. However, it was in the seventeenth and

G.Vasi dis.et.
1 Antichaglie nel giardino di detto Palazzo, a. Appart. nuovi del medesimo Palazzo per uso della famiglia g.Chiesa dei XII SS Apostoli, q.Palazzo Muti

Palazzo Colonna

Palazzo Colonna in an engraving by Vasi. Here the stable wing (foreground) still has its Rococo façade, now replaced by a Neoclassical one. Vasi has inserted some of the ancient marbles from the villa Colonna into the right-hand corner.

eighteenth centuries that the palace underwent a massive consolidation to turn all the disparate parts of it into a unified complex. Marcantonio II's great-grandson Cardinal Girolamo (1604–66) put together the core of the art collection, and Girolamo's nephew Lorenzo Onofrio Colonna (1637–89) constructed the glittering setting for it, the Galleria Colonna, with Antonio Del Grande (1625–71) and Gianlorenzo Bernini (1598–1680) as architects followed by Girolamo Fontana (fl. 1690 –1714), who completed the gallery in 1703. The building received a rococo finish under the architects Mario Michetti and Paolo Posi in 1730: Michetti created the front facing on to piazza Santi Apostoli and Posi the back, with the bridges into the villa Colonna across the street. In the late nineteenth century Michetti's stable wing and the edge of the palace facing the new via IV Novembre were both remade by Andrea Busiri Vici, who stripped off the rococo window arrangement on the piazza and elaborated it on the new road elevation. From the via IV Novembre, the Colonna emblem of the Siren can be seen decorating the western front of the Galleria wing.

The palace remained a centre of Roman high society for centuries and continues to be a relatively exclusive bastion of aristocratic privilege. Colonna banquets were famous for their sumptuousness, like the one given for the son of the king of Poland by the High Constable Fabrizio in the 1730s, of eighteen courses. Male guests were, however, required to undergo the strange ritual of urinating into one of two antique vases decorated with myrtle and orange branches placed by the front door, perhaps as a preventative measure to stop them from performing the same function in corners of the palace. This went on until the fall of the Papal States in 1870. Perhaps the advent of the kings of Italy brought adequate plumbing.

II   THE PRINCESS ISABELLE APARTMENT
Entrance from piazza Santi Apostoli 66. Tel. 06 678 4350; fax 06 679 4638; website: www.galleriacolonna.it; e-mail: galleriacolonna@tin.it. Open upon advance request only to groups of ten or more. Admission €15 per person

This part of the palace is only open to groups and is sometimes used as banquet space for corporate functions. The entrance to the apartment, which is named for the twentieth-century Colonna princess who restored it, is inside the first great courtyard, which is reached from the *portone* on piazza Santi Apostoli. It is a ground-floor suite, a summer apartment; the lower floors, darker and cooler, were much more desirable residences in the heat of July than during the dank cold of the winter, when the occupant would move upstairs to the *piano nobile*. Lavishly decorated, it contains a further selection of the family art, displaying Prince Lorenzo Onofrio's taste for landscapes with no less than three rooms decorated by masters of the genre like Gaspard Dughet (1615–75) and Pietro Mulier (*c.* 1637–1701), called Il Tempesta from his skill at seascapes. Another room displays small panel paintings by Gaspar Van Wittel (1653–1736), Italianised to Vanvitelli, who was employed as a painter by three generations of the Colonna family. The paintings show scenes of Roman landmarks as well as Colonna properties outside Rome and some *capricci*, imaginative scenes with ruins.

III   THE GALLERIA COLONNA
Entrance at via della Pilotta 17. Tel. 06 678 4350; fax 06 679 4638; website: www.galleriacolonna.it; e-mail: galleriacolonna@tin.it. Open Saturday mornings, 9–13, closed in August. Admission €7. Open at other times upon advance request

To visit the Galleria Colonna is to enter one of the most grandiose expressions of late Baroque display in Rome. The Galleria is more than a collection of art: it is, most properly, the dazzling setting for the court of the Colonna princes of Paliano. In this setting the art is merely one component and, to understand it, the visitor should not separate the art from the rooms themselves, as together they form a coherent cultural artefact created for one purpose: to demonstrate the wealth and power of the Colonna. As such it reflects the will of its three principal builders, Cardinal Girolamo Colonna, his nephew Lorenzo Onofrio and the latter's son, Filippo II, who inaugurated the gallery in 1703. The collection itself is of less interest than the overall effect of the magnificent state apartment, chronologically the last in this book and the culmination of a long development which we will explore in detail in later chapters.

Modern visitors have a reversed view of the sequence of rooms seen by guests of Don Filippo. We enter from via della Pilotta, up a set of servants' stairs into what is today called the vestibule and from there suddenly into the grand state rooms. This is confusing, rendering the original sequence meaningless. Instead of encouraging you to explore each room as you arrive in it, I suggest you go immediately to the last room in the sequence, the Room of the Primitives, where the itinerary begins.

As we will see in the Barberini chapter, the main building block of a Baroque palace was the living and working space of a noble, the state apartment. Palazzo Colonna offers us only a partial visit to Don Filippo's state apartment, reserving both the original entrance and the private suite for the family's own use. From the Room of the Primitives a door opened into another ante-room and the main staircase, which admitted guests from the courtyard. The **Room of the Primitives**, so called from its smattering of early paintings, was one of the first reception rooms, an antecamera (antechamber). Here the visitor would have noticed the collection of paintings, though the present hang is entirely modern. One of the most remarkable works in this room is by Pietro da Cortona (1596–1669), the *Resurrection of Christ with Members of the Colonna Family* (**143** in the present numbering of the collection) commissioned in 1623 by Filippo I Colonna for the family funerary chapel at Paliano. Christ soars heavenwards in triumph, admired by angels and God the Father, while below, Filippo I, his wife Lucrezia Tomacelli and his mother Anna Borromeo ease themselves politely out of their coffins. The portraits of Lucrezia and Anna were posthumous, as Lucrezia had died the year before and Anna in 1582, and the painting represents an affectionate tribute from a bereaved husband and dutiful grandson. Another small portrait in this room is one by Gaspar Netscher (1639–84) of *Maria Mancini Colonna* (**130**), the unhappy wife of Lorenzo Onofrio, resplendent in ermine-trimmed robes and depicted in the French court manner, as befitted a woman who had been Louis XIV's lover.

The next room, the **throne room**, necessarily stood at the beginning of the great sequence of state rooms. This, the papal throne room, was merely one of several throne rooms in the palace. The portrait of Martin V Colonna above the throne seems to suggest that he was the pope for whom the throne was meant, but this was certainly not the case, as the palace post-dates his reign by almost three centuries. This throne room had a specific function in Roman etiquette. When a pope came to visit the Colonna princes, he naturally outranked them. Thus the pope was ushered into this room, where he could function as the host and welcome his subordinates to their own event. The throne is kept turned to the wall when a pope is not visiting. The room is strangely plain: it had no function except when a pope was present and the family concentrated its energies in decorating the rest of the apartment, where their own authority was supreme.

The eighteenth-century guest would be ushered into the next room, the **Room of the Apotheosis of Martin V**, just to be reminded of how glorious the Colonna's own pope had been. The ceiling decoration, by Benedetto Luti (1666–1724), who also did an altarpiece for Santi Apostoli next door, shows the pope welcomed in heaven. This room contains some of the gallery's most important paintings, including the treasure of the collection, the *Bean Eater* (**43**) of Annibale Carracci (1560–1609), much admired for its sketchy, energetic depiction of a peasant at supper.

From here the visitor arrives in the first of the sequence of three grand rooms that comprise the major gallery space. This is the **Room of the Landscapes**. Prince Lorenzo Onofrio's passionate interest in landscape painting has its strongest expression in this room, which displays paintings by Gaspard Dughet, as well as works by other prominent artists in the same genre. Lorenzo Onofrio once owned no less than nine huge landscapes by the most prestigious artist of the genre, Claude Lorrain (1600–82), but these were sold in 1798, along with many of the other greatest works in the collection, to help the pope meet the terms of the Treaty of Tolentino. The room also contains two lavish desks, one with an ivory relief copy of Michelangelo's *Last Judgement*. Even more important, the spectacular ceiling fresco, by Sebastiano Ricci (1659–1734), is an *Allegory of the Victory of Marcantonio II Colonna at Lepanto* and the furniture here has a recurrent Turkish-prisoner motif. For the remainder of the state rooms, allusions to the family pope disappear in favour of the great secular family leader, Marcantonio II, to underline the power of the Colonna prince receiving guests at the other end of the gallery.

From here, steps lead down to the **Great Gallery**, the architectural centrepiece of the state apartment. Recent studies have shown that the gallery's design is due to no less a genius than Gianlorenzo Bernini himself, who had been a guest of Louis XIV at Versailles in 1665 and returned to recreate a Hall of Mirrors for the Colonna. The ceiling is frescoed with scenes from the life of Marcantonio II, including the central *Battle of Lepanto*, by Giovanni Coli (1636–81) and Filippo Gherardi (1643–1701), two painters from the Tuscan republic of Lucca who always worked together. All the scenes are painted to be seen from the Room of the Landscapes end of the gallery. This ceiling is a Venetian effusion of colour and perspectival effects; the rich, brightly coloured silk of captured Turkish standards is vividly represented. Five pairs of windows face each other across the gallery, and between them are Venetian glass mirrors, painted with putti by Carlo Maratta (1625–1713) and flowers by Mario Nuzzi (1603–73), called Mario de' Fiori for his stock-in-trade. These are peeling now, but must have created a great sensation when they first appeared, paintings full of reflected and mobile light. The paintings on the mirrors served a practical purpose as well: the mirrors were made of several panes of glass and the painting concealed the joins. Paired sets of ancient statues are set between the windows, subtly attesting to the antiquity of the family and to their taste.

At the far side of the room a cannonball lies on the steps leading up from the Great Gallery, resting where it landed in the French siege of Rome on 24 June 1849. At the top is the **Room of the Column**, the throne room of Prince Filippo II Colonna and his successors. His throne, and that of his wife Princess Olimpia Pamphilj, would have been placed to either side of the ancient spiral column that forms the room's centrepiece, while above, the ceiling is frescoed with a scene of *The Apotheosis of Marcantonio Colonna* by Giuseppe Chiari (1654–1727), in which the victor of Lepanto is received into heaven, the final stage in the natural progression of scenes in his story. Behind the column a set of doors open on to a bridge leading to the Villa Colonna (never open) and the culmination of this grand view is a triumphal arch dedicated to Marcantonio II, with his statue in the centre. Set here in front of the light, surrounded by art glorifying his family, Prince Colonna must have appeared to visitors almost as a god. The last scene in the film *Roman Holiday*, which was shot here, approximates this effect, with Audrey Hepburn's throne resting where Don Filippo's would have been.

This room contains a number of portraits of the Colonna family. A depiction perhaps of *Vittoria Colonna* (37) shares space with Lorenzo Lotto's (1480–1557) *Cardinal Pompeo Colonna* (106) here. A portrait perhaps by Anton van Dyck (1599–1641) of *Lucrezia Tomacelli Colonna* (66) hangs here, made in the year of her death, 1622; she was the wife of Filippo I Colonna, grandson of Marcantonio, the victor of Lepanto. A portrait by a follower of Dosso Dossi (c.1489–1542) is said to depict the ferocious *Sciarra Colonna* (53). Two portraits by Pietro Novelli (1603–47) depict *Marcantonio V Colonna* (131) and his Sicilian wife *Isabella Gioeni Colonna* (132) with their son, the youthful Lorenzo Onofrio himself, contrasted against the dark tent of his mother's skirts.

After these magnificent rooms, the **vestibule** and **stairs** come as something of an anticlimax. They contain a series of historical portraits, many of Colonna family members, and a number of copies of paintings by great artists.

6 Piazza Santi Apostoli and the basilica of Santi Apostoli
Basilica open daily 8–12, 16–19

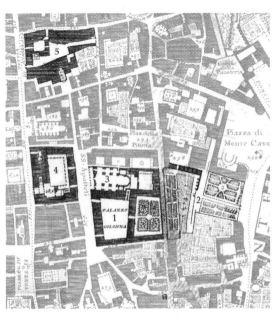

Colonna sites in and near piazza Santi Apostoli

Key:
1 palazzo Colonna
2 villa Colonna
3 basilica of Santi Apostoli
4 palazzo Colonna di Zagarolo
  (today's palazzo Odescalchi)
5 palazzo Sciarra

The long, thin piazza Santi Apostoli more closely resembles a wide street than a piazza. It was, for many centuries, the very heart of the Colonna-dominated territory of Rome. Both palaces facing each other along the long sides of the piazza were Colonna palaces; only one still is today. The other palace, today palazzo Odescalchi, belonged to the Colonna dukes of Zagarolo, who were forced to sell it in 1622 to the new family of the Ludovisi. They raised enough money to buy back the palace, which had been restructured by Carlo Maderno in the meantime, six years later. When the Zagarolo branch died out in 1661, it was sold to the Chigi and rebuilt for them by Bernini (for which see the Chigi itinerary); eventually it passed into the hands of the Odescalchi family, who had it enlarged in the eighteenth century by Nicola Salvi (1697–1751), the designer of the Trevi fountain.

The piazza has been a scene of Colonna ceremony since the Middle Ages, when the family sponsored jousts there; the diarist Giacinto Gigli recounted that on 4 July 1653 Cardinal Girolamo, ambassador of the Holy Roman Emperor, 'made celebration for three days because of the election of Ferdinand III as the new King of the Romans [the traditional title of the Holy Roman Emperor before his coronation as emperor], and in the piazza of the Santi Apostoli in front of his palace he caused fountains of white and red wine to flow, and divers fireworks, mortars and fanfares'.

The colossal basilica of the Holy Apostles, **Santi Apostoli**, is of ancient origin. It was founded by Pope Pelagius I around AD 560 to celebrate the eastern emperor Justinian's general, the eunuch Narses, who had just successfully reconquered Rome for Byzantium from the Goths who had held it for almost a century. Martin V Colonna restored it, as did the Greek cardinal John Bessarion, while Cardinal Giuliano della Rovere built the entrance loggia. There, beside the right-hand door, is the unmarked funeral monument of a handsome youth, accompanied by two cherubic Geniuses of Death, with reversed torches; above, in a scalloped curve, rises the Colonna column. This is the tomb monument of Lorenzo Oddone Colonna, executed for rebelling against Sixtus IV in 1484. Sixtus had, in fact, promised to spare Lorenzo Oddone, but he then gave permission for his beheading in the Castel Sant'Angelo. The youth's funeral took place in this basilica. During the ceremony his mother snatched the severed head from the coffin and shouted, 'This is the head of my dear son and such is the faith of Pope Sixtus!'

The basilica, inside, bears a more than passing resemblance to the rooms of the Galleria Colonna. It was reconstructed by Francesco Fontana in 1702–8 and after his death his father Carlo continued the work until its completion in 1714. It was decorated in late Baroque style by many of the artists who worked in palazzo Colonna. Most notable is the chapel of St Francis, a **Colonna chapel** since 1464. Its previous decoration was late sixteenth century, with an altarpiece by Durante Alberti (1538–1616), but this was cleared out in the eighteenth-century rebuilding. The new altarpiece was by Giuseppe Chiari, last seen frescoing the *Apotheosis of Marcantonio II Colonna* on to the ceiling of the Room of the Column in the Galleria Colonna; the painting depicts *St Francis Supported by Angels*. On the left wall of the chapel is the Baroque tomb from 1753 of Cardinal Carlo Colonna (d. 1739) and on the right is that of a relative of the family, Maria Lucrezia Rospigliosi Salviati (d. 1749). Outside the chapel on the wall to the left is the tomb of Prince Filippo Colonna, of 1822, a more restrained monument. The decorative scheme of the Colonna chapel, though late, still reflects a thoroughly Baroque taste.

Directly to the left is the chapel of San Giovanni da Copertino, formerly under the patronage of the Mancini family, Colonna relatives by marriage; across the nave is the **Orsini chapel**, with an altarpiece by Corrado Giaquinto (1703–65). By the eighteenth century the rivalry between the two houses had long since dissipated, but it is interesting to find two significant chapels of Rome's most famous warring clans nearly facing each other across the great polished stone floor.

7 Other Colonna sites in Rome

I PALAZZO SCIARRA-COLONNA; PALAZZO MASSIMO-
COLONNA

Two other Colonna palaces can be identified. The first is **palazzo Sciarra-Colonna**, of the branch of the family that took its name from Boniface VIII's great enemy, Sciarra Colonna. The Colonna di Sciarra, as they were known, were princes of Carbognano, the last heirs of the old main branch of Palestrina. The palace, at via del Corso 239, where they lived, was constructed at the end of the sixteenth century by Flaminio Ponzio (1560–1613), an architect working mostly for the Borghese family. In the Middle Ages another Torre Colonna rose on this site and traces of it still remain in the interior walls. The palace, today a bank office (no admission), is distinguished by its great seventeenth-century *portone* or main entrance (said quite falsely to have been carved from a single block of marble), decorated with columns whose bases have columns carved on them and fantastical masks above. This branch of the family intermarried with and eventually took the name of the Barberini, and it is from that union that the present Barberini family descends. In the late nineteenth century, when times were hard, it sold its considerable art collection illegally at auction in Paris. Several pieces, including a Bronzino portrait of Stefano Colonna di Sciarra from 1546, are now in the Galleria Nazionale. At the same time the family sold this palace; it was the headquarters of a newspaper called the *Giornale d'Italia* before being bought by the Cassa di Risparmio di Roma.

Another palace of the family is **palazzo Massimo-Colonna**, at piazza d'Aracoeli 1 (no admission). This was a late acquisition, which the Colonna obtained when the heiress Maria Massimo married Prospero Colonna, twice mayor of Rome, in the nineteenth century. Even today the Colonna own the building, which has, however, undergone major changes due to its location on the corner of piazza d'Aracoeli and via del Teatro di Marcello.

When Mussolini made the latter street, he demolished all the buildings that huddled at the base of the Capitoline hill on the other side of the street from the palace, including the house of Michelangelo. In the process of making a large avenue leading to piazza Venezia suitable for military parades, he also had the corner of palazzo Massimo-Colonna lopped off. The palace has a cool and shaded courtyard with a grand Berninian fountain, a triton spouting water from a conch. Above is a strange crenellated tower, the former observatory of the astronomer Duke Mario Massimo in the early nineteenth century, and written on it is the word MAXIMA, another reference to the Massimo family. The large and enviable terrace and upper-floor apartment is, it is said, the possession of the actress Sophia Loren.

II OSPEDALE DI SAN GIACOMO DEGL' INCURABILI
Church of San Giacomo on via del Corso, close to the corner of via Canova. Open 9–12, 16–18; hospital open twenty-four hours; courtyard entrance on via Canova

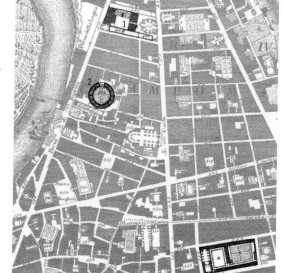

Colonna monuments in the *tridente*

Key:
1 Ospedale di San Giacomo
2 Mausoleum of Augustus (a Colonna stronghold in the Middle Ages)
3 church and convent of San Silvestro

In 1326 Cardinal Pietro Colonna, the third important cardinal in the family's history, desired to make his peace with God. To make up for his sins, among which he may have counted his opposition to Boniface VIII, he endowed a large poor hospital named for his uncle's patron saint, James. The new hospital stood in the family domain near the mausoleum of Augustus; from this position, the hospital was called *San Giacomo in Augusta*. Still in full operation today, it stood not far from the great northern gate of the city, the porta del Popolo, and its position on the via del Corso, the main north–south thoroughfare of Rome, ensured a constant stream of patients. In the late fifteenth century it received the discouraging appellation 'of the Incurables', due to the influx of sick people suffering from the new disease being spread by the French army, the *morbo gallico* (syphilis), which could be treated (with mercury, more harmful than helpful) but not cured.

The church was rebuilt at the end of the sixteenth century by Cardinal Antonio Maria Salviati. It has no Colonna emblems in it and, to find traces of the family, we must enter the courtyard of the hospital from via Canova. Once inside the otherwise uninteresting courtyard, halfway along the left-hand wall is a small monumental arrangement of sculpted medieval stonework. At the top is a fragmentary inscription dating from 1329, which refers to the 'lord Petrus de Columpna, Cardinal Deacon of Sant'Angelo', the founder. At the bottom of the doorway-shaped collection of stonework is a badly damaged effigy of a knight, certainly an old tomb from the medieval church. At the back of the courtyard is an archway, probably early fifteenth century, with Colonna crests and bishops' mitres in the corners, which suggests that their patronage did not end with Cardinal Pietro's bequest.

III   PAVILION AND FOUNTAIN OF THE VIA FLAMINIA
       Via Flaminia 162, on the corner with via della Villa Giulia. No admission

Outside the walls of Rome, on the via Flaminia before it enters the city at the porta del Popolo, on the corner of the via della Villa Giulia, rises a building of mid sixteenth-century date. The façade cuts across the corner of the block and is dominated by a central fountain with the Colonna arms, a large inscription of Filippo Colonna above. On the level of the floor above, a beautiful pair of stucco angels hold the crest of Pope Pius IV de' Medici, of the Milanese Medici family (no relation to the Florentine), the name of whose nephew, Cardinal Carlo Borromeo, is inscribed below. This façade is a monument to the alliance between two great families, the Borromeo of Milan and the Colonna of Rome.

This building is the so-called **palazzina of Pius IV** and it was part of the outbuildings of the great Renaissance villa built by Julius III del Monte (1550–5), the villa Giulia, which we can see at the end of the via della Villa Giulia. When this property was expropriated from the pope's family after his death, it was given by Pius IV de' Medici (1559–65) to his nephew Carlo

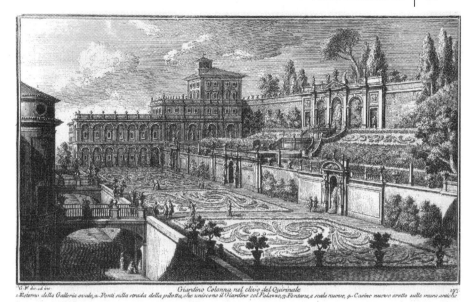

'G.V.... ... ...   Giardino Colonna nel clivo del Quirinale   ...
... Esterno della Galleria ovale, 2. Ponti sulla strada della pilotta, che uniscono il Giardino col Palazzo, 3. Fontane, e scale nuove, 9. Casino nuovo eretto sulle mura antiche

The Villa Colonna in the eighteenth century, built over the site of the palace depicted by Dupérac. These terraces were laid out like the *giardino segreto* of Villa Doria-Pamphilj.

Borromeo. Today it houses the Italian embassy to the Holy See (no admission), and the main apartments contain a stucco frieze of battle scenes interspersed with the crests of Colonna and Orsini, which suggests it was decorated for Marcantonio II Colonna and his wife Felice Orsini. Carlo Borromeo gave it to the Colonna to mark a wedding between the two families: Anna Borromeo (d. 1582), the cardinal's sister, became the mother of Filippo I Colonna, the builder of the present fountain, whose central element is a crest from which the Colonna column has been carefully excised by some later owner, perhaps the Italian state itself. Crests were once used as evidence of legal ownership: hence they were sometimes obliterated following a sale.

IV   A MISCELLANY

The ornamental entrance to the **Villa Colonna** is on the modern via XXIV Maggio, which leads from via Nazionale to piazza del Quirinale. The great gateway, with a more modern staircase leading to it, constructed when the road level was lowered in the nineteenth century, was built at the order of Filippo I Colonna, Duke of Paliano, Tagliacozzo and Marsi, in 1618, and decorated with the Colonna Siren which we have already seen on the Torre Colonna. The villa itself is not open to visitors.

Among other buildings with contributions by the Colonna family are the church of **San Lorenzo in Panisperna** (via Panisperna, open 16–18), whose convent was reconstructed by Cardinal Giacomo Colonna in *c*.1290 ; the convent and its gardens, which once stretched over this part of the Viminal hill, were expropriated in 1878 and destroyed to build the Ministry of the Interior. Now the only hint of a Colonna presence is Cardinal Giacomo's crest, furthest on the left on the front wall of the church enclosure facing the via Panisperna. This was, like San Silvestro in Capite, a comfortable society convent. The church itself contains an underground chapel, which is meant to open on to the very spot where Lawrence was grilled to death: his place among the comic saints was assured with his last words, 'Turn me over, I'm done on this side.' The building was reconstructed in 1585 and contains an enormous, though mediocre, fresco of the martyrdom of the saint, by Pasquale Cati (1537–1612).

A little further east, into what were once the wilds of the Esquiline hill and which is now the slightly run-down *rione* Esquilino, the **church of San Vito** was thoroughly reconstructed at the expense of Federico Colonna (1601–41), uncle of the great Prince Lorenzo Onofrio. A plaque inside explains why this out-of-the-way and insignificant church was the beneficiary of Colonna largesse:

FEDERICUS COLONNA

PALIANI PRINCEPS

A RABIDO CANE ADMORSUS

B. VITO LIBERATORE SUO

AEDEM RESTAURAVIT

AN MDCXX

(Federico Colonna,
Prince of Paliano,
having been bitten by a rabid dog,
restored this shrine to the blessed Vitus, his liberator,
in the year 1620)

St Vitus was invoked against rabies, a disease that gives the sufferer's movements a jerky, uncontrolled quality that used to be called 'St Vitus's dance'. Don Federico, having escaped rabies, was one of the warlike Colonnas and died at the siege of Tarragona in 1641. The church later underwent thorough alterations and now it is an airy, white, cool container for prayer, in which parishioners are not distracted by a superfluity of art.

The ancient convent of **Santa Maria della Concezione in Campo Marzio** (entrance from piazza in Campo Marzio; admission to courtyard only) was originally constructed for Greek nuns fleeing persecutions in Constantinople in 726. Their large and macabre wagon train, full of the mummified corpses of saints and various different holy body parts, bogged down in the mud on this site. This event, whether miracle or traffic accident, determined the location of the new convent. One of its altar paintings, a *Haghiosoritissa* or image of the Virgin as intercessor, dates from the middle of the twelfth century and is now in the Galleria Nazionale in palazzo Barberini; another, the *Blessing Christ*, is in the Vatican Pinacoteca. In time the property passed to the Benedictines and their convent received a rich new rebuilding in 1563 by the wealthy abbess Chiara Colonna. However, the new church was torn down less than a century later to make way for the current church of Santa Maria della Concezione, an elegant Baroque edifice of 1668–85 (rarely open). The graceful courtyard is usually accessible; through a glassed-in gate at the far end you can see the fifteenth-century cloister and a surprisingly exuberant fountain, as well as the little façade of the church of **San Gregorio Nazianzeno** and its thirteenth-century bell tower, which are entirely contained within the conventual complex. The convent was expropriated by the state at the end of the nineteenth century and half of it is now a convention centre and offices for the House of Deputies, the lower house of the Italian parliament. The other half retains its ancient connection with the Greek rite, as it is the Roman office of the Patriarch of Antioch.

Carlo Borromeo, a Colonna relative by marriage (and once the tenant of palazzo Colonna's Princess Isabelle apartment), was canonised in 1610 for his good works and exemplary pastoral care. He became the great Counter-Reformation saint of Milan. The first Roman church dedicated to him, **San Carlo ai Catinari**, was the mother church of the Milanese order of Barnabite fathers, who were seeking space in the crowded centre of Rome to carry out their missionary work to the poor. Gregory XIII gave the fathers a decrepit church near the present site in 1575. By 1611 a new church was under construction, finally completed in 1648. The façade is by the Borghese family architect Giovanni Battista Soria (1581–1651). In 1631 the Barnabites found a patron to endow the high altar: Filippo I Colonna of Paliano, the saint's nephew through his mother Anna, and after him his son Cardinal Girolamo Colonna. The family commissioned Pietro da Cortona (1596–1669) to paint the impressive altarpiece, *St Charles Borromeo with the Holy Nail*, perhaps as late as 1657. The crowned column of the family crest appears on the presbytery rail and on the marble surround of the altarpiece.

The ceiling of the great Franciscan church of **Santa Maria in Aracoeli** (open 8–19) was remade in 1572–80 to commemorate Lepanto, and it accordingly has a military and triumphal theme (piles of weapons and armour) which might seem out of place until one remembers that the miraculous intervention of the Virgin in her aspect of Our Lady of the Rosary was given credit for the victory, which took place on her feast day. A side chapel (just before the left transept) was under Colonna sponsorship, but contains no family monuments.

The **Capitoline Museums** show some traces of the Colonna. In the Hall of Statues in the Apartment of the Conservators (palazzo dei Conservatori) is a statue of Marcantonio II Colonna by Nicolò Pippi, dating from 1595. In the Room of the She-Wolf, where the famous symbol of Rome, the *Lupa Capitolina*, is kept, a wall plaque commemorates Marcantonio's victory amid emblems of triumph. One other Colonna monument remains on the Capitoline: the tower on the back corner of the palazzo Senatorio, to the left as one faces the façade, the **torre di Martino V** was built around 1427 to guard the approach up the hill along the street today called via di San Pietro in Carcere, which was originally part of the papal procession route, the via Papalis. At a glance it is unimpressive, but a closer look shows that its base is far down, on the level of the Forum itself, and it must once have been a striking sight.

The chapel of the family in **Santa Maria sopra Minerva** (piazza della Minerva; open 8–19; the Colonna chapel is the second in the right aisle), like the palazzo Colonna, underwent a decorative phase in the late seventeenth century; the theme was of the first saint of the New World, St Rose of Lima, a fitting Dominican saint for this mother church of the Dominican order. The chapel belonged to the Colonna di Sciarra and the painter was Lazzaro Baldi (1624–1703), a prolific painter who worked in the Chiesa Nuova, San Marco, San Silvestro al Quirinale and many other churches. Here his theme was, of course, St Rose of Lima. This chapel also has the tomb of a Colonna princess, Isabella Alvaria Colonna da Toledo, and her infant, both of whom died of cholera in an 1867 epidemic.

In Rome's cathedral, **San Giovanni in Laterano** (piazza San Giovanni in Laterano; open 8–19), the family chapel (usually closed, but visible through glass windows) opens off the left transept of the huge basilica and is called the **winter choir**. It was built by Carlo Rainaldi in 1625 at the order of Lorenzo Onofrio's father, Marcantonio V (1603–59). Marcantonio V commissioned the tomb of his mother Lucrezia Tomacelli Colonna here, almost the only decoration in the unexpectedly austere interior. The wooden stalls of the choir are beautifully carved and the centre of the floor is marked with a slab decorated with the family emblem: beneath it is the Colonna mausoleum. The very simple bronze floor **tomb of Martin V Colonna**, by Simone Ghini (1406–91), has pride of place in the *confessio* in front of the cathedral's high altar. It is covered with reflective glass, which makes it hard to see, and before it was moved to this exalted position it must have been exposed to centuries of passing feet, for it is much worn. Romans sometimes throw money on it for luck. An inscription at his feet gives the legend FELICITAS TEMPORUM SUORUM (happiness in his times). The Cosmatesque floor paving of the cathedral is also punctuated, at intervals, along the middle of the floor, with the great inlaid crest of the Colonna, the crowned column now so familiar to us. Its presence in the floor of Rome's most senior church reflects the power and splendour of this ancient family.

Intermezzo:
The fifteenth century

The successor of Martin V Colonna, **Eugenius IV Condulmer** of Venice (1431–47), inherited a Rome that was less a papal than a Colonna capital, and his efforts to unseat the family from power resulted in his own defeat and flight to Florence, where he stayed for nine years, returning only in 1443. Clearly he had no energy, or capacity, to rebuild the city. The Rome of the mid fifteenth century was barely functional. A terrible disaster on the Castel Sant'Angelo bridge, in which hundreds of people died in a panic-stricken crush in the jubilee year of 1450, underlined the lack of basic services: not only safe and sufficient bridges, but also properly paved roads, sewers that worked, a functioning water supply. The holy year of 1450, during which pilgrims to Rome received special remission of their sins, was a spur for further building. **Nicholas V Parentucelli** (1447–55) was the most ambitious of Renaissance town planners, and his ideal scheme encompassed massive renovations in the Borgo, including the creation of a large avenue from the river to St Peter's, demolishing the irregular series of city blocks called the *spina di Borgo*, a plan finally put into place by Mussolini beginning in the 1930s. He also intended to restructure, though not entirely rebuild, the basilica of St Peter's itself, on the advice of the great Florentine architect Leone Battista Alberti (1404–72), with new transepts and apse. This plan, though it came to nothing, influenced other church building in fifteenth-century Rome. Nicholas established an important principle for papal building:

> If the authority of the Holy See were visibly displayed in majestic buildings, imperishable memorials and witnesses seemingly planted by the hand of God himself, belief would grow and strengthen like a tradition from one generation to another, and all the world would accept and revere it.

Nicholas died, leaving most of his own plans incomplete or unstarted, and his successor, the Spaniard **Calixtus III Borgia** (1455–8), deplored Nicholas's spending on art and learning, preferring to focus his financial resources on an attempt to rouse a crusade against the Turks, who had conquered Constantinople, the old capital of the Byzantine Empire, two years before he took office. In his brief three-year reign his nephew, Rodrigo Borgia, was made the Curia's Vice-Chancellor. Borgia accumulated wealth

Palazzo Venezia is to the right, in this eighteenth century engraving. The only parts of this scene still recognisable today are the main façade of palazzo Venezia and the tower (both far right). The palazzetto Venezia (centre) was rebuilt around the corner, while palazzo Bolognetti (left) and the tower of Paul III (background) were demolished to enlarge piazza Venezia and build the monument to Vittorio Emanuele II.

and influence, and became one of the main players at the papal court. The next pope, **Pius II Piccolomini** (1458–64), was a complete contrast: an Italian from Siena, and a well-educated and well-travelled diplomat, with a chequered past that included the writing of erotic plays. His successor, **Paul II Barbo** (1464–71), was a luxury-loving pope, building the first great palace of Renaissance Rome, the palazzo Venezia, a colossal building attached to the Venetian national church of San Marco and thus also known as the palazzo San Marco. This was still more than halfway to being a fortress, in its sober and forbidding design, with a large tower and battlements. Its warlike appearance speaks to us eloquently of the violence and disorder of the Roman streets in the second half of the fifteenth century.

3 The della Rovere

The popes of the fifteenth century made small steps towards renewing the city after its long decadence, but it took an outsider named Francesco della Rovere, from Savona, a small town on the coast of Liguria near Genoa, to make significant changes. The two della Rovere popes, Sixtus IV (1471–84) and Julius II (1503–13), dominated Italian politics and Roman life in the late fifteenth and early sixteenth centuries. Sixtus's nephews also endowed Rome with several important palaces and the flood of their relations left traces across the city. With the della Rovere we find a new phenomenon among papal families: the desire not merely to dominate Rome, but to found an independent dynastic state carved from the domains of the pope. The family of Sixtus IV launched two attempts at this goal. One failed, the other succeeded, and the fortunes of the della Rovere provided a blueprint for the ambitions of other Renaissance families like the Borgia and, more triumphantly, the Farnese.

POPE SIXTUS IV (1471–84)

The origins of the della Rovere family are somewhat obscure. Sixtus IV's librarian, the scholar Platina, wrote a laudatory biography of the future pope, born *Francesco della Rovere* (1414–84), which recounted implausibly miraculous stories about his childhood spent scratching a living from the barren Ligurian coast. It seems, however, that the della Rovere family was of moderately successful bourgeois rank: Francesco's father, *Leonardo della Rovere* (d. 1430), held government offices in Savona and married his children into similar families of the town. In the increasingly rigid social structures of the fifteenth century, upward mobility was offered either as a soldier or as a priest and Francesco chose the latter, entering the Franciscan order. He attended the university of Padua, gaining a degree in logic and philosophy, and thereafter (from 1445) embarked on a stellar career as an academic, teaching first at Padua, then Perugia. His career in the Franciscans was similarly accelerated: in 1446 he was already assistant to the general of the

Franciscan Minorites and less than three years later he had become the private confessor to the great Greek cardinal John Bessarion. In 1464 he was elected general of the Franciscan order and three years later he was created cardinal of San Pietro in Vincoli by the Venetian-born pope Paul II Barbo. Despite the simplicity of his habits, he accumulated benefices like an expert and aligned himself with the dukes of Milan, in whose territory della Rovere's home town of Savona then lay.

The conclave that followed Paul's death was split between two factions, the *Paoleschi*, cardinals chosen by Paul himself, and the *Pieschi*, who had been

A sixteenth-century engraving of Sixtus IV. Francesco della Rovere's erudition and eloquence propelled him from obscurity to the papal throne.

created by his predecessor Pius II. Della Rovere, a compromise candidate from the ranks of the *Paoleschi*, emerged on 9 August 1571 as the victor, with thirteen votes of a total of eighteen. He chose the name of Sixtus, following the saintly and educated Sixtus III of the fifth century.

Sixtus made his initial focus the war against the Turks, but if the pope's first thought was for a crusade, his second was for his family. The della Rovere were poised to launch themselves into the Roman nobility and Sixtus had ambitions even beyond that, of establishing della Rovere signories or hereditary lordships within the papal territories. The Papal States were, at the time, very loosely controlled by the pope. Individual cities might have local lords, *signori* or titled nobles such as counts, marquesses or dukes, nominally drawing their authority from the pope but in reality independent princes. The further from Rome the more independent the prince, and nowhere was more free from papal control than the distant provinces of the Romagna and Emilia, to the north-east of Rome along the ancient via Flaminia.

In attempting to overthrow some of the *signori*, Sixtus disturbed the balance of power in the region and the republics of Florence, under the guiding hand of Lorenzo de' Medici, and Venice, which was seeking to expand its territory on terra firma, soon took an interest in the pope's activities. Medicean interference in the Romagna incited Sixtus to involve himself in 1478 in a sacrilegious plot to murder Lorenzo de' Medici and his brother Giuliano at Mass in Florence's cathedral. This plot, the Pazzi conspiracy, was to have as its trigger the holiest point of the Mass, the transubstantiation of the Host. The assassins, themselves priests, botched the job and Lorenzo got away, locking himself in the sacristy, though his brother was cut down in front of the high altar. The Pazzi family's revolt against the Medici failed and the outraged Florentine government went to war with the Papal States. Two years elapsed before peace returned, after much bloodshed. Sixtus also schemed to depose the Este rulers of Ferrara and hoped to incite the Venetians to attack the city, but this plan backfired as well and the pope placed an interdict on the city of Venice to punish it for its disobedience.

Sixtus's main interests – the enrichment of his family and the restoration of Rome – went hand in hand and he was careful to ensure that his family emblem, the oak tree with its entwined branches (*rovere* is one of the Italian words for oak), was set over all his works. In order to prevent the 1450 disaster on the Castel Sant'Angelo bridge from recurring, in 1473 he built a new bridge, the ponte Sisto, downstream from the castle bridge. At the same time he ordered the regularisation of a street leading from the castle to the Vatican, the Borgo Sant'Angelo, to facilitate the passage of pilgrims. He also gave new powers to the urban planning authority, the *magistri viarum*, in 1480, remarking in the bull that 'it seems to us fair to place communal utility before individual convenience'. His most significant urban decree was, perhaps, his bull permitting clerics to will real estate to their relatives; this opened the field for cardinals and other rich priests to build palaces without the worry that the Vatican would take them from their heirs – this decree, more than any other, permitted the redevelopment of Rome. A similar decree permitted the builders of great palaces to expropriate neighbouring buildings of lesser size, to encourage greater grandeur.

Sixtus's two principal foundations of churches were both dedicated to the Virgin: the first, Santa Maria del Popolo, was intended as a family mausoleum, and the second, Santa Maria della Pace, as a thank offering for the end of the Pazzi war. He also restored and altered a number of other churches, paying particular attention to the most ancient and decrepit; his interest in the early church had pious and antiquarian motives. His relations with the Roman barons, however, were violent. Sixtus understood that the only way towards papal control was to crush the power of the Colonna, the most obstreperous clan of the time.

From the beginning of his reign, Sixtus was interested in reviving the antique splendour of Rome and to this end, in 1471, he donated a small group of ancient statues to the city government, including the bronze Capitoline

Wolf, the *Spinario* or Thorn-puller, and a massive bronze Hercules, as well as the famous stone head of Constantine's statue from the basilica of Maxentius. These works formed the core of what was to become the Capitoline Museums, the first museum of the modern world. However, Sixtus's most lavish building was at the Vatican. The relatively modest palace there, enlarged by his predecessors, was enhanced with the creation of the Vatican Library in December 1471, but, even more important, Sixtus decreed that a new chapel be built there for the use of the papal court. This Sistine Chapel, built to the dimensions of the temple of Solomon, was dedicated to the Assumption of the Virgin and its decorative scheme, whose object was the exaltation of the authority of the pope, offered some clear responses to his political situation.

Sixtus's own character is still somewhat controversial. A fierce and austere man, he nonetheless threw himself and the papacy into Italian politics. His enrichment of his relatives was unprecedented: previous popes had contented themselves with creating one or at most two cardinals from their own family, but Sixtus gave four of his relatives the red hat, six if we include two, Domenico and Cristoforo della Rovere, who were probably unrelated to him. The Colonna partisan Stefano Infessura, whose diary recounts every anti-papal rumour, asserts that Sixtus was much given to homosexual activity and, indeed, that his advancement of his nephews was based on his incest with them. Sixtus's nephew Julius II also faced similar accusations, as did members of the Farnese family.

Sixtus's death in August 1484, in the malarial heat of the Roman summer, brought an end to his furious campaign against the Colonna and transferred power from the hands of his secular nephew, Girolamo Riario, into those of his cardinal nephew, Giuliano della Rovere. It was to be Giuliano's influence in the college of cardinals that would swing the next papal election.

THE *NIPOTI* OF SIXTUS IV

Sixtus gave two of his nephews the red hat on 16 December 1471. The elder of the two, *Giuliano della Rovere* (1443–1513), was already a Franciscan and had been a scholar at Perugia under his uncle's guidance, though he showed little propensity for study, being a hot-tempered and undiplomatic man; his irascibility was only to develop over time, until his rages became legendary. He said of himself that he would have made a bad monk, as he was too restless to stay still. He was given the pope's own titular church, San Pietro in Vincoli, and heaped with an astonishing number of rich bishoprics: Carpentras, Lausanne, Catania, Coutances, Mende, Viviers, Sabina, Bologna,

Ostia, Lodève, Savona, Vercelli and the archbishopric of Avignon. The younger, *Pietro Riario* (1445–74), was his uncle's favourite, the son of the pope's youngest sister Bianca, and he received the cardinalate church of his uncle's namesake, San Sisto. In this first cardinalate creation the principal tensions in the pope's family appeared. Pietro was the apple of his uncle's eye and the pope did not stint in giving him benefice after benefice. The struggle between Pietro and Giuliano, and, on a wider scale, that between the Riario and della Rovere branches of the family, were to take on a Rome-wide significance and shaped the doom of one branch and the triumph of the other.

Pietro was twenty-six when he was raised to the cardinalate; he had been his uncle's servant in the conclave, fetching his food and drink. Perhaps he had involved himself in some of the election negotiations; whatever his role, it was clear that he was to be the principal cardinal nephew. The German historian Ludwig von Pastor summed up Pietro's character:

> He was intelligent and cultivated, courteous, witty, cheerful and generous, but his good qualities were counterbalanced by a lust [for] power, a boundless ambition and pride, and a love of luxury which rendered him utterly unworthy of the purple [. . .] He seemed to vie with the ancients in pomp and grandeur – and, it may be added, in vices. Instead of the habit of Francis, he went about in garments laden with gold, and adorned his mistress from head to foot with costly pearls.

There was, on the surface of it, little to differentiate Pietro's behaviour from that of Giuliano, apart from the scope afforded to greater wealth: Giuliano was no angel, with a string of mistresses and at least one child, a daughter, *Felice* (1483–1536). However, Giuliano was distinctly less important to the pope; and Pietro's brother, *Girolamo Riario* (1433–88), waited in the background for the pope's favour as well. Three years after the pope's election, when young Cardinal Pietro died of a fever, Girolamo rose to take his place at the pope's side, again bypassing Cardinal Giuliano.

Girolamo Riario was, by all accounts, a thoroughly unpleasant man. Niccolò Machiavelli referred to him as a man *'di bassissima e vile condizione'* (of a very low and contemptible nature). Pastor observed that Girolamo 'was, as it were, Sixtus's evil daemon'. He quickly took his brother's place in the pope's affections and became the focus of Sixtus's dynastic plans. As early as 1473, before his brother's death, Girolamo had been chosen to marry an illegitimate daughter of the Duke of Milan, *Caterina Sforza* (c.1462–1509); the couple were given the city of Imola to govern, part of the Papal States which had become a Milanese dependency. Ambassadors learned to pay court to Girolamo and he was set firmly against his cousin Giuliano.

Giuliano's influence in the curia was further diminished when, in December 1477, Sixtus nominated three more of his relatives as cardinals: *Cristoforo della Rovere* (d. 1478) was at best a distant cousin, from a della Rovere family in Piedmont, but the other two were a nephew, *Girolamo Basso della Rovere* (1434–1507), the son of the pope's sister Luchina, and a Riario great-nephew, *Raffaele Riario Sansoni* (1460–1521), who had the distinction of being the Renaissance papacy's first teenaged cardinal. The brother of the Piedmontese Cristoforo, *Domenico della Rovere* (d. 1501), was made cardinal in Cristoforo's place after his death in 1478. The Riario were to be the most significant beneficiaries of papal favour. Sixtus worked tirelessly to establish Girolamo Riario as lord of Imola and of a nearby city in the Romagna, Forlì, which was rid of its hereditary lords, the Ordelaffi. The pope also found an advantageous marriage for Giuliano's brother *Giovanni della Rovere* (1457–1501) with Giovanna da Montefeltro, the daughter and heiress of the Count of Urbino, in 1474. The following year Giovanni received from the pope the hereditary title of prefect of Rome, which nominally made him chief secular noble of the papal domains. This title would survive in Giovanni's branch of the della Rovere family until its extinction in the seventeenth century.

By 1477 the dislike between the pope's two nephews came to a dangerous point. Two of Giuliano's protégés were imprisoned in the Castel Sant'Angelo and confessed to a plot to poison Girolamo. Sixtus may have suspected Giuliano's hand in the scheme, for he took away the cardinal's suite of rooms in the Vatican palace, but they were returned when the affair fizzled out a few months later. The rivalry extended outwards from the papal palace. In the chequerboard of Italian politics, Giuliano was allied with the French, while Girolamo was a stalwart of Milan; in Rome itself Giuliano was most closely associated with the Colonna family, another indication of his distance from the pope, while Girolamo was linked with the Orsini.

Sixtus supported Riario and waged a furious campaign against the Colonna, culminating in the execution of Lorenzo Oddone Colonna on 30 June 1484 (as we have seen, contrary to his promise of amnesty). The Colonna houses were sacked and their cardinal was imprisoned in the Castel Sant'Angelo. The aged and ailing Sixtus witnessed a furious argument between his two nephews: Riario accused the cardinal of harbouring rebels against the pope in his own house, to which Giuliano retorted that they were no rebels, but loyal servants of the pope, and that it was Riario himself who would bring the pope and cardinals to destruction. Riario snapped back that he would like to drive Giuliano out of Rome, sack his palace (which was suspiciously close, indeed next door, to the Colonna fortress) and burn it, as he had done to the house of Cardinal Colonna. Giuliano's arguments were in vain and the pope ordered his troops to mass against the Colonna strongholds in southern Lazio. However, a scant three months later the pope was dead and Girolamo Riario was stuck with the troops in the hilly wilds of Colonna territory. It was a tactical mistake from which he never recovered.

Upon Sixtus's death in 1484, Girolamo's position suddenly became much weaker. The college of cardinals, interim rulers, ordered him to desist from his attacks on the Colonna and he and his army withdrew from the conflict. It took less than a week for the industrious Colonna to reoccupy their lost lands. Riario wanted to influence the conclave. His wife, the spirited Caterina Sforza, though heavily pregnant, took his place as castellan of the Castel Sant'Angelo, riding in through the gate waving a sword in one hand and, more persuasively, a bag of money in the other. The soldiers quickly accepted her leadership and an anxious stalemate ensued for some days. The conclave was unable to meet, due to the insecurity in the streets: cardinals were afraid to leave their palaces in case they were set upon by Riario's supporters and his allies, the Orsini. With no conclave, there could be no pope elected, favourable to Riario or otherwise, and he realised with frustration that he had no choice but to accept the college's command and withdraw to his Romagnol estates. Caterina Sforza, who had also been outmanoeuvred (eight cardinals had peaceably entered the castle and politely commanded her and her troops to leave), joined him there.

The power that had been held by Riario in Sixtus's lifetime devolved quickly upon the dead pope's other nephew, Giuliano, whose position as senior cardinal gave him the determining voice in the conclave. The papal election of 1484 resulted in the elevation of Gianbattista Cibò as **Innocent VIII** (1484–92). Innocent was another man of relatively low origins, this time Neapolitan but of Genoese parents, and, like Giuliano della Rovere, had fathered illegitimate children. He was, like Sixtus IV, keen to advance his family and arranged for his worthless son, Franceschetto Cibò, to wed the daughter of Lorenzo de' Medici, 'il Magnifico', the de facto ruler of Florence. A flood of Cibò relations descended upon Rome to enjoy the rich pickings, but none of them achieved lasting importance. The pope's main counsellor was Cardinal Giuliano della Rovere, who achieved under Innocent an authority he never had under Sixtus.

The Cibò pontificate was not, however, particularly good for the della Rovere or the Riario. In 1488 Girolamo Riario was assassinated by noblemen of Imola, to no one's surprise, as he had made himself universally hated. Thereafter, his widow Caterina Sforza ruled as regent for her son; she remarried twice, the second time to a Florentine de' Medici to whom she bore a son, Giovanni 'delle Bande Nere' or of the Black Bands, who became a famous condottiere (mercenary). Her grandson in the Medici line became Cosimo I, the first Grand Duke of Tuscany, in the mid sixteenth century.

Innocent's death on 25 July 1492 took place following a violent argument, witnessed by the pope from his deathbed, between Cardinal Giuliano della Rovere and the other powerful cardinal of Innocent's pontificate, Rodrigo Borgia of Valencia, the Vice-Chancellor. Borgia objected to the pope's gift of the entire cash reserve of the Papal States, 47,000 ducats, to Innocent's relatives and Giuliano defended the gift. If the animosity between the two began then, it soon heated up into a European conflagration. After the next conclave elevated Borgia to the papal throne as **Alexander VI** (1492–1503), relations between pope and cardinal quickly grew acrimonious. Upon hearing that Alexander had created twelve new cardinals, including the brother of the pope's mistress, Giulia Farnese, and the pope's own son Cesare, Giuliano left the gambling table where he was entertaining himself and rushed to his room, 'shouting and bellowing'. By the beginning of 1493 he had left Rome, first for Ostia, of which he was bishop, then for France.

For the next two years Giuliano della Rovere waited in France, stirring up the French king against the Spanish-born pope and encouraging the weak-minded Charles VIII to press his dynastic claims to inherit the kingdom of Naples. Alexander VI was a good administrator, clever and even devout in his own way, but his view of the office of pope was notably secular and he unblushingly legitimised his children in order to build them a hereditary state in central Italy. His eldest son Juan was made a grandee by the king of Spain, while his second son Cesare became a cardinal and his daughter Lucrezia became his principal pawn in the diplomatic game of marriages: she was married three times in the course of Alexander's pontificate, the first marriage being annulled when her husband lost his political value, the second brought to a violent conclusion when Cesare had her spouse murdered. Other of the pope's children were married into the Neapolitan and Roman nobility.

In September 1494, in large part due to Giuliano's urgings, Charles VIII brought his army south into Italy. This invasion marked the beginning of the Italian Wars, which signalled the end of the independence of Italy's patchwork of small republics and princedoms, and turned the peninsula into a battlefield between the two European giants of France and Spain. At the time, of course, no such terrible consequence was expected. Cardinal Giuliano was present as French troops occupied Rome and the pope made every sign of concession to the shambling, nearly imbecilic Charles VIII.

However, the pope did not acknowledge Charles's claim to the crown of Naples and, to Giuliano's disgust, the king was still persuaded to reverence Alexander as true pope: della Rovere had been agitating for his overthrow, on the grounds of immorality and simony, the sale of church offices. Alexander also promised the king that Giuliano could return to live in Rome unmolested: the cardinal did not, however, place much value in his word and with good reason, for as soon as Charles VIII left for Naples, with Cesare Borgia as hostage, the pope abandoned all his guarantees and Cesare escaped.

The opposition to the French advance was nearly non-existent and Charles entered Naples on 22 February 1495; he waited there in vain for the pope to confirm his investiture as its king. Alexander, meanwhile, had been busy arranging alliances against the French. Charles soon faced an intimidating alliance of pope, emperor, Spain, Venice and Milan blocking his re-entry into France. By the end of the year Charles was back in Paris, licking his wounds. Not long afterwards he died, after hitting his head violently on a low beam in a dark palace corridor. His successor, Louis XII, was a different character altogether, a wily and ambitious man who would remember his family claims to Naples and plunge Italy into further war. In Rome, Giuliano della Rovere was prepared to negotiate with Alexander. The cardinal's principal concern was to protect the lands and titles of his brother Giovanni, the prefect of Rome, whose son, *Francesco Maria I della Rovere* (1490–1538), through his mother, stood to inherit the important city of Urbino, now raised to a dukedom. However, Giuliano did not return to Rome until after Alexander's death, remaining instead in the north, particularly in Avignon, of which he was the singularly unpastoral archbishop.

Alexander, for his part, decided that the only way to maintain order in his own realm was to crush the Roman barons once and for all. To that end he waged war against both the Orsini and the Colonna. His warlike son Cesare was offered the French title of Duke of Valentinois the following year and was received in Avignon by Giuliano, where they feasted together without noticeable enthusiasm. (Both were, however, suffering severely from the effects of what the Italians called the 'French pox', syphilis.) Cesare was given a French bride, whom he left to commence a campaign of conquest through the Romagna, with the aid of French troops. The aim was to carve out a Borgia dominion, with Cesare as Duke of the Romagna, a new title created for him by his indulgent father. Louis XII himself took Milan in 1500.

In that year this war lapped at the gates of the Riario domains of Imola and Forlì. Caterina Sforza defended her cities with her customary ferocious will: at one point, when her children were taken hostage and presented to her as she stood on the battlements of her fortress, she raised her skirts and cried defiantly, 'Do you think I cannot make others?' Her toughness won her the title of 'virago', a woman with the strength of a man. However, her courage did not prevent her cities from capitulating and she was taken to the Castel Sant'Angelo: in her year there, her hair turned stark white. When she was released she went to Florence, where she spent her last decade litigating with her husband's relatives for possession of the palazzo Medici and intriguing unsuccessfully to have her son Ottaviano returned to power in Forlì. The Riario adventure in the Romagna was over. Cesare Borgia was a remarkably successful general, ruthless enough to impress the Florentine observer Niccolò Machiavelli, who made him the model for the Prince of his handbook of the same name, and he rapidly reduced the independent cities of the northern Papal States to obedience. The stage appeared to be set for a new Borgia dynasty, with a larger territory than envisioned by any previous papal family. But this was not to be.

In the summer of 1503 Alexander VI fell ill, probably with the usual Roman scourge, malaria, and Cesare was laid low at the same time. The older man died, the younger barely survived and, as with Girolamo Riario after the death of Sixtus IV, the conclave refused to meet until Cesare had withdrawn with his troops to a safe distance from Rome. Cardinal della Rovere returned from France and was present at the next conclave, which elected, as a compromise, the frail Cardinal Piccolomini as **Pius III** (1503). However, the gout-ridden Sienese pope did not survive beyond thirty-four days from his election and the cardinals returned to the conclave. This time Giuliano was determined to compromise no more.

POPE JULIUS II (1503–13)

Giuliano had received the majority of votes in the first scrutiny of the previous election, but had been forced to step back when it was clear he would not be able to win over the block of Spanish cardinals, appointees of the Borgia pope. To overcome their opposition in this conclave, he met with them on 29 October 1503, and with Cesare Borgia, and promised to support Borgia and maintain him in his territories in the Romagna; the next evening, 30 October, all the cardinals came to him en masse to tell him they had decided unanimously to elect him pope. He had been so confident of the outcome that he had brought in his own papal ring, made in advance. It was the briefest conclave in papal history.

His contemporary, the politician and historian Francesco Giucciardini, commented:

IVLIVS II.Iulia..... ...nus de Ruuere Sa:
uonens. creat.die i.   Nouemb. ann.1503.
Sedit 9.an. men.3.   dies 20. Obijt die
20.Februarij ann   1513.Vac.Sed.dies 18

Julius II in a sixteenth-century engraving.
Giuliano della Rovere was the first pope in
centuries to wear a beard, against canon law,
as a sign of mourning after the revolt of
Bologna.

Great, certainly, was the universal amazement that the papacy should have been given up, without a dissenting voice, to a cardinal who was notorious for his very difficult nature, which everyone found formidable, and who, always unquiet, and having spent his life in continual turmoil, of necessity had offended many and aroused hatreds and enmities with many important men. But on the other hand, the reasons were clear why, having overcome all difficulties, he was raised to such an elevated position. Because, having been for a long time a very powerful cardinal, and owing to the magnificence in which he had always outshone all others, and to his rare spirit, he not only had many friends but also deep-rooted authority in the court, and he had gained the reputation of being a leading defender of ecclesiastical dignity and liberty.

More than those virtues, however, what really assisted in Giuliano's election was the enormous amount of benefices he held, which were in his gift and which he scattered liberally to ensure his victory. The new pope, who took the name of Julius II, was to make and break alliances with an almost Borgia-like unreliability. Julius had as his two main political purposes the consolidation of his power over the Papal States and the expulsion of the foreign powers which, as cardinal, he had done so much to bring into the Italian peninsula. In short order Julius arranged for the ejection of Cesare Borgia from the Papal States: Cesare hired himself out as a soldier of fortune and was killed not long afterwards in a skirmish in Spain.

Julius was remarkably fortunate in his campaigns in the north-east of the Papal States. He acted as leader of his own troops and success followed success, most notably when he drove out the Bentivoglio family, rulers of Bologna, in 1506. He formed a league against Venice and helped to drive them back out of their cities in the northern Romagna. He then turned his attention to the French threat and joined forces with Venice in 1511 in a so-called Holy League, which eventually included distant England as well, always eager to strike a blow against the French. A rebellion in Rome by the old baronial families, with the pope's old Colonna allies at its forefront, was brutally suppressed. By 1512 the French had been driven out of Italy and Julius had subjugated rebellious Bologna once again, as well as adding the cities of Parma and Piacenza to the Papal States. At his death in 1513, Julius II could look back with satisfaction on a successful military career that had unquestionably, if bloodily, reasserted the pope's authority over his own domains.

He was satirised by the great humanist scholar Erasmus of Rotterdam, the author of the *Julius exclusus* (Julius Excluded from Heaven, 1514), in which the dead pope leads an army to the heavenly gates, to be rebuffed by St Peter himself:

PETER: Immortal God, what a sewer I smell here! Who are you? [. . .]

JULIUS: [. . .] So you know what sort of prince you're insulting, listen a little. [. . .] I neglected nothing in accumulating money; when Bologna had been occupied by the Bentivogli, I restored it to the Roman See. The Venetians, previously not conquered by anyone, I crushed in battle. [. . .] I drove the French, who were then the terror of the whole world, completely out of Italy [. . .] What if you could see today so many buildings erected by kingly wealth, so many thousands of priests everywhere (many of them very rich), so many bishops equal to the greatest kings in military power and in wealth, so many splendid palaces belonging to priests, [. . .] what would you say?

PETER: That I was looking at a tyrant worse than worldly, an enemy of Christ, the bane of the church.

Erasmus's observation about the 'splendid palaces belonging to priests' pointed to the pope's colossal building programmes. Indeed, Julius II was the greatest patron of art and architecture of the High Renaissance in Rome. His principal architect was Donato Bramante (1444–1514), who also took charge of urban design. The two nearly parallel riverside streets of via Giulia and via della Lungara were built under his guidance, with a large building, the palazzo dei Tribunali, planned on the via Giulia to contain the papal law courts, only sections of which were ever begun. Bramante also contributed the first design for rebuilding the ancient basilica of St Peter's, extended the Vatican palace by two long corridors to incorporate the Belvedere villa of Innocent VIII and added a new apse to the della Rovere church of Santa Maria del Popolo. Julius II used the architect Giuliano da Sangallo (c.1445–1516) as well, one of the architectural dynasty whose principal member, Antonio the Younger, would become architect to Paul III Farnese.

With an unerring eye for talent, Julius employed Michelangelo

Buonarroti (1475–1564) as painter and sculptor, though their relationship was often acrimonious. The artist worked most notably on the ceiling of the Sistine Chapel and also received the commission for the pope's tomb, which was conceived as a massive free-standing pyramidal structure in the apse of New St Peter's, but ended up in Julius's old cardinalate church of San Pietro in Vincoli, much reduced in form. From 1508, Julius hired the most important artists to decorate the Vatican: foremost was the young Raffaello Sanzio, Raphael (1483–1520), whose frescoes in the pope's private apartments are among his greatest works.

Unlike his uncle, Julius II was distinctly uninterested in nepotism. He did make a number of family cardinals, including two of his nephews, *Galeotto Franciotti della Rovere* (1471–1507) and Galeotto's half-brother, *Sisto Gara della Rovere* (1479–1517). Despite this, his nephews were neither over-beneficed nor significant advisers. Julius worked hard on behalf of his brother Giovanni, prefect of Rome, to have Giovanni's son Francesco Maria adopted as the heir of the duchy of Urbino, and even made a rather half-hearted effort at reconciliation with the Riario Sforza branch, Girolamo Riario's family. However, Julius refused to reinstate the unremarkable Ottaviano Riario Sforza as *signore* of Imola and Forlì, preferring to send out papal governors rather than install hereditary lords. He also married his daughter Felice to Gian Giordano Orsini, Duke of Bracciano, in 1506, as a sign that the old enmity towards the Orsini family was at an end. He supported the construction of a family dynasty in Urbino, but he was notably free of the extravagant family favouritism that preceded, created and followed him.

The second della Rovere pope was famous for his irascibility, which made him appear almost a force of nature to his contemporaries: they knew him as *il papa terribile*, the overwhelming pope. The Venetian ambassador thought him insane; he was certainly both violent and unpredictable. Julius's personal life came under a certain amount of whispered criticism, not least due to the sinister influence exerted over him by his very close friend Francesco Alidosi (1450–1511), who was even said to be his lover. Alidosi, created cardinal in 1505, was one of Julius's most important advisers; he was a sponsor of Michelangelo and was as thoroughly secular as Julius himself; the poet and future cardinal Pietro Bembo wrote of Alidosi that 'faith meant nothing to him, nor religion, nor trustworthiness, nor shame, and there was nothing in him that was holy'. He was murdered in 1511, at the hands of the pope's own nephew, Francesco Maria of Urbino, who had accused Alidosi of misgoverning Bologna into revolt. Different contemporary commentators observed that Julius preferred the company of his own sex: the hostile Venetian diarist Girolamo Priuli wrote that 'he used to bring his Ganymedes with him, that is, certain very handsome young men, with whom it was publicly said that he had enjoyed carnal relations'.

On 8 January 1513 Julius took to his bed and he died, calm and conscious to the last, on the evening of 20 February. He was buried next to his uncle Sixtus IV in St Peter's, where he was meant to lie until his own tomb was completed. As he lay in state, the Romans came in great numbers to see his body and the papal master of ceremonies, Paris de Grassis, wrote, 'I have never seen, nor indeed has ever been seen, such a huge crowd of people flocking to the body of any pope.' He observed that the people kissed the feet of the dead pope, praying aloud, 'through their tears, for the salvation of his soul, who had been a true Roman pope and vicar of Christ, upholding justice, extending the Apostolic Church, punishing and conquering tyrants and powerful enemies'.

THE DELLA ROVERE DIASPORA

After Julius's death, the most powerful member of his family was undoubtedly Raffaele Riario Sansoni, the Vice-Chancellor, whose massive palace attached to the church of San Lorenzo in Damaso is today known as the Cancelleria. He was the man who introduced Michelangelo to Rome in 1496: Raffaele was a passionate antiquarian and bought an apparently ancient statue of a *Cupid*, which turned out to be a clever fake made by the young Florentine artist. Raffaele played host to Michelangelo for almost a year and commissioned another faux-antique piece from him, a *Bacchus* now in the Uffizi in Florence. Weighed down with rich benefices, Raffaele was a significant force, until his involvement in a plot against Julius's successor, Leo X de' Medici (1513–21). The Riario Sforza family became nobles of Bologna and dukes in the kingdom of Naples. They only relinquished their presence in Rome in 1736, when Duke *Nicola Riario Sforza* (1743–96) sold his palace on the via della Lungara to the Corsini family. The Riario Sforza now have their principal residence in Naples.

The Riario Sforza success was eclipsed, however, by the fortunes of the della Rovere of Urbino. Francesco Maria I was unseated from his duchy but was later reinstated and founded a line of dukes that lasted into the following century. His son, *Guidobaldo II della Rovere* (1514–74), and grandson, *Francesco Maria II della Rovere* (1549–1631), both remained in their territories, which they administered more or less independently of the pope. The wily Francesco Maria II, all too aware of the grasping nature of the pope of the time, Urban VIII Barberini (1623–44), secretly sent his huge family art collection to Florence in the 1620s, where his granddaughter and heiress, *Vittoria Feltria della Rovere* (1622–94), was engaged to Ferdinando II, Grand

Duke of Tuscany. The della Rovere collection from Urbino now fills the Pitti and Uffizi galleries.

A granddaughter of Francesco Maria I married into the aristocratic Lante family of Rome and their descendants took the name Lante della Rovere. They are Roman nobles even today and one of their number, *Lucrezia Lante della Rovere* (b. 1966), is a well-known film star. Another branch of the fecund della Rovere family is part of the nobility of Genoa. The family is in no danger of extinction, having succeeded in becoming aristocrats in far-ranging cities across all of Italy, far from their humble beginnings as merchants of an insignificant coastal town.

DELLA ROVERE ITINERARY

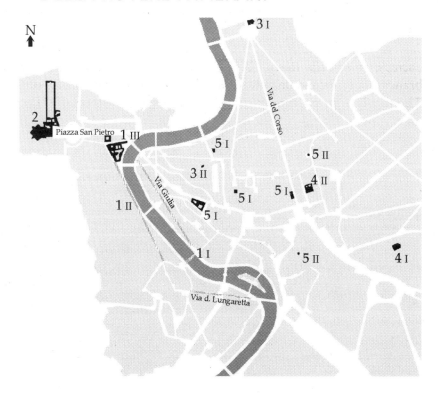

Immediately obvious in the monuments of the della Rovere family are two preoccupations: the restoration of Rome as a functioning capital and the elevation of papal grandeur. The family's artists were among the greatest of the Renaissance, beginning under Sixtus IV, whose chief architect was the Florentine Baccio Pontelli (c.1450–c.92) and whose favoured painters included Bernardino Betti, 'il Pinturicchio' (c.1454–1513), and Melozzo da Forlì (1438–94). In the decoration of the Sistine Chapel he employed Tuscan masters like Sandro Botticelli, Domenico Ghirlandaio, Piero di Cosimo and the Umbrian artist Luca Signorelli. From Pontelli Sixtus commissioned a new bridge, the ponte Sisto, and a great poor hospital at San Spirito in Sassia.

The della Rovere and Riario cardinals built lavishly, but in three cases, at San Pietro in Vincoli, Santi Apostoli and San Lorenzo in Damaso, they built in the knowledge that palaces attached to cardinalate churches could not be willed to family members and would revert to the control of the Holy See after their deaths. They were excluded from the freedom granted to other palaces built by clerics which, according to a decree of Sixtus IV, could be willed to heirs normally instead of being subject to expropriation.

Giuliano della Rovere's eagerness to build began with his two great cardinalate palaces at San Pietro in Vincoli and Santi Apostoli, with related constructions in the attached churches, employing Pontelli as architect and Melozzo and others as painters. He commissioned the extraordinary tomb of Sixtus IV (made 1484–93) from the Florentine sculptor Antonio del Pollaiuolo. After Pontelli's death, Giuliano's chief architect was another Florentine, Giuliano da Sangallo (1445–1516), who moved his family to Rome on the strength of his connection. However, upon Cardinal Giuliano's election as pope, Sangallo had to take second place to Donato Bramante of Urbino. Bramante's grandiose plans and powerful personality were to shape many of Julius's commissions, particularly his urban planning, which was stretched between two poles established by Sixtus IV, the ponte Sisto and the ospedale Santo Spirito.

Julius also served as Michelangelo's most significant patron, though the clash of their personalities made the relationship stormy. The pope's initial project for the sculptor was his tomb, but Julius, distracted by Bramante's project for St Peter's, lost interest in the tomb and instead commissioned the unwilling Michelangelo to paint the ceiling of the Sistine Chapel. He also hired Bramante's countryman Raphael to decorate his private apartments in the Vatican palace. Though Julius was not by any means the greatest of the papal dynasts, he was always careful to ensure that the della Rovere emblem of the oak tree figured in his commissions. Like his uncle, he was proud of his place of origin, and his inscriptions often describe him as 'LIGURE', from Liguria. Other popes would follow his lead.

▌ A walk around the della Rovere rectangle

Start: piazza San Vincenzo Pallotti, the southern end of the via
Giulia, at the intersection with ponte Sisto

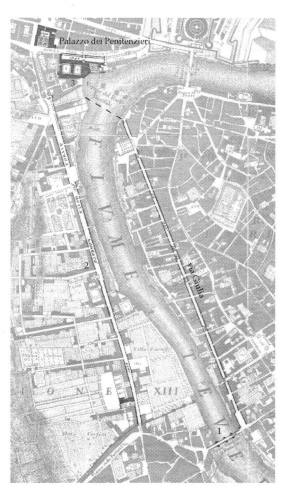

The della Rovere rectangle, seen in
Nolli's map of 1748. The dashed
line indicates a possible course for
Julius II's unbuilt bridge; another
course would extend across the
river along the line of the via Giulia
to the Santo Spirito hospital.

Key:
1 ponte Sisto
2 via della Lungara
3 Ospedale di Santo Spirito

The physical changes brought about by the della Rovere popes can best be
appreciated on foot, following the circuit of streets and public works
projects that form a rectangle enclosing the lower diagonal of the Tiber
bend. Despite the neighbourhood's drastic transformation with the building
of the river embankments, the achievement of Sixtus IV and Julius II is
still visible, spanning the Tiber and cutting streets through the tangle of
medieval alleys on the crowded east bank.

Our walk begins by the Tiber, where today the traffic of the *Lungotevere* roars past the mouth of a footbridge. The banks of the river were teeming with urban life in the fifteenth century. Two sandbanks, the *Arenula* on one side and the *Renella* on the other, narrowed the Tiber at this point: fishing and swimming were popular from the sandbanks. A ferry crossed here, navigating the ruins of an ancient bridge. Above this riverside scene rose the large Franciscan convent of San Salvatore in Onda, more or less on the site of the present building of the Pallottine fathers, who succeeded the Franciscans in ownership of the little old church (entrance from via dei Pettinari; open 9–12, 16–18), heavily redecorated in the nineteenth century. In the old convent, in a high room overlooking the river, the Franciscan general, Francesco della Rovere, had his offices.

However, it took until 1473 for him to begin building a new bridge on the site of the ruined one, which was not sufficient time for the 1475 jubilee; the bridge was finally finished in 1479. His architect was the young Florentine, Baccio Pontelli, and together they created the first bridge built in Rome since antiquity, fulfilling the ancient mandate implied in the pope's title of *Pontifex Maximus*, the great bridge builder. The bridge, of four arches, was constructed in perfect ancient Roman style, with a core of tufa stone and a facing of travertine. At the Rome (as opposed to the Trastevere) side, two large inscriptions, composed by the pope's librarian Platina, greeted the traveller. On the left, the inscription, recently replaced with a copy (where has the original gone?), says in Latin: 'Sixtus IV, Pontifex Maximus, for the utility of the Roman People and the multitude of pilgrims participating in the Jubilee, rebuilt this bridge, which for good reason had been called 'broken', from its foundations, with great care and cost, and wishes that from his name it should be named "Sisto".' The pope was taking more credit than he deserved, as the money for construction came from a bequest of the Dominican cardinal Juan de Torquemada. The right-hand inscription says: '1475. You who pass by merit of Sixtus IV, pray to the Lord to preserve for us this best of high priests, for a long time and in good health. Go in peace, whoever you are, after you have recited this prayer.'

As we cross the bridge, at the highest point, underneath our feet and invisible from where we stand, the great oculus of the bridge marks the centre of the structure. This oculus served not only as a safety valve for water in times of flood, but also as a flood warning – as soon as the waters of the river reached the bottom of the oculus, nearby residents were warned that the lowest level of habitation was under threat and the sewers were already backing up.

The ponte Sisto, by Vasi. This view shows some of the monuments along the della Rovere rectangle: on the left, part of the villa Farnesina, on the right, the massive pile of palazzo Farnese.

The bridge has been restored and repaired several times, most heavily during the construction of the embankments. Restoration of the ponte Sisto was only completed in time for the jubilee of 2000, when a new balustrade was built, approximating a lost Renaissance one. At the far end we can see the two fountains of Paul V Borghese.

II   THE VIA DELLA LUNGARA

If we cross piazza Trilussa and follow via di Ponte Sisto to our right, and straight through the little piazza di San Giovanni della Malva to the corner of via di Santa Dorotea and via di Porta Settimiana, by turning right we will look down one of Julius II's great new boulevards, **via della Lungara**. Julius also built Trastevere's other main Renaissance street, the via della Lungaretta, stretching from piazza Santa Maria in Trastevere to the ancient bridge today known as the *ponte Rotto*.

The porta Settimiana, which arches over the road here, was constructed by Alexander VI on the site of an old gate in the ancient city wall, which enclosed Trastevere but not the stretch of land along the Tiber below the Janiculan hill. The nature of the via della Lungara, which extends northwards from the gate, was conditioned by its position outside the walls. It was meant as an auxiliary route to the Vatican from Sixtus's bridge, straight and broad, with buildings on either side of a recreational nature, as befitted a 'suburban' space. It was left to Julius II to build the street, which runs almost exactly parallel with the same pope's via Giulia on the other side of the river. A patchwork of properties in its path were bought and cleared, and the work took four years, from 1508 to 1512.

Immediately outside the gate, on our left, we pass the ex-Museo Torlonia, the former seat of the Torlonia family's legendary collection of classical sculpture, which closed 'for restoration', reopening in 1978 as ninety-eight mini-apartments. This unique approach to museum design met with the outrage it deserved but, as so often in Rome, to no effect, although negotiations for the re-establishment of the museum are 'in progress'.

The next block contains, on both sides of the street, two buildings by members of Julius II's court. On the right is the villa of Agostino Chigi, 'il Magnifico', the pope's stupefyingly rich banker, now the **villa Farnesina** (for which see the Chigi chapter). On the left is palazzo Corsini, which has, as its nucleus, the **palazzo Riario**.

In 1492 Cardinal Raffaele Riario Sansoni, nephew of Girolamo Riario of ill fame, purchased from a monk, Fra Agostino Maffei, a plot stretching up the Janiculan hill. Two years after the Lungara opened in 1508, work on the palace began, with an unknown architect in charge, certainly a member of Bramante's workshop. The palazzo Riario was a U shape, with loggias facing the garden, taking its inspiration from the villa of the banker Chigi across the road. Like the villa, the palazzo was conceived as a unity with its gardens, which are today separated from the palace as Rome's botanical gardens (entrance from via Corsini). Cardinal Riario left this palace to his cousins, the Riario Sforza, and Cardinal Alessandro Riario Sforza (1543–85) lived here from 1565 to 1585. To him is owed the decoration of the Sala dell'Alcova, a bedroom whose vaults are frescoed with stories of the lives of Moses and Solomon. The Riario Sforza dukes lived principally at Naples and rented the palazzo out: its most august tenant was the eccentric Queen Christina of Sweden, who lived here for thirty years from 1659. She turned the palace into a centre of cultural and social life, filling its rooms with her art collection, now sadly dispersed.

From the outside, only the arrangement of the windows on the wing facing via Corsini remains from the original building. In 1736 Duke Nicola Riario Sforza sold the palace to the Florentine family of the Corsini, from which the palace takes its current name. The Corsini redeveloped the site, vastly enlarging the palace and rearranging the gardens. In the late nineteenth century the palace and its contents, including the great Corsini library, were sold to the state, coming into the possession of the Accademia dei Lincei, an academic society which also runs the villa Farnesina. The fine

Corsini art collection (open 9–13 daily, closed Monday; admission €5), part of the Galleria Nazionale, is on the *piano nobile* and the Sala dell'Alcova, where Queen Christina slept, can be visited.

Further along the via della Lungara the terrain becomes almost exclusively seventeenth century, though the old nunneries of Santa Maria Regina Coeli and Santa Maria della Visitazione were demolished and replaced with the imposing Regina Coeli prisons (1881–1900), today Rome's most prestigious penal address. Under Urban VIII Barberini (1623–44) a new circuit of walls banded the back of the Janiculan summit, and this street developed into a quiet district of religious communities and, towards the northern end, smaller houses. The last sixteenth-century building we pass is palazzo Salviati (at number 82–83; no admission), designed by Raphael's pupil Giulio Romano and now the property of the Italian Armed Forces.

III THE OSPEDALE DI SANTO SPIRITO IN SASSIA, THE PALAZZO DEI PENITENZIERI AND THE VIA GIULIA
Entrance from borgo Santo Spirito 1 and 2. Admission by appointment with the agency Giubilarte, tel. 06 6835 2433, 06 6821 0854; Monday–Friday 9–13, 15–18; €7.50 per person, minimum ten persons

At the traffic-ridden piazza della Rovere we diverge to follow the curve of the river, passing for an entire block the modern buildings making up part of the huge hospital of Santo Spirito in Sassia. This, the oldest hospital in the city, was founded by Innocent III in 1204 and given to the order of the Holy Spirit, which came to found or inspire as many as 500 daughter hospitals across Europe. It stood on the site of the old *schola Saxonum*, the settlement of Anglo-Saxons first created by Ine, king of the West Saxons, in AD 727. He, 'exchanging an earthly for a heavenly crown', abdicated and lived his final years here, founding the papal suburb called the Borgo. The English *schola* had died out by the thirteenth century and the building was rededicated to the Holy Spirit. By the reign of Sixtus IV, however, the old hospital was in a grievous condition, as the pope himself noticed: 'crumbling walls, gloomy, airless and narrow buildings, without any kind of comfort, giving rather the impression of a prison'. Sixtus decided to demolish it and build what was, at the time, one of the largest and most important hospital complexes in Europe, in 1473–82. He assumed control of it himself, asserting in a 1477 bull, 'Our hospital of Santo Spirito in Sassia of the Alma Urbe, which we have recently reconstructed from its foundations and extended with lavish works, giving aid and shelter to the poor, has as Superior none other than the Pope of Rome.'

As we reach the corner of borgo Santo Spirito, we overlook a building of greater age than the ones we have been passing. It is composed of a portico and a façade above with four gothic windows. This is the end of the long building called the *corsia Sistina*, the 'Sistine Wards'. Across the river, the mouth of the via Giulia opens, stretching in a straight line all the way back to the ponte Sisto. This spot was meant to be the site of a great new bridge, the ponte Giulio or ponte Trionfale, which was to complete the della Rovere rectangle, linking Julius II's great show street of the via Giulia with Sixtus IV's hospital in a grandiose display of family power and generosity. Unfortunately, the bridge was never constructed, though a ferry crossed here for many centuries and at this point, the Tiber bend, a famous watermill floated in the river, the *mola dei Fiorentini*.

The hospital's façade facing the river is a fake, made in 1926–8, deriving from a building in one of Botticelli's frescoes in the Sistine Chapel. It reuses the original fifteenth-century windows and the original portal whose marble frame was carved by Andrea Bregno (1421–1506), one of the great sculptors of the Roman Quattrocento; it replaces a wing built by Benedict XIV Lambertini (1740–58) and demolished, along with much else, during the construction of the Lungotevere. The Sistine constructions here are enormous along the whole initial stretch of the borgo Santo Spirito, down which we now turn.

Until the year 2000, patients were still housed in the rather dilapidated wings of the *corsia Sistina*. Now the entire 120-metre-long stretch has been closed and isolated from the living hospital and, under the name of the *Complesso Monumentale di Santo Spirito in Saxia*, has been given into the hands of a tour agency. Only tour groups of ten or more will be accommodated, but it is often possible to join groups that have already been assembled. The site is of such interest and is so rarely visited by tourists, that it is worthwhile to arrange a tour, if at all possible. What we may visit without paying is also interesting: only the *corsia Sistina* is closed.

The two long wards of the *corsia Sistina* are surrounded by porticoes, in which the ill could take their ease; they were walled up by Benedict XIV in the eighteenth century but one has had its arches reopened. Just before the main entrance at number 2 is a grille with a round hole in it, behind which sits a sort of turning barrel with an aperture in one side. This was the foundling deposit, where unwanted babies could be abandoned without giving away the identity of the abandoner. The main door was remade by Gianlorenzo Bernini during the reign of Alexander VII Chigi (1655–67) and the Chigi crest rises above the portal; it incorporates the della Rovere oak tree, a privilege granted by Julius II to his banker, Agostino Chigi. The building further along, the **palazzo del Commendatore** or palace of the hospital governor, dates from the late sixteenth century and sports a beautiful courtyard with a two-level loggia, the upper decorated with frescoes depicting the coats of arms of the noble governors of the hospital.

Inside, the **corsia Sistina** is a huge space, now divided by glass partitions into three areas. The two wards, the **Sala Baglivi** and **Sala Lancisi**, named after great doctors of the seventeenth century who worked here, are decorated with frescoes between the windows in the uppermost register of the walls. Some were remade in the late sixteenth century, but the ones in the *Sala Lancisi* are fifteenth century (1477–81) and were made by the studio of Melozzo da Forlì. The frescoes are in a really terrible condition, waiting to be restored, but they represent the first and decidedly lesser, major fresco cycle commissioned by Sixtus IV, preceding the great cycle in the Sistine Chapel. They depict the history of the site, including the foundation of the hospital by Innocent III, following a nightmare he had of river fishermen catching dead babies in their nets.

The majority of the paintings, thirty-seven in total, show scenes from the life of Sixtus himself. Most interesting are the twelve scenes of his urban projects in Rome: repairing and constructing streets, piazze, walls, the Acqua Vergine aqueduct, the port of Ripa Grande, the ponte Sisto, churches like Santa Maria del Popolo, rebuilding the hospital and founding the Vatican Library. The final scene in this glorious progress shows St Peter himself conducting the pope to the door of Paradise.

Dividing the two wings of the *corsia Sistina* is the **vestibule**, a tall and striking space which functioned as a chapel, with a free-standing altar and ciborium from *c*.1546, which are purportedly the only Roman works of the great Renaissance architect Andrea Palladio (1508–60), though decorated with the arms of Clement VIII Aldobrandini (1592–1605). The octagonal drum contains four beautiful gothic windows, which open above twelve niches containing statues of saints, surmounted by a fine coffered wooden ceiling with the emblem of the Order of the Holy Spirit in the centre, a double-barred cross.

The rest of the complex is more readily accessible. From the riverward façade we proceed round the portico through some tiny patches of garden before arriving at another portico containing huge fragments of stone carvings, crests and cherubs; from here is the entrance to the **National Historical Museum of Medicine** (open Monday, Wednesday and Friday, 10–12; admission €5), which contains a rarely visited but interesting collection.

Further on, we find an open corridor sloping downwards, which leads to two cloisters opening on either side, both constructed at the order of Sixtus IV. To the right is the **Cortile dei Frati** (Monks' Courtyard), protruding from one wall of which is a rather frightening half-length portrait bust in bronze of Clement XII Corsini, who looks as if he might tear himself from his niche and lay waste to all in his path; to the left is the larger **Cortile delle Suore** (Nuns' Courtyard), with a pretty fountain in the centre, possibly the work of Baccio Pontelli. The nephews of the last papal nepotist, Pius VI Braschi (1775–99), stripped the reused ancient columns of these cloisters (twelve from the monks' court, ten from the nuns') to put them in the grand staircase of palazzo Braschi, now the Museo di Roma. Most of the present columns are travertine replacements.

Continuing along the edge of the same building, we pass round a corner and through a narrow gate into the courtyard of the palazzo del Commendatore and straight through to leave by the main *portone*. The beautiful complex of Santo Spirito in Sassia, amply provided with courtyards, expresses the power and wealth of this great confraternity, which was to provide the initial capital and security for the papal bank at the beginning of the seventeenth century, the Banco di Santo Spirito. Next to the palazzo del Commendatore is the church of Santo Spirito in Sassia, the final part of the complex, which belongs more properly to the itinerary of the Farnese family. However, across the borgo Santo Spirito, under an arch labelled with the name of the Knights of the Holy Sepulchre of Jerusalem, we may enter the courtyard of a della Rovere family palace, the **palazzo dei Penitenzieri**.

This courtyard appears strangely fresh and bright, hardly one's idea of the fifteenth century, but this is due to restoration work undertaken in 1948 and again in the 1990s to bring the palace back to life after centuries of decay. Unusually, it is divided in two: this part, the rear of the courtyard, is at a higher level than the front part, a compromise to take into account the change in ground level from the front to the back. The Hotel Columbus now occupies most of the building and its restaurant has its tables in the courtyard. The surrounding walls are painted with false columns, restored decorations that resemble Melozzo's frescoes in palazzo Altemps, roughly contemporaneous with this palace. If we leave the courtyard and go round the building, we will arrive on the via della Conciliazione, barren and ugly, generously endowed with tour buses and souvenir shops. At this point it is worth crossing the first lane of the street and standing on the travertine median to look at the palace and its surroundings.

Before Mussolini's architects did away with the *spina del Borgo*, the irregular spine of buildings running towards piazza San Pietro from the river, to build this street, two old and narrow thoroughfares ran through this densely built area, the borgo Vecchio and the borgo Nuovo, opening into a small square here called piazza Scossacavalli. The piazza was framed by two fifteenth-century palaces, this and palazzo Giraud Torlonia, home of the Torlonia princes. In the latter palace, in the early seventeenth century dwelt the great cardinal nephew Scipione Borghese, whose presence was marked by a fountain bearing the family emblems in the middle of the piazza (now in front of Sant' Andrea della Valle). In the late fifteenth century, piazza Scossacavalli must have made a tremendous impression on visitors coming from the Castel Sant'Angelo bridge.

It was here that the newly created cardinal Domenico della Rovere, a distant cousin from a Piedmontese branch of the della Rovere family, decided to build his palace in 1478. The architect was perhaps Baccio Pontelli and he seems to have taken his inspiration from the first great palace of Renaissance Rome, palazzo Venezia, constructed only about fifteen years previously and similar to this one in many details, particularly in the design of the windows and the tower which stands on the left hand of the façade. Inscriptions above the windows give the cardinal's name and his cardinalate church: 'DO. RUVERE CARD. S. CLEM.' (Domenico della Rovere, Cardinal of San Clemente). On the upper-floor window frames appear the words 'SOLI DEO' (to God alone).

If we enter the courtyard, we will see a fifteenth-century well with the della Rovere arms on it. The palace today is owned by an order of Catholic knights, the Order of the Holy Sepulchre, but we may enter the left-hand half and ask the hotel clerk if it is possible to be shown the principal rooms. Some of the bedrooms retain their fifteenth-century friezes, thought to be by Pinturicchio. The restaurant is in a frescoed loggia and one other room, formerly a library or study, has a ceiling frescoed with a scene of the *Chariot of Apollo* by Francesco Salviati. Around the side, on via Scossacavalli, a large fragment of the original exterior decoration can be seen.

In 1501 the palace fell into the gift of Cardinal Giuliano della Rovere; he gave it to his favourite, the future cardinal Francesco Alidosi, who thereby had one of the most modern and comfortable palaces near the Vatican. Alidosi lived there, though travelling frequently as Julius II's envoy, until his murder in 1511. Remarkably, the next tenant was his murderer, the future Duke of Urbino, Francesco Maria I della Rovere, the pope's nephew. However, the della Rovere never inhabited this palace again, and it passed into the hands of the wealthy hospital of Santo Spirito across the road and their tenants.

We return to the river and cross it by the anti-papal ponte Vittorio Emanuele II (*c.*1911), decorated in the somewhat oppressive *'stile Liberty'* favoured at the time, with four sculpture groups in travertine celebrating *Victory over Oppression, Italian Unity, Loyalty to the Law* and *Freedom* (the flame of which is being protected from extinguishing winds apparently blowing from the Vatican). We will cross the traffic-ridden Lungotevere and turn right along it, where we turn again down the via della mola de' Fiorentini, the name of the last stretch of the via Giulia and cross the via Acciaioli into piazza d'Oro.

The church of San Giovanni dei Fiorentini, which forms the monumental decoration of this end of the via Giulia, post-dates the della Rovere papacies, being first constructed under Leo X de' Medici. Late fifteenth-century houses face towards the church's eighteenth-century façade, with round-arched windows. From here we have a clear view down Renaissance Rome's most characteristic street, the **via Giulia**.

Bramante and his papal patron intended this to be the principal state street of the city. To that end it was to be wide and straight, both qualities that emphasised the power and wealth of the pope who built it, cutting through the knot of old property ownership in this heavily built-up part of the Campus Martius. It bears a close similarity to Renaissance stage-set streets visible in sixteenth-century theatres, with a strong perspectival effect. As a street, it is unquestionably both beautiful and impressive, '*una bella strada longa*', the most prestigious sort of street to live on, according to the canons of the Renaissance; but it did not work out as Julius II planned. On the western side, between vicolo del Cefalo and via del Gonfalone, the heavy Bramantean base of Julius's failed project for the **palazzo dei Tribunali** is testament to his vast ambition. The travertine base, which at via del Gonfalone rises as high as the bottom of the first floor, is now interrupted by two churches and a street. The palace was intended to form the heart of a new administrative district for pontifical justice and for the city government, to replace the forbidding old fortress on the Capitoline. A large piazza in front was also planned.

Julius II intended that this become the principal residential street for the papal court, and the buildings on both sides by and large conform to this plan, though in constructing the street he incurred the anger of the local great family, the Incoronati Planca. Their traces are now hard to see, especially since Mussolini demolished the greater part of the '*monte degl' Incoronati*' (Incoronati neighbourhood), to build the Virgilio high school. Julius, too, had long ago demolished Incoronati property, and in revenge the family built up their remaining properties as small shops and apartments, rather than expensive palaces, and rented them not to courtiers, but to courtesans. The via Giulia thus had a strangely dual character: it was both a desirable residential address and a famous red light district. In the seventeenth century the Incoronati buildings were expropriated by Innocent X Pamphilj (1644–55) to build his New Prisons (*Carceri Nuove*) and the prostitutes were replaced with criminals. Only the name of the cross-street, the vicolo del Malpasso, 'of the Mis-step', remains to hint at the identity of the former residents.

2 The della Rovere in the Vatican

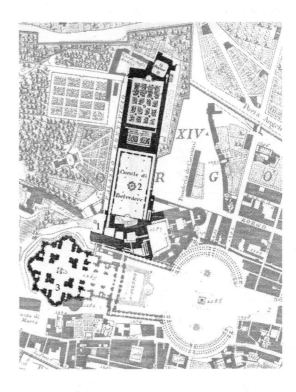

The della Rovere in the Vatican

Key:
1 Sistine Chapel
2 Vatican Palace
3 New St Peter's, with the Michelangelo-designed section highlighted

As the papal court expanded in the later fifteenth century the Vatican palace needed to be enlarged and both the della Rovere popes applied themselves to this task, Julius II even more than Sixtus IV. Julius took the radical decision to demolish Old St Peter's and construct a vast new basilica, a task which was to take the better part of the next century and a half. He also developed the papal palace, perhaps remembering the palais des Papes at Avignon where he had lived as legate, which was much larger and more commodious than the Vatican. He set about remaking the Vatican in the image of the Avignonese residence, though with an architectural vocabulary that was modishly classical, an imperial style well suited to the self-image of the Renaissance papacy.

The Sistine Chapel in a nineteenth-century image, complete with Victorian gawkers. An expression of papal claims to supreme authority, it proclaims the glory and taste of the della Rovere family's great commissioners of art, Sixtus IV and Julius II.

I   THE SISTINE CHAPEL
Entrance included in admission to Vatican Museums. Open 8.45–16.45, 1 April to 31 October; 8.45–13.45, 1 November to 31 March. Admission €12

By the reign of Sixtus IV the size of the papal court required a new palace chapel and Sixtus took the opportunity to mend a political fence: originally he had intended to employ only Umbrian artists, but after the end of the Pazzi war in 1480 the magnanimous Lorenzo de' Medici allowed the best Florentine artists to go to Rome to serve him. Thus the new chapel became a showcase of Tuscan talent, with the Umbrian school under Pietro Vannucci, called Il Perugino (c.1450–1523), relegated to second place. The Tuscan–Umbrian rivalry was to reassert itself again under Julius II.

Constructed from 1475 to 1481, from the outside the Sistine Chapel is remarkably like a fortress, with its bleak high walls and crenellations; indeed, it was by far the tallest construction of the complex and served as a defensive bastion. Sixtus's Tuscan architect, Baccio Pontelli, designed the chapel on a monster scale that was soon to be matched by the plans for New St Peter's under Julius II. The proportions were set out in no less authoritative a source than the biblical First Book of Kings: the length of the chapel is twice its height and three times its width, the dimensions of the temple of Solomon. However, what Solomon covered in gold and cedar Sixtus intended for fresco, an appropriate decoration to mark it out as different from the other great meeting halls. The plain box of a chapel was divided into two sections, the part closer to the altar being reserved for priests, the other, slightly smaller section for the laity. A cornice, halfway up from the floor to the apex of the vault, marks another clear visual break: above the cornice, the wall is measured out with windows and shallow pilasters. Two further windows in the altar wall were blocked up by Michelangelo when he painted the *Last Judgement* for Paul III Farnese. These two windows, though now vanished, have left a trace, as the principal Sistine cycle of frescoes are all painted as if being lit from them. The basic design of the chapel was well suited to fresco decoration: plenty of wall space was matched with plenty of light.

Whole libraries have been filled with books discussing the Sistine Chapel, the most famous room in the world. We will confine ourselves here to a consideration of Sixtus's and Julius's intentions. Sixtus IV, though he dedicated the chapel to the Assumption of the Virgin, caused two fresco cycles to run along the middle register of the walls, beginning with two panels above the altar (now, of course, destroyed) and ending over the entrance: the right-hand cycle facing the altar depicts episodes in the life of Jesus, while matching episodes in the left-hand cycle represent the life of Moses. Thus the Old and New Testaments were both represented, with Moses as precursor of Christ. Work was under way by July 1481 and rapidly completed by May 1482.

Sixtus had a clear political motive, to indicate the progression of authority and legitimacy, through the Old and New Testaments, to St Peter and his successors, the popes. It was thoroughly informed by Sixtus's own beliefs: the pope wrote that 'Moses was our Christ'. Added to this scheme is the old theme of the transmission of Christ's authority to the popes, the *traditio legis* ('tradition of the law'). The two most prominent and important frescoes are in the centre of both long walls: on the right, *Christ Giving the Keys to Peter* by Perugino and on the left the *Punishment of Korah* by Sandro Botticelli (1445–1510), a warning to those who would disobey the pope: Moses's lieutenant Aaron, in the latter painting, is wearing a conical blue cap surrounded by three gold crowns, easily recognisable as a papal tiara, and in the della Rovere colours, while the censers falling from the hands of the rebellious Korah, Dathan and Abiram are in the form of Riario roses. In all the frescoes in this room figures wearing the della Rovere colours of blue and gold should be considered possible portraits of family members. In the background of both the central frescoes is the arch of Constantine, alluding to that emperor's legendary gift of temporal power to the papacy. On one of the twin arches in Perugino's fresco the inscription says 'To Sixtus, in wealth less [than Constantine], in religion greater'.

The frescoes contain many contemporary portraits. In Botticelli's *Temptation of Christ and Healing of the Leper* (second from the altar on the right-hand wall), the figure of the cardinal in the foreground, looking rather glum, is Giuliano della Rovere, while the seated figure in the green cloak gilded with oak leaves is probably his brother Giovanni, prefect of Rome. Perugino and Pinturicchio's *Baptism of Christ* (next to the former, beside the altar wall) also seems to contain a group, in the right foreground, of Riario portraits the haughty figure in the middle of the group, with a red hat and cloak, might be Girolamo Riario. By contrast, the *Calling of the First Apostles* by Domenico Ghirlandaio (1449–94) has a crowd of prominent members of the Florentine community in Rome in the right foreground. The walls of the chapel are vivid with fifteenth-century faces.

By the time of the death of Sixtus IV most of the decoration he had envisioned was complete and the two popes who followed him contented themselves with finishing minor details. Under Julius II, however, a second phase began, which was to mark the astonishing appearance of Michelangelo as a fresco artist.

In May 1504 a large diagonal crack appeared across the vault of the chapel, damaging the simple painted pattern of stars on a blue sky that had been the choice of Sixtus IV. The chapel was closed for six months. Julius summoned Bramante to fix the structural damage, which was due to subsidence caused by other building work nearby, and the architect suggested that Michelangelo be employed to make a new fresco. Michelangelo, who had been summoned to Rome to make Julius's tomb, was far from delighted with this suggestion and suspected Bramante of trying to sabotage the tomb project; there was rivalry involved, all the more because Bramante, from Urbino, had received the commission to rebuild St Peter's that Michelangelo's friend and fellow Florentine Giuliano da Sangallo had hoped for. It took until 1508 for the artist to accept the commission and the work was not completed until 1512, though half the scaffolding was removed in 1510 to placate the impatient pope, revealing the vast and spectacular work finished to that point.

Julius probably left the iconographic programme to the artist, though there has been much academic discussion of other possible authors;

Michelangelo seems to have settled on a fairly clear scheme uniting the Bible with church tradition. The central scenes depict episodes from the Book of Genesis, while around the sides of the chapel roof are alternating prophets and sibyls, the former being Jewish foretellers of Christ and the sibyls being pagan prophetesses who nonetheless, according to legend, also saw the coming of Christ. The prophet Zacharias is probably a portrait of Julius himself. In the 'sails' above the windows and the rainbow-shaped spaces below them on the walls are the ancestors of Christ. In accordance, perhaps, with Julius's lesser interest in nepotism, there is relatively little by way of allusion to the pope's family: only the famous *ignudi* who decorate the fictive architecture surrounding the central scenes bear garlands of the della Rovere oak, with acorns in bunches. The whole ceiling, instead, alludes to the biblical force of papal power, continuing the theme set by Sixtus IV.

II   THE VATICAN PALACE
Admission as for the Vatican Museums

The palace of the popes was, by the accession of Julius II, larger and grander than ever before, but it still required enlargement. In addition to the main body of the palace close to the piazza San Pietro, on the height of the Vatican hill, Innocent VIII Cibò had built a villa called the Belvedere. In 1505, under the direction of Bramante, construction began on a colossal extension to the main body of the palace: two long wings clambering up the hill to unite the villa of Innocent VIII with the main papal residence, 300 yards away. There were to be three terraces to even out the space of the colossal courtyard, known as the **Belvedere courtyard**, flanked by porticoes acting as corridors, the upper enclosed floor serving as a link between the palace's second floor and the villa's ground floor. However, only the right-hand corridor was completed during the pope's lifetime and perhaps that was as well for Julius's purposes, as he really seems only to have been interested in the construction as a passageway to the villa, where he kept his collection of ancient sculpture. A huge inscription on the eastern exterior wall, visible if you glance through the porta Sant' Anna (the working entrance to the Vatican City, on the via di Porta Angelica), asserts proudly in Latin that 'Julius II, sixth pope from Liguria, of the city [*patria*] of Savona, nephew of Sixtus IV, built this way [*via*] for the convenience of the popes'. Bramante's design for the inner side of the courtyard, which was carried out with modifications by later popes, seems to have owed much to ancient Roman theatre architecture: the façades closely resemble the *scenae frons* or ornamental backdrop that would stand behind a stage. In its theatricality

The Bramante-built arm of the Belvedere courtyard in the Vatican palace, sixteenth-century engraving by Philippe Galle, showing some of Julius II's sculpture collection.

it has much in common with the via Giulia, also designed under the supervision of Bramante. It was completed only in 1563.

In 1508, Julius decided to add a grandiose porticoed façade overlooking the piazza. This was also a project of Bramante's, though it was only brought to completion after the death of both pope and architect, by Raphael, and decorated with frescoes by Raphael and his workshop. The loggia on the second floor leads out of the papal apartment decorated by Raphael for Julius and his successor Leo X. The pope moved up to these rooms in 1507, abandoning the apartment of his predecessor Alexander VI on the floor below, saying he couldn't bear to see the face of the detested Borgia pope every day. The rooms of this apartment, now called the **Raphael Rooms**, were lavishly decorated; the principal room, today called the *stanza della Segnatura*, was probably Julius's library, with four frescoes by Raphael that are among his most famous: the *Disputa*, representing the discussion of the Eucharist, the *School of Athens*, representing the triumph of philosophy, the *Parnassus*, referring to the art of poetry, and on the window wall representations of civil and canon law. The next room, the *stanza d'Eliodoro*, contains two frescoes from Julius's time, the others being completed under Leo X. The first fresco, the *Expulsion of Heliodorus from the Temple*, bears two portraits of Julius, one as himself, witnessing the action from the left, and another as a participant, the high priest in front of the altar. It probably alludes to Julius's expulsion of foreign powers from the Papal States. The second, the *Mass at Bolsena* over the window, refers very obliquely to the pope's campaigns against Bologna, for it was at Orvieto, on the way to Bologna, that the relic of the Mass of Bolsena was kept: the miracle was of the Host, which bled to prove the real presence of Christ. Here is the most splendid and characteristic portrait of the *papa terribile*, furiously at prayer, one of his Swiss guards regarding us curiously across the centuries. This room's decoration has a more explicitly political subtext: the *Liberation of St Peter from Prison* alludes both to the main relics of Julius's cardinalate church of San Pietro in Vincoli, St Peter in Chains and to Julius's 'liberation' of the Papal States from occupation by French troops.

The palace houses two famous works of ancient sculpture, the *Apollo Belvedere* and the *Laocoön*. Both were discovered during the lifetime of Julius II and he brought them here to the **octagonal courtyard**. The two pieces stand in contrast to each other, the *Apollo* for its serenity and the *Laocoön* for its agitation.

One other significant della Rovere memorial is in the Pinacoteca Vaticana, the Vatican picture gallery, a detached fresco by Melozzo da Forlì removed in the nineteenth century from the site of the first Vatican Library, founded by Sixtus IV. Its nominal subject is the *Investiture of Platina as Vatican Librarian* (1477) but it really serves as a papal family group; the pilasters that frame the picture have the della Rovere oak symbol weaving up along their length, while the coffered ceiling of the painted room displays the Riario rose. Apart from the kneeling figure of Platina in the centre, who is pointing to a laudatory inscription below praising Sixtus and his works, the fresco is populated solely with the pope and his relatives. Sixtus IV, seated in profile to the right, is looking up towards his nephew, Cardinal Giuliano della Rovere, while the tonsured head of Raffaele Riario Sansoni, not yet a cardinal (his elevation took place in December of that year, 1477), is facing in the same direction. To the left, behind Platina, the tall figure in a blue robe is none other than Girolamo Riario of Imola and Forlì, and the shorter figure at the far left is Giovanni della Rovere, the prefect of Rome. The fresco can be seen as a hierarchical expression of each member's position relative to the pope, a group, like the family, riven by tensions.

In the same room of the Pinacoteca are more detached frescoes by Melozzo, this time part of the colossal decorative programme commissioned by Cardinal Giuliano for his church of Santi Apostoli. The great apse fresco, of which these details form a tiny part, was badly damaged in an earthquake and only these lovely *Music-making Angels* were preserved, along with some other pieces now in the Quirinal palace and in Madrid, when the basilica underwent a major renovation in 1711.

III   NEW ST PETER'S AND THE TOMB OF SIXTUS IV
       Basilica open 7–19 daily. Admission to Treasury Museum April to
       September 9–18.30, October to March 9–17.30; €2.50

According to Michelangelo's biographer Condivi, the spur for the papacy's most expensive and long-lasting architectural project, the building of a new basilica over the presumed site of St Peter's grave, was Julius II's desire for an appropriately august site for his own tomb. In reality, the project had already been considered by popes from Nicholas V (1447–55) onwards. Sixtus IV had built his own funeral chapel on to the old basilica, a thoroughly della Rovere monument with a maiolica tile floor covered in oak tree emblems and a ceiling in green and gold with oak branches and acorns, in the centre of which was Cardinal Giuliano's most important sculptural commission, the **tomb of Sixtus IV** himself.

Today the della Rovere funerary chapel, where Julius was also eventually interred, no longer exists, and the tomb of Sixtus IV, after residing for centuries in one of the large side chapels off the nave of New St Peter's, has been moved to the Museo del Tesoro, the Treasury Museum of the basilica. This tomb is the masterpiece of the Florentine sculptor Antonio del Pollaiuolo (1431–98), made at the height of his powers in 1484–93, with the assistance of his brother Piero. It has an unusual shape, the form of a catafalque or bier, all in bronze, with concave sides divided by acanthus volutes, between which are reliefs of seated female figures representing the sciences: Rhetoric, Grammar, Perspective, Music, Geometry, Theology, Philosophy, Mathematics, Astrology and Dialectics. The presence of so many semi-clad female figures may have raised some eyebrows, and the parallels made between classical goddesses and the sciences are surprising: Theology, for instance, is represented by the almost nude goddess Diana. The supine figure of the pope, his dead cheeks fallen in, is beautifully represented, and around the body is a strip of low reliefs with the personifications of the cardinal and theological virtues, interspersed with the della Rovere crest. It shows the Renaissance enthusiasm for study, as well as reflecting Sixtus's own academic career. It also stands out as strikingly different from other papal tombs, both before and after; here the pope's effigy shows tremendous realism and every fold of his garments is rendered with exquisite care. An inscription praises the sculptor: 'Antonio of Florence, famous for his work in silver, gold and painting'.

St Peter's as it stands today shows almost none of its della Rovere-era construction. Julius II's architect, Bramante, submitted a series of different plans, in close consultation with the pope, and Julius settled upon a Greek cross plan, with four arms of equal length and space for his tomb in the apse. Bramante ruthlessly demolished the venerable basilica's north side, discarding much that could have been saved and thus winning for himself the nickname, given him by his countryman Raphael, of 'Bramante Ruinante'. His demolitions, perhaps more than his designs, gave an irresistible impetus to the construction of the new basilica, for subsequent and more cautious pontiffs might have chosen merely to repair the old Constantinian fabric rather than build an entirely new structure. This plan was subject to regular changes, and construction went through long phases of inactivity, being finally finished only in the seventeenth century.

Though it was begun by Julius II, it was left to others to complete his greatest project. The French writer Stendhal observed in his journal that 'if the foreigner who enters St Peter's attempts to see everything, he will develop a furious headache and presently satiety and pain will render him incapable of any pleasure'. This sensory overload, a common experience for many cultural tourists, is called Stendhal's Syndrome and indeed it is wise not to try to see it all at once.

3　Sixtus IV and the Virgin Mary

During his academic career Francesco della Rovere often debated subjects related to the Virgin Mary. In 1470, before he became pope, he published a concordance between the works of two medieval theologians, Thomas Aquinas and Duns Scotus, in an attempt to prove that they both believed the same thing about the Virgin's conception without original sin (the Immaculate Conception, a vexed topic that will recur in these pages). As we have already seen, Sixtus dedicated the court chapel of the Vatican palace to the Assumption of the Virgin. The pope's enthusiasm for the cult of Mary extended to his founding two of Renaissance Rome's greatest churches, Santa Maria del Popolo and Santa Maria della Pace.

I　SANTA MARIA DEL POPOLO
Piazza del Popolo. Open 8–12, 16–19

In 1472 a small chapel on the site of this church, originally built in the eleventh century on the reputed site of the tomb of the Emperor Nero, came into the possession of the Augustinians of the Lombard Congregation. Soon afterwards Sixtus IV decided to make it into a showpiece of his pontificate. His motive was in part spiritual, in part political and in part familial. Spiritually, Sixtus's devotion to the Virgin played a large role in his personal faith. Politically, it was a compliment to the Duke of Milan to beautify the church of the Lombard Augustinians and for his family the church was to serve as a mausoleum. Furthermore, Sixtus knew that the city needed to present a modern face to visitors arriving from the north and that pilgrims would be impressed by a great new church to pray in as they entered.

Work began in 1472 and ended in 1478. The name of the architect is unknown, but the plan was based on Nicholas V's unrealised scheme for St Peter's: the nave, with equal side chapels, reached a crossing under a dome, from which the transepts and apse branched out, all of equal length. This produced a grand canopied space, solemn and serene; the stone was not exotic marble but local travertine, quarried near Tivoli.

The **façade**, though rather altered under Alexander VII Chigi in the 1650s (for which see the Chigi itinerary), retains its fifteenth-century solemnity. Two smaller side doors, whose lintels are inscribed with the pope's name (one misspelled as 'SIXUS') and the date 1477, lead into the aisles, while the main door frame is delicately carved, following classical examples. In fact, the whole church front is a good example of the way Renaissance churches adapted the plan of ancient temple façades: two temple silhouettes are combined, a lower one that includes the side aisles and a narrower, taller one that accounts for the higher central nave. The effect is made a little Baroque with seventeenth-century curved pediments and volutes above the aisles, but originally a simple sloping pediment here joined the nave façade. Two large inscriptions on either side of the main door announce Sixtus's authorship of the building and enumerate its various privileges, and on the lintel of the central portal is carved the della Rovere oak crest.

The **interior**, also somewhat changed from its fifteenth-century appearance, nonetheless vividly expresses Sixtus's intentions. This monastery church was not meant to be of lavish materials, but was designed to underline the simplicity of the contemplative life. The central dome is octagonal, following Sixtus's scheme to symbolise the resurrection of Christ on the eighth day after his entry into Jerusalem.

This church's character as a court mausoleum is immediately apparent in its side chapels. To the right, as we enter, is the **della Rovere chapel**. Its decoration remains almost as it was in the fifteenth century: the graceful marble balustrade is by Bregno, with extremely beautiful carvings of the family oak emblem in different guises, while the altarpiece, a *Nativity*, is by Pinturicchio and one of his pupils, Tiberio d'Assisi (c.1460–1524). The altar itself bears particularly graceful carved decorations of ewers and bundles of fruit, and above the altar table is a dedicatory inscription by Cardinal Domenico della Rovere. The pilasters measuring out the walls of this chapel are decorated with among the first examples of a style which we will find throughout Rome, the *grottesche*, derived from ancient Roman wall paintings discovered not long before in the ruins of Nero's palace, the Golden House: as this palace had been buried and filled with earth, Renaissance explorers saw only the vaults, which formed dark but glittering grottoes full of fresco and stucco, all of which greatly influenced Roman art from the fifteenth century onwards. On the left wall is the tomb, by Bregno, of the two Piedmontese della Rovere brothers who were successively made cardinals by Sixtus: Cristoforo, who died in 1478, and Domenico, builder of the palazzo dei Penitenzieri, which we have already visited, who died in 1501. The ceiling of this chapel, an umbrella vault, is a tiny version of the Sistine Chapel ceiling before Michelangelo: deep blue with golden stars.

Next is the Baroque **Cibò chapel**, belonging to the family of Innocent VIII, and beside it is the **Basso della Rovere chapel**, which has wonderful monochrome *trompe-l'oeil* benches with books on them, also by Tiberio d'Assisi. The frescoes in the lunettes, with *Scenes from the Life of Mary*, are by the same painter, with an assistant. Set into the right-hand wall is the tomb of Giovanni Basso della Rovere (d. 1481), Sixtus's brother-in-law, husband of the pope's sister Luchina, who herself was buried in greater pomp in St Peter's. The floor here, as in the previous della Rovere chapel, preserves some of its original and lovely Deruta ceramic floor tiles. The most prominent monument in the **Costa chapel**, next door, was moved from another position in the church: this is a free-standing tomb of 1480, an interesting precursor of Pollaiuolo's tomb of Sixtus IV. It commemorates Pietro Foscari of Venice, created cardinal by Sixtus in 1477, and is one of the last works of the Sienese sculptor Lorenzo di Pietro, called Il Vecchietta (1412–80). The other principal tomb in this chapel is that of Jorge de Costa (d. 1509), Archbishop of Lisbon, created cardinal by Sixtus in 1476. Though not belonging to the della Rovere, this is unquestionably a courtier's chapel, owing its presence here to the gravitic weight exercised by the papal family.

The **transepts** are now almost wholly seventeenth century in appearance, but from a door in the south transept we can visit a corridor in which a few of the tomb monuments from the cloister of the now demolished monastery, also built by Sixtus, have been preserved. The monastery, which used to extend across the whole eastern part of today's piazza del Popolo, housed Martin Luther when he came to Rome. At the end of the corridor is the **sacristy**, which contains a beautiful marble altar by Bregno, the church's original high altar, commissioned by Rodrigo Borgia while still a cardinal.

Returning to the church, we now enter the **presbytery**. A piece of inlaid stone gives the date 1263, the earliest inscription in the church. Raphael's portrait of Julius II, now in London's National Gallery, used to hang here, along with a cannonball that narrowly missed the pope when it was fired at him in the siege of Mirandola. If we explore behind the altarpiece with its Byzantine Madonna from the early thirteenth century, we find ourselves in a second phase of della Rovere patronage: this is the **choir**, constructed by Bramante, first in 1500 at the order of Alexander VI, when the beautiful shell vault of the apse was made, then transformed 1505–9 at the order of Julius II as a funerary chapel for his cousin Girolamo Basso della Rovere and Julius's old rival, Cardinal Ascanio Sforza of Milan, the pope maker of the conclave that elected Alexander VI. The two tombs, with Sforza on the left and Basso della Rovere on the right, were conceived of as twins by their sculptor, the Venetian Andrea Sansovino (1460–1529). Set into two elegant triumphal arches, the deceased are depicted as if sleeping, and not very comfortably at that, Sforza leaning heavily on his elbow as if at a particularly dull dinner party: this emulates Etruscan tomb figures, which were often represented as asleep. Above the tombs are two beautiful stained-glass windows from 1509, extremely rare in Rome, depicting the *Childhood of Christ* and *Episodes in the Life of the Virgin*, by the French master Guillaume de Marcillat (c.1468–1529). Surmounting the ensemble is the ceiling frescoed by Pinturicchio 1508–10, with the *Coronation of the Virgin* in the centre, surrounded by a programme of sibyls, evangelists and prophets that should remind us of the Sistine Chapel ceiling, being painted at the same time. A comparison of the two underlines the revolutionary nature of Michelangelo's accomplishment.

The north or **left transept** has two lovely chapels, including the Cerasi chapel of c.1600 with its famous paintings by Caravaggio and Carracci. Back down the left aisle (the first chapel we will pass, by the transept, has a fifteenth-century crucifix, a gift of the Cibò family), the only chapel which concerns the della Rovere is the one closest to the entrance wall, which functions as a baptistery, with the reliefs round the font niche and ciborium being made from pieces of Andrea Bregno's original high altar.

II   SANTA MARIA DELLA PACE
      Entrance from piazza Santa Maria della Pace. Open Tuesday to Friday
      10–12.45, Monday and Saturday 16.30–17.50, irregularly

In 1482, not far from piazza Navona, in a tangle of medieval alleyways, stood a small and dilapidated church. It was old, having been noted in the church lists of 1188 and 1192, the first time as 'Sant' Andrea *de Aquarenariis*' and the second time as 'Santa Maria *de Aquarenariis*'. Both names referred to an important civic task: in the Middle Ages, when fresh water was scarce and the fountains in this district were few and far between, *acquarenari* (water carriers) sold fresh water, generally barrelled at the medieval basin at the Trevi fountain or, less scrupulously, taken from the Tiber and allowed to settle. This was the water carriers' church. However, by 1482 it was in a terrible condition. Moreover, something strange had happened outside it. In the portico, where one of the columns was frescoed with an image of the Virgin, some young men were fighting. By accident, a thrown stone struck the fresco, which immediately began to bleed. This miracle prompted the rebuilding of the whole church, and its rededication, with the consequent enshrining of the sacred image, was to St Mary of Peace.

This miracle was also exceedingly opportune. Sixtus's attempt to isolate and crush the Florentine republic following the failure of the Pazzi conspiracy had initially included most of the republic's neighbours and the powerhouse of Naples in the south: only Lorenzo de' Medici's highly risky personal diplomacy succeeded in convincing the king of Naples to turn the tables on Sixtus. An ugly and inconclusive war then consumed Italy for two years. Sixtus, having failed by conspiracy and then by war to unseat the Medici, decided to seek a peaceful solution, all the more because the threat from the Turks was intense: Sultan Mehmet II had pushed his ground troops into Venetian territories and in 1480 the Turkish fleet captured Otranto in the heel of the Italian peninsula. To celebrate its recapture and the end of the Pazzi war, Sixtus took the miraculous bleeding image from the porch of the water carriers' church and glorified it into a wider celebration of the new peace.

The architect is, again, unknown, though this time more possibly Baccio Pontelli. Work seems to have been completed by 1484, but then again, the church was and is small. Its original front was a tall version of the central section of Santa Maria del Popolo's façade; this church was designed without aisles, so only one temple front was needed, now hidden under seventeenth-century reworking.

Inside, the church has a very unusual plan: a short nave with four side chapels opens into a large octagonal drum, as at Santa Maria del Popolo, with four more chapels off it, and the presbytery, altar and choir at the far end. Inside the octagonal drum, only the crucifix in the chapel to the left of the main altar is fifteenth century, with its altar by Bregno, a commission of Innocent VIII. The high altar and the little choir behind were remade in 1612 by Carlo Maderno, the greatest of Paul V Borghese's architects. The medieval fresco of the Madonna of Peace is the only thing inside the church that Sixtus IV would have recognised without any difficulty.

Adjoining is the old monastery of the Dominicans who were given this church by Sixtus IV. Its serene **cloister** (now used as a concert and exhibition space: entrance either to the left of the church, in the piazza, or at number 5 arco della Pace) is the first work of Bramante in Rome. Dating from 1500–4, it is surrounded by an arcade on the ground floor and a colonnade with a flat trabeation above. It was commissioned by Cardinal Oliviero Carafa, the Neapolitan general of the Dominican order, who also built his family a wonderful funerary chapel in his order's mother church of Santa Maria sopra Minerva. Bramante made his reputation with this cloister; on the strength of its success he was hired by Julius II as the pope's principal architect.

4 Julius II and his cardinalate palaces

You yourself are a great builder; build yourself a new Paradise!

Erasmus, *Julius exclusus*

Giuliano della Rovere was an energetic builder even as a cardinal: with his revenues, he was able to build on a truly lavish scale, and he did. Naturally, one of the principal sites for development was his titular church of San Pietro in Vincoli (St Peter in Chains), where he renovated the basilica and added a monastery and a small palace on either side, creating a complex that united all the functions of a cardinalate church. When his cousin Pietro Riario died in 1474 of his excesses, Giuliano inherited Riario's cardinalate palace, which stood in the fifteenth-century hot spot of piazza Santi Apostoli, the Colonna stronghold. Here, too, Giuliano renovated the church and completed the palace, which was subsequently given to the Franciscan order and now serves as the order's mother house in Rome.

The passage of time has altered these constructions considerably. Both churches were radically reconstructed in the eighteenth century, while the complexes surrounding them were subsumed into later buildings: the monastery of San Pietro in Vincoli was partially digested by the university of Rome's faculty of engineering, while half of the magnificent palace at Santi Apostoli was devoured by palazzo Colonna, as we have already seen. However, both sites retain unexpected traces of Giuliano's presence. San Pietro in Vincoli also houses Giuliano's final monument, his tomb.

I   THE COMPLEX OF SAN PIETRO IN VINCOLI
Church in piazza San Pietro in Vincoli, metro station Colosseo.
Open 8–12, 16–19. Faculty of Engineering, entrance from via
Eudossiana 16. Usually open

The piazza San Pietro in Vincoli, occupying the height of the Oppian hill, commands good views over the centre of Rome. It is also full of parked cars and even tour buses bringing groups to visit the statue of Moses by Michelangelo. However, in the fifteenth century it was decidedly on the edge of built-up Rome, a zone of *vigne* and farms.

It is unclear what sort of buildings surrounded the fifth-century church in the Middle Ages; across the piazza a fortified tower rose over the steeply inclined *vicus sceleratus*, today's via San Francesco di Paola. In the second half of the fifteenth century Cardinal Nicholas of Cusa (1400–64) replaced the roof with a new wooden span, sections of which have now been mounted on the nave walls. It was to this church that Francesco della Rovere, general of the Franciscan order, was elevated as cardinal in 1467. It was to remain a della Rovere family seat for half a century.

Sixtus IV, while a cardinal, had contented himself with finishing the work begun by Nicholas of Cusa. When it was given to Giuliano della Rovere at his creation as cardinal in 1471, the cardinal vaulted the roof over the altar and transepts, inserted apses into the ends of the aisles and placed an arched portico at the front of the church, all perhaps under the direction of Meo del Caprino (1430–1501), a Tuscan sculptor and architect responsible for the façade of Santa Maria sopra Minerva. This building work was completed by 1481, when the cardinal ordered the construction of a modest new palace for his own use, attached to the northern side of the church. It seems to have had three storeys, with a loggia of arches running along the length of the top floor; this building still survives, as the present monastery of the church (no admission) and every door inside on the *piano nobile* still carries his oak tree emblem. He liked this palace and stayed here for short periods even while pope, though the building was said to be small and stuffy. Perhaps he appreciated it as a retreat from the court.

On the southern side of the church the university of Rome's faculty of engineering stands on the site of Julius II's great Franciscan monastery. However, if we enter the building by via Eudossiana, to our left is the beautiful **cloister** of the monastery, recently restored and graceful though rather stark. The architect was probably Giuliano da Sangallo, the cardinal's preferred collaborator before Bramante. The cloister contains a well-head of *c*.1500, elegantly carved; the whole thing, full of students strolling under the arcades, still has a monastic air and della Rovere crests abound.

Michelangelo's monument to Julius II, a failed commission and an empty tomb: the body of the pope remains under a blank slab in the chapel of the Holy Sacrament in St Peter's. It was exhumed and abused in the 1527 Sack of Rome.

The church **interior** is disappointing, a tedious eighteenth-century make-over having deprived it of its fifteenth-century character. The columns of the nave are ancient and of great beauty; they all match, indicating that they were collected during the glory days of architectural scavenging, in late antiquity, when intact sets of columns were still available. Julius II would recognise the medieval mosaic of St Sebastian above an altar in the left aisle; he would have seen the doors covering the tabernacle containing the holy chains, as they were his commission in 1477 from the goldsmith Cristoforo Foppa (1457–1527), known as Il Caradosso. The floor tomb of Cardinal Nicholas of Cusa, transferred to the wall, and an altar nearby, commissioned by him from Andrea Bregno (1464), also survive.

One object that the pope would not have recognised is, paradoxically, the one which is most closely associated with his name and which is the reason most people visit: the **tomb of Julius II** by Michelangelo. This project, which was to consume a large part of the artist's life, was his greatest disappointment. No less than five different projects over forty years involved Michelangelo first with the irascible pope himself, who lost interest when he began rebuilding St Peter's, then with his executor, Francesco

Maria I of Urbino. The tomb changed location from the apse of St Peter's to the end of the south aisle of San Pietro in Vincoli, from free-standing to a wall tomb and from forty fully rounded figures to seven. Michelangelo expended years of effort and creativity on the nude *Slaves*, now in the Louvre and the Accademia in Florence, that were excluded from the final version. By the time the tomb was being assembled the cultural climate no longer greeted male nudes in art with innocent rapture.

The outrageously grandiose scheme of 1505 comprised a free-standing pyramidal composition surmounted by an effigy of the pope, surrounded by figures including one of a weeping angel, sad for humanity left behind at Julius's death, and one of a laughing angel, happy for the pope's soul, and many other allegorical figures. What was installed in 1544–5 is a design completely altered and pared down to what amounted, for the old artist, to a 'tragedy of a tomb'. The Duke of Urbino, who was paying, required that three fully rounded figures (a far cry from the original forty) were to be from the hand of the master himself, with the rest to be made under Michelangelo's close supervision by a younger and stronger hand. Michelangelo chose to complete the three figures on the lower register of the two-tiered tomb: the central one, the famous *Moses*, had been finished already, and Michelangelo set his hand to completing *Rachel* and *Leah*, representing the contemplative life and the active life respectively. The upper register is completed with the statues of a *Prophet* and a *Sibyl*, above the two female figures below, the reclining effigy of the pope (possibly the worst part of the monument) and a *Madonna and Child* above the effigy: these are principally by Raffaele da Montelupo (1505–57), a mediocre sculptor. The *Moses* inevitably draws the eye: the prophet, who as in the Sistine Chapel is here used as an emblem of papal power, is depicted in the moment of having discovered the Israelites adoring an idol, after coming down from Mount Sinai with the Ten Commandments, the two stone tablets of which have slipped down under his arm. Moses has the *terribilità* of Julius II and of Michelangelo himself; his angry glance and tense musculature must have reminded many of the artist's older contemporaries of both artist and patron.

II   THE COMPLEX OF SANTI APOSTOLI

Entrance to church from piazza Santi Apostoli, open 8–12, 16–19; entrance to monastery at piazza Santi Apostoli 51. Ring at porter's lodge for admission to courtyards, 9–18. Closed Sundays

We have already seen the basilica of Santi Apostoli in its role as a Colonna church. However, it was meant as a della Rovere and Riario church,

Albert Clueri. inven.   *Forum SS. Apostolorum.*   *Philipp. Gall. excud.*

Philippe Galle's view of piazza SS. Apostoli in the early sixteenth century. The two wings of the della Rovere-Riario palace, flanking the portico of the church, form a rough unity destroyed when the right-hand wing was given to the Colonna.

attached to a palace which enclosed it on three sides. The palace had two wings, north and south of the church (left and right as one faces the entrance portico). The southern half had been commenced by Cardinal Pietro Riario and Giuliano greatly expanded it by adding the northern wing, which survives intact. The church's gracious entrance portico by Baccio Pontelli was probably built *c*.1482: its upper arcade linked the two wings of the della Rovere palace at the level of the principal residential floor. The upper loggia was enclosed in the seventeenth century; it remains part of the palace today called palazzo dei Santi Apostoli. This is the north wing of Cardinal Giuliano's palace, while the south wing has vanished, except for a pavilion formerly in the gardens, now incorporated in palazzo Colonna.

Inside the **portico**, as well as the della Rovere crest, is an ancient relief of an eagle with wings outstretched, holding a laurel wreath that frames it. This emblem of ancient Roman victory bears an inscription naming Giuliano, cardinal nephew of Sixtus IV, as the one who placed the relief here. The relief is an important one: it provided a model for many subsequent representations of the eagle, a favourite image of authority.

The church **interior** also bears some memories of the della Rovere. In the **apse** are two monuments to Riario cardinals: to the right is the earlier tomb, of Pietro Riario, Cardinal of San Sisto (d. 1474), by Rome's greatest stoneworkers of the late fifteenth century, Andrea Bregno, Giovanni Dalmata and Mino da Fiesole. Across the presbytery stands the tomb of Raffaele Riario Sansoni (d. 1521), possibly to designs by Michelangelo, though very little is known about its provenance. The apse originally held other monuments of Sixtus IV's family, but they were moved to an underground chapel when the **confessio** was built under the high altar area in 1873–81.

Steps in front of the presbytery lead down into the confessio. Directly beneath the high altar is a small reliquary containing the presumed remains of the apostles Philip and James the Less. To the left of the reliquary niche is the **della Rovere–Riario chapel**, arranged here in the late nineteenth century. The walls and vaults are painted to resemble a catacomb, but the tombs range from the fifteenth to the nineteenth centuries. On the right-hand wall is the tomb, by Bregno, of Raffaele della Rovere (d. 1477), brother of Sixtus IV and father of Julius II. Cardinal Alessandro Riario Sforza (d. 1585) lies across the chapel in a reused ancient sarcophagus and Cardinal Tommaso Riario Sforza (d. 1857) has a floor tomb here.

Behind the false shell of the southern transept's apse, constructed in the eighteenth century, the fifteenth-century curve of the Renaissance structure was rediscovered in 1959. It was excavated to the level of the original floor, placed by Justinian's general Narses in c.560 and large fragments of the fifteenth-century fresco decoration survive, by Antoniazzo Romano (c.1452–c.1512), a local competitor of Pinturicchio's, and the young Melozzo. This was the **Bessarion chapel**, commissioned by the Greek cardinal. The frescoes, retelling stories of the Archangel Michael, express his religious and political goals: union between the Catholic and Orthodox Churches, and a crusade against the Turks. Portraits of his contemporaries include those of the future Sixtus IV and his young nephew, Giuliano della Rovere. Special application can be made to the sacristan to see these frescoes, which vividly suggest the appearance of the church during Giuliano's tenure.

To the left of the basilica is the large **palazzo dei Santi Apostoli**. This was Giuliano della Rovere's main residence as a cardinal and it bears his stamp very clearly. On the outside, it has the familiar late fifteenth-century regular windows and tall tower on the corner. We may compare this with its contemporary, the palazzo dei Penitenzieri, near the Vatican, built by Cardinal Domenico della Rovere in 1478, the year Giuliano began work here. The palazzo dei Santi Apostoli was one of the most luxurious of late fifteenth-century Rome, the site of diplomatic banquets and the place where, in the late reign of Sixtus IV, Giuliano hid his Colonna friends from papal and Riario wrath. The surviving section of the palace was built by Giuliano da Sangallo.

Inside (ring for admission at the porter's lodge), a long porticoed corridor runs straight ahead from the entrance, forming one side of two successive courtyards. The **first courtyard**, today containing a collection of sculptural fragments, was the nucleus of Giuliano's building – it is serene and beautiful, barely ornamented, with arcades springing from a set of reused ancient columns. Upstairs, in the state rooms (accessible sometimes upon request to the porter), Giuliano's crest is carved into the window embrasures. These rooms are dignified and graceful; though adapted to more humble use as a Franciscan monastery, they still serve as the occasional residence of the titular cardinal of the basilica, usually an absentee. The **second courtyard** is larger, with a tinkling sixteenth-century fountain in the middle; this was an addition of Julius II after he became pope. The palace was never a della Rovere possession, but belonged as a cardinalate palace to the church adjoining it. As well as continuing as the residence of the cardinal of Santi Apostoli, it now serves as a house for the Franciscan order.

5 Other della Rovere sites in Rome

I 'SO MANY SPLENDID PALACES . . .'

The nepotism of Sixtus IV created a series of different power centres in Rome connected to his family. We have already seen four of them, the palazzo Riario begun by Cardinal Raffaele Riario for his Riario Sforza cousins, the palazzo dei Penitenzieri belonging to Cardinal Domenico della Rovere, the palace of San Pietro in Vincoli of Cardinal Giuliano and the more significant palazzo dei Santi Apostoli, a creation of Cardinal Pietro Riario and Cardinal Giuliano in succession. These were far from the only residences constructed by family members – the remainder still comprise some of the most grandiose and important palaces of Rome.

Chronologically first is the palazzo Altemps, named after the family of a later owner, Cardinal Marco Sittico Altemps, who radically rebuilt it in the later sixteenth century. It was begun some time around 1477 and completed some time before 1484, when it was sacked upon the death of the pope. The Riario part of **palazzo Altemps** (piazza San Apollinare 46; now a seat of the National Roman Museum, open 9–19.45 daily except Mondays; admission €5) extends along the east side of via dei Soldati, a street so named because it was the border between the districts controlled by the Orsini and the Colonna. Rather provocatively, perhaps, given that Girolamo Riario was an Orsini ally, the palazzo stands on the Colonna side of the street.

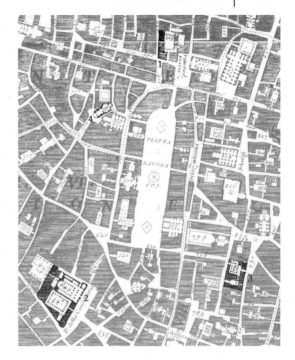

Della Rovere sites around piazza Navona

Key:
1   palazzo Altemps (ex-palazzo Riario part highlighted)
2   palazzo della Cancelleria
3   palazzo Lante della Rovere
4   Santa Maria della Pace

The palace seems to have had the standard regular windows and a tower at one end, on the corner towards piazza di Tor Sanguigna. This was the home of the newlyweds Girolamo Riario and Caterina Sforza from the late 1470s onwards, and their conjoined crests can be seen on many of the ceilings on the ground floor, in the keystone of the vaults. The walls of one of the ground-floor rooms show that the Riario palace incorporated an earlier house: the surface of one wall has been removed in two places to reveal the medieval painted decoration. Upstairs, the *sala della piattaia* is the only room that retains significant traces of its Riario phase: on the west wall, between the windows, is a large fragment of a fresco by Melozzo da Forlì and his studio, of a *piattaia* (silver cupboard). This must have been painted in 1477, as a commemoration of the wedding gifts of the Riario–Sforza couple: a lavish collection of silver dishes is laid out on a stepped cabinet in front of a floral tapestry, which has been attached to a wall panelled in pink and green marble, with a column in the centre whose capital bears the Riario rose. The room must have been similarly frescoed all round. For the modern visitor, however, the magical quality of this fresco lies in its representation of one moment in the history of a family, captured in paint and somehow surviving for more than five centuries.

Even more impressive is the colossal **palazzo della Cancelleria**. This palace, which will figure prominently in several other family histories, is unfortunately closed to the public except for special exhibitions, as it belongs to the Vatican, which uses it as offices of the Rota, the high court which judges marriage annulment cases and other Church matters. It is the cardinalate palace par excellence, for many centuries the residence of the second most powerful cleric in Rome, the Vice-Chancellor.

Change was in the air for the old buildings surrounding the church of San Lorenzo in Damaso when the ancient basilica was given in 1483 to Raffaele Riario Sansoni, the teenaged great-nephew of Sixtus IV, as his titular church, along with San Giorgio in Velabro, which gave him his more commonly used title, 'Cardinal of San Giorgio'. The old church, the most important in the Tiber bend, was soon demolished along with the dilapidated cardinalate palace next to it, and the whole complex was rebuilt and incorporated, as at Santi Apostoli (and at San Marco two decades previously, by the Venetian cardinal Marco Barbo), into a single unit. Funds came from an unorthodox source: Raffaele won 60,000 scudi at dice with Franceschetto Cibò, son of Pope Innocent VIII, and immediately spent it on this building, so the pope could not make him pay it back. He took a further loan of 120,000 scudi from a friendly banker, and completed both palace and church by 1514.

The architect of the palace is unknown, perhaps Antonio da Montecavallo, the brother of Andrea Bregno. The **façade** is extraordinary, marking a break with the standard fifteenth-century typology we have seen so far: instead of a plain stucco front, the palace has a monumental travertine surface (made with stone from the Colosseum) on its principal entrance side, to the east, divided into three main horizontal fields broken up by shallow pilasters. Above each window on the main floor is a Riario rose, and the finely carved balcony by Bregno on the corner with via del Pellegrino bears another Riario crest, while the crests of the cardinal's relatives, Sixtus IV and Julius II, adorn the north-east and south-east corners. The tower, sign of prestige in palace construction, has here been reduced: there are four 'towers', but they are only slight protrusions at each corner and none projects over the building. The long inscription above the *piano nobile* reads: 'Raffaele Riario of Savona, cardinal deacon of San Giorgio, chamberlain of the Holy Roman Church, built this palace and temple, dedicated to St Lawrence the Martyr, from its foundations, with honest fortune, under Alexander VI'. The *portone*, however, dates from almost a century later, under Sixtus V Peretti, with its balcony, and the inscription 'Corte Imperiale' dates from the Napoleonic occupation, when the Cancelleria was used as the supreme court. The secondary façade, on via del Pellegrino, has openings for shops along it, providing a source of maintenance income for the building. The great courtyard, built in 1496,

PALAZZO DELLA CANCELLERIA FATTO FABRICARE DAL CARDINAL RAFAELLE RIARIO
Architettura di Bramante da Urbino.

The Cancelleria, an eighteenth-century view by Alessandro Specchi. The left-hand façade, along via del Pellegrino, is home to vendors of gold and silver. A nearby street, vicolo del Bollo, Silverstamp Alley, records their presence.

perhaps reusing columns from the theatre of Pompeii nearby, has a grandeur hitherto unseen in Rome, with two levels of open arcades, the Riario rose omnipresent between each arch as well as in the central drain of the pavement.

From the main façade of the palace, through a secondary door, you can visit the basilica of **San Lorenzo in Damaso** (8–12, 16–19). Before Raffaele demolished it, this was an ancient foundation, by Pope St Damasus I (366–84), dedicated to one of Rome's enduring favourites, the deacon Lawrence. Excavations beneath the church and courtyard have rediscovered the outline of the ancient basilica. The present one still has the shape given by Cardinal Riario, although it was thoroughly renovated, first in the seventeenth century under Cardinal Francesco Barberini and then again in the nineteenth century by the barbarous Pius IX, when most of its previous decoration was stripped out. The church, sadly, contains very little from the period of its construction.

The palace seems to express the ambitions of its builder. Raffaele Riario Sansoni put his name in huge letters across the front, with the crests of his family popes on the main corners of the building; as this was certainly one of the greatest buildings of the time, it could hardly have appeared as anything other than the residence of a would-be pope. However, it was not to be. Implicated in a conspiracy against Leo X de' Medici in 1516, the cardinal was disgraced and lost the use of his palace, which was turned into the bureaucratic headquarters of the papal administration, the chancellery, from which it derives its name.

Two other palaces deserve a brief mention. The first is **palazzo Lante della Rovere** (piazza dei Caprettari 70; no admission). The main part of this palace was constructed in 1513 by Leo X de' Medici and his brother Giuliano, Duke of Nemours. During Leo's pontificate Francesco Maria I della Rovere was chased from his duchy of Urbino in favour of the pope's nephew Lorenzo, who was temporarily installed in his place. Thus it was somewhat awkward that Leo's brother was building his house right next door to a house of the della Rovere family (entrance at via Monterone 84; no admission). The family were probably relieved when it passed out of the hands of the Medici, being purchased in 1558 by the Lante family, who finished it, rather beautifully, with details in coloured marble, including the name LVDOVICVS LANTES above the principal door. When Lucrezia della Rovere, granddaughter of Francesco Maria I, married Marcantonio Lante in 1609, she brought with her the della Rovere house next door and the two buildings were unified internally, though they remain externally separate. The della Rovere façade bears the familiar oak tree crests beside the door. Today the palace belongs to the Aldobrandini family.

The Aldobrandini also acquired the main palace of the della Rovere dukes of Urbino in Rome, palazzo Santoro-Aldobrandini, today's **palazzo Doria-Pamphilj** (via del Corso 304). Its history is treated in greater detail in the Pamphilj itinerary, but the nucleus of the palace dates from the decade after 1489, when Giovanni Fazio Santoro, a canon of the nearby church of Santa Maria in via Lata, bought a number of houses and constructed a large residence, which he expanded further after Julius II made him cardinal of San Lorenzo in Lucina in 1505. He began a grand courtyard along the lines of the Cancelleria and his palace was reputed to be among the most luxurious in Rome, even competing with Julius's palazzo dei Santi Apostoli a block away. Julius, visiting the cardinal, remarked that it was '*più degno per un duca che per un cardinale*' (more suited to a duke than a cardinal) and requisitioned it from the unfortunate Santoro. The cardinal retired sadly to the run-down palace attached to his cardinalate church and left this fine palazzo to Julius, who gave it to his nephew Francesco Maria I della Rovere. The dukes of Urbino lived here when they came to Rome and enlarged the property by buying nearby houses, until in 1601 the family sold it to Pietro Aldobrandini, the cardinal nephew of Clement VIII Aldobrandini (1592–1605). From the entrance on the Corso it is possible to glimpse the beautiful Santoro courtyard, whose upper arcade has been enclosed, altering its fifteenth-century appearance.

II   SIXTUS IV AND THE PEOPLE OF ROME

To accommodate the growing Benedictine community, Sixtus IV vastly enlarged the already significant complex of **San Cosimato** in Trastevere (now the Regina Margherita hospital; entrance to cloisters from via Roma Libera, closed Sundays). To the evocative Romanesque first cloister, constructed in *c*.1246, he added a second storey with the characteristic octagonal brick columns of the fifteenth century and a second cloister, again with octagonal columns. The rarely open church of San Cosimato, in the same complex, was revised from its Romanesque condition by Sixtus. Once standing in rolling fields cultivated by the Benedictine brothers, the ex-monastery is now almost unrecognisable under its ugly modern hospital crust, but the cloisters remain, a haunting testimony to a vanished rural Trastevere.

Two public works of Sixtus IV had a profound effect on the city. The first, and certainly the more important to most, was the restoration of the **Acqua Vergine**, the one aqueduct that survived from the ancient city. Rome had a dearth of fresh water and the Acqua Vergine was in urgent need of restoration, having been reduced to a trickle before it opened into a little basin, the predecessor of today's great Trevi fountain. Not long after his accession, Sixtus sent workmen into the ancient underground channels to clear them of the accumulated debris of a millennium of neglect, and to chip away the calcium deposits that caked the walls and floor. On via del Nazareno, just off via del Tritone, there is a fence through which can be seen the ancient arches of one of the old distribution centres of the aqueduct, built by the Emperor Claudius in AD 46. Across the road, set into a later building, is a fifteenth-century arched doorway, quite small, with the della Rovere arms above. This is the access channel and stair which the pope's workmen cut to mend the aqueduct. The massive increase in fresh water provided the impetus for the first spate of fountain building in the sixteenth century. A Latin poem of *c*.1477, 'Lucubraciunculae tiburtinae' ('Little Night-time Thoughts at Tivoli'), by an Englishman, Robert Flemmyng, Dean of Lincoln, praises Sixtus for this work:

> [The aqueduct was] almost fallen in, and the healthful streams
> Almost lost, and earth dried up where once
> The water wantoned through the dark conduits.
> This aqueduct Sixtus purged of its debris,
> Digging out stones, mud, wood and drawing together
> All the filth collected over the years.
> So he restored it and redirected the water

So long lost; and again from the Quirinal hill
Built a permanent pipe at notable expense
To bring the water to the Trevi fountain
For the great pleasure of both Roman and traveller.

Also 'for the great pleasure of both Roman and traveller' was Sixtus's foundation of the civic collection of antiquities, the **Capitoline Museums**. This was created in the first year of his pontificate, 1471, and the small collection included some important bronze statues, such as the *Lupa Capitolina* (She-Wolf), dating from the fifth century BC, the *Spinario* (Thorn Puller), probably from the first century BC, and the gigantic bronze *Head of Constantine*, from the fourth century AD, and a few other pieces, mostly from a collection at the Lateran that had been known as '*tesaurus romanitatis*' ('treasure of Romanness'). They were moved to the Capitoline hill, seat of the civic administration, and given formally to the Roman people. This museum has been added to ever since and forms one of Rome's most magnificent collections of art.

Intermezzo:
the early sixteenth century

Apart from motives of affection, there was a pragmatic root to the Renaissance papacy's endemic nepotism: the only government a pope could trust was one run by dependent relatives. Despite their power, papal families had to struggle to insert themselves permanently into the aristocracy of Rome. For example, the two Borgia popes, Calixtus III (1455–8) and Alexander VI (1492–1503), worked hard to arrange advantageous marriages with different Roman patricians and Italian ruling families, but the Borgias, detested as much for being Spanish as for their flagrant misuse of papal power and their war against the barons, disappeared from Rome after Alexander's demise.

Following the death of Julius II in 1513, Rome fell for nearly two decades under the control of the ruling family of Florence. The two popes of the Medici family, **Leo X** (1513–21) and **Clement VII** (1523–34), presided over the flowering of the High Renaissance in Rome and, at the same time, over the beginning of the Protestant Reformation in Germany. The Medici popes had a profound effect on the cityscape; the pope who came between them, **Adrian VI Florensz** (1521–3), was an austere cleric from the Low Countries who made no impression on the city. The Medici popes, in contrast, were great street builders, creating the branching thoroughfares of what is today called the *tridente*, the two streets that depart from the piazza del Popolo on either side of the via del Corso. Leo X constructed the via di Ripetta, which ran from the piazza to the northern river port of Rome and then, changing its name to via della Scrofa, ended at the colossal corner of the Medici palace today called palazzo Madama. Clement VII built the via Clementina Trifaria, the third street of the trident, today called via del Babuino. Medici sites proliferated: a palace near palazzo Madama, today's palazzo Lante della Rovere; the villa Madama on the hill of Monte Mario, half built before the Sack of Rome in 1527 permanently ended its construction; the completion of the Raphael Rooms in the Vatican palace; and the mortuary chapel of the family popes behind the high altar of Santa Maria sopra Minerva, to name a few. The family never sought to establish a permanent branch in Rome, remaining proudly aloof as befitted the ruling house of Florence. Thus though the two Medici pontiffs modified the streetscape and built a number of important monuments, as a family the Medici had an ambiguous presence in the city, almost akin to a foreign occupier. It was in contrast to this that Cardinal Alessandro Farnese presented himself as a 'Roman' candidate for the papacy.

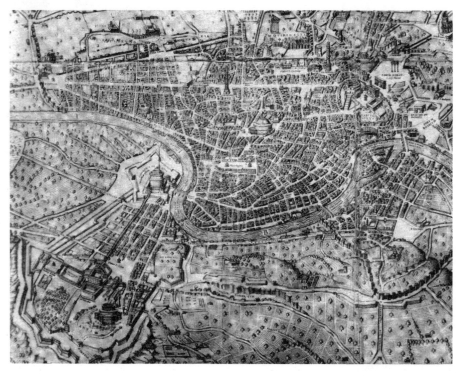

This sixteenth-century map shows the built-up area of Rome. North is to the left, and the Vatican is prominent at the bottom; at the right, the Forum clearly stands at the edge of the inhabited area inside the city walls.

4 The Farnese

The Farnese were originally a family of soldiers and landholders from northern Lazio, on the border with Umbria near the town of Orvieto. They probably assumed their family name from their feudality of Castrum Farneti, in around 1100, a property they received for battling the Normans who rampaged through Italy in the mid eleventh century. The family's initial ambitions seem to have been directed towards Florence. Their crest, six irises (*gigli,* or fleurs-de-lis, often inaccurately called 'lilies') of blue on a gold background, derived from the *giglio* emblem of the Guelf or papal party in Florence, and the first certain record of a Farnese, *Pietro Farnese* (d. 1383), describes his captaincy in the Florentine army, then ranged against Pisa.

The first really important warrior, however, was *Ranuccio Farnese* (*c.*1390 –*c.*1450) – who fought to subdue the northern Papal States for Martin V and Eugenius IV: whose efforts were repaid by the great papal honour, the Golden Rose, in 1435. The Farnese reoriented their ambitions Romewards during Ranuccio II's life: the papacy rewarded him with prosperous feudalities in the hills surrounding his family territories, in Cassano, Montalto, Latera, Marta, Capodimonte, Valentano, Gradoli and Camino, all in the area around Viterbo. His tomb, the first of the family, was built on Isola Bisentina in Lake Bolsena, in the newly founded convent there. Both Ranuccio and his brother *Bartolomeo Farnese* (*c.*1395–*c.*1460) married noblewomen from the Monaldeschi of Orvieto, a family with a presence at Rome. Bartolomeo's family became the secondary Farnese line, the dukes of Latera.

Ranuccio's third son, *Pier Luigi Farnese* (*c.*1435–87), made the family's first important marital alliance within the Roman patriciate when he married Giovannella di Onorato Caetani, of the powerful but declining family of Boniface VIII. Pier Luigi's eldest son *Angelo* (1465–94) was a soldier, leading the armies of Naples and Florence in succession; he married an Orsini. Pier Luigi's second son, *Alessandro I Farnese* (1468–1549), the future Pope Paul III, was destined for an ecclesiastical career, while his daughter *Giulia* (1475–1524) wed another Orsini. One of Pier Luigi's sisters married a Colonna. These marriages signalled the direction of Farnese ambitions; but the Farnese fortunes were soon to owe more to love than to marriage.

POPE PAUL III (1534–49)

Alexander VI, the Borgia pope, set aside his long-term mistress, Vannozza de' Catanei, when he met the beautiful Giulia Farnese in early 1493. Roman satires of Alexander's reign were particularly scathing about this and made use of his heraldic emblem, the bull, to mock his affair:

> *Europen Tyrio quondam sedisse iuvenco*
> *Quis neget? Hispano Julia vecta tauro est.*
> *Ille sed astringeri partem vix occupat orbis:*
> *Hic coelum atque deos sub ditione tenet.*

> (Europa sat upon the Tyrian bull,
> Who could deny it? Giulia is set upon the Spanish bull.
> The former bull has its place among the constellations,
> The latter rules over heaven and over gods.)

Pasquino, the 'talking' statue to which satires were attached anonymously, accused Alessandro Farnese of being little better than a pimp for his sister: 'You should attach horns to your hat' 'because of that slut, your sister Giulia; for that point where she meets the sixth Alexander, when she lies under him, is the point where your own life is touched.' Giulia was also mockingly described as the 'bride of Christ' and was said to have given birth to at least one child by the pope. Her beauty was undeniable and it is thought that the principal female figure in Raphael's great and final painting, the *Transfiguration*, depicts her in profile.

Perhaps Giulia's efforts did permit the elevation of Alessandro, in 1493, to the title of cardinal deacon and then, five years later, to the bishopric of Montefiascone and Corneto, despite his not having been consecrated as a priest. Alessandro, cardinal at twenty-five, was known as the 'petticoat cardinal' due to his sister's role in his elevation, and this epithet followed him throughout his career. A cascade of benefices compensated for the teasing, though none of these ecclesiastical preferments got in the way of the cardinal's principal relationship with a woman whose identity is disputed but who was likely to have been the Roman noblewoman Silvia Ruffini (1475–1561). Together they had four children, *Costanza* (1500–45), whom Alessandro married into the family of the Sforza of Santa Fiora, *Pier Luigi* (1503–47), *Paolo* (1504–13) and *Ranuccio* (1509–29). In 1505 the cardinal's children were legitimised, with the consent of Julius II. In 1509 Alessandro became bishop of Parma, a city upon which his dynastic intentions soon became fixed.

Alessandro, who cleverly identified himself as a Roman in contrast to the many foreign cardinals at the papal court (and to the Spanish Borgias and Florentine Medici), was a candidate in the papal elections of 1521 and 1523, both times being defeated, and it was only in 1534, when he was sixty-six years old, that he was able to ascend to the papal throne as Paul III. If the electing cardinals had hoped that the relatively old cardinal would have a brief reign as pope, they were to be disappointed: Alessandro's pontificate, at fifteen years, was the longest of the sixteenth century. His reign was marked by the first concerted attempt to address the criticisms of the Church set forth by the new Protestant churches in

This engraving after Titian captures something of the cleverness of Paul III Farnese.

Germany: he convened the Council of Trent, which gradually redefined Catholic belief and practice. Paul gave his permission for the formation of the Jesuit order, the new militant arm of the Catholic Church, and he put leading Catholic reformers in positions of authority; less benignly, he instituted the Roman Inquisition in 1542.

Paul's policies suffered from obvious contradictions. In ecclesiastical affairs he conscientiously tried to respond to the Protestant threat, but simultaneously poured the wealth of the Church into his grandsons' coffers. Similarly, he claimed a high-flown papal neutrality in the wars between France and the Empire, but attempted, with maximum venality, to carve out a Farnese state for his heirs in north-central Italy. By his death in 1549 these contrasts had undermined his moral prestige and destroyed his capacity to mediate between Europe's Catholic princes.

In the Papal States, Paul III combined great peacetime public works, such as the construction of an enormous aqueduct at Spoleto, with preparations for war, like the Rocca Paolina at Perugia. The pope's ambitious plans even involved the refoundation of entire cities, like Frascati and Castro. Castro, rebuilt by the Farnese under the supervision of Antonio da Sangallo the Younger, was perhaps the most perfect expression of Renaissance urban planning ever made.

Paul III's works within Rome were also significant. He appointed

Michelangelo as head of the Fabbrica of St Peter's, the office in charge of construction of the basilica; he confirmed Clement VII's commission for Michelangelo to paint the great *Last Judgement* on the altar wall of the Sistine Chapel (1536–41) and the frescoes of the private chapel of the popes, the Pauline Chapel (1542–50), and he also ordered the construction of the papal audience hall, the Sala Regia, in the complex of the Vatican palace. Remembering the disastrous Sack of Rome in 1527, the pope decreed that the city be properly fortified against any possible subsequent attacks. To this end he cast a huge wall around the Borgo and the enlarged Vatican Palace and commissioned Sangallo to reconstruct the ancient city walls, a task that was completed only in one tiny section, from the porta San Sebastiano towards the river. Paul's interest in the remains of ancient Rome, which had fascinated him since his youth, was expressed in his revival of the office of Commissioner of Antiquities, but the continual need for building materials meant that this office failed to protect many ancient monuments from falling to the prospector's pick or the lime burner's kiln.

In 1540 Paul III took more destructive action against ancient monuments than any of his predecessors, when he granted the Fabbrica of St Peter's a monopoly on the profits of despoiling ancient buildings and even gave it the right to sell digging permits to others. The destruction that we see today in the Forum was committed not by barbarians in the Dark Ages, but by the agents of St Peter's in the third decade of the sixteenth century: what is left are the ruins of ruins. Very little of this was done for the purposes of tidying up the appearance of the Forum, though that was the motive of the demolitions undertaken by the Commissioner of Antiquities himself, a cultivated courtier named Latino Giovenale Manetti, in 1535–6, on the eve of Charles V's visit. Temples still intact at the beginning of the 1530s, like that of Mars Ultor in the Forum of Augustus and that of Minerva in the Forum of Nerva, were unrecognisable stumps by the end of the 1540s. Paul's reign was one in which antiquity, cherished in theory, was sacrificed without qualms in order to further the development of the modern city.

Charles V's visit was the pretext for another large public work, the reordering of the Capitoline hill. Paul III had already made it the site of his summer palace, north of the Aracoeli church on the crest now occupied by the monument to Vittorio Emanuele II, but the hill was otherwise shabby, an undistinguished spot on the edge of inhabited Rome. In 1536 the Campidoglio was considered too dilapidated to merit a stop on the emperor's processional route. The following year Paul III moved the ancient statue of Marcus Aurelius from the Lateran to the Capitoline piazza. The pope then commissioned Michelangelo to design both a pedestal for the statue and a complete renovation of the city's administrative buildings around the piazza. This project entailed the reconstruction of much of the medieval palazzo del Senatore, the principal building of the communal government, and the regularisation of the façade of the palazzo dei Conservatori; to match this last he designed a mirror-image façade, the palazzo Nuovo. Though the project was not completed until long after both Paul's and Michelangelo's deaths, it strongly expresses the ambitious urban planning of the Farnese pontificate. Paul died in 1549, having set his children and grandchildren among the European aristocracy. If his legacy as pope was mixed, his success as a dynast was unambiguous.

THE *NIPOTI* OF PAUL III

After only one year on the throne, Paul III raised two Farnese youths to the cardinalate, *Alessandro II Farnese* (1520–89), his grandson through his son Pier Luigi, and Guidantonio Sforza of Santa Fiora, his grandson through his daughter Costanza; both of these boys, fourteen and sixteen years old respectively, were richly beneficed. A third grandson, Alessandro II's brother *Ranuccio II* (1530–65), was elevated to the cardinalate not long afterwards.

In the secular world, advancement was more difficult. Paul III set his sights on the central Italian cities of Parma and Piacenza. Charles V, the emperor, at first opposed the pope's investiture of his son Pier Luigi with these cities, which were of key strategic importance as gates to south-central Italy, but in 1538 the emperor appeared to relent, with the marriage of his illegitimate daughter *Margherita* (1522–86) to Pier Luigi's second son, *Ottavio* (1524–86). Pier Luigi's family was badly divided against itself, however, with Ottavio aligned with imperial Habsburg interests and his cardinal brothers Alessandro and Ranuccio preferring the French cause.

In 1545, against the emperor's wishes, Paul III invested Pier Luigi with the ducal title of Parma and Piacenza. Pier Luigi was widely known as an unpleasant person, a reputation consolidated in the autobiography of the sculptor and goldsmith Benvenuto Cellini who claimed the pope's son had been the driving force behind his imprisonment in the Castel Sant'Angelo on trumped-up charges. Pasquino, the 'talking statue' which provided an anonymous outlet for anti-papal satires in an age without a free press, had a gleeful time describing Pier Luigi's misadventures: famous as a sodomite, the pope's son was said to have raped and murdered a young bishop, Cosimo Gheri of Fano; Pasquino saw Pier Luigi's image in Michelangelo's *Last Judgement* as the damned soul wrapped round with a snake biting his private parts:

Ligato ne l'Inferno
Con una serpe che li morde il cazzo
Per peccato di rompere il quaderno.
Per questo, in sempiterno,
Cristo condanna i bugironi al foco,
E star con una serp'al triste loco.

(Bound in Hell
With a snake that bites him in the prick,
For the sin of breaking arses.
For this, in eternity,
Christ condemns the buggerers to the fire,
And to stand with a serpent in this sad place.)

Few tears were shed for Pier Luigi when he was assassinated by the Landi, nobles of Piacenza, very possibly with imperial approval. Paul III's dynastic ambitions suddenly looked as if they might collapse like Alexander VI's.

A little while before Paul's death in November 1549, Ottavio, Pier Luigi's son and heir, occupied Parma and closed the gates against an imperial army, much to the pope's displeasure. The next pope, Julius III Del Monte (1550–5), strove to deprive the Farnese of the two cities and only Cardinal Alessandro II's diplomatic skill, along with some discreet pressure from the French, prevented Parma and Piacenza from incorporation into the Papal States.

In 1556, after years of uncertainty, the Farnese were confirmed by Charles V's heir, Philip II of Spain, in their possession of Parma and Piacenza, though Philip II installed robust Spanish garrisons in both cities, to ensure that his interests would not be neglected. By now, there was a long-standing family alliance between the Habsburgs and the Farnese, via the frankly unhappy marriage between Margherita and Ottavio. Margherita lived separately from her husband after a very few years, in her beloved territories in the Abruzzo and, for a key period between 1559 and 1567, as regent for her half-brother Philip II in the Low Countries. She and Ottavio produced one heir, *Alessandro* (1545–92). Ottavio busied himself with state building, creating, in effect, a sort of proto-absolutist state in Parma, with a council of state with wide-ranging powers: he opened mines, summoned Jewish bankers to his duchy to ensure a source of credit, prepared a property census and sought piously to apply the decrees of the Council of Trent to his subjects. In this he was helped by the bishops of Parma, always chosen from the secondary family lines of Farnese–Latera or the Sforza of Santa Fiora, and by the Jesuits, whose order was practically a family foundation and who opened a famous college in Parma in 1564, to be followed in 1582 by another in Piacenza.

The problems faced by the new dynasty were geographical and genealogical. Farnese properties did not comprise a unified territorial state. The new duchies of Parma and Piacenza were far from the original centres of Farnese power near Lake Bolsena and there was a scarcity of male heirs partly due to the risky tendency of the family to put its males into the Church. Only the marriage of Alessandro, Ottavio's heir, to Maria of Portugal (1538–77) ensured the dynasty's continuity.

The two Alessandros, the *Gran Cardinale* and his nephew, the future Duke of Parma and Piacenza, were among the most important figures in international politics in the later sixteenth century. Cardinal Alessandro acted as Paul III's prime minister, a position soon to become traditionally known as the *cardinal nipote*, the cardinal nephew (or grandson). For forty years after the death of his grandfather Alessandro was Rome's most important cardinal: the richest, the most well-informed and -connected, the most powerful. He had a reputation as an intelligent and cultivated man, and Emperor Charles V said of him that 'if all the members of the Sacred College resembled Farnese, it would be the greatest assembly in the world'. As Alessandro grew older, he became more and more involved in the Catholic reform movement and was, unlike most of his contemporaries, unfettered by the restrictions and directives imposed by the Council of Trent. He did as he pleased.

Cultivated, charming and clever, he achieved the rare victory of fooling the wily pope Sixtus V Peretti (1585–90). Sixtus issued edicts against the bearing of arms within the city, which ensnared one of Alessandro's nephews. The young man was condemned to death. The cardinal sent his men to silence all the clocks in Rome, including the one in the pope's own bedroom, and as the execution was set to take place at the ringing of the hour, the hour passed without the deed being done. The cardinal presented himself to the pope, requesting that the boy's body be consigned to him, and the pope, thinking the execution had taken place, agreed: thus the cardinal secured his nephew's release. When the story got out, the pope, once the head of the Franciscan order, laughed and said, 'A cardinal has fooled a mere monk.' He summoned Cardinal Alessandro and imposed on him the light penance of saying the 'Our Father' and the 'Miserere', though he also delivered a warning: 'This is the penance given by a monk – next time, mind you, watch out for the penance given by a pope.'

The cardinal was also famed for the occasional act of spectacular generosity. Once a poor woman asked five scudi from him in alms and he sent her fifty. The woman, imagining this to be a mistake, sent it back and the cardinal agreed in a message: 'I mistook a zero,' he wrote and sent along five hundred scudi in place of the original fifty. He was much loved by the

Romans for his generosity and good heart. His patronage did not end with the sponsorship of art, but extended over the protection of the Jews in their newly enclosed ghetto and over different charities as well. Titian's portrait of Alessandro in the Capodimonte gallery in Naples reveals a sensitive, sensual face, full-lipped and handsome, the very image of a Renaissance prince of the Church. His sexual life was also more Renaissance than Counter-Reformation. He had an illegitimate daughter, Clelia, a famous beauty, who married twice, first into the Roman family of the Cesarini, then into the Savoia family, which 300 years later became Italy's royal family. She was also the lover of Cardinal Ferdinando de' Medici, whose court painter Jacopo Zucchi painted her portrait (today in the Galleria Nazionale in palazzo Barberini). In his later life the cardinal developed a deeply felt piety, which expressed itself in enormous donations; each year, of his income of 120,000 gold scudi, he gave 30,000 to various good works, a vast sum. At his death the Romans mourned him extravagantly.

Alessandro was an accomplished diplomat, in 1540 and 1552–4 in Paris, and in 1544 at Worms, where he discussed the reopening of the Council of Trent with Charles V. The principal obstacles to his becoming pope were familial problems: the attachment to the French cause, the problematic duchies of Parma and Piacenza, and the memory of Paul III's nepotism. Perhaps to compensate for his failure to achieve the highest position, Cardinal Alessandro surrounded himself with a vast, near-royal court.

His nephew, Alessandro Farnese, Duke of Parma and Piacenza, had a more unambiguously glorious career. The greatest of the family warriors, Alessandro showed early promise as a soldier in Parma and even more so at the court of his uncle, Philip II of Spain, who had summoned him as a sort of hostage in order to guarantee Farnese good behaviour. Two years after his marriage to Maria of Portugal in 1565, he returned to Parma and in 1571 took part in the great defeat of the Turkish fleet at Lepanto, as one of the most able lieutenants of the supreme commander, Don Juan of Austria. When Don Juan became regent of the rebellious Spanish holding of Holland in 1577, it was natural that Alessandro should follow him. It was one of history's ironies that this scion of a famously pro-French house should thereafter, upon the unexpected death of Don Juan, assume the regency of Holland himself, under the command of France's great Habsburg enemy. At the time, only one of Holland's seventeen provinces was still in Spanish hands; using his skills both as diplomat and military commander, Alessandro succeeded after ten years in extending Spanish control from the sea to the Rhine. The ever cautious Philip II, however, kept Alessandro on a tight leash, both financially and in terms of official authority, perhaps in order to reduce any temptation to claim the Low Countries as his own. Duke

Alessandro was Philip II's principal agent of destabilisation in northern Europe: he was intended to lead a Spanish army across the English Channel to subdue the Protestant Elizabeth, after the projected success of the Spanish Armada. When this failed, Alessandro supported the Catholic League in France, a semi-rebellious army under the control of the ambitious Duke of Lorraine. His death at Arras in December 1592 laid to rest any anxieties Philip II might have had about his nephew's ambitions. Through his military efforts he was the father of modern Belgium, which he created from the Catholic provinces of the Netherlands.

Alessandro, duke of Parma and Piacenza. This commander was widely acknowledged to be the greatest threat to the Protestant cause in northern Europe.

Paul III's efforts on behalf of his own family at Rome had been left unfinished at his death in 1549, most notably his plans for palazzo Farnese, whose construction he had pushed forwards as if it had been an affair of state, once again under the direction of Michelangelo. It was occupied by Cardinal Ranuccio II after 1550 even though incomplete, and was only finished by Cardinal Alessandro in 1589. Until then, the Gran Cardinale had lived in the palazzo della Cancelleria not far away, in his capacity as papal vice-chancellor. His nephew *Odoardo* (1573–1626) was the last important cardinal of the family to add important pieces of art to palazzo Farnese, most notably the great gallery painted by Annibale Carracci and his brother Agostino.

In 1579 Cardinal Alessandro expanded the family holdings with the purchase of the villa Chigi on the other side of the Tiber. Alessandro was the initiator of another great Roman property, the Farnese Gardens on the Palatine hill, the components of which he began to acquire as early as 1537. A further site of primary importance both to the family and to the architectural history of Italy was the Farnese villa at Caprarola, in northern Lazio. The cardinal did not neglect religious constructions in Rome either: the great church of the Gesù (1568–84), the chief church of the new Jesuit order, was built at his expense and he completed the Oratory of the Santissimo Crocifisso, begun by his younger brother Cardinal Ranuccio II.

THE FARNESE SUCCESSION

The Farnese held sumptuous court for centuries in their duchies of Parma and Piacenza. They won the game played by previous papal families to carve out an independent dynastic territory from lands held by the pontiff and to rule it legitimately as sovereigns. The family decisively transferred itself out of Rome and, though the dynasty survived until 1731, the last cardinal resident of the great family palace in Rome was *Francesco Maria* (1619–47). The last Farnese cardinal, *Girolamo* (1599–1668), was of the Latera branch's final generation. As prefect of the Vatican palace under Alexander VII Chigi, he did not live in palazzo Farnese and his death seems to have put an end to all interest the Farnese had in the city.

In 1599 Duke Ranuccio I (1569–1622) wed Margherita, a member of the papal house of the Aldobrandini, family of Pope Clement VIII (1592–1605). The Farnese considered this a misalliance, as the new pope's grandfather had been the major-domo of the Farnese under the first Cardinal Alessandro. But the family's pretensions did not match their European significance, which dwindled through the seventeenth century. And their loyalty to Spain suffered a reverse with Duke *Odoardo I* (1612–46), who fought for the French in the war over the succession of Mantua against the viceroy of Habsburg Milan. This war cost the state of Parma dearly and brought no gain politically. But worse was to come.

The duchy of Castro, under papal suzerainty, had been placed in pawn to the Papal Camera at the time of Duke Ranuccio's wedding to Margherita Aldobrandini, as surety for the duke's massive debts. These remained unpaid even under the pontificate of the Barberini pope Urban VIII (1623–44) and, even more offensively, the duke refused to arrange a marital alliance with the Barberini. As a result, in 1641 Urban VIII annexed the duchy forcibly to the rest of the Papal States. Duke Ranuccio claimed this was a barefaced robbery by the pope in favour of his avaricious Barberini nephews, and formed a league with Florence, Modena and Venice. In 1642 he led a cavalry attack into northern Lazio and the following year the league terrified the pope into a compromise. Although Urban VIII succeeded in breaking up the league in 1644, the price was the restitution of Castro to the Farnese, the gift of a cardinal's hat to Ranuccio's son Francesco Maria and a five-year stay on the debt. In 1649, when the debt again fell due, the new duke, *Ranuccio II* (1630–94), provoked the next pope, Innocent X Pamphilj (1644–55), who decided to retake the duchy once and for all. Papal troops besieged Castro and razed it to the ground after evacuating the inhabitants. The duchy was dissolved and absorbed into the Papal States.

The last years of the dynasty had a surreal quality. The hugely fat

Francesco Maria (1678–1727) failed to produce heirs perhaps due to his enormous corpulence, and his family became extinct in 1731 with the death of his brother, *Antonio Francesco* (1679–1731). Duke Antonio left no heirs beyond his niece *Elisabetta* (1692–1766), who had married the Bourbon king of Spain, Philip V, in 1714. In 1732 her son, Charles V Bourbon (1716–88), made his entry into Parma as regent for his mother, the last Farnese duchess of the territory, and used it as his base for the conquest of the kingdom of Naples. When he left Parma for Naples, he took with him the Farnese archives (destroyed by German bombing in the Second World War), the picture gallery, which is now the pride of the Capodimonte gallery in Naples, and the state library of Parma. The treasures of the neglected Farnese palace in Rome were also soon transferred to Naples. In 1748 the new lateral line of Bourbon-Parma was at last recognised as the legitimate successor of the Farnese. Over the centuries the remaining Farnese collections were mismanaged and dispersed, leaving behind them in Rome only the memory of the family's greed, wealth and opulence.

FARNESE ITINERARY

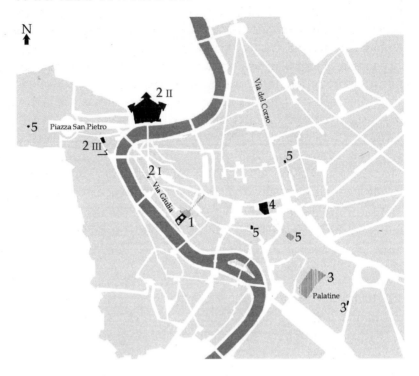

The Farnese presence in Rome bears a certain similarity to that of the della Rovere. As with the family of Sixtus IV, a double twist of fate took the family out of the city as independent princes of another territory, then brought the line to an end. The Farnese's Bourbon heirs stripped all the family's Roman properties: their possessions fill the Naples Archaeological Museum and the

Capodimonte gallery. Other works found their way to the Neapolitan royal palace at Caserta, some to Spain and to France, and still more remain in Parma and Piacenza. Within Rome, very little of the Farnese treasure is to be seen. Moreover, the great palace of the family is now the French embassy; its fantastic fresco decoration and the Carracci gallery, one of the city's most spectacular virtuoso displays of skill and invention, are reserved for the appreciation of the ambassador's guests.

Nonetheless, the Farnese left an impressive legacy. The list of the artists they employed is remarkable: the Zuccari brothers, the Carracci, Francesco Salviati, Domenichino, Lanfranco. Equally significant were the family architects, Vignola, della Porta, Antonio da Sangallo the Younger and Michelangelo. This hoard of talent outshines that of almost any other Roman family, excepting, perhaps, the Barberini. The Farnese imposed their presence on their neighbourhood, carving new streets and a piazza from the medieval jumble of buildings around the Campo de' Fiori and ornamenting them with fountains. We can see a preoccupation with antiquity in the one Farnese palace accessible today, the Castel Sant'Angelo, and in the still magnificent Farnese Gardens on the Palatine hill. The great church of the Gesù with its attached Jesuit residence, the Casa Professa, is the city's most prominent testimonial to the role played by a patrician family in the religious resurgence of late sixteenth-century Rome. That the religious impulse could also be more private and perhaps more deeply felt is evident in the little Oratorio del Santissimo Crocifisso, which was sponsored by Cardinals Alessandro II and Ranuccio, and in the frescoes in the church of Santa Maria dell'Orazione e Morte, which came from the private prayer rooms of Cardinal Odoardo.

Paul III's efforts to remake Rome are also still visible today, in his decorations in the Castel Sant'Angelo, his new street, the via Paola and his colossal fortifications, all of which made Rome more monumental while addressing practical needs.

▌ Palazzo Farnese and its neighbourhood

All was sovereign pomp, blended with death.

Emile Zola, *Rome*

I   THE PALACE AND ITS DEVELOPMENT

Standing in front of the great main portal of palazzo Farnese, surmounted by its huge family crest, one is left in no doubt about the ambitions of the builders. This is unequivocally a royal palace. At the time of its construction, no other family inhabited a palace as large; only the Vatican Palace, the

Piranesi's engraving of palazzo Farnese evokes the dampness and gloom described by Zola. The raised path leading to the *portone* crosses the piazza to become via de' Baullari.

palazzo Venezia and the palazzo della Cancelleria could compete with it for size, and none of them was in private hands. Indeed, for a long period Cardinal Alessandro II himself occupied the Cancelleria, two piazze away, while waiting for the completion of his family palace. Thus two of Rome's great Renaissance palaces were in Farnese hands.

Palazzo Farnese has a long building history. To begin with it was constructed piecemeal on a site that had been partially occupied by a previous cardinalate palace, palazzo Albergati-Ferriz, which took up the right-hand half of the present façade. In the rear part of this earlier palace Cardinal Alessandro I lived while the building works continued. The future Paul III, raised to the cardinalate in 1493, bought the palazzo Ferriz two years afterwards and soon began acquiring neighbouring properties.

Alessandro Farnese seems to have appreciated that his new palace was in a highly desirable and developing neighbourhood. This zone was, however, already thick with other baronial families, each with their region of influence. To the east lay the *contrada* of the Capodiferro family, ancient nobles of the area. To the west was the Corte Savella prison, bastion of the once-powerful Savelli family; and to the north was the piazza called the Campo de' Fiori, traditional territory of the great Orsini. Farnese's decision to build where he did constituted an assertion of his family's arrival at the pinnacle of the aristocratic Roman world. This was also a thriving area full of the houses of other members of the papal court and close to the major papal procession route. The palace garden backed on to the via Giulia, the newly created and ultra-fashionable road decreed by Julius II della Rovere, a wide, straight, paved street a kilometre long. Palazzo Farnese was thus built in the very heart of early modern Rome.

The larger social purpose that justified the construction of vast residences like palazzo Farnese had been set out by the theorist Paolo Cortesi, Alessandro Farnese's tutor, in his 1510 treatise *De Cardinalatu* (*On the Cardinalate*). Cortesi maintained that to build great houses (*domus magnae*), in an ordered style and with appropriate grandeur, was the responsibility of princes of the church, not only as an expression of the respect owed to the church but also because such houses, through their large size and rational appearance, had the asserted (if not proven) effect of contributing to civic order. The theory – if not the outcome – was that the endemic violence of Roman society would be quelled through the awe and stupefaction they inspired.

The palace was constructed in two phases. The first phase, which began in 1514–15, was undertaken by the Florentine architect Antonio da Sangallo the Younger (1484–1546). The front part of palazzo Ferriz was systematically demolished as the new building grew; the famous delays in the construction were in part due to the enormous cost (one wag tied a beggar's tin cup to the scaffolding at one point and affixed a sign above: 'Alms for the building of the Farnese'), as well as the logistical difficulty of building a palace on the site of another that was continuously inhabited. Giorgio Vasari, in his biography of Sangallo, said that the cardinal's intent was not merely to 'restore' his old palace and enlarge it, but also to provide housing space for his own large *famiglia* (household), and to create spacious and dignified apartments for his sons Pier Luigi and Ranuccio; the apartments were to be entirely separate. Vasari also observed that the construction, though slow, proceeded 'every year' in 'a measured manner', which argues for a set building schedule, not merely one determined by the availability of funds. This first plan changed after 1540, for two reasons: first, the death of Ranuccio in 1529, which permitted the modification of the plans for the *piano nobile* as a unity; and second, Cardinal Alessandro's election in 1534, which, Vasari noted, allowed the Farnese to build 'a palace no longer of a cardinal but of a pope', doubling its size.

The style of the building expresses the fundamentals of Roman palace design in the Renaissance: foursquare, it sits round a central courtyard reached by a corridor leading from a great central door, the *portone*; from the courtyard, a passage directly opposite the entrance corridor leads to the large garden in the rear of the building, surrounded by a high fence and faced, across the street behind, with the palace stables. The ground floor was used as service spaces, the principal family members lived in state on the first floor or *piano nobile*, the noble floor, and the second floor was reserved for lesser family members and retainers. Above the second floor, various attics also housed servants, though these storeys do not make an impression from the piazza. The building owes many of its features to the designs of the great architect of the early Renaissance in Rome, Donato Bramante (1444–1514). His preference for the large-scale, matched with a new interest in classical proportion, made him the most influential architect of his generation. His great follower and collaborator was the Florentine Antonio da Sangallo the Younger, whose education included a close study of Roman ruins, many features of which appeared in the designs for palazzo Farnese.

In true Renaissance fashion, Sangallo planned the palace along principles set out by the ancient Roman architect Vitruvius: 'the front of the place divided into [equal] parts', specifically four parts of equal size; the proportion of the front to the sides was four to five. Each floor is separately marked by a string-course, a line of stonework that suggests the floor level, supporting, on bases of different kinds, rows of windows framed in classical aedicules or protruding window frames, inspired, it seems, by similar aedicules in that essential ancient building, the Pantheon. In 1514 the pope gave permission to reuse ancient marbles, travertine, columns, capitals and bases taken from the ruins around the old basilica of San Lorenzo fuori le Mura. The entrance vestibule quickly became famous for its double row of columns, two of a very rare grey Egyptian granite. The columns of *verde antico* within the palace came from the bath house of Zenobia of Palmyra, who lived in exile near Tivoli after her defeat at the hands of Emperor Aurelian in AD 271. Sangallo seems to have completed the first two floors of the principal façade and the wing on the left, to the same height, as well as the first level of the courtyard and part of the second, before he died in 1546. He had succeeded in combining the classical Roman precepts of his predecessor Bramante with his own experience of Florentine palace architecture, and palazzo Farnese may justly be considered his masterpiece and signature.

The second phase of construction began in 1540, and moved steadily forwards based on a new and more spacious plan for the *piano nobile*. In 1546 the already legendary Michelangelo Buonarroti was given the charge of completing the palace's courtyard and top floor. Michelangelo and Sangallo had hated each other, the former reserving particular scorn for the latter's plans for New St Peter's, and it must have been a further annoyance for Michelangelo to be constrained, as he was, to keep most of the carved stone aedicules for the top-floor façade, which had been designed by Sangallo and were already cut, waiting to be installed. Michelangelo, however, seems to have been responsible for the strange scrolling double brackets acting as pedestals for the window frames.

Michelangelo was certainly responsible for the palace's most important innovation, the *cornicione* or great cornice, the huge jutting ledge that surmounts the building. The *cornicione* sticks out six feet into the piazza and acts in a masterly way as a sort of hat, crisply delineating the building from the sky above and anchoring it to the earth. He is also credited with the ambitious plan to extend a private bridge from the palace all the way across the Tiber to the Farnese villa on the other side, but this never came to fruition. In 1549, three years after he had reluctantly accepted the papal commission to finish palazzo Farnese, Michelangelo gave it up at the death of Paul III, leaving it to his pupil Jacopo Barozzi da Vignola (1507–73), who completed the right-hand wing, finally obliterating the last traces of palazzo Ferriz. Vignola also designed the rear façade in a Michelangelesque manner, with a beautiful loggia, though this was completed by another of Michelangelo's followers, Giacomo della Porta (1533–1602). Finally in 1589 the structure was complete; it remained only to be decorated.

II   THE INTERIOR OF THE PALACE

The palace is decorated with sculpture and different pictorial programmes: the first sequence begins with the courtyard, which displays two ancient sarcophagi, the one on the right-hand side purportedly from the tomb of Cecilia Metella on the via Appia and the one facing it from the Baths of Caracalla. The Farnese owned these ruins even under the first Cardinal Alessandro, and they proved to be a rich and almost endless mine of ancient sculpture. In the garden behind the palace stood one of the greatest of the sculpture groups found in the Baths by the cardinal's treasure hunters, the group of the *Farnese Bull*, while the great *Farnese Hercules* stood in the centre of the courtyard, visible from the street when the *portone* was open.

Upstairs, the apartments of the *piano nobile* similarly reflect the Farnese interest in antique glory. The entire left-hand side of the façade is taken up with the Salone d'Ercole, the principal reception room and audience hall, which contains a copy of the *Farnese Hercules* and, on either side of the monumental fireplace, two statues by Guglielmo della Porta removed in the seventeenth century from the tomb of Paul III, *Peace* and *Abundance*. Quite often the room above the *portone* is lit up at night and one can see from the piazza the decorations of the Room of the *Fasti Farnesiani*, the Room of the Farnese Deeds. This was created as a pictorial history of the family, with its emphasis on the activities of Paul III as peacemaker between France and the Empire; its wall frescoes (1558–63) are among the masterworks of the painter Francesco Salviati (1510–63), whose skill we have already seen in the Galleria Colonna and in the della Rovere palazzo dei Penitenzieri. Salviati, whose last work this was, was assisted by the Zuccari brothers, Taddeo and Federico (1529–66 and 1540–1609). These two brothers, who rose to prominence through the patronage of the Farnese, also executed the main decoration of the colossal family country house at Caprarola. The bedroom of Cardinal Ranuccio has a frieze painted by Daniele da Volterra (1509–66), another pupil of Michelangelo, making the palazzo one of the most eloquent expressions in Rome of the school of Florentine Mannerism.

The decorations sponsored by Cardinal Alessandro II were to be profoundly influential upon artists of the Roman scene until the end of the sixteenth century and beyond. They were, in fact, largely directed by a highly intellectual circle of Farnese retainers, including the writer Annibal Caro and the antiquarian Fulvio Orsini, the cardinal's librarian, who was responsible for much of the more elaborate symbology. In part on the strength of his Farnese patronage, Federico Zuccari rose to act as a conservative, rather repressive force within the guild of artists in Rome, the Accademia di San Luca. (The power of the guild was not to be dismissed: the president, or *principe*, had the right to imprison disobedient painters.)

Further decorative work was taken up in 1597 by the next, and last, great cardinal of the family, Odoardo. He commissioned a painter from Bologna, Annibale Carracci (1560–1609), then unknown in Rome, to decorate the long gallery at the back of the main block. In seven years of work Carracci and his brother Antonio, along with younger artists such as Domenichino (Domenico Zampieri, 1581–1641), also from Bologna, and Giovanni Lanfranco (1582–1647), from Parma, produced the most dazzling frescoes of the period. The theme was love, not divine love but the loves of the pagan deities.

Carracci's ceiling produced a sensation when it was unveiled: there in palazzo Farnese were the kernels of the Baroque style, bright and expressive, full of virtuoso perspectival effects. The gallery, conceived as a room for the display of sculpture, was a manifesto of Carracci's, asserting the superiority of painting to sculpture by offering a comparison between the two, often involving painted representations of the sculptures displayed in the niches on the wall. An eighteenth-century English visitor, the painter Jonathan Richardson, saw in the gallery

> a Copious and Rich, a Solid, and Judicious way of Thinking, Strong and Just Expressions, a Colouring between the Gravity of Rafaelle, and the Gaiety of Guido, and inclining to that of Correggio . . . the nobile [*sic*] Attitudes, and Contours of the Antique, and the Roman Schools somewhat reduc'd toward Common Nature, but very Great and Open . . . In a Word all that . . . can be Wish'd for in Painting is here to be found.

Perhaps more impressive is the fact that the ceiling was painted this way at all, given that the repressive pope of the time, Clement VIII Aldobrandini, was stringent in observing the Council of Trent's dictums about propriety in painting. The Carracci gallery, with its joyous tumble of pagan nudes, harks back to an earlier period of art unconstrained by the responsibility of moral teaching. It may also express the Farnese cardinal patron's own contempt for his jumped-up superior, since the pope belonged to a family of former Farnese retainers.

The 'Bolognese school', the studio of Carracci, was to produce some of the greatest names in art of the seventeenth century. The patronage of Cardinal Odoardo proved fatally disappointing to Annibale, whose payment for his years of hard work amounted to only five hundred scudi (delivered, like a tip for a waiter, on a saucer): this sent him into an alcoholic depression from which he never emerged, dying only a few years later. When Odoardo commissioned a fresco cycle for the abbey of San Nilo at Grottaferrata outside Rome in 1608, his specifications were '[da trovare] un buon giovane e da spendere poco' (to find a good young man and to spend little money). Annibale recommended his pupil Domenichino, who thereby made his first dazzling appearance as an independent painter. Both Annibale and Domenichino did other work in the palace and its outbuildings, particularly in the so-called Camerini, rooms built on the bank of the Tiber behind the stables, which Odoardo used as reception rooms and for religious meetings. The buildings no longer survive, due in part to the construction of the Tiber embankment, but some of the decorations have been preserved, including canvases by Lanfranco now in Naples and frescoes by Domenichino now in the main palace building.

III   THE PALACE IN HISTORY

The period in which the family lived here was surprisingly brief: Cardinal Alessandro II barely had time to occupy it in its completed form before his death in 1589, and the secular members of the family, preoccupied with their affairs in Parma and Piacenza, rarely inhabited it: the last cardinal of the main Farnese line, Francesco Maria (1619–47), lived here briefly during the difficult times of Urban VIII's war against the duchy of Castro and after that it played host to Farnese family members only sporadically. It was nonetheless one of the famous glories of Rome and with its majestic piazza it was an obvious choice for powerful ambassadors to rent; thus it had a double life as family palace and as an embassy.

The Farnese lived in near-royal state and Cardinal Alessandro II was said to have put up a court of 391 persons in the palazzo, including priests and chaplains, gentlemen-in-waiting, pages, litter bearers and other household members including a huge kitchen staff. The cardinal lived for much of his life in the Cancelleria not far away – to him the Cancelleria owes its beautiful chapel, frescoed by Salviati, and Vasari's famous great hall, the Sala dei Cento Giorni – but his personality is imprinted upon palazzo Farnese more than any other.

The palace was rented by the French ambassador after the death of Cardinal Odoardo in 1626 for a period and in 1655 Queen Christina of Sweden (for whom see the Chigi itinerary) stayed here before she moved to palazzo Riario on the other side of the Tiber. It was rented by the French ambassador in the later seventeenth century, and during the political tumults of the century the piazza and the palace were the scene of riots and demonstrations. When Giuseppe Garibaldi conquered the Kingdom of the Two Sicilies in the 1840s as part of the movement towards the unification of Italy, the royal family, the Bourbons of Naples, the exiled King Francesco II, his queen, Maria Sofia, and their children came to palazzo Farnese, where they lived quietly. After the fall of Rome to the forces of unification in 1870, the surviving Bourbons left for exile elsewhere and rented the palace to the French. In Emile Zola's 1896 novel *Rome*, a character considers the building in rather unflattering terms:

> Ah! That colossal, sumptuous, deadly dwelling, with its vast court whose portico is so dark and damp, its giant staircase with low steps, its endless corridors, its immense galleries and halls. All was sovereign pomp blended with death. An icy, penetrating chill fell from the walls. [. . .] The only part of the building which was at all lively and pleasant was the first storey, overlooking the Tiber, which the ambassador himself occupied.

The French bought it from the Bourbons soon afterwards, but sold it to the Italian state in 1936 (doubtless for tax reasons) and have rented it back from them ever since, at a not exorbitant rent of one lira every ninety-nine years. The French, for their part, returned the favour by offering the Italians a similar deal for their embassy in Paris. Even today the piazza is the scene for demonstrations and public spectacles.

IV   THE PIAZZA FARNESE AND ITS SURROUNDINGS

The whole neighbourhood surrounding palazzo Farnese reflects the importance of the palace, which has a gravitational pull that draws important streets towards it. The **piazza** itself is a Farnese creation: Paul III, both before and after his election, bought up two city blocks of irregular size and demolished them, making an open space where previously none had

Palazzo Farnese and its
neighbourhood, from the Nolli
map of 1748

Key:
1 palazzo Farnese
2 via de' Baullari, on axis with the portone
   of palazzo Farnese
3 the *isola* of the Massimi, on the via
   Papalis
4 the first section of via di Monserrato, on
   axis with the windows of the palace's
   corner rooms

5 stable wing of the Farnese property,
   Cardinal Odoardo's *Camerini*, and the
   ferry to the villa Farnesina (see Chigi
   itinerary)
6 palazzo della Cancelleria, a Farnese
   residence under Cardinal Alessandro II
   Farnese

existed. After being made pope, he also caused a new street, on an axis with the *portone* of the palace, to stretch from the piazza to the papal procession route, the via Papalis. The piazza was the scene of great family ceremonies and celebrations, and bullfights and jousts were held in it.

The **original street plan** of the area was a creation of both the ancient and the medieval periods. The street running along the façade of palazzo Farnese followed the course of an ancient roadway, tentatively identified as the *vicus stabularius* (Stables Street), named because the stables of the imperial chariot factions, blue, green, white and red, lined it. Mosaics discovered under the palazzo tend to confirm this theory, as they depict charioteers of the *factio russata*, the Reds; another place-name, San Lorenzo in Prasino (an old name for today's nearby church of San Lorenzo in Damaso, built into the fabric of the Cancelleria), bolsters this identification, as *prasinus* means leek-green, the colour of another faction. Supporters of these teams could be violent in their partisanship, and were a source of civil disturbance in the late imperial period. The *vicus stabularius* was an important street, running parallel to the river bank from the Tiber Island bridge, the ancient *Pons Fabricius*, to the Castel Sant'Angelo bridge, the ancient *Pons Aelius*. Its course seems never to have been lost and, apart from a peculiar divergence along the via Monserrato where it bulges out and then back again, it still conforms to the ancient plan, though from six to twelve metres above its ancient level. Parallel to it, towards the river, Julius II's via Giulia had been created only a few years before, while streets running across these main arteries were often of medieval origin. One block away from the piazza Farnese was the western end of the Campo de' Fiori, the central market square of medieval and Renaissance Rome, selling hay and animal fodder.

The section of the ancient street to the right of the palace façade, the via Monserrato, was the object of frustrated plans by Paul III in 1541. He intended to straighten it all the way to where it joined the major arterial via del Pellegrino, eliminating the bulge that obstructed the view of his palace's corner from that point. The bulge, however, was the site of the English hospice. The street was straightened to the point where the English property began. Today, at the end of the first house on the street, the Swedish nunnery of Santa Brigida, you can see how the street suddenly narrows as the obstreperous English building thwarted the Farnese plan.

In front of the main doors of palazzo Farnese a slight ridge can be detected in the surface of the square, running from the beginning of the **via de' Baullari** to the *portone*, which further emphasises the door. If you stand with your back to the palace, you can see at the far end of the street another coat of arms on the distant wall opposite: it is the crest of the Massimi family, whose contemporaneous block of palaces, the *isola dei Massimi*, prevented the extension of the via de' Baullari to piazza Navona beyond. The Massimo crest confronts the Farnese crest across the length of the street, a frozen expression of the competition between one of Rome's oldest families, the Massimi, and the new and powerful Farnese.

The two **fountains** in piazza Farnese have a long history as well. The two bath-like basins of granite are ancient and come from the Baths of Caracalla, though they are more likely to have been fountains than bathtubs. They were discovered in 1466 by Paul II Barbo, the Venetian pope who built palazzo Venezia, where he installed one of them as a decoration in the piazza in front. Paul III brought the other to piazza Farnese, still dry and used as an ornament rather than a fountain, and placed it directly in front of the palace's main doors, where it can be seen in a print of 1545. Perhaps it functioned as a sort of royal box where Farnese family members could sit safely, watching the spectacles that were held in the piazza. It seems to have been Cardinal Alessandro II who brought the second basin to piazza Farnese, but it was left to Cardinal Odoardo to put them in their current positions and to turn them into the beautiful fountains we see today. By 1627, when the basins were thus modified, the new aqueduct of the Acqua Paola had been brought to the city. Pope Paul V granted his permission and the fountains were designed, probably by the influential architect Girolamo Rainaldi (1570–1655), the author of the façade of the nearby church of San Girolamo della Carità. The elegant carved central jet represents the Farnese fleur-de-lis and the water from it falls into a four-

Henri Cluen inuen.   *Farnesiorum palatium .*   *Philipp Gall extud.*

A mid sixteenth-century engraving showing a bullfight in piazza Farnese, then known as piazza del Duca after the Farnese dukedoms of Parma and Piacenza. Note the basin in the middle, filled with Farnese spectators.

leaved basin before trickling down into the granite tub from the Baths; other jets spring upwards from the tub and from the lower basin which completes the ensemble, though these are not always playing. A print of 1652 shows a man wading through water in the piazza, which might indicate that the piazza was occasionally flooded intentionally for sport, as piazza Navona was later to be, but may also depict one of the Tiber's disastrous floods.

The street to the left of the front, via del Mascherone, takes its name from the third fountain sponsored by Cardinal Odoardo, the *Mascherone* or Big Mask, which stands at the Tiber end, by the back of the Farnese palace. The huge marble face which disgorges the fountain's water is ancient, and possibly comes from an old downspout or even a drain cover of late antique date. Two other similar ancient faces still peer out at Rome: one is the *Bocca della Verità* (Mouth of Truth), a drain cover now in the porch of Santa Maria in Cosmedin, the other is a fountain on the Aventine, just outside the church of Santa Sabina.

Behind the palazzo, along the via Giulia, the old Farnese stables can still be seen, and behind them, where the Lungotevere now roars with traffic, stood the **Camerini** or 'little rooms', built as a retreat for Cardinal Odoardo and decorated by the Bolognese school. Some of the rooms functioned as an oratory for the adjacent church of **Santa Maria dell'Orazione e Morte** (St Mary of Prayer and Death, open Sundays 16–18), a church housing a confraternity whose responsibility was to collect and bury the bodies of the poor dead. Though Cardinal Odoardo was one of the church's sponsors, the church building itself is eighteenth century, a beautiful elliptical work of Ferdinando Fuga (1699–1781). Cardinal Odoardo's presence is still evoked by two frescoes of saintly hermits by Lanfranco, *San Simeone Stilita* and *San Antonio Abate* (from c.1617): these were once in his prayer room in the Camerini, which he rented to the confraternity and from which, through a screen, he could look into the church to take part in Mass without ceremonial fuss. A room in the basement of the church, open on request, contains what is left of the underground cemetery: shelf upon shelf of skulls and a macabre cross of skulls in front of which is a *prie-dieu* with a skull resting upon it. Separating the stable block, which now contains offices and apartments (most of which are occupied, like the palazzo itself, by members of the French embassy), from the church is the so-called **bridge of Michelangelo** over the street, now festooned with ivy: its single span over the road forms a sort of Farnese triumphal arch complete with the family *gigli* in the corners.

Next to Santa Maria dell'Orazione e Morte is another ex-Farnese palace, the present **palazzo Falconieri**. It was purchased in 1606 from the Odescalchi family to serve as the Roman residence of the Latera branch of the Farnese family, though it was sold only thirty years later to the noble Florentine family of the Falconieri, when it was impressively expanded and reimagined by the brilliant architect Francesco Borromini (1599–1667). Little remains from its Farnese occupancy, though over the entrance arch on the façade can be seen the familiar *giglio*. Today it houses the Hungarian Academy and can, on special occasions, be visited. Ask to see the *altana* (rooftop loggia), from the top of which, accessed via a wrought-iron spiral stair, you have a spectacular and unusual view over palazzo Farnese and all of Rome.

2 Walking with Paul III

Start: via Giulia 93, almost a kilometre down the via Giulia from Santa Maria dell'Orazione e Morte

A walk through the tip of the Tiber bend and across the river is one of the best ways to understand the effect that Paul III Farnese, through the talents principally of Antonio da Sangallo the Younger, had on the urban plan of Rome. To cover all the works of these two figures, patron and architect,

Walking with Paul III

Key:
1 piazza d'Oro and San Giovanni
   dei Fiorentini
2 via Paola
3 end of the *via Trinitatis*
4 Castel Sant' Angelo
5 bastions of Paul III
6 porta Santo Spirito
7 church of Santo Spirito in Sassia

would require a walk across most of downtown Rome, but this relatively self-contained selection typifies the skill of Sangallo and the ambition of the pope.

I   THE STREETS OF PAUL III

Our starting point is at the north end of the via Giulia, whose width and straightness must have influenced Paul when he was planning his great new street, the *via Trinitatis* (see below). It was also Rome's most fashionable address.

The house in front of which you are standing bears the familiar crest of the Farnese family, because it was built by Paul III for his daughter, Costanza Farnese, who married into the Sforza of Santa Fiora. It remained a Farnese property for at least another century and Cardinal Alessandro II, it is said, lodged his own daughter Clelia here, in a strange echo of his grandfather's action. After her marriage, Costanza Farnese bought another, larger house further back on this street, which is today called Palazzo Ricci (the main entrance façade is on piazza de' Ricci, covered with *grisaille* frescoes by Polidoro da Caravaggio). Further on, you will enter an irregular open space that marks the end of the via Giulia, the piazza d'Oro.

In this piazza stands the large parish church of **San Giovanni dei Fiorentini**. Several architects, including Antonio da Sangallo the Younger, submitted plans to the pope for this church. The architect chosen was Jacopo Sansovino (1486–1570), but the works, begun in 1519, took a long time and Sangallo took them over for a while. The nave is the work of Giacomo della Porta and the dome is by Michelangelo and Carlo Maderno, who brought the work to its conclusion in 1620, and is buried inside the church along with his relative and fellow architect Francesco Borromini. The church of San Giovanni formed the heart of the old Florentine district of Rome, and all around stand the palaces of the Roman branches of Florentine families, the most visible being the palazzo Medici Clarelli (via Giulia 79), built originally as a house for the Sangallo family, then sold to the Medici rulers of Florence, which they used probably as offices connected with Florentine business affairs. The large fifteenth-century house across the street was the Consolato, a minor law court for the Florentine community in Renaissance Rome, whose privileges, granted by the Medici pope Leo X, extended Florentine jurisdiction over law cases involving claims against property, though not over felonies against persons. The Florentines were important here, principally as bankers, and in recognition of this, Cardinal Alessandro I Farnese, with the assent of the Medici pope Clement VII, planned a new street, linking San Giovanni with the ponte Sant'Angelo. Demolitions for this began in 1533, and by the time it was finished, Cardinal Alessandro had become pope: the street still bears his name, the **via Paola**.

The whole area around this end of the via Giulia was severely altered during the *ventennio*, the twenty-year rule of the fascists in the 1920s and 1930s. The busy via Acciaioli that runs from the Lungotevere towards corso Vittorio Emanuele II was rudely hacked through the Florentine quarter in the 1920s, and the raw edges of semi-demolished buildings are still notable, as well as the ugly parish hall of San Giovanni, to the right of the church. Cross the via Acciaioli and the corso Vittorio Emanuele II, and follow the via Paola along its brief length.

This street ran to what was, for many centuries, the most important piazza in the whole Tiber bend, the piazza di Ponte, named after the bridge which joined the city to the Borgo of the Vatican, under the supervisory eye of the Castel Sant'Angelo. The piazza has now vanished under the Lungotevere, so that it no longer resembles a piazza at all. However, in the early sixteenth century it had four streets going into it, all major arteries; the earliest was the central street, the via de' Banchi or Canal di Ponte, now the via del Banco di Santo Spirito, followed by Alexander VI's via dell'Orso, now partially lost under the Lungotevere, which ran from the via del Corso directly to the piazza di Ponte. Following that, Clement VII de' Medici intervened dramatically with his creation of a street on a diagonal, stretching from the piazza di Ponte to the old Orsini fortress of Monte Giordano, today's via di Panico. The via Paola was opened as a counterpart to the via di Panico, leading, as we have seen, to the important Florentine district and the via Giulia.

At this point the viewer should cross the Lungotevere and stand at the beginning of the bridge, looking back towards the city, where the three streets can best be seen. This trident of streets, the *zampa d'oca*, or goose-foot as it was locally known, is one of the earliest expressions of a concept of town planning that was soon to become central: the radiating street plan which focuses on one important site, in this case the piazza di Ponte. This design responded well to the particular needs of Rome. The city, with its huge transient population of pilgrims, had to be navigable by strangers who could often neither read nor speak the local language. All these pilgrims needed to be guided towards the main pilgrimage centre of St Peter's, and this piazza was essential because the ponte Sant'Angelo was the only means of crossing the river for a great distance both up- and downstream. Pilgrims crossing the bridge were met, at the castle end, with a toll-booth, so the whole design was also, in a sense, a machine for making money.

Paul III made further alterations to the via dell'Orso in 1544, widening and straightening it and extending it across the city to the base of the Pincio hill: this street, known as the via Trinitatis (Trinity Street) in the sixteenth century, is now the major artery of the via Condotti–via Fontanella Borghese, and today's via dell'Orso intersects with this at the old inn that is still called the Hostaria dell'Orso.

During Paul III's reign (1534–49), only the two statues of Saints Peter and Paul adorned the bridge; as the piazza was also a principal site for the execution of criminals, many human heads on pikes decorated the bridge too, an impressive if not pleasant sight for pilgrims. The angels were added in the 1670s, but the Castel Sant'Angelo, our next destination, is much as it was in Paul III's time, despite the alterations that buried the river front of the castle in order to construct the Tiber embankment.

Crossing the bridge and noting on the base of one of the angels' statues the mark of a cannonball (which, fired during the half-hearted papal defence of the city in 1870, knocked the statue into the river), we come to the entrance of the **Castel Sant'Angelo**.

II   CASTEL SANT'ANGELO
Open in winter 9–19, summer 9–20, closed Mondays. Admission €5; tours available, also in English; opening of the *passetto* and of the Historic Prisons at set times at weekends for an extra fee

A thorough tour of this colossal pile of masonry should take at least half a day. It began life as a mausoleum, the Hadrianeum, constructed by the Emperor Hadrian around the year AD 123 and was used as an imperial burial site until after the death of Caracalla in 217. The stone drum upon which the castle sits, which today has a very rough appearance, is the surviving part of the mausoleum, but its transformation into a castle took place relatively

CASTELLO·ANGELO·DI·ROMA

The exterior aspect of the Castel Sant' Angelo under Paul III was fearsome, yet the papal apartment atop the castle became airy and stylish under Farnese redevelopment.

early. It was incorporated into the city walls by the Emperor Aurelian in 271 and then, in the fifth-century Gothic sieges, its statues were broken up and lobbed at the invaders. It soon became Rome's most important fortress; in 590 a procession approached the castle, led by the newly elected pope Gregory the Great, who was making a formal visit to all the great churches of Rome to call upon God to lift the plague from the city. A vision was granted to those present: a mighty angel appeared over the castle, sheathing its sword, to signify that the plague would come to an end. Since then, it has carried the name of the Castle of the Holy Angel.

Though Alexander VI Borgia undertook major reconstruction around 1500, it fell to his successors, and particularly to Paul III, to complete the task: the Medici pope Clement VII had some of the papal apartments frescoed by pupils of the recently deceased Raphael and then had to occupy them uncomfortably during the terrible Sack of Rome in 1527, when German and Spanish troops devastated the city for a year. Paul III completed most of the decoration of the castle's residential areas, culminating in a loggia at the back, looking towards the hill of Monte Mario. This loggia was the work of Antonio Sangallo the Younger and is the companion piece to the earlier loggia of Julius II at the front of the castle, constructed by Antonio's father Giuliano da Sangallo.

As an official papal residence, the castle required an apartment for the use of the pope, either in emergency or during state occasions. A visit to the state apartment of the Castel Sant'Angelo affords us a glimpse of what a Renaissance papal palace must have looked like. Other such palaces have been either demolished or vastly altered over the centuries, but the castle, too small to contain the papal court and never a favourite residence, has retained most of its sixteenth-century decoration. It could certainly have provided the Farnese pope with a place to retreat from the court, especially during the summer: it was well positioned not far from the Vatican, and its altitude made it cool and breezy even in August. Paul III's main summer palace was on the height of the Capitoline hill, also making the most of the breeze, but unfortunately it was destroyed at the end of the nineteenth century for the construction of the monument to Vittorio Emanuele II. The Castel Sant'Angelo alone survives and it strongly shows Paul III's antiquarian taste in interior decoration, the last word in chic, 1540s style.

Upon entering the castle and ascending through the ancient drum, the first courtyard is the **cortile dell'Angelo**, whose eponymous angel, carved by Michelangelo's pupil Raffaele da Montelupo, was commissioned under Paul III in 1544 to stand at the summit of the castle, where its successor now rises. The **Sala d'Apollo**, on the first floor of the castle's papal apartment, is accessible from this courtyard. Its *grottesche* wall and ceiling frescoes are among Rome's best and most purely classical imitations of ancient Roman painting. They were begun in October 1547 by Raphael's old pupil Perino del Vaga (1501–47), only one month before his death; the work was completed by his followers. Rooms off the Sala d'Apollo, now usually closed, were Clement VII's residence during the 1527 siege and also sport ceilings covered in Medici emblems; when open, the rooms contain some of the castle's art collection. Paul III's apartments were on the floor above, where he transformed Clement VII's semi-finished rooms into a dignified palace. The pope commissioned Antonio da Sangallo the Younger, already at work on palazzo Farnese, to demolish the old chapel of San Nicola in 1542, in order to build a large audience hall, the *Sala Regia* or **Sala Paolina**, completed two years later and frescoed in 1545.

The room represents a moment of flux in Roman art. The master in charge of the decorative scheme was Perino del Vaga, whose fellow alumnus of Raphael's workshop, Giovanni da Udine, had contributed much to the decorations of the apartment in the time of Clement VII. Perino's painted *grottesche*, his mainstay to this point, never suggested he was capable of the startlingly virtuoso design of the Sala Paolina frescoes. His main inspiration was Michelangelo's Sistine ceiling: the larger pictorial spaces are separated by painted and illusionistic architecture and at regular intervals the main paintings are punctuated by lesser scenes, painted in roundels held up by allegorical figures. But Perino retained Raphael's preference for bright and elegant figures and the style of the room is wonderfully assured and skilled. Vasari, in his *Lives of the Artists*, described this room as 'the most beautiful and rich room that had hitherto been seen in the world', and indeed, though it receives little attention in guidebooks, it is an extraordinary accomplishment.

The frescoes depict scenes from the life of Alexander the Great, in tribute to the other great Alexander, Alessandro Farnese, Paul III: Alexander makes peace between two of his fellow soldiers; Alexander consecrates the twelve altars; Alexander has the works of Homer placed in a desk; Alexander cuts the Gordian knot; The family of Darius at the feet of Alexander. In the centre of one of the two short walls, the Archangel Michael appears, sheathing his sword, as in the vision of Gregory the Great; this figure, distinguished by a powerful Michelangelesque strength, was by Perin's assistant Pellegrino Tibaldi (1527–96), who may also have made the matching figure of the Emperor Hadrian that faces the archangel across the room. The stuccoed ceiling, too, depicts the life of Alexander the Great and, in the centre of the ensemble, the great crest of the Farnese.

Unusual details set the room apart: the two baboons, court pets, who sit sharing an apple beneath the angel; the courtiers coming out of false doors, a little dog next to the figure of Christian Faith. The room shows Roman art as it was at mid century, halfway between the classic naturalism of the High Renaissance and the complex, allegorical Mannerist style, with its focus on inventive *disegno* that can be seen in its final stages in palazzo Farnese.

The smaller room, called the **Sala del Perseo** from its frieze (again by Perino) of the legend of Perseus and Andromeda, is decorated as a small reception room of the sixteenth century, including a surround and a small dais for a throne, whose place has rather ignominiously been taken by a metal folding stool. The Farnese emblem is prominent on the ceiling. The following room, the **Camera di Amore e Psiche**, also with a frieze by Perin, has been fitted out as a bedroom, with a large sixteenth-century bed in the middle of it, under a wooden ceiling bearing the name of Paul III and his *gigli*. (The furnishings of these rooms come from the state collections, principally from a bequest of 1916.) Probably the outer room, the Sala del Perseo, had been the papal bedroom, as a little-noticed door (now an emergency exit) near the entrance from the Sala Paolina leads down a staircase to the bathroom of Clement VII; the Camera di Amore e Psiche was most likely a *retrocamera* (private retiring room).

Another exit from the Sala Paolina leads into a corridor beautifully frescoed with *grottesche*, whose windows offer a view of St Peter's. It leads to the **Sala della Biblioteca**, the northern reception room, whose ceiling is delicately decorated with stucco reliefs and frescoes depicting scenes from Roman history. Again, the Farnese emblem is prominent. Two smaller rooms, sometimes closed, lead off this one: the **Camera dell'Adrianeo**, named for the mausoleum itself, which is imaginatively depicted in the frieze; and the **Camera dei Festoni**, named for the garlands in its frieze. Both these rooms were decorated under Paul III, perhaps as a winter apartment. Today they host part of the art collection of the Castel Sant'Angelo, a dusty and strangely random series of paintings. Also opening from the Sala della Biblioteca is the **Camera del Tesoro**, the former papal treasure house, built into the topmost room of the Hadrianeum's central tower and containing a vast sixteenth-century treasure chest and the beautiful walnut cabinets of the old *Archivum Arcis*, the most secret part of the Vatican Archives, now in the Vatican Palace itself. A curved staircase leads up to the terrace and a spectacular view of Rome.

From the loggia of Julius II down the steps from the Sala Paolina, we can identify and appreciate even better the *zampa d'oca* of three streets converging on the ponte Sant'Angelo on the other side of the river.

III   PAUL III IN THE BORGO

Leaving the castle and turning right to continue downstream along the Lungotevere, which at this point is restricted to pedestrian use only, on the right is the vast complex of the hospital of Santo Spirito in Sassia, which we have visited in the della Rovere itinerary. At piazza della Rovere, where a bridge goes over the river, we will cross the now car-infested Lungotevere and approach the gigantic **bastions of Paul III** towards the road tunnel under the Janiculan hill.

Though the Vatican had never been included within the Aurelianic circuit of city walls, in 847–52, after a disastrous sacking by the Saracens, Leo IV constructed a set of walls around St Peter's and the Vatican guest house (not yet a palace). By the time of Paul III these walls were both old and unadapted to the exigencies of modern warfare, and were reconstructed, at the corner we are now looking at, to the designs of the indefatigable Antonio da Sangallo the Younger. In yet another argument, Michelangelo and Sangallo disagreed vehemently about the kind of fortification necessary to repel cannon fire, and because the arguments of both had some validity, Sangallo's gate, the **porta Santo Spirito**, was suspended in mid construction in 1544 and, as we can see, was never completed. Sangallo regarded this as nothing less than sabotage and never forgave his fellow Florentine.

Proceed along the via dei Penitenzieri, named after the papal penitentiaries or confessors of St Peter's, whose palace at the far end of the street is described in the della Rovere itinerary. At the corner with the borgo Santo Spirito is the **church of Santo Spirito**. The church we see today (open 9–12, 16–18) is the third on the site: the first, built as the church of the Anglo-Saxon community in the early Middle Ages, was dedicated to the Virgin, but by the time Sixtus IV rebuilt the complex it had already been reconsecrated to the Holy Spirit. Only his tall bell tower, which we have already passed along the via dei Penitenzieri, survives: a little more than sixty years later the church was torn down and reconstructed again, by order of Paul III, in 1538–45. The architect, of course, was Sangallo, though the façade was only finished in the 1580s by the architect Ottaviano Nonni, 'il Mascherino'.

The church has a plan that prefigures that of the much more important Gesù, whose construction only started in 1568: instead of the traditional basilica style, with a nave separated from side aisles by rows of columns, Santo Spirito has a single nave and side chapels in place of aisles. The Council of Trent, which opened in the year of this church's completion, was to place new stress on the importance of the main altar and in Santo Spirito we can see precisely how prominent the altar, and the officiating priest, were soon to be. The interest of the pope in this new construction is apparent in the wooden ceiling that contains the Farnese crest in a huge flourish directly above the altar. The organ, too, reflects Paul's role here, with another crest and beside it a smaller Farnese crest surmounted by a cardinal's hat, the emblem of Cardinal Alessandro II, soon to be the founder of the Gesù. Most of the rest of the decoration dates from the 1580s, a later Mannerist phase, though even in that period there is a Farnese presence: somewhere in the church was once a painting by Jacopo Zucchi containing a portrait of the beautiful Clelia Farnese, Cardinal Alessandro's daughter, depicted as St Helena discovering the True Cross. On the entrance wall are two frescoes from the 1540s, a *Visitation* by Marco Pino da Siena (*c.*1517–*c.*1579) and, matching it on the other side of the main door, a *Conversion of St Paul* begun by Francesco Salviati (1510–63) and finished by his Spanish pupil Francisco Ruvial (1511–82). The presence of a work by Salviati, Farnese family painter par excellence, is the final stamp of the taste of Paul III and his grandson Alessandro.

3   The Orti Farnesiani on the Palatine

The Palatine hill. Open 9–sunset. Admission €8, joint ticket with admission to the Colosseum. Entrances from via di San Gregorio (where the visit begins) and from the Forum above the arch of Titus

The Palatine hill, the site of ancient imperial palaces, was by the sixteenth century a mound of half-visible ruins and underbrush. Different families owned property there, which they used either as vineyards or as farms. The eastern half of the hill, facing on to the Forum, was transformed by successive members of the Farnese family into a spectacular garden, the **Orti Farnesiani**, whose traces still survive. Richard Lassels, a traveller in the later seventeenth century, described his visit briefly:

> Going from hence on the right hand still, I came to the dore of the Farnese garden. This garden stands upon the Mount Palatin, where anciently the Emperors had their Palace; [. . .] Entering into this garden I found some pretty waterworks and grottoes at the entrance, and fine high walks aboue overlooking the place where the Circus Maximus stood anciently.

The three sons of Pier Luigi were the driving force behind the acquisition of the property. By 1542 Cardinal Alessandro II owned some land on the Palatine, and after 1565 he built the Forum side into a series of terraces, and surrounded the property with a huge, featureless wall with a grand gate on to the street that ran through the Forum, the via Papalis, whose Vatican end we have seen at the ponte Sant'Angelo. He determined the general plan of the garden, with its avenues, and the little grotto called the Ninfeo degli Specchi. Later, Cardinal Odoardo, from 1600 to his death in 1626, transformed part of the terraces facing the Forum into a summer dining room dug into the earth, and subsequently into another fountain house called the Ninfeo della Pioggia. On the topmost terrace he built a large aviary, which he filled with exotic birds. The final Farnese to build here was Odoardo, Duke of Parma, from 1627 to 1635, who built another aviary as a twin to the first and covered both of them with exotic pagoda roofs of wire mesh: he completed the series of structures up the Forum side of the hill, decorating them with *sgraffito* frescoes in monochrome, and also undertook various fountain constructions.

The gardens later fell into abandonment and decline, especially with the extinction of the Farnese dynasty and the inheritance of the Bourbons, who removed most of the ancient statuary either to Parma or to Naples. Much of the garden returned to the wild. The English traveller Samuel Rogers, at the beginning of the nineteenth century, experienced the gardens in their desolation:

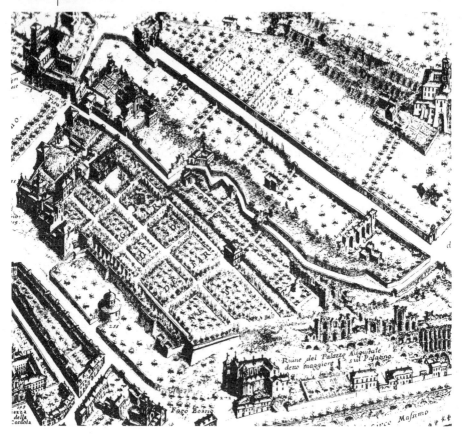

The Orti Farnesiani in 1676. The ordered parterres of the Italian garden fell into neglect before their destruction at the hands of Napoleon III's archaeologists.

Now in the Orti Farnesi you see fractured capitals and rich cornices half hid in the long grass; [. . .] The Orti Farnesi themselves have now given way. The terraces are dismantled – the aviaries a ruin, and the fountain designed by M. Angelo no more to be seen – but its situation is unrivalled. The Capitol, the Forum, and the Coliseum are striking objects here.

Under the Napoleonic occupation the gardens were rearranged as a public park. Finally, Napoleon III, who bought the gardens from the king of Naples, destroyed the whole Farnesian plan when he commissioned the archaeologist Pietro Rosa to uncover the remains of the *Domus Tiberiana*, the earliest great palace on the hill, thought at the time to be a construction of Tiberius. Rosa adapted the aviaries as a house for himself and built in the gap between them. In 1870 the Italian state took over the excavations: the surrounding wall was obliterated and the great gate was dismantled, to be set up again, in a different location, in 1957. In the first decade of the twentieth century, the archaeologist Giacomo Boni finished the excavations of the Julio–Claudian palace, refilled the site with earth and replanted the gardens.

Our visit begins at the **great gate of the Orti Farnesiani** in its modern site on via di San Gregorio. The gate (completed for the jubilee of 1575), thought to be the product of the family architects Vignola and Del Duca, is decorated with a frieze of Farnese *gigli*, the inscribed legend 'ORTI PALATINI FARNESIORUM' and, at the very top, the crest of Cardinal Alessandro II. In its original position it lined up with the series of platforms overlooking the Forum across from the central vault of the ruins of the basilica of Maxentius. Up the stairs to the right, a path leads round the side of the hill towards the via Sacra. On the left at the top of the stairs are the window frames that were demolished along with the great gate: thus we can duplicate Samuel Rogers's experience of seeing 'fractured capitals and rich cornices half hid in the long grass'. This time the ruins are not ancient, but Farnese.

Around the curve of the hill, a small tunnel leads under the public street to emerge at the *Clivus Palatinus*, the ancient street leading up the Palatine hill. A short distance further on, we branch up the steps to the right to reach the second level of the **Farnese terraces**. In the sixteenth and seventeenth centuries these terraces were lavishly landscaped, and the area we are crossing was once stocked with wild boar and game birds, so that the Farnese and their guests could enjoy the pleasures of the hunt.

A staircase descends through the trees. At the bottom, in a dark and damp porch opening out towards the Forum, is the gated entrance to the **Ninfeo della Pioggia**, the Nymphaeum of the Rain, perhaps named for the moisture that even today makes the ceiling of the grotto damp. This was a summer dining room for Cardinal Odoardo in 1601, which he adapted as a fountain house in 1612. It was frescoed with garlands (traces of which can still be seen) and the ceiling was decorated with a false pergola filled with musicians. As recently as 1960 these painted embellishments were photographed in a reasonably good condition, but today they are almost invisible. Plinths with the Farnese emblem on it once bore ancient statuary, now in either Parma or Naples, and a door in the back of the room connected it with the *cryptoporticus* of Nero, a subterranean passage that linked the front of the hill to the back, overlooking the Circus Maximus. In front of the gateway is a little porch, once decorated with statues, overlooking the ramp that leads down towards where the great gate used to stand: at the foot of the ramp a semicircular space opened up, filled with statues and little fountains, just within the gate. The untended, decaying nature of this part of the gardens is still evident, with ugly temporary fences erected long ago still blocking access to large areas formerly covered by formal flowerbeds and now the home of pines and deciduous saplings. Yet this lovely spot can still be appreciated, especially on a hot summer's day, when the shade is welcome and the trickling fountain inside the nymphaeum offers the cooling sound of water.

Back up the stairs, another access ramp leads up to the third terrace of the gardens, the **Teatro del Fontanone**. Baroque architects and designers often conceived of open spaces in terms of theatres, not necessarily as places to put on plays, but as stages for the theatre of human life. The Teatro del Fontanone takes its name from the big fountain at its back, whose run-off we have already seen below in the nymphaeum. The design of this space is attributed to Vignola and its execution to Girolamo Rainaldi, who was the designer, for Cardinal Odoardo, of the fountains in piazza Farnese. The *teatro* does have a distinctly stage-like nature, with its entrances to right and left, its twin staircases rising to the top terrace, and its ramp down, as well as its dramatic fountain and *sgraffito* wall frescoes. The fountain itself is nineteenth-century: in the seventeenth century it would have been a series of basins, one above the other. A rather forlorn bare rectangle in the centre of the lip of the fountain's basin marks the spot where, until recently, an ancient lion statue stood. Its unexplained disappearance is another testament to the lack of interest the archaeological authorities take in the monumental remains of the Farnese gardens.

Up the flight of stairs to the right of the *fontanone* is the highest terrace, the site of the **Uccelliere** or bird houses. The fantastical cage roofs have gone, probably when the bird houses were converted into a residence for Pietro Rosa in the 1860s, and simple tile roofs replace them.

The Orti Farnesiani were foremost among Rome's original botanical gardens, beginning around the year 1600. Cardinal Odoardo's botanical collection derived from his wide-ranging agents, the members of the Jesuit order, whose travels in the Orient and in the New World brought seeds of the most exotic plants to flower on the Palatine: the yucca, the Floridian aloe (whose first blossoms appeared in the Orti in 1616), tuberoses, narcissi, amaryllis and the famous acacia from the Caribbean island of Santo Domingo, which in Italy took on the secondary name of 'farnesiana'.

The gardens were the scene of a good deal of botanical research in the seventeenth century, by such gentleman scientists as Fabio Colonna of the Academy of the Lincei, one of Rome's most prestigious intellectual societies. All these exotic plants were, sadly, dug up during the late nineteenth century for the excavations of the *Domus Tiberiana*, but when

An eighteenth-century view of the Orti shows the birdhouses with their cage-roofs intact. Hans Christian Andersen, seeing the gardens in their nineteenth-century decadence, was still enchanted: 'so green and sweet-smelling that we cannot believe it is winter . . .'

Giacomo Boni had the excavations refilled, he laid out a new garden, which he called the *Vivarium Palatinum*, with two distinct didactic sections: the first was a section devoted to plants identifiable in ancient Roman wall paintings, from Pompeii and from the House of Livia not far away on the Palatine hill itself, and the second section was a remaking of the Farnese plantings. Only about a quarter of the previous area of the gardens was replanted, so the size and complexity of the original arrangement are hard to imagine. Subsequent custodians added the avenue of orange trees that greets visitors at the top of the steps to the aviaries, and a rose garden, in the middle of which is the little cenotaph marking the site where Giacomo Boni's ashes were interred, in the gardens he loved. Despite these changes, the Orti Farnesiani, in their current condition, still have few rivals in Rome as regards the beauty of their flowering bushes and above all their splendid location.

Two further sites on the hill still recall the Farnese and their gardens. The first, the **Casino del Belvedere**, stands isolated at the back of the hill, overlooking the Circus Maximus. The Casino del Belvedere (Pavilion of the Beautiful View) rises beyond the excavated right-hand fountain of the huge dining room of the *Domus Flavia*. Its interior, on two levels, is small and simple. There is no admission, but the internal frescoes can be glimpsed from the ground. Facing the north-west is a two-storey loggia, the upper decorated by the school of the Zuccari with *grottesche* frescoes for Cardinal

Alessandro II. Landscapes describe the various territories of the Farnese, while a picture cycle tells the story of the struggle between Hercules and Cacus. Cacus was a giant thief who lived in a cave in the flank of the hill not far away and robbed Hercules of his cattle. The hero, discovering this, met and fought Cacus and killed him. This cycle alludes to a struggle between the Farnese and the pope who followed Paul III, Julius III del Monte (1550–5). In this allegorical reading, determined by Cardinal Alessandro's court intellectual Fulvio Orsini, Cacus was Julius III, who strove to deprive the Farnese of the family duchies of Parma and Piacenza, and Hercules was the cardinal, overcoming the thief and triumphing, as Cardinal Alessandro did, persuading the pope to restore the territories to the young Duke Ottavio.

From the *Domus Flavia*, return towards the Forum side of the hill, following the path that leads into the little valley in front of the palace, now covered with briar roses, and keep to the left-hand side until you reach a small paved space and a ramp leading upwards to the aviaries again. The final Farnese site is here, the rather sad ruin of another fountain house. This is the **Ninfeo degli Specchi**, the Nymphaeum of the Mirrors. Today this consists of a small hemicycle of niches decorated in pebble mosaic, which stands just off the *Clivus Palatinus*. At one time it was a covered grotto with little fountains, forming the base of the terrace that supported the so-called Garden of the Plane Trees above, now vanished. Sixtus V conceded water from his new aqueduct, the Acqua Felice, to Cardinal Alessandro in 1588 so that both the Farnese fountain projects here, the Fontanone Ninfeo della Pioggia and this fountain house, would be well-supplied with water. The Ninfeo degli Specchi also possessed the quintessential sixteenth-century fountain, the *giochi d'acqua* (water games), a pavement with tiny jets of water concealed within it. When unsuspecting visitors were led on to it, and a hidden lever was pulled, water would douse them from below. (Just as well it is definitively out of order.)

The Garden of the Plane Trees also had a fountain and it was here, from 1693 to 1699, that the Academy of the Arcadia had its seat: this was the final *teatro* of the Orti Farnesiani, the *Teatro degli Arcadi*. This Academy, which was devoted to classicism in both art and literature, acted as a sort of club where artists and writers could meet with each other and with patrons. The conceit was that in the Arcadia everyone took on the name of a classical shepherd or nymph (women, too, were members). Meetings took place out of doors, as befitted a society that took its name from the semi-mythical bucolic paradise of ancient poems, and members recited their poetry or discoursed on classicism to an audience of their peers. All this was fine, but when members began to read satires as well, Francesco Maria took umbrage. In an edict of 27 May 1699, the duke declared that he would 'no longer tolerate that his garden [. . .] would serve as an outlet for private passions, and even less as a theatre for the recital of satires and ill-sayings'. The Arcadian Academy eventually found a permanent seat in a garden it still owns, on the slope of the hill overlooking Trastevere.

4 The Gesù

Piazza del Gesù. Open 8–12, 16–18. Rooms of Sant' Ignazio, Casa Professa dei Gesuiti, piazza del Gesù. Open weekday evenings 16–18, Sunday mornings 10–12. Admission free, but the explanatory booklet (in English) costs €2 and is worth it as exhibits are not labelled. Casa Gesuita della Provincia d'Italia, entrance on via degli Astalli, ring buzzer 'Curia Provinciale' to ask for access to the Cappellina Farnese

Though in general the secular works of the Farnese are most spectacular, the massive church of the Most Holy Name of Jesus, the Gesù, is testament to their spiritual patronage. Two successive Farnese cardinals were responsible for the construction of the church, and the order of Jesuits itself owed its foundation to the Farnese pope Paul III. The story of the Gesù is thus also the story of the early Jesuit order and it shows a different side to the Farnese family.

The piazza in which the church stands was, and is, otherwise dominated by the property of the ancient family of the Altieri. The great palazzo Altieri on the northern edge of the piazza dates from the late seventeenth century, but earlier Altieri buildings surrounded the site of the present church on the north and east sides of the piazza, which was then called, of course, piazza Altieri. A small church nearby, Santa Maria della Strada, acted as a local focus, and piazza Altieri was the centre of the busy and highly populous *rione* Pigna. The church was also called Santa Maria degli Astalli, after another family whose residence nearby, in what is today called via degli Astalli, was established as early as the year 1000. Thus the church had a long tradition of noble patronage. This patronage was not, however, enough to save it from the powerful forces of Counter-Reformation religious reform.

Iñigo de Loyola was born in 1491, the youngest son of a Basque nobleman. He lived as an aristocrat and soldier until he was wounded in the siege of Pamplona in 1521. It was in his convalescence that he converted to a religious life and had a vision of the Virgin Mary, and thereafter, during a peripatetic life, he surrounded himself with Catholic intellectuals and wrote his great devotional work, the *Spiritual Exercises*, in a conscious attempt to shape a new kind of Catholic spirituality. Loyola, who changed his first name to Ignatius, went to Rome to obtain papal approval for the foundation of his new religious order, the Society of Jesus. Paul III ratified the new Society in September 1540; at the same time an Italian follower of Loyola, a high official at the papal court, arranged to become parish priest of Santa Maria della Strada. Loyola rented a little house nearby, and a further bull of Paul III in 1541 granted the church to the Jesuit Society in perpetuity. The stage was set for a triumphant reconstruction of the building. The only thing lacking was money.

Two false starts in 1550 and 1554 came to naught due to lack of funds and only in 1568 did a wealthy patron finally appear: Paul III's grandson Cardinal Alessandro II. The cardinal took a precise and personal interest in the details of construction, ordering that the façade of the church should be orientated towards what is today largo Argentina, facing on to the via Papalis. The church would thus have a tremendous prominence from afar, just as the front entrance of palazzo Farnese itself did, when viewed from further along the via Papalis. The cardinal also ordered that the ceiling should be vaulted, not roofed with wooden beams and coffers in the style of the time: he wanted the church to be like an audience hall, and the vaulted ceiling would give 'more solemnity' to the nave, which was to be constructed, like Santo Spirito in Sassia, without aisles. Although building work was not finished, the church was open to the public in the jubilee of 1575. The church of the Most Holy Name of Jesus, the Gesù, was finally consecrated on 25 November 1584. Jesuit documents make no doubt about its familial connection: it is referred to as the 'Farnese temple' and 'your church' in letters to Cardinal Alessandro.

The Farnese family architect Jacopo Barozzi da Vignola was chosen to design the church; strictly in line with the decrees of the Council of Trent, emphasis was placed on pulpit and high altar, and in order to accommodate the largest possible number of worshippers the side aisles were done away with and side chapels of uniform size opened directly off the nave. However, a series of arches lined up in an enfilade joined the side chapels to each other, forming a sort of vestigial aisle. The basic plan of the church was a Latin cross, with the transepts shorter than the nave, but the plan was itself a derivation of earlier Renaissance centrally planned churches rather than a remaking of a medieval Latin-cross plan.

However, the cardinal was dissatisfied with Vignola's project for the **façade**. He opened a new competition for the design of the church front and in 1570 he chose Vignola's pupil, the thirty-year-old Giacomo della Porta. Vignola was shocked and affronted and withdrew to take over the management of the Fabbrica of St Peter's. Della Porta's façade was extremely influential in subsequent church construction in Rome and across the Catholic world. It was thought to combine both solemnity and energy, in the simple way it builds towards a climax in the central section of the façade, with double pediments and, at the top, the huge crest of the Farnese above a well-defined central window. The crest itself has been obliterated, but *gigli* survive over both the side doors and on the cornice running round the whole eastern half of the Casa Professa attached to the church.

Inside, the vast symphony of decoration expresses the late Baroque, much as in the Colonna family church of Santi Apostoli. A lot of the immediately visible decoration of the **interior** is from 1672–85, though the boring high altar dates from the mid nineteenth century. The original aspect of the Gesù was a rather austere building, white and huge, with decorated side chapels. Above the front entrance the original dedicatory plaque can still be seen and can be translated as follows: 'Alessandro Farnese, Cardinal, Vice-Chancellor of the Holy Roman Church, grandson of Pope Paul III, by whose authority the Society of Jesus was first received and decorated with broad decrees, built this temple from its foundations, as a monument to religion and posterity, according to his will, in the year of the Jubilee, 1575.'

Farnese *gigli* can barely be seen inside, unusually for a family monument. Little of the church's art dates from the time of Cardinal Alessandro, though the third chapel on the left, from the entrance, the **chapel of the Most Holy Trinity**, includes an altarpiece by Francesco Bassano the Younger (1540–91) from 1582. Other wall decorations in this chapel are by Durante Alberti (1538–1613) and Scipione Pulzone; Pulzone also had a hand in the decoration of the chapel to the left of the presbytery, the **chapel of the Madonna della Strada**, perhaps at the order of Cardinal Alessandro. Of a similar period are the rather weak statues in the third chapel on the right-hand side (directly across the nave from the Trinity chapel), the **chapel of the Angels**, whose walls are entirely covered in frescoes by Federico Zuccari, a Farnese family artist. The next chapel in the direction of the high altar is in fact a vestibule leading to the **sacristy**, a construction of the next Farnese cardinal, Odoardo. Here at last are *gigli* in abundance, even spangling the panels of the doors. Within, paintings depict various points where the order and the Farnese interacted. In the sacristy's inner room is an altarpiece by Annibale Carracci, another family painter, depicting *Sant' Ignazio*: on the ceiling is the *Adoration of the Holy Sacrament* by Agostino Ciampelli (1578–1640), whose work we will also meet in Santa Bibiana, in the Barberini itinerary. In the pavement, in front of the high altar, are the simple tomb slabs of the Farnese cardinals Alessandro and Odoardo, unexpectedly humble in death. Cardinal Alessandro's funeral was held here in the spring of 1589 and his catafalque had to be surrounded by a guard corps, so insistent was the homage of the public who remembered him for his generosity and piety.

Cardinal Odoardo was responsible for the construction of the new Jesuit house, the **Casa Professa**, attached to the Gesù. This building, which encloses the original house in which St Ignatius lived, was begun in 1599 and Odoardo gave 100,000 scudi towards it; the architect was Girolamo Rainaldi. He laid the foundation stone on the corner of via degli Astalli and via di San Marco, where an inscription and a little wall shrine of the Virgin commemorate the event. Inside, the halls are cool, large and austere. Here, on the *piano nobile*, Cardinal Odoardo maintained a small private apartment, now an administrative office. A small doorway leads to a little room with a grille opening into the Gesù below, so the cardinal could watch the services unobserved. The apartment also contains a tiny and beautiful chapel, the **cappellina Farnese**, full of gilded stucco work and paintings by the school of Domenichino (accessible sometimes upon request). When the property of the religious orders was expropriated by the Italian state in the late nineteenth century, the Jesuits were allowed to keep only the rooms above Cardinal Odoardo's apartment, where his servants had resided. The property, even today, belongs to the state, though it is leased back to the Jesuits. This is a standard settlement in Italy and ensures that the financial burden of maintaining the property lies on the wealthy Italian state, rather than on the declining religious orders.

5   Other Farnese sites in Rome

The original appearance of the Gesù, before the late Baroque interventions, can be appreciated in a church of the same period, **Santa Caterina dei Funari**, not far away on via dei Funari, beside the *isola* of the Mattei. The church (open irregularly on Sunday mornings) preserves its late sixteenth-century appearance inside and out, and its white vaulted ceilings and richly decorated side chapels show how the Gesù's own side chapels must have blazed out rhythmically from the edges of the worshippers' vision, which would have been concentrated on the high altar. This was, in fact, a Jesuit church in the mid sixteenth century, one of the order's first. Also in this church, the first chapel to the right of the entrance, the **Bombasi chapel** (*c.*1600), was endowed by a member of the huge household of Cardinal Odoardo Farnese. Perhaps through the cardinal's influence, the chapel has an altarpiece by Annibale Carracci, *Santa Margherita*, with a frame that also incorporates another decoration by Carracci, the *Coronation of the Virgin*.

A more intimate and personal expression of the faith of the Farnese can be found in the little **Oratorio del Santissimo Crocifisso** (open 16–19) in piazza dell'Oratorio behind palazzo Sciarra. This oratory, founded to celebrate the miraculous crucifix that alone had survived a terrible fire in the nearby church of San Marcello al Corso, was designed by Giacomo della Porta: it forms a simple box without side chapels, whose elegant façade is decorated by the Farnese arms surmounted by a cardinal's hat, and an inscription naming the patrons as Cardinals Alessandro and Ranuccio Farnese. It was commissioned by Cardinal Ranuccio in 1562 and completed by his brother Alessandro in 1569. The **interior** is a small gem of late Mannerist painting: its decorative scheme was planned by the intellectual nobleman Tommaso de' Cavalieri, Michelangelo's beloved, and executed in 1578–90 by the best painters Rome had to offer, including the Pomaranci (father and son), Cesare Nebbia, Paris Nogari and Baldassare Croce, all depicting episodes in the story of the Cross.

The famous **villa Farnesina**, across the Tiber from palazzo Farnese, bears almost no sign of its occupancy by the Farnese beyond its name, as the family, starting with Cardinal Alessandro who purchased it in 1581, were careful to preserve the frescoes installed by the villa's builder, Agostino Chigi (which form part of the Chigi itinerary). Just to the right of the present entrance gate an enclosure contains a very decayed fountain with a Farnese *giglio* on its top. Similarly, the huge white monoliths of the Italian Foreign Ministry, just below the hill of Monte Mario to the north of the Vatican, are called collectively **La Farnesina** because originally the site had been occupied by farms belonging to the family. Not a trace of them remains there, however.

On the **Capitoline hill**, the Farnese have less presence than one might expect: after all, it was Paul III who gave the initial order for the redesign of the piazza del Campidoglio and who commissioned Michelangelo as the architect. However, the work was so slow that Paul III was a mere memory by the time it was finished and as a result Farnese emblems barely appear at all, though the centrepiece of the piazza, the great statue of Marcus Aurelius (a modern copy of the ancient bronze, now in the Capitoline Museums), has the *gigli* on the pedestal. In the church of **Santa Maria in Aracoeli** a plaque honouring Alessandro Farnese, Duke of Parma and Piacenza, can be found high on the wall in the left-hand transept, and in the **Capitoline Museums**, in the Room of the Captains stands an antique statue of a Roman commander which was given a head portraying the same Alessandro in 1593; in the nearby Room of the She-Wolf, an honorary inscription lauding Alessandro was inserted in 1588, where it keeps company with a grandiose inscription commemorating Marcantonio II Colonna.

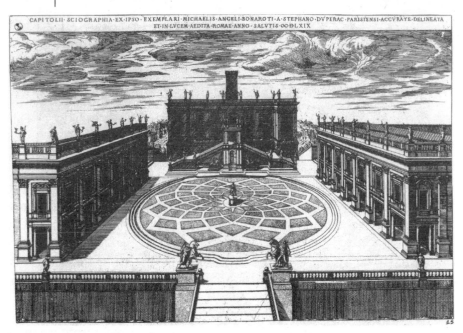

Etienne Dupérac's famous engraving of the Campidoglio omits the roof of the palazzo Nuovo (to the left): this palace was not built until long after Michelangelo's death, and is shown here as part of a theoretical scheme.

In the **Vatican**, many interventions of Paul III exist, most notably the works commissioned by the pope from Michelangelo: the fresco of the *Last Judgement* in the Sistine Chapel, which had originally been commissioned by Clement VII but executed under the Farnese pope, and the two frescoes of the Pauline Chapel (closed to the public), *The Conversion of St Paul* and *The Martyrdom of St Peter*. Within St Peter's, the **tomb of Paul III** by Guglielmo della Porta (1515–77), father of the Farnese architect Giacomo, depicts the pope between two female figures, *Justice* and *Prudence*, who are alleged to be, respectively, portraits of the pope's sister Giulia and his mother, Giovanella Caetani. The tomb was rearranged in the seventeenth century and two of its figures were removed to palazzo Farnese. The figure of Giulia-Justice was carved as a semi-nude (one satire about the statue said Giulia was 'born naked and was afterwards partially clad'), but under Clement VIII Aldobrandini it was covered 'decently' with a dress of bronze, painted white to look like marble. Even after death the Farnese could cause a scandal.

Intermezzo:
the middle and late sixteenth century

Of the papal families of the later sixteenth century, only a scant few succeeded in inserting themselves into the Roman aristocracy for longer than the duration of their pope's pontificate. Following the death of Paul III Farnese in 1549, a series of popes focused their efforts on confronting the two principal challenges of the day: responding to the Protestant revolution in northern Europe and adapting Rome as the capital of the increasingly centralised Papal States. **Julius III del Monte** (1550–5) was a lazy, pleasure-loving pope, whose main contribution to Rome was his huge retreat outside the porta del Popolo, the villa Giulia. This was expropriated from his heirs by **Paul IV Carafa** (1555–9), who succeeded Julius after the very brief interregnum of **Marcellus II Cervini** (April–May 1555).

Paul IV was best known for his passionate heresy-hunting, his establishment of the Index of Forbidden Books and his enclosure of the Jewish ghetto. *'Accidenti, che vino forte che c'è in questa carafa!'* ('My, what strong wine there is in this carafe!'), said Pasquino. Marforio, his interlocutor, replied, *'Ti sbagli; è aceto'* ('You're mistaken; it's vinegar'). His reign was one of fanatical orthodoxy, mingled with a disastrous foreign policy of opposing the Spanish who ruled the kingdom of Naples to the south. In 1557 Rome was in serious danger of a second sacking by the troops of Philip II of Spain. Paul's puritanical attitude extended in all directions but one: he was intensely indulgent to his two nephews. When he finally discovered their ransacking of the papal treasury and numerous other crimes, he repudiated them and stripped them of their wealth, but the public shame of his apparent hypocrisy contributed to his death. Paul was buried in the Carafa family chapel in Santa Maria sopra Minerva, in the south transept, which had been decorated by the Florentine artist Filippino Lippi (c.1457–1504) at the behest of Paul's relative and mentor Cardinal Oliviero Carafa (1430–1511). His tomb, smashed into a wall, destroyed part of the decorative cycle, and the portrait of the wild-eyed and terrifying pontiff evokes in the viewer a sense of relief that there is, after all, an end to even the worst career.

Paul's successor, **Pius IV de' Medici** of Milan (1559–65), no relation to the Florentine Medici but bearing the same coat of arms, was an enthusiastic urban redesigner whose principal gift to Rome was the *strada Pia*, now via XX Settembre. His nephew Marcus Sittich Hohenemps established himself as a Roman prince under the name of Marco Sittico Altemps and his family palace, formerly that of Girolamo Riario, is now one of the seats of the Museo Nazionale Romano. Pius IV and the next pope, **Pius V Ghislieri** (1566–72), were both devoted to instituting the reforms of the Council of Trent, in response to the Protestant Reformation; Pius V saw the turning back of the Ottoman Turks in the sea battle of Lepanto in 1571. **Gregory XIII Boncompagni** (1572–85) was a vigorous champion of Catholic orthodoxy who founded religious colleges under Jesuit supervision, among them the Collegio Romano and the English College, whose graduates were intended to reconvert Protestant Europe. The family of Gregory XIII, the Boncompagni, intermarried with a later papal family, the Ludovisi, and even now play a leading role in Roman high society; their collections of antique sculpture are the property of the nation, housed in palazzo Altemps.

The most important of the later sixteenth-century popes for the city of Rome was **Sixtus V Peretti** (1585–90), whose brief pontificate saw the conclusion of many of the earlier papal urban schemes as well as new initiatives. Like his namesake Sixtus IV, Peretti was from a humble family and rose through the Franciscan order to the cardinalate and then the papal throne. An enemy of his predecessor, Gregory XIII, he hid himself away in the Vatican Library during Gregory's pontificate and emerged into the conclave, wheezing and leaning heavily on a stick, clearly not long for this world. This made him a favourite candidate among the other cardinals, since a brief pontificate would give them a chance to consolidate their position and perhaps be the next man elected. However, once enthroned, Sixtus tossed away his cane and only took it up again, so the story goes, in order to belabour his opponents about the head. He was quite merciless: on the day after his coronation, he was asked to give the traditional pardon for all prisoners in his jails, but he replied, 'While I live, every criminal must die'. And die they did, in droves. The heads of executed criminals were displayed on the Castel Sant'Angelo bridge, where they were said to be 'more numerous than melons in the market'.

Sixtus was a fascinating character: autocratic and irascible like Julius II, he also resembled the second della Rovere pope in the ambitions of his urban schemes. These included the construction of a new aqueduct, the Acqua Felice, which permitted development of the previously waterless hills of Rome for the first time since antiquity, and a great new street, the *strada Felice*, named, like the aqueduct, after the pope's birth name, which stretches from the church of the Trinità dei Monti (at the top of what are now the Spanish Steps) all the way to the great basilica of Santa Croce in Gerusalemme. On its

The many accomplishments of Sixtus V's five-year reign are celebrated in this contemporary engraving. Clockwise from top left: the Sistine Chapel in Santa Maria Maggiore; an armorial bearing; the library wing in the Vatican Palace; another armorial bearing; the new fleet; the benediction loggia at San Giovanni in Laterano; the obelisk in front of that loggia; the restoration of the Column of Marcus Aurelius; the obelisk behind Santa Maria Maggiore; the fountain of the Acqua Felice near Termini; new streets; the Scala Santa and the new Lateran palace; the church of San Girolamo dei Croati; the obelisk of St Peter's; the restoration of Trajan's Column; the ceremonial burial of Pius V; and the hospice next to the ponte Sisto.

way it crosses the *strada Pia* at a spot where Sixtus caused four fountains to be built on each corner of the intersection, the *Quattro Fontane*. Sixtus also carried out a plan of Nicholas V, from the previous century, of placing obelisks at various key locations as markers for pilgrims making their way around the basilicas of Rome. These obelisks had been looted from Egypt by different Roman emperors and in Sixtus's time lay buried or half buried around the city (two in the Circus Maximus alone), until Sixtus sent his architect Domenico Fontana (1543–1607) to dig them up and re-erect them, in piazza del Popolo, at the Lateran, in front of the new papal summer palace on the Quirinal, and, most famously, in piazza San Pietro. The stamp which Sixtus put on Rome with his new roads, his obelisks and his fountains made the city reflect his personality more than any previous pope's.

Throughout the later sixteenth century, the phenomenon of the *cardinal nipote* (the cardinal nephew), who took on the role of prime minister, continued to be elaborated. The successful example of Cardinal Alessandro Farnese, the Gran Cardinale, provided an instructive role model. The most glamorous of these cardinal nephews was Alessandro Damasceni Peretti, called Cardinal Montalto (1571–1623), Sixtus V's nephew, whose wealth rivalled that of Cardinal Farnese; it was Cardinal Peretti who constructed the vast church of Sant' Andrea della Valle, not far from the Gesù, and the extensive Villa Montalto-Peretti, which stood on the site of today's Termini train station.

The final pope of the century, **Clement VIII Aldobrandini** (1592–1605), has already made his appearance in the stories of the Cenci, Santacroce and Farnese. He was of a mercantile Florentine family whose pro-French political sympathies placed them in the camp of the Farnese; upon his election he set about enriching his family in the standard way, showering titles and properties in the Papal States on his *cardinal nipote*, the ambitious Pietro Aldobrandini. Pietro commissioned the construction of a huge family villa in the Alban Hills at Frascati and was a great collector of art, part of which he kept at his villa on the Quirinal hill, the Villa Aldobrandini. Today a public park, the villa has lost its seventeenth-century appearance. The Aldobrandini family will play a central role in the history of the Borghese and the Pamphilj.

Noble Roman families during this period were undergoing a great expansion in their displays of wealth and taste. The late sixteenth century was responsible for many new palaces, churches and chapels, in the densely inhabited urban core around the Pantheon and the Campo de' Fiori, and new villas in the stretches of lightly populated hilly space within and just outside the walls, to which Sixtus V's new aqueduct provided fountain water. The stage was set for the astonishing conspicuous consumption of the seventeenth century.

5 The Borghese

The Borghese family were of Sienese origin and relatively modest, though their traces are visible in Siena from around 1200 onwards. They were *borghesi* in truth, not feudal nobles like the Colonna or the Farnese but bourgeois bureaucratic nobles active in the civic administration of Siena. Their training was traditionally not military but legal and they held respectable positions in the Sienese signory, including diplomatic posts. The first significant member of the family, *Marcantonio I* (1504–74), was employed as the Sienese ambassador to the pope and spent most of his life in Rome. Marcantonio achieved the position of consistorial lawyer, one of the highest a lay person could reach in the papal administration and even served as one of Rome's chief civic officials, one of the two annually chosen conservators, in 1554. Six years previously he had married Flaminia Astalli, of the ancient noble Roman family whose property bordered on to the back of the Gesù. All these signals indicated the arrival of the Borghese within the aristocracy of the city. During Marcantonio's lifetime, Siena lost its independence after its conquest by Florence; in that struggle, the Borghese in Rome remained neutral and thus won the approval of the conqueror, Cosimo I de' Medici.

Marcantonio's sons were to carry the family to the heights. *Camillo Borghese* (1552–1621) and his younger brother *Orazio* (1553–90) both entered the church. Orazio bought the post of Auditor of the Camera, an important job dealing with papal finance, but died before he could recoup the cost of the post; the family fortunes, at a low ebb, depended on his older brother Camillo. The latter was a practised career cleric: papal legate to Spain, diplomat, vicar of Rome under Clement VIII and doctrinally orthodox. Camillo's skill at negotiating the complex politics of life at the papal court stood him in good stead when, during the deadlocked conclave of 1605, after the death of the twenty-six-day pope, Leo XI de' Medici, he appeared as a compromise candidate between the two great cardinals Alessandro Peretti and Pietro Aldobrandini, both former cardinal nephews and consequently both rich and powerful. 'He who enters the conclave a pope', says an old Roman proverb, 'leaves it a cardinal'; that is, the expected candidate is rarely elected. In this case no one was more surprised than

Camillo Borghese that he had slipped through the crack between the two dominant factions.

POPE PAUL V (1605–21)

Let the irrepressible Pasquino have the first word.

> *Dopo i Carafa, i Medici, i Farnese*
> *Or si deve arrichir i Borghese.*
> (After Carafa, Medici, Farnese
> Now we must enrich Borghese.)

This prediction, inevitably, proved accurate. Camillo took the name of Paul V, perhaps to signal his determination to follow in the severely Counter-Reformation footsteps of the austere Paul IV Carafa. Like his predecessor, Paul V continued the programme of ensuring Catholic orthodoxy. He upheld the authority of the Roman court with unbending strictness, even to the extent of placing the state of Venice under an interdict, an excommunication, for new Venetian laws which placed restrictions on the power of the clergy over property. A long and ugly controversy broke out between the two Italian powers, which was only resolved by a faint face-saving agreement by Venice 'to conduct itself with its accustomed piety', without repealing its offensive laws; the republic's main advocate, Paolo Sarpi, was gravely wounded by the hands of Roman assassins (surely not sent by His Holiness!). The episode underlined the diplomatic eclipse of the papacy, a fact of which Paul V was doubtless aware.

PAVLVS V. C*am*manus creat. die 17. an.is. mens.8.dies nuarij an.1621.Vac illus Burghesius Ro Maij an.1605.Sedit 12. Obijt die 28 Ia: Sed.dies 12.

Paul V Borghese's ill-advised interdict against Venice backfired, diminishing papal prestige. Seventeenth-century popes could no longer use their spiritual authority as a lever with secular states.

This unwelcome truth was disguised by a massive programme of construction, restoration and reconstruction by both the pope and his cardinal nephew. Paul V's urban plans were in large part an elaboration of the schemes of Sixtus V: to Sixtus's aqueduct, the Acqua Felice, Paul made a partner in the Acqua Paola; to Sixtus's funerary chapel in Santa Maria Maggiore, Paul built a pendant for himself and his predecessor, the cappella Paolina. Paul's work to enlarge papal grandeur included not only his famous completion of the basilica of San Pietro but also the enlargement and decoration of the papal summer palace founded by Sixtus V on the Quirinal, now the residence of the President of the Italian Republic. He also was active in the creation of saints, canonising Carlo Borromeo and Francesca Ponziani (Santa Francesca Romana), and beatifying Ignatius Loyola, Francis Xavier, Filippo Neri, Teresa of Avila, Louis Bertrand, Tomas of Villanueva and Isidore of Madrid.

Paul was relatively restricted in his nepotism: the more distant branches of his family, and his relatives by marriage, received little or nothing, in contrast to previous pontificates in which Rome was overwhelmed by a tidal wave of obscure papal relatives. In the climate of Counter-Reformation Rome, and particularly with the scandal of Paul IV's nephews still in mind, Paul V focused his patronage of family members on the children of his siblings: in the secular world, the pope's nephew, *Marcantonio II* (1601–58), was the main recipient of the pope's largesse; he was granted the title of prince of Sulmona. In one of his first consistories with the College of Cardinals, Paul gave the red hat to his nephew, *Scipione Caffarelli Borghese*, son of his sister Ortensia. Scipione was twenty-six years old when he achieved this eminence and embarked on his career as patron and collector of art.

SCIPIONE BORGHESE (1579–1633)

The son of a family alliance between the Borghese and the Caffarelli, an old noble family whose palace on the via Papalis had been designed by Raphael, Scipione Borghese was raised in an environment of great culture. His arrival at the centre of the papal power network brought Rome one of its most cultivated, if unscrupulous, patrons of art. For his patronage, his jovial nature and the splendour of his court, he was known as the '*Delizia di Roma*' (Delight of Rome). He was quickly given a large number of lucrative church offices, as well as being made abbot *in commendam* (without the responsibility of residency) of several rich monasteries both inside and outside the city; a veritable Croesus of the church, his annual income was about 200,000 ducats. In direct competition with the previous arbiter of papal taste, Clement VIII's nephew Cardinal Pietro Aldobrandini, he gathered a stellar collection of art, both of contemporary artists and of ancient sculpture, which he kept first in his palace in the Borgo, today's palazzo Giraud Torlonia, and then in a specially designed villa-palace outside the city walls by the porta Pinciana, the Villa Borghese. He also commissioned work on two other palaces for himself and his family: one was a series of garden pavilions in the grounds of today's palazzo Pallavicini Rospigliosi, next to the papal palace on the Quirinal, and the other was palazzo Borghese in Campo Marzio, built with a façade along Paul III's great *via Trinitatis*, an axis known today as via Condotti and via della Fontanella di Borghese.

No great diplomat, in his work for his uncle, Scipione did little that was either dramatically brilliant or especially foolish: however, as Paul V's reign drew to its end, Scipione concentrated on works that would put him in a favourable light with the Romans. The cardinal was aware of the resentment that the populace generally felt towards a cardinal nephew, particularly one who had fattened himself for two decades on the profits of the church; and though he indisputably had a religious side to his nature, policy as well as piety led him to sponsor a large number of ecclesiastical building projects, including the reconstruction or redecoration of such prominent old churches as San Gregorio al Celio, San Crisogono in Trastevere and San Sebastiano fuori le Mura, as well as the new church of Santa Maria della Vittoria.

It was, however, as a patron of art that Cardinal Scipione won his fame. He was one of the first patrons of the young Gianlorenzo Bernini (1598–1680), a startlingly precocious artist who dominated the Roman artistic scene until the end of his life, placing his stamp on the city more than any other single person, whether artist, architect, or pope. Scipione was Bernini's principal patron for the first part of his career, which was marked by a number of large free-standing statues of extraordinary virtuosity, on mythological themes, now conserved in the cardinal's suburban retreat, the Villa Borghese. However, Scipione's interests ranged widely. He was a tireless and discerning collector of ancient sculpture, most of which now forms the nucleus of the state collection of the Louvre in Paris, and he also collected paintings, both of his contemporaries and of their sixteenth-century predecessors. His preference for bright colouristic effects led him to commission or buy work from painters inspired by the Bolognese school of Carracci: among the most prominent of this soon to be dominant Baroque style were Domenichino, Guercino (1591–1666) and Guido Reni (1575–1642). The cardinal was also an avid collector of paintings by Caravaggio, who worked in a radically different idiom of dramatic light and shade mixed with intense naturalism. To obtain his art collection, Scipione Borghese was prepared to use the full power of his position and that extended to confiscation and even theft, as we shall see.

After his uncle's death in 1621, the powerful cardinal more or less retired from public life. The pope who succeeded Paul V, Gregory XV Ludovisi (1621–3), was an opponent of Scipione's, though he himself had been raised to the cardinalate by Paul V; to sweeten the temper of the pope and of his cardinal nephew Ludovico Ludovisi, Cardinal Scipione commissioned a *Pluto abducting Proserpina* from Bernini and gave it to Ludovico. The Borghese cardinal could have returned to power with the accession of Urban VIII Barberini (1623–44), his great friend, but he preferred to remain in relative retirement, enjoying the wealth of his benefices and continually enriching his palaces and collections with new treasures.

THE BORGHESE SUCCESSION

When he died in 1633, Scipione left 3.5 million ducats to his cousin Marcantonio II, a quarter of which was in art and property. Marcantonio's fortune, estimated at 6 million ducats, made him not only the richest man in Rome but one of the richest in all Italy; the future of the Borghese family at the summit of the Roman aristocracy was secure. Most of this money was invested in trustworthy landholdings, which the Borghese prince purchased from the more established families, principally the Savelli, the Conti, the Orsini and the Colonna, who underwent a serious economic crisis in the seventeenth century. Thus many of the lands surrounding Rome left the possession of the old fractious medieval barons and entered the more compliant hands of new papal families, who took care not to oppose papal sovereignty.

A direct line of succession – father, son, grandson, great-grandson and so on, for many generations – made the Borghese family an enduring feature of Roman aristocratic society but, like all new nobles, they were concerned to ally themselves by marriage with the older families: thus Paul V more or less forced Marcantonio II Borghese to wed Camilla Orsini, both bride and groom being opposed to the union and the bride herself strongly inclined towards the convent. This unhappy union resulted, late in life, in a son, *Paolo Borghese* (1624–46), who wed the exceedingly rich heiress Olimpia Aldobrandini, the last of the family of Clement VIII. Paolo sired a son before dying at the age of twenty-two; Olimpia remarried. Paolo's great-grandson *Marcantonio IV* (1730–1800) allied himself with the French, whose revolution in 1789 sent shock waves through Europe and finally resulted in the Napoleonic empire, which spread to Italy in the last years of the eighteenth century. Marcantonio's two sons, *Camillo* (1775–1832) and *Francesco* (1776–1839), were even more intimately linked with the revolutionary movement, in stark contrast to most of the rest of their class, which remained conservative supporters of the pope.

VENERE VINCITRICE

All' Illustre Mylord Cawdor che ad esempio della presente Statua incoraggi l'Autore alla Scultura di una Ninfa giacente in diversa attitudine

Antonio Canova

Napoleon's sister was depicted by the sculptor Canova as Victorious Venus, but the Apple of Discord she holds in the statue was all too effective in real life.

PAOLINA BORGHESE (1780–1825)

Camillo became a member of Napoleon's family itself, through marriage to the emperor's sister Pauline, in Italian Paolina, in 1803. The relationship between husband and wife was initially passionate and Paolina commissioned a portrait of herself as Venus from the leading sculptor of the time, Antonio Canova (1757–1822), as a private gift for her husband. However, the marriage turned sour. She made a name for herself with her eccentricities, which included using her ladies-in-waiting as footstools and being carried to her bath by her colossal African footman; she soon took a series of lovers, and she and Camillo led separate lives. Paolina asked Napoleon to give her husband the governorship of Piedmont: 'Camillo is an imbecile, no one knows that better than I do. But what does that matter, when we're talking about governing a territory?' Napoleon soon gave Camillo the desired appointment, and while governor of the region the Prince Borghese was responsible for tending to Napoleon's prisoner, the pope, Pius VII Chiaramonte (1800–23), a particularly unbecoming task for a scion of a Roman papal house.

Napoleon constrained Camillo to sell a large portion of the Borghese family collection, 344 pieces, to the French state. Most of these were works of ancient sculpture, which Camillo replaced with other pieces excavated from Borghese family properties around Rome, so that even after the Napoleonic depredations the collection was still considered one of the world's finest. Like his father before him, he took an interest in the family villa at porta Pinciana and gave it a new monumental entrance gate outside the porta del Popolo; he also rearranged the family collection of art in the palazzina or main villa building.

The writer H. V. Morton recounts the devotion that existed between imperial brother and Borghese sister:

> After the battle of Wagram a special messenger was sent by Napoleon to Pauline to tell her he was safe. When the courier returned, Napoleon asked him: 'Did she give you a present?'
>
> 'No, sire.'
>
> 'I thought she wouldn't, the stingy little beast!' was Napoleon's brotherly comment. Yet when he was in need the 'stingy little beast' gave him all her jewels. She went to live with him on Elba, and when his travelling coach was captured at Waterloo her diamonds were discovered in a secret drawer. One wonders what became of them.

Paolina lived contentedly without Camillo during the period of the French Empire, but after her brother's fall from power she was an embarrassment to her husband and he moved to Florence to keep his distance from her. With the title of Duchess of Guastalla, Paolina passed, as one author has said, from one spa to the next, from *malades imaginaires* to real illnesses, from one lover's arms to those of another. In the last years of her life she lived quietly in Rome, visiting her mother Letizia who lived in a palace on piazza Venezia, and occupying a villa just inside the city walls, the Villa Paolina, which she had decorated in her favourite Egyptian style. At the end of her life a crisis either spiritual or financial caused her to try for a reconciliation with her estranged husband, yet another embarrassment to him, as by that time he had been contentedly living with a mistress in Florence for a decade. However, with the help of the pope she prevailed and Camillo received her once again, whereupon she died, probably of cancer, three months later. Though Camillo mended his fences with the pope so skilfully that none of the Borghese properties was sequestered as punishment for his allegiance to Napoleon, he still spent the latter years of his life engaged in secret and futile Bonapartist plots until his death in 1832.

THE LATER BORGHESE

Meanwhile, Camillo's younger brother Francesco, who inherited the right to assume the surname Aldobrandini after the extinction of that family, became a general in the French army and fought bravely at Wagram and Austerlitz, finally marrying into the French noble family of the La Rochefoucauld. Camillo and Paolina had no children, and in 1832 Francesco inherited the family wealth and titles, giving up his Aldobrandini surname, which he bestowed upon his second son. Francesco's first-born son, *Marcantonio* (1814–86), married an Englishwoman, Gwendolen Talbot, daughter of the Earl of Shrewsbury, but the twenty-two-year-old princess came to a tragic end, dying along with her two infant children in 1840. The Borghese fortune continued with strength throughout the nineteenth century, but in 1891, when the Bank of Italy crashed, much Borghese wealth was lost and *Paolo Borghese* (1844–1920) was constrained to sell his family villa and its park to the state, along with the collection of art that had made it famous for centuries. Though Paolo's son *Scipione* (1871–1927) had some success in recouping the family wealth, the power of the Borghese family had by the period of fascism faded into near insignificance. *Junio Valerio Borghese* (1906–74) was implicated in a failed right-wing putsch in December 1970, the infamous *golpe Borghese*. Today the family retains its prominence among the high society of Rome and still occupies at least one apartment in its colossal Baroque palace in the Campo Marzio as well as properties outside the city, principally the castle at Artena to the east of Rome.

BORGHESE ITINERARY

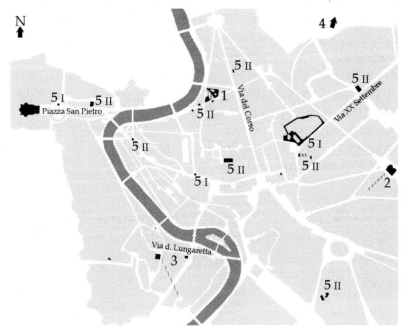

In general, the Borghese expressed in their patronage the glory of the papacy, the exaltation of specific saints canonised by Paul V, and their own wealth and taste. They made up for their lack of pedigree by never mentioning it: not until two centuries of wealth had placed them beyond reproach did they claim the *fainéant* grandeur of an imaginary genealogy. Instead, piety and culture received equal emphasis in the early days of the family's power.

The Borghese emblems of eagle and dragon dominate Rome like few others. Paul V was a monumental builder and was greatly concerned with the pomp of the papal monarchy. As head of the Borghese dynasty, he built up his family palace in the Campo Marzio, carved out a piazza which was surrounded by buildings belonging to his family and scrupulously preserved it as a semi-private family precinct.

Rome in the early seventeenth century was still composed of a nucleus of inhabited land within the Tiber bend, surrounded by a band of undeveloped, or underdeveloped, properties including *vigne* (vineyards), farms, cottages and noble villas. Following the example of his predecessor Clement VIII, Paul V sought to make these outlying areas, newly habitable due to these new roads and Sixtus V's new aqueduct, into thriving residential and mercantile districts. His first area of interest was the node of Santa Maria Maggiore itself, where he built a colossal and sumptuous funerary chapel, and its environs. At the same time the pope wanted to redevelop the depressed district of Trastevere on the other side of the river, a rough part of town where sailors and other transients lived. In both these marginal areas Paul V sponsored the construction of new streets and in Trastevere the pope was aided by his nephew Scipione, whose titular church of San Crisogono was the recipient of a new façade.

Cardinal Scipione's greatest legacy was the villa that, in emulation of Sixtus V's Villa Peretti and the previous papal nephew's Villa Aldobrandini, he caused to be built outside the Pincian gate of the ancient city walls, the porta Pinciana. The cardinal also sponsored the building or renovation of several other church complexes, with the result that the proud name of SCIPIO CARD BURGHESIUS can be seen as often as that of his uncle.

▍ Palazzo Borghese and its neighbourhood

Largo della Fontanella Borghese 19. Closed to the public, but the courtyard is sometimes visible

The colossal palazzo Borghese so strongly expresses the will of its most important builder, Paul V, that it seems hard to believe it is the combination of a number of pre-existing buildings. It is famed as the *cembalo di Roma* (harpsichord of Rome), due to its odd shape, with its 'keyboard' on via di Ripetta, facing the Tiber and spreading out in a grand-piano-like triangle of ground, cut off by the largo Fontanella Borghese at the front. In fact, the site was predetermined by a series of prior papal street systems: the early sixteenth-century via di Ripetta, which ran from piazza del Popolo to palazzo Madama, was the riverside boundary, while the slightly later (1523)

PALAZZO DELL ECC.^o SIG.^r PRENCIPE BORGHESE.
Architettura di Martino Longhi il vecchio.
1.*Facciata principale verso la Piazza* 2 . *Altra Facciata verso la strada de Condoti* 3.*Logoni verso Ripetta.* 4.*Palazzo della Famiglia di sua Ecc.^{za}*

An eighteenth-century engraving showing piazza Borghese as a private forecourt, surrounded by family buildings and closed off with chains: this extravagant space declared the family's wealth and power.

grid of streets around piazza di Monte d'Oro, laid out in alignment with the nearby church of San Giacomo degli Schiavoni (dei Croati), determined the northern and western edges. Paul III's *via Trinitatis* formed its southern edge, and the eastern side was governed by the trace of a medieval lane, now vanished, that snaked towards the river. So the site itself was partially the product of the random medieval street system and partially that of the determined scheme of popes and property speculators in the early sixteenth century: as such it expresses in a nutshell the conditions of urban design in Rome at the beginning of the seventeenth century.

The first nucleus of the palace was a cardinal's residence, as with palazzo Farnese. Cardinal Giovanni Poggio sold his house or palace to another papal official. In the second half of the sixteenth century, this man, Monsignor Tommaso del Giglio, hired the Farnese architect Jacopo Barozzi da Vignola to rebuild it, before selling it to Pedro Dezza, a Spanish cardinal. Dezza commissioned Martino Longhi the Elder (d. 1591), the first in a family of Lombard architects that was to make a strong impression on Rome, to enlarge it. No sooner had this work begun, however, than the building was acquired by that industrious and politic member of the papal court, the first Camillo Borghese, recently made a cardinal. Camillo immediately ceded the building to his lay brothers, making sure that it could not be expropriated by the papal Camera (treasury) after his death.

Though the lay branch of the Borghese family nominally took over the responsibility for the palazzo, there can be no doubt that Paul V himself had a hand in commissioning the architect Flaminio Ponzio (1560–1613) to make it a spectacular expression of papal and familial power. Ponzio was the first of a series of Borghese-sponsored architects to rise to prominence; after his career was cut short by his premature death, other architects finished the palace, which was substantially complete by 1623. The earliest part, the old palazzo del Giglio, faced largo Fontanella Borghese; in 1608 another building was added along its eastern side and the task of unifying the appearance of the two fell to Ponzio, who made the first bend in the façade looking on to what was to become piazza Borghese, but which was at the time still simply a medieval lane. Finally, when the loggia facing the Tiber was built (1612–14), the second bend was created, forming the distinctive 'harpsichord' shape.

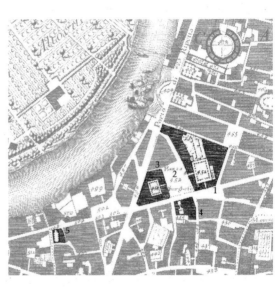

Palazzo Borghese
and its neighbourhood

Key:
1 palazzo Borghese
2 piazza Borghese
3 palazzo della 'famiglia'
4 palazzo Borghese-Caetani
5 Santa Lucia della Tinta

The Borghese stamp had only begun to be put on the area. Having started with the palace, Paul V continued with grander plans. In 1609–10 he purchased a block of houses on the other side of the alley and demolished them to create today's piazza Borghese. The Borghese family had the right to close the piazza with chains and to forbid neighbours from creating windows opening on to it: the new space was not exactly public, but a sort of royal forecourt for Borghese family retainers and petitioners to gather in. This new piazza was meant not only as a public display of family wealth and power, but also as a point on a new processional route planned to link the papal summer palace at the Quirinal to the Vatican. This was a more ambitious, but similar, plan to that of Paul III Farnese to dominate a papal procession route. Paul V also planned to cut a new road from the largo Fontanella Borghese diagonally south-east to join the Corso at the via Frattina, allowing for another distant viewpoint of the family palace from a major street. This plan, however, was never executed. All the money spent on these projects left the palace itself uncompleted, and its side façade on via Monte d'Oro has the by now familiar jagged teeth of masonry rising above a smaller building adjoining it.

The pope was also careful to protect the piazza from other aspirants to visual domination: records exist of plans from 1609–10 by the Medici Grand Duke of Tuscany to enlarge his palace, palazzo Firenze, so it would have a façade on piazza Borghese. The pope quickly bought up the intervening property and built a wall there (now long vanished) to block the view and the Medici plans came to nothing. The buildings surrounding the piazza Borghese on three of its four sides also originally belonged to the family: across the piazza from the curved side of palazzo Borghese is the former **palazzo dei famigliari**, where the family retainers lived, and another palace on the south side still displays the dragon and eagle on ornamental door knockers.

The **palazzo Borghese** itself is still in part a Borghese family possession and the prince maintains an apartment there, but mostly it is given to other tenants. These include the Spanish ambassador, whose residence occupies half of the *piano nobile* and whose presence explains the permanent police guard; the other half of the main floor is an exclusive private club, the Circolo della Caccia or Hunt Club, which once barred Prince Charles from membership on the grounds that his ancestry was not quite noble enough. The ceilings of the main rooms (closed to the public) were frescoed by a series of Baroque artists, notably Ciro Ferri (1634–89) and Gaspard Dughet. The **summer apartments** on the ground floor, accessible from the *tastiera* (keyboard) façade on the via di Ripetta, can sometimes be visited: the flaking but sumptuous decoration of the rooms remains impressive.

The **courtyard**, visible through the Fontanella Borghese entrance, is a vast and sumptuous space surrounded on all four sides by a double loggia of paired columns supporting arches, with two colossal statues facing the entrance and a third on the right-hand side. The upper-floor loggia has been enclosed in glass on three sides, but the fourth is open on both sides, for behind the rectangular courtyard is a huge triangular **garden**, whose main decorative feature is a monumental set of three late seventeenth-century fountains, by Carlo Rainaldi and Johann Paul Schor, who also worked for the Colonna. The fountains depict three goddesses, Flora, Venus and Diana, but the whole ensemble is generally referred to as the *Bagno di Venere* (Bath of Venus). The courtyard and garden are occasionally open for concerts and on other special occasions, but in general palazzo Borghese maintains its privacy.

2 The Cappella Paolina in Santa Maria Maggiore and the settlement of the Suburra

Entrance to the basilica from piazza Santa Maria Maggiore. Open 9–19, no midday closure

We have already visited Santa Maria Maggiore in conjunction with the Colonna and their sponsorship of the magnificent mosaics of the apse and medieval façade. However, the basilica is no longer entirely medieval. Under Sixtus V it was the focus of a great deal of interest, not only as the site of the pope's funerary chapel but also as a centrepiece for the urban design of the surrounding streets: Sixtus's great new avenue, the *strada Felice*, leads directly to the apse of the basilica all the way from the church of the Trinità dei Monti at the top of the Spanish Steps (which had yet to be constructed), and his via Panisperna leads here from near Trajan's Column. The dome of the Cappella Sistina was also the focus for his street joining Santa Maria Maggiore with the Lateran, the via Merulana.

These plans, vast though they were, served only as a prelude for the work of Paul V in the basilica and the surrounding region. In the piazza in front of the entrance, the most prominent feature is the colossal column which supports a statue of the Virgin: this was a column from the basilica of Maxentius in the Forum, one of the two that had survived the building's collapse in a ninth-century earthquake. The column of piazza Santa Maria Maggiore rises here to celebrate the Catholic devotion to the Virgin. Its dedicatory inscription commemorates the Borghese pope, as do many of the inscriptions on the outside of the basilica; this one refers to the pope removing the column from what was thought at the time to be the temple of Peace, built by Vespasian to commemorate his crushing of the Jewish revolt, and this error is recorded in the inscription. One also notes that the pope's name is in larger script than even the Virgin's. The fountain at the base of the column is proudly decorated with the Borghese emblems of eagle and dragon.

The whole area surrounding Santa Maria Maggiore was reworked by Paul V and his architect, Flaminio Ponzio, beginning with the church itself. Paul also had Ponzio construct a new administrative building attached to the right of the old church façade, which was mirrored in the following century by a matching palace on the left-hand side: the different dates are shown on the façades, the right-hand one commemorating Paul V in 1605.

Within the basilica, to the left-hand side of the nave is the **Cappella Paolina**, the Pauline Chapel, constructed in 1605–11 at the order of Paul V as his funerary chapel, aligned with the funerary chapel of Sixtus V across the nave. This is one of the richest and most splendid papal chapels in the city: the Cavalier d'Arpino (1568–1640) painted the pendentives of the dome and the lunette above the altar, while Guido Reni frescoed the side vaults and lunettes. The overall scheme of the chapel commemorates Paul V's bull of 1617 on the doctrine of the Immaculate Conception of the Virgin, insisting that no one should teach that Mary was conceived with original sin. The **dome** is frescoed with the *Assumption of the Immaculate Virgin* (1612) by Ludovico Cardi, called Il Cigoli (1559–1613), a Tuscan artist of some renown; the Virgin, rolling her eyes in modest delight, stands with the crescent moon under her feet and wears a crown of twelve stars, all part of the accepted depiction of Mary. This type of dome painting, with concentric circles of clouds opening up to a heavenly populace of saints, angels and cherubs, was popular throughout the seventeenth century. In Baroque church decoration the object was to give the worshipper a vision of the other world, and the ceilings seem to give way to infinite spaces of sky through which messengers of God soar and beckon; this is the intention in the Borghese chapel.

The rest of the decoration is a combination of fresco, relief work and free-standing sculpture. In the pendentives directly beneath the dome are four prophets; further down, the frescoes reflect the carrot-and-stick Catholicism of the early seventeenth century: those who praise the Virgin and her majesty are rewarded, while those who criticise her or deny her Immaculate Conception, are punished. In the latter category we will see, for example, the death of Leo IV, who destroyed Marian images, and the death of the Byzantine emperor Constantine IV, another iconoclast. The statues also represent figures linked with the Virgin, like St Joseph, her husband, and St John the Evangelist, to whom Jesus linked Mary when he was on the cross, saying 'Mother, this is your son', Mary's priestly ancestor Aaron, the adjutant of Moses, her royal ancestor King David, St Dionysus the Areopagite, present at the Virgin's death, and St Bernard, the composer of the 'Salve regina', her greatest hymn.

The **altar** is famed as one of Rome's richest, as it is covered with a number of semi-precious stones: the background for the sacred image of the Virgin is a veneer of lapis lazuli, while the columns on either side of the image are of Sicilian jasper. The icon itself is contained in a frame of gilded bronze, studded with agates and amethysts. Why pray at anything less? The image itself is subject to some controversy. It is an icon of Byzantine manufacture, but different authorities give it different dates: the faithful claim implausibly that it is a portrait painted by St Luke the Apostle, patron of artists, while more sceptical scholars date it variously as from the fifth, sixth, tenth, twelfth, or thirteenth centuries AD. The later attributions are more likely, but considering the number of times it has been restored and repainted, a specific date is hard to arrive at. The principal image of the Virgin in the church is called 'Santa Maria ad Nives' (St Mary at the Snow), a name which recalls the foundation myth of the church (for which see the Colonna itinerary), and also 'Salus Populi Romani' (the Salvation of the Roman People), for its purported intervention in 1527, that violent year, when the holy image quelled an outbreak of the plague. Whatever its miraculous powers, it is a lovely image, whose two figures have a weight and presence matched with great delicacy. Atop the lapis lazuli frame of the altar is a strange bas-relief that apparently depicts a pope playing hockey or golf, but in reality shows Pope Liberius drawing the outline of the basilica in the miraculous snow that the Virgin caused to fall in August.

The two **papal tombs** of Paul V and his patron Clement VIII Aldobrandini, both of which were designed by Ponzio and carved by a number of sculptors, follow the plan of the tombs of Pius V and Sixtus V in the chapel across the nave that we have already seen in connection with the Colonna. Paul V is shown kneeling in prayer to the sacred icon of the Virgin, and reliefs around the main figures show events in the lives of the popes. Eleanor Clark, in her book *Rome and a Villa* (1950), observed acidulously of the Borghese pope's portrait that 'the face is fat, piglike but authoritarian, shrewd, with a look of rabid highhandedness that seems to have been comically interrupted, at the moment of the portrait, by an effort to appear spiritual'. In the upper register are relief-work scenes from the pope's life, including the arrival of an ambassador wearing a turban. Paul V was very proud to have the papacy's status as a world authority confirmed by exotic embassies, so much so that he had the main reception hall in his summer palace, the Quirinale, frescoed with scenes depicting the same subject.

The other work of Paul V in Santa Maria Maggiore is the **baptistery**, also built by Flaminio Ponzio and decorated with a similar richness: its main altarpiece, by Pietro Bernini, Gianlorenzo's father, represents the *Assumption of the Virgin* and is considered to be his masterpiece; the ceiling is frescoed with the same subject by Domenico Cresti (1559–1638), called Il Passignano from his home town. The ceiling decorations and the stuccoes in the window embrasures still proudly display the Borghese emblems, as do the very door handles. Also of interest in the baptistery is the **tomb of the Congolese ambassador** in 1604, Antonio Ne Vunda, sent by King Alvaro II of the Congo to the papal court. His three-year journey was full of misadventures and, after presenting himself to Clement VIII, who died soon after, he fell into an irreversible decline and died in the early months of Paul V's reign. His portrait in polychrome marble presides over the room, installed there by Urban VIII; he also appears, as we will see, in a fresco in the Quirinal palace.

The **basilica museum**, in the basement (entrance through the baptistery and to the left through the bookshop; admission €4, open 10–18), contains a sumptuous reminder of the lavish court of Paul V, in the extraordinary vestments and cloth decorations made for the Borghese pope: his faldstool (the folding stool provided for him when he presided over ceremonies in the basilica), his cope and all his other vestments are on display, all in glittering cloth of gold covered with the dragon and eagle emblems. The private altarpiece (c.1650) from the sacristy of the Cappella Paolina is also there, as well as portraits of Paul V and Cardinal Scipione, not very good but vividly conveying the wilfulness and physical presence of the art-loving cardinal and his uncle.

Outside the basilica of Santa Maria Maggiore, Paul V's hand is evident in his restructuring of the street plan. His most significant new street in the area is the **via Paolina**, which is aligned on the altar wall of the Cappella Paolina, affixed to the exterior of which is a commemorative plaque announcing the devotion to the Virgin professed by Paul V, her 'humble servant'. A stroll through the neighbourhood shows a beautiful and functional residential and artisanal district, which is only now starting to be gentrified. Paul's main work was, once again, a supplement to that of his great predecessor Sixtus V: he created a new artery from a pre-existing street (today's via degli Zingari) by adding to it at both ends, linking it to the so-called Arca Noe or Arch of Nerva at one end, and at the other end to Sixtus V's via Panisperna.

3   The Borghese in Trastevere

Since the late fifteenth century the mercantile and seafaring district of Trastevere had been a focus for different urban schemes. The two della Rovere pontiffs, Sixtus IV and Julius II, were the most important redesigners, building the ponte Sisto and the streets called the Lungara and the Lungaretta, both using the district's central square, piazza Santa Maria in Trastevere, as an end point. The via della Lungaretta, cut through by Julius II, stretched from there to what is today called the ponte Rotto, the broken bridge, but which linked Trastevere to the other bank until 1598 when it was finally destroyed in a flood.

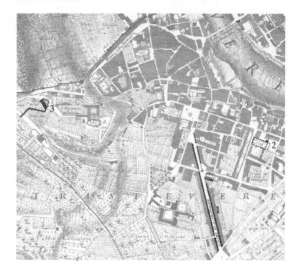

Borghese sites in Trastevere,
from the Nolli map of 1748

Key:
1 via di San Francesco a Ripa
2 San Crisogono
3 Fontanone of the Acqua Paola

Paul V recognised the need to make new thoroughfares in this flourishing area. Three large monastic communities, at San Cosimato, Santa Cecilia and San Francesco a Ripa, occupied huge blocks of land that seemed to prevent further development: one of the pope's main tasks was to extend the street network past these obstacles and towards the southern city gate on this side of the river, porta Portese. To achieve this he created two streets, roughly corresponding to via di Porta Portese and via Jacopa da Settesoli. These were linked to the extant street network through his main construction in the district, **via di San Francesco a Ripa**.

The two main streets here were now the via della Lungaretta and the via dei Vascellari, which met the Lungaretta in a V at the ponte Rotto and led to the nunnery of Santa Cecilia and the Franciscan church and monastery of San Francesco a Ripa. The Borghese pope transformed the V into a triangle with the construction of via di San Francesco a Ripa, which linked the church of St Francis with Santa Maria in Trastevere. The new street quickly became a major thoroughfare and the map of Rome made by G. B. Falda in 1676 shows three-storey houses along its length. Like the area around Santa Maria Maggiore, this district owes its existence to Paul V but does not bear much in the way of Borghese family monuments.

Closer towards Santa Maria in Trastevere and occupying a prominent position on the new (nineteenth century) main street, viale di Trastevere, the ancient **church of San Crisogono** was given new life and a new appearance by Cardinal Scipione Borghese. Its origins date back as far as the fifth century, but in the twelfth century the old basilica was levelled and filled in to form the foundations of a Romanesque construction. It was Cardinal Camillo Borghese's titular church: when he ascended the papal

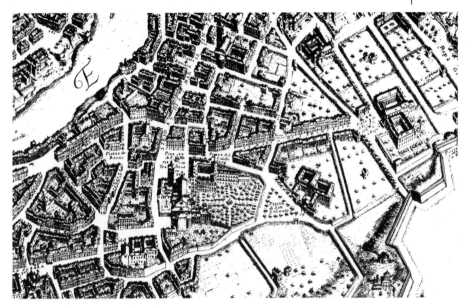

Paul V's new street, via di San Francesco a Ripa, from the Falda map, 1676. The street was responsible for extending the inhabited area of Trastevere toward the former country church of San Francesco.

throne as Paul V, he invested his nephew with it. In 1623, after the death of his uncle, Cardinal Scipione ordered the old twelfth-century basilica to be renovated, with a new façade and a rearrangement of the interior. The architect was another Borghese artist, the family cabinetmaker Giovanni Battista Soria (1581–1651). The façade is a restrained and beautifully classical work, with a simple portico of reused ancient columns supporting an inscription recording the name of Cardinal Scipione: as in the more grandiose façade of St Peter's, made by Paul V, the name 'BURGHESIUS' is in the very centre of the design.

Inside, the ceiling contains a copy of Guercino's *Glory of San Crisogono*; the original, having been stolen in 1808 and now in England, was a commission of the cardinal. Above the columns of the nave a frieze of dragons and eagles signals the Borghese presence, as do the heraldic mosaics inserted into the spectacular thirteenth-century Cosmatesque pavement in front of the high altar. The *baldacchino* (canopy) over the high altar was also designed and built by Soria, on four antique columns of alabaster which came from the interesting fifth-century church underneath.

The renewal of the entire zone was made possible by the one great Borghese monument of Trastevere, the **fontanone dell'Acqua Paola**. This is the grandiose display fountain of Paul V's new aqueduct, the Acqua Paola, which the pope resurrected from the ruins of Trajan's ancient *Aqua*

Alsietina. In 1608 the pope bought the rights to the ancient springs that had once fed the aqueduct of Trajan, more than thirty miles north of Rome, from the Orsini Duke of Bracciano and set his engineers to rebuilding the course of the aqueduct. The pope reserved a strip of land alongside the new aqueduct where, in accordance with the rules of the ancient engineer Frontinus, no trees were to be planted, as their roots would disturb the channel of the water. However, by 1616 Paul V found it necessary to impose a huge fine of 200 scudi on people whose plants were found to infringe on the sacrosanct area; this fine was raised fifty years later to 300 scudi and various tortures and consignment to the galleys. Paul and his successors were very serious about maintaining the water supply to Rome. In 1679, water from Lake Bracciano itself was channelled to join the aqueduct, though with a resulting decline in the quality of the water, and in 1829 the waters of Lake Martignano, a small volcanic crater lake next to Bracciano, were added as well. The water of the Acqua Paola was rather bitter and unpleasant, and is today not considered fit to drink. However, it is excellent fountain water and its fountains can be found throughout Trastevere, in piazza San Pietro and across the river (where the water is carried in a channel under the pavement of the ponte Sisto) in *rione* Regola, the most prominent being the fountains in piazza Farnese. Paul V was so famous as a fountain builder that he was nicknamed Fontifex Maximus.

The display fountain that announces the water's arrival in Rome is called simply the Fontanone, the Big Fountain. It stands in a prominent position not far inside the porta San Pancrazio, the city gate leading across the Janiculan hill to the via Aurelia. From there it is visible from many points in the city. In appearance it closely resembles the fountain of the Acqua Felice, on the other side of Rome not far from piazza della Repubblica in largo Santa Susanna. Both fountains are principally architectural rather than sculptural and both are based on an ancient Roman triumphal arch. Flaminio Ponzio was responsible for the design of the Fontanone, a free-standing structure with three large arches flanked by two smaller ones.

Work was concluded in 1612, as the inscription, a perfect imitation of ancient Roman monumental script, proudly states: 'Paul V, High Priest, gathered this water, taken from the purest springs of the fields around Bracciano, and brought it for 35 miles from its source over the ancient channel of the Aqua Alsietina, which he restored, and over new ones, which he added.' At the summit of the monument, below a simple cross, two large angels present the Borghese family crest. The two side fountains in the smaller arches are of water gushing from the mouths of two comically stunted-looking dragons, while more dragons and eagles adorn the upper corners of each level of the monument. The fountain had one final addition,

The Fontanone before the construction of the basin in 1690. The four central columns come from Old St Peter's.

in 1690, when Carlo Fontana (whom we have already met as the final architect of Santi Apostoli) added the large basin that we see today.

Behind the fountain is a little garden, rather neglected, which serves as a theatre in the summer. Inside the portico behind the great arches is a plaque which states how many *oncie* (a measure of water) were to be allowed to different bodies, from the distribution station behind the fountain: a significant amount was given for the use of the 'most illustrious House of Borghese'.

The last fountain of Paul V in Trastevere, the **fontana di piazza Trilussa**, was not originally meant for its present location. It was intended as the first fountain of the Acqua Paola on the other side of the Tiber. The fountain was originally set into the side of the Ospizio dei Mendicanti, built by Sixtus V to house poor beggars, and the splashing waters formed the end point of the long perspective down the straight via Giulia. Like its larger sibling on the hill above, the fountain is a triumphal arch, with the water entering from the upper part and trickling down from a basin set high up. Two Borghese dragons spurt water towards each other from the lower sides, providing accessible (if bitter) drinking water to passers-by. When the ospizio was demolished to build the Lungotevere, the fountain was taken apart and only after great public outcry was it rebuilt at the other end of the ponte Sisto in 1897.

4   The Villa Borghese and its collections

Of all the villas of Rome, none is more famous than the magnificent Villa Borghese. Its gardens have survived many vicissitudes, to emerge triumphantly in the twentieth century as Rome's public park par excellence. Indeed, it was always intended as a park for the benefit of the public, as Cardinal Borghese's former inscription inside the enceinte of the Parco dei Daini, the deer park, stated: 'I, the custodian of the Villa Borghese on the Pincian hill, publicly declare: whosoever you may be, so long as you are a free man, fear not the hindrance of regulations; go wherever you will, ask whatever you wish . . . In this golden century in which freedom from danger has made everything excellent, the owner refuses to impose strict rules on the guest who pauses here awhile, respectful of the place.' The park was expanded and redeveloped over time, its principal sponsors being Cardinal Scipione, the eighteenth-century Prince Marcantonio IV Borghese, and his son Prince Camillo in the early nineteenth century. The family sold the villa to the state in 1901 and it has been altered and adapted since then, with playgrounds, theatres and even a colossal underground car park and shopping centre now among its amenities.

| A VISIT TO THE VILLA BORGHESE PARK
Start: entrance gate on piazzale Flaminio. Never closed

The **monumental entrance** just outside the porta del Popolo, in the form of a pair of Greek propylaea, marks the westernmost point of the villa grounds. It was constructed by order of Prince Camillo Borghese in 1827 by the artist and amateur archaeologist Luigi Canina (1795–1856). Its inscription asserts that 'Prince Camillo Borghese remade his suburban villa in greater and larger form than before', alluding to Camillo's purchase of the ex-villa Giustiniani and other properties beside the porta del Popolo. Prior to the construction of this great entrance, whose width matches that of the main palazzina of the villa, the architect Giuseppe Valadier (1762–1839) had redesigned the piazza del Popolo and the Pincio park above it, so there is a consistency of style in this part of Rome, which became all the more providential when the Pincio was linked to the villa soon after the latter's acquisition as a public park. Just inside the entrance to the Villa Borghese a large artificial lake briefly provided visitors with an immediate vision of the relaxation and natural beauty of the park; this was done away with, however, within a few years, as it was thought to be malarial.

Proceeding along the gravel path beside viale Washington, we pass, on

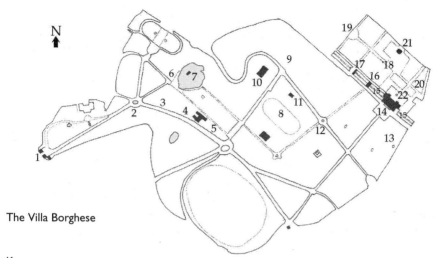

The Villa Borghese

Key:
1 monumental entrance
2 fountain of Aesculapius
3 Egyptian propylaea
4 Aranciera
5 Portico dei Leoni
6 Arch of Severus
7 lake and temple of Aesculapius
8 Piazza di Siena
9 tempio di Antonino e Faustina
10 Fortezzuola and Museo Canonica
11 casina dell'Orologio

12 Fontana dei cavalli marini
13 Grotta dei Vini
14 Palazzina, Galleria Borghese
15 giardini segreti
16 Uccelliera
17 Meridiana (information desk)
18 parco dei Daini
19 teatrino
20 statue of Dacian
21 Serbatoio
22 Italian garden

our left, a staircase leading to a fountain in a grotto, with a river god who seems to have had his head sawn off. A thin curtain of water falls across the mouth of the grotto from a little basin above; the river god and the grotto are both meant to recall one of the Baroque villa's most impressive fountains, that of the *Mascherone* (Great Mask), where a similar river god reclined behind a shower of water emanating from a fantastical mask emerging from raw stone. This now vanished fountain stood near the main building itself, but was eliminated during the eighteenth-century remodelling. Above the fountain, a governmental building, the Consiglio Nazionale dell'Economia e del Lavoro, occupies part of the old gardens of the Giustiniani family. The next fountain is more encouraging, Canina's **fountain of Aesculapius**, made in 1830–4 but harking back strongly to Marcantonio IV's eighteenth-century taste, with a basin of water spilling into a false-natural pool, featuring an ancient statue of the god of healing.

Here the street turns to the right and continues uphill, through Canina's **Egyptian propylaea** of 1827, in the Egyptomaniac style beloved of Paolina

Borghese. Further along is the **Aranciera** (Orangery), of late eighteenth-century origin though now much altered, as it houses the offices of the park authorities. Once the focus of the park's redesigns under Marcantonio IV in the late eighteenth century, it was almost completely destroyed when this part of Rome was bombarded by French cannons in 1849. A monument to Victor Hugo across the road dates from the early twentieth century, when the civic authorities decided to use the Villa Borghese to commemorate great foreigners, a practice which still fills corners of the park with generally ugly statues. Further along, is the **portico dei Leoni**, a neoclassical loggia of arches, with lions in front of the columns, carved by Canina. Also damaged in the French bombardments, which were part of the papal recapture of the city following the short-lived Roman Republic of 1848, the portico has recently regained its original prominence, though a wrought-iron gate prevents strollers from sitting in the shade.

Immediately following the portico is a street junction: the road leading to our right, viale delle Magnolie, crosses a bridge to the Pincio park, which overlooks northern Rome. We turn left and left again through a gate, to enter the **Giardino del Lago**. This, the jewel of the eighteenth-century redesign, was completed in about 1787. Under the supervision of the Scotsman Jacob More (*c.*1740–93), from Edinburgh, Marcantonio IV Borghese sought to recreate the park as a relaxed and natural *giardino inglese* after its century and a half of rigid formality as an Italian garden, doing away with the old box-hedge avenues and freeing nature from its ruthless subordination to human design. Following along the gravel path parallel to the wall to the left, we pass through a tall pine forest before reaching, on the left, the upper part of the Aranciera (now with public washrooms helpfully installed) and, on the right, a small coffee bar. Ahead is a false triumphal arch, the **Arch of Severus**, with an inscription on its far side that claims to celebrate that emperor's victories. We will not go so far as the arch, but continue past a grassy space containing the bizarre **fountain of the satyrs** or **fonte gaia** (1929), to the edge of the **lake**, a small ornamental sheet of water with a path going off to the left. If we look into the somewhat brackish depths, we may be rewarded by the sight of the Villa Borghese turtles, a whole gathering of which live in this lake. They sometimes sun themselves on the rocks at the water's edge, piled three or four turtles high for maximum exposure to the warmth, a sight that never fails to provoke the cynical Romans to lose their worldly edge for a moment.

Following the side of the lake, we find another gravel path stretching to the right. Before turning along it, we are rewarded with a view of the **temple of Aesculapius**. This temple, the work of Marcantonio IV's trusted architects Antonio and Mario Asprucci (1723–1808 and 1764–1804 respectively), dates to 1787 and is of simple classical form; it contains an ancient statue of the god of healing, though the figure has been much restored. Back along the wide gravel path in front of the temple, we walk through the rest of the Giardino del Lago and out through the gates on to viale Pietro Canonica. Before we turn left we see, in the distance, the pretty **tempio di Diana**, built by Antonio Asprucci in 1789, the year of the French Revolution, which was eventually to involve even the Borghese family: the interior of the temple has a dome decorated with delicate stucco emblems of the Zodiac, though there is no longer any statue to Diana.

Along viale Canonica, with the fence round the Giardino del Lago to our left-hand side, we soon reach the large oval open space of **piazza di Siena**, a name which recalls the home town of the Borghese family and the Sienese annual horserace, the Palio, for the piazza di Siena was constructed for outdoor exercise, especially of the equestrian variety. Operas are now sometimes held here in the summer, as well as horse shows and various sporting events. At the end of the viale Canonica is a false ruin, the **tempio di Antonino e Faustina**, and on the left-hand side of the end of the street is a large, apparently medieval building, the **Fortezzuola** (little fortress), a seventeenth-century *gallinaro* (henhouse), used by Cardinal Scipione to breed his flocks of ostriches and peacocks; this was converted in the late 1790s into a fake medieval fortress. Inside is housed the surprisingly charming **Museo Canonica** (closed Mondays; open 9–18; admission €5), with works of sculpture by the sculptor Pietro Canonica (1869–1959): he was a society artist, and here you can see a few aristocratic faces. Upstairs, Canonica's **private apartment**, full of antique furniture, shows how well an artist (he was a senator of Italy by the end of his life) could live in a more civilised age.

At the tempio di Antonino e Faustina we turn right along viale dei Cavalli Marini, past the charming and recently restored **Casina dell'Orologio**, modified to its current appearance at the same time as piazza di Siena was built and destined as the new museum for the sculptures formerly scattered throughout the villa grounds, which now must be conserved indoors for reasons of security. This is not an inappropriate use of the building, however, as in Cardinal Scipione's day it was a sculpture gallery and Marcantonio IV converted it for use as a museum of statues excavated from the ancient town of Gabii; this museum had a life of only ten years before Napoleon carted almost all its contents to the Louvre. In front of us is the appealing **fontana dei Cavalli Marini**, the fountain of the seahorses, from 1791, in which the marine beasts rear up good-naturedly, laughing like dowagers at a comic opera. Continuing along the viale dei Cavalli Marini, we reach another junction, this time with a street called viale del Museo Borghese.

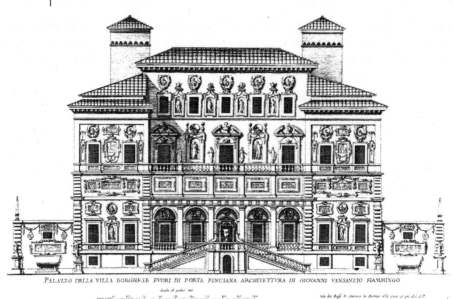

PALAZZO DELLA VILLA BORGHESE FVORI DI PORTA PINCIANA ARCHITETTVRA DI GIOVANNI VANSANZIO FIAMMINGO

The lavish relief work encrusting the façade of the palazzina of Villa Borghese was stripped off by Napoleon's men in 1807, with French soldiers keeping the outraged Romans at bay.

Now we are in the heart of the original nucleus of the villa, whose extent was much smaller during the lifetime of Cardinal Scipione. Turning left, we can see, through the trees of the Pineta, the villa building itself. Before we go to it, though, we will make a detour: a path to the right leads to a semi-buried round building consisting of a set of rusticated arcades. This is Cardinal Scipione's summer dining room, the **Grotta dei Vini** (Grotto of the Wines), linked to the main palazzina by a tunnel. It is much decayed from its Baroque glory and sits here neglected, behind a fence, waiting for princely diners who will now never arrive.

Returning to the viale del Museo Borghese, we pass through a gate made of two fountains of satyrs' faces spouting generous fans of water, and enter the piazza in front of the villa building itself, the **palazzina**.

Here Cardinal Scipione charged his family architect Flaminio Ponzio to construct the villa and planned a dramatic Italian garden with parterres and fountains, a stage set for the display of his pieces of classical statuary. After Ponzio's untimely death, the main building was completed by his assistant, the Flemish cabinetmaker Jan van Santen, known in Rome as Giovanni Vasanzio (1550–1621). Vasanzio's original trade was evident in the surface finish of the building, which was covered in classical reliefs that gave the appearance rather of a large veneered cabinet or desk. These reliefs have mostly been removed, either during the Napoleonic sale of Borghese treasures to the French state or subsequently, some perhaps even stolen after the villa became public property in 1901. The present statues are casts. To the right and left of the palazzina, extending in a long narrow line, are the **giardini segreti** (secret gardens), secret in the sense that they were separate from the rest of the park and accessible only from the palazzina itself, for which they formed a sort of outdoor series of rooms. Until the twentieth century they were enclosed with high stone walls; these were demolished when the park became public, at which point the gardens sank into a century-long decline before being revived in the year 2000. Now it is possible to take a free guided tour of the secret gardens (Saturdays, 11 a.m.), which have been restored to a semblance of their seventeenth-century appearance.

Turning left along the road in front of the museum, we can follow the edge of the secret gardens; in a moment we arrive at one of the most fantastical creations of the Borghese, the **Uccelliera** (Aviary), built by Vasanzio or, as is traditionally said (without documentary evidence), by Girolamo Rainaldi in 1617–19. Unlike Rainaldi's bird houses in the Orti Farnesiani, this Borghese bird house retains its extraordinary cage roof. Inside are traces of frescoes representing birds in flight: in the seventeenth century the Aviary was famous for its tumble of exotic birds. Further along, the secret gardens were extended in 1688 with the construction of the **Meridiana**, by Girolamo's son Carlo Rainaldi (1611–91), which prominently displays a sundial over its main arch. Past the Meridiana we turn right, with a large gate to our left that opens into a final garden in the series, this one originally for kitchen herbs and now a nursery for plants. We continue up through another gate into the **parco dei Daini**, the deer park, which during Cardinal Scipione's tenure was a densely forested preserve punctuated with paths and long monumental vistas. Only two of these remain, and the park now has a strangely tonsured quality, with a fringe of young trees surrounding a large expanse of gravel.

If we continue into the parco dei Daini we will come to a crossroads: to the left we can see the monumental **Teatrino**, a now rather denuded open-air theatrical structure also created by Rainaldi for Cardinal Scipione, and to the right, mirroring the position of the Teatrino, the great statue of the **Dacian**, a cast of an ancient fragment which probably once adorned the Forum of Trajan. Turning towards it, we can see an odd, tall building in the park to our left: this is the **Serbatoio** or water-tower built here in 1922–5 in neo-Baroque form to distribute water to the nearby neighbourhood of Parioli. Continuing on towards the Dacian, we turn left and soon approach the rear façade of the palazzina, entering the final area of the park, the **Italian garden**, with its carefully trimmed topiary and its central fountain, the **fontana di Venere**. The present statue is a cast, inserted when the garden was recreated in early 2000, a copy of the original which is soon to be displayed in the new Villa Borghese sculpture museum. However, the large herms which measure out the boundary of the parco dei Daini are original and are now thought to be partially by the hand of either Pietro Bernini or his more famous son Gianlorenzo.

Our path takes us round the far corner of the palazzina and back into the piazzale. The appearance of the main façade of this building has been very greatly changed, not only through the despoliation and subsequent replacement of some of the antique relief work, but also in the colour of the stucco itself. In the nineteenth century, according to the fashion of the time, the palazzina was painted an ochre colour, but in the restorations of the 1990s the villa building was returned to its original seventeenth-century marble white: the building was meant to be a white, classical vision that hovered over the green of the park, and its exterior no less than its interior was intended to be full of light. Prince Marcantonio IV also removed the original double staircase and replaced it with a pyramidal one; this was taken off in the restorations and a replica of the original one was recreated in its stead, even to the extent of recarving marble copies of the antique vase and cornucopiae that adorn it. The entrance to the museum is now through the new door at ground level set into the staircase.

II   THE BORGHESE GALLERY
      Open 9–19, closed Mondays. Admission €8.50, timed entrance every two hours; bookings 06 328 101

The palazzina of the Villa Borghese was never intended as a residence, but only as a retreat for the space of a day, before the cardinal or the prince would retire once again to the palazzo Borghese. The building has been through several decorative phases, but its current appearance reflects the taste of Marcantonio IV Borghese and his son Camillo. Cardinal Scipione decorated the interior walls with light colours, travertine door frames and fireplaces, and wall coverings of stamped leather in blue and gold; this must have been quite decrepit by the late 1700s, when Marcantonio IV commissioned Antonio and Mario Asprucci to redecorate the palazzina in lavish style, halfway between Baroque and neoclassical.

In the rooms on the ground floor, a new emphasis was given to the lineage of the Borghese family, something that the arriviste Cardinal Scipione never would have attempted, but which was possible after the family had spent almost two centuries at the pinnacle of Roman society. In this, the decoration of the palazzina strongly resembles that of the Galleria Colonna, which also trumpets the power and antiquity of the owner's family. The entrance hall's ceiling fresco, for instance, celebrates the ancient hero Marcus Furius Camillus and his battle with the Gauls, in tribute to the birth name of Paul V, Camillo Borghese, and to the family heir, Paolina Bonaparte's future husband Camillo. Through the name Camillo the family claimed a spurious ancestry in an ancient hero, de rigueur among Roman nobles; this presumed antiquity of lineage was celebrated in other frescoes on the ground floor ceilings, all of which have ancient themes derived from myths and poems. The upper floor retains, in the great room which is the first to be entered from the stairs, one of Cardinal Scipione's original decorations, a 1624 ceiling fresco by Lanfranco depicting the *Gods of Olympus*. Otherwise the vast majority of decoration work is eighteenth century.

The collection can be roughly divided into two parts: the Museo Borghese on the ground floor, consisting of ancient and later sculpture, mosaic and paintings, and the Galleria Borghese on the upper floor, which consists principally of paintings. The art historian Francis Haskell wrote that the Borghese collection can be characterised as 'cheerful chaos', there being no obvious thematic or stylistic thread. At base it reflects the discerning, omnivorous eye of Cardinal Scipione, with many additions and deletions. Perhaps the one clear desire of the cardinal's that remains visible today is that of amazing his guests with spectacular pieces.

THE MUSEO BORGHESE On the ground floor, some characteristic pieces stand out. To begin with, the great collection of statues by Gianlorenzo Bernini reflect the cardinal's patronage of the young sculptor. The Bernini pieces all date from the sculptor's youth, from his teens to his early thirties. Each has some remarkable illusionistic effect: the *David* in Room II shows the Old Testament hero in the very act of slinging a stone at the Philistine champion Goliath, and the expression of determination on his face is said to be a self-portrait, with Cardinal Maffeo Barberini, the future Pope Urban VIII, himself holding the mirror for the artist. In Room VI, the *Aeneas and Anchises* has a twisting motion to it that recalls Florentine sculpture, while the spectacular *Apollo and Daphne* in Room III is a virtuoso display of technical skill in which every leaf of the branches springing from Daphne's fingers is carved so thinly as to be translucent. There were certainly political and moral messages to these works: *Aeneas and Anchises*, with its young man supporting and protecting an old man, appears to be a reference to Cardinal Scipione's support of his uncle the pope – in Latin, *scipio* means a staff for leaning on and this subtlety was not likely to be lost on the educated visitor. The *Apollo and Daphne* has on its pedestal a moralising epigram written by Maffeo Barberini: 'whosoever, being fond of pursuing the joys of fugitive forms, reaches out to pick fruit, will instead reap sorrow'. The great

Bernini *Pluto abducting Proserpina*, the present for Cardinal Ludovico Ludovisi commissioned by the Borghese cardinal, only joined the collection early in the twentieth century. Bernini's *Truth unveiled by Time* was also a late acquisition, sold by the artist's heirs in the twentieth century, and its position in the Salone offers the visitor an opportunity to compare the unfinished statue with a painted example of the same metaphor on the ceiling.

In Room VIII are six of the original twelve paintings by Caravaggio that Cardinal Scipione possessed; the others were sold or have vanished. The austere *St Jerome* was a commission of the cardinal's, which is an interesting light on his spirituality, especially in comparison with a similar interest in hermit saints in Santa Maria dell'Orazione e Morte commissioned by Cardinal Odoardo Farnese, an older contemporary of Scipione's. Cardinal Scipione, as we will see, did not always acquire his paintings in a fair and open manner; it may be that his will lay behind the removal of Caravaggio's great altarpiece from St Peter's, now hanging in this room, the *Madonna dei Palafrenieri*, which had been up in the basilica for about a week before the Guild of Papal Litterbearers (Palafrenieri), who had commissioned it, rather mysteriously took it down and sold it to the cardinal. Scipione also bought the moody *St John the Baptist* and got his hands on two early Caravaggios, the *Boy with a Basket of Fruit* and the *Self-Portrait as Bacchus*, when he expropriated the entire art collection of the painter Giuseppe Cesari, the Cavalier d'Arpino, who had been thrown into prison by Paul V in 1607 on a pretext: his extensive art collection was confiscated by the cardinal. D'Arpino had not only a good selection of his own work, but many works from younger artists who had worked in his studio, among whom was Caravaggio. One of the latter's final paintings, the *David with the Head of Goliath*, may have entered the cardinal's collection directly from Caravaggio's personal effects after his death.

The Museo Borghese is also famous for its collection of antiquities. Among the best known are the mosaics found on the Borghese estate at Torrenuova, on the via Casilina outside Rome, in 1834, in a villa dating from AD 320–30. They were set into the floor of the salone soon afterwards. They depict scenes of hunting and a gladiatorial contest. Note particularly the figure of 'Licentiosus', the Lustful One, perhaps a favourite with the ladies. The other prominent antique work remaining after the Napoleonic depredations is the *Hermaphrodite* in Room V. In fact, this is a replacement for the original *Hermaphrodite*, which had been in Cardinal Scipione's collection (see below, section on Santa Maria della Vittoria), but which made its way to the Louvre along with much else from the Borghese collections in 1807. Fortunately the Borghese also owned this version, discovered in 1781 and dating from the second century AD. The strange figure of the hermaphrodite is a representation of an idea of Plato's, concerning the human condition before humans were split into different sexes. Its possession of both male and female sexual characteristics is, however, primly concealed, with the tell-tale side of the figure set facing the wall.

The final piece that vividly expresses the Borghese family patronage is the portrait of Paolina Borghese as Venus by Antonio Canova in Room I. Paolina commissioned it for her husband Camillo in 1806; she appears on a couch, nude to the waist, and holding in one of her dainty hands (the statue is life-sized) the Apple of Discord that was the prize in the celestial competition Venus won, declaring her the most beautiful of goddesses. Her face bears a remarkable resemblance to that of Napoleon. The statue has undergone some peregrinations, from Rome where it was carved to Camillo's home in Turin, then via Genoa back to the palazzo Borghese, finally arriving in the villa around 1838. When Paolina was asked whether she had not felt uncomfortable posing in a state of semi-undress, she famously replied, 'Of course not! The room was quite warm.' This is often used as evidence of her tendency to *épater les bourgeois* (or, in this case, shock the Borghese), but it was probably a double tease, since Canova almost certainly never saw this particular princess nude, instead working from preparatory sketches. The elegant Greek-style couch the statue reclines upon is made of wood and the platform underneath conceals an apparatus for turning the statue so it could be admired from all angles without the viewer moving.

THE GALLERIA BORGHESE In the Galleria upstairs, a few small works by Bernini, including a set of three paintings, further display the artist's skill. His small sculpture of *The Goat Amalthea*, who in Greek mythology suckled the infant Zeus, king of the gods, was already in Cardinal Scipione's collection by 1615, at which time Bernini was only seventeen. In this work, the artist's earliest known free-standing sculpture, Bernini's ability in achieving different painterly textured effects in stone is evident. Three other pieces of his are also famous: a miniature portrait bust of Paul V and two larger ones, nearly identical, of Cardinal Scipione. Of these, Eleanor Clark wrote:

There is a strong family resemblance between [Paul V] and his nephew, [. . .] of whom there are two busts by Bernini in the museum. This one seems a shade more genial but like his uncle has the kind of flesh a cannibal would not like; worldly bossy sensuous intemperate clever men the both of them, with no humility it appears, except that which gave them good judgement for the art that would perpetuate their glory.

The story goes that Bernini had no sooner finished one of the busts of the cardinal than he noticed a black streak flawing the marble across the portrait's forehead: he quickly made the copy that stands nearby, though more likely in three weeks than in the three days sometimes credited him.

For the rest of the gallery, whole volumes have been written. We will confine ourselves, briefly, to a look at Cardinal Scipione's tendencies as a collector: as we have already seen, he was ruthless. He put Domenichino in prison when he protested that a painting in his studio, *Diana at the Hunt* (Room XIX), had been commissioned by Cardinal Pietro Aldobrandini, the formerly all-powerful papal nephew of the previous reign. Scipione suggested the artist reconsider the sale and, after three days in jail, Domenichino was happy to offer the painting to the Borghese cardinal instead. The most shocking act of collecting, however, was his commission of the theft of Raphael's *Entombment of Christ* (now in Room IX) from the church of San Francesco in Perugia on the night of 19 March 1608. The painting, which had hung in the Baglioni chapel in that church for a century, was considered one of the jewels of the city. Its theft provoked a near rebellion against the pope and his nephew. The Perugians were finally placated with tax concessions, and d'Arpino, prudently obedient after the sequestration of his collection the year before, painted a copy of Raphael's masterpiece to take the place of the stolen original. Some of the remaining paintings here derive from d'Arpino's confiscated collection. A portrait of *Paul V* in the entrance vestibule is an interesting counterpoint to Bernini's portrait in marble: here we see the Borghese pope eyeing the viewer suspiciously, with a somewhat censorious expression. It appears to be based at least partially on a Caravaggio portrait which still belongs to the Borghese family and is not on display. A portrait of the same pope by Marcello Provenzale (1577–1639) in micro-mosaic, in the same room, is more flattering; the room also contains a pair of views of the palazzina of the Villa Borghese in the seventeenth century, when it still had its full complement of antique statuary on the façade.

5 Other Borghese sites in Rome

The Borghese imprint appears so strongly across Rome that it would be easy to imagine that Paul V and Scipione Borghese were the greatest builders in the history of the city, but this is not so. Both uncle and nephew did manage to complete a number of grand projects, which were in many cases begun by others, the pope focusing on monuments to pontifical authority, the cardinal on lesser churches and palaces. Both also delighted in adorning Rome with fountains, which bear the omnipresent eagle and dragon.

| PAUL V AND PAPAL SPLENDOUR

The efforts of Paul V included two major building works. The first concerned the **basilica of St Peter's**. The apparently endless saga of construction, redesign, demolition and reconstruction of the principal basilica of Rome (though not its cathedral, which is San Giovanni in Laterano) was brought to completion by the Borghese pope, who finally abandoned Michelangelo's centrally planned Greek-cross floor plan for a Latin cross. In the course of this redesign, made for liturgical reasons and in order to ensure that the whole area of the original Constantinian basilica was included in the new building, a recently built façade had to be demolished. Carlo Maderno (1556–1629), another of the great Borghese-sponsored architects, was commissioned to build the new nave of three chapels each side and a new façade. He sensibly continued the exterior appearance determined by Michelangelo, with a colossal order of pilasters that unites the whole gigantic exterior surface, and a ground-floor loggia that draws heavily on Michelangelo's plans for the palazzo dei Conservatori on the Capitoline hill. Though the dedicatory inscription on the frieze says the work was completed in 1612, it was not finished until 1614. The same inscription proudly trumpets the name of PAULUS V BORGHESIUS ROMANUS: 'Strange,' observed Pasquino, 'I had always thought it was dedicated to St Peter.'

The **fountains** of piazza San Pietro also owe their existence to Paul V: though he only ordered the construction of the right-hand one, it was mirrored sixty years later by a partner. Carlo Maderno was the architect, replacing a fountain of a hundred years before, and its unusual design of an upturned, leaf-carved basin over which water splashes into a lower one, effortlessly conveys the copiousness of the Acqua Paola, which feeds it. The diarist John Evelyn, visiting in 1644, wrote of the fountain that from it

> . . . gushes a river rather than a stream which, ascending to a good height, breaks upon a round emboss of marble into millions of pearls that fall into the subjacent basin with great noise; I esteem this one of the goodliest fountains I ever saw.

The second great building work of Paul V was the papal summer palace, the **Palazzo del Quirinale** (free tours of the state rooms every Sunday, 8.30–12.30). Though the building had been used as a summer retreat since the time of Sixtus V and had been greatly enlarged by Gregory XIII

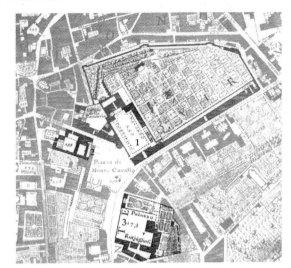

Borghese sites on the Quirinal hill

Key:
1 palazzo del Quirinale
2 palazzo della Dataria
3 palazzo Pallavicini Rospigliosi
 (ex-palazzo Borghese)

Boncompagni, Paul V set out to make the palace a suitable seat for the government of the Papal States. The architects were Flaminio Ponzio, until his death in 1613, then Maderno. Paul V used this as his residence from 1613 onwards and built a palace nearby (palazzo della Dataria, rebuilt in 1860) to house part of the pontifical bureaucracy. Three great rooms reflect the pope's taste. The first is the **Sala dei Corazzieri**, the former Sala Regia or Royal Audience Hall. Two huge shields in the ceiling bear the Borghese arms, and the spectacular frieze was painted in 1616–17 by Agostino Tassi (1580–1644), Giovanni Lanfranco and Carlo Saraceni (1579–1620). Among Borghese emblems, a painted loggia shows the arrival of an embassy from the East in the early years of Paul V's reign. The ill-fated Congolese ambassador, whose tomb we have already seen in Santa Maria Maggiore, is represented as well.

The second important room opens from the Sala dei Corazzieri: this is the **Cappella Paolina**, built to the exact dimensions of the great Sistine Chapel in the Vatican, which was to serve as the Papal States chapel during the Pope's residency, and also as the site for papal elections when the pope died in the Quirinale. Its wall decoration dates from the nineteenth century: under the Borghese it was merely hung with red damask, but the ceiling stucco survives from Paul V's reign. The stucco work, of the highest refinement, was made by the Ticinese artist Martino Ferrabosco in 1616 and is full of the familiar emblems; in the corners allegorical figures hold representations of buildings erected or completed by Paul V. Off to the right-hand side of this chapel an inconspicuous door opens into a tiny closet-like room, lavishly decorated, where the pope could attend Mass unseen. The third important room is a private chapel, the **Cappella dell'Annunziata**, for the pope's own use. It is not generally open to the public, so special permission must be obtained. Its frescoes, by Guido Reni, are among his most beautiful work.

A third building received alterations under Paul V: this was the **Papal Mint** at the juncture of via del Banco di Santo Spirito and via dei Banchi Nuovi, a building of Paul III Farnese. Paul V furnished it with a pair of allegorical statues at the summit of its façade and put it under a new authority, the **Banco di Santo Spirito**. The new papal bank was created on 31 December 1605 for public deposits, which were secured by the massive wealth and lands of the rich confraternity of the Holy Spirit, which ran the Ospedale di Santo Spirito. The bank was one of Paul V's most successful and enduring creations. With its sister institution, the Monte di Pietà or papal pawnbrokers (housed, as we have seen, in a former palace of the Santacroce family), the Banco di Santo Spirito lasted until the fall of the pontifical state in 1870, when its buildings were taken over by the new Banca di Roma, which holds them even today.

II   CARDINAL SCIPIONE AT WORK AND PLAY
Palazzo Pallavicini Rospigliosi, via XXIV Maggio 43. Palazzo never open to the public. Casino dell'Aurora open on the first day of every month, 10–12, without charge, or upon request to the Amministrazione Pallavicini, tel. 06 481 4344, to groups of no less than ten, with admission charge

While Paul V was rebuilding the Quirinal, not far away his nephew, Cardinal Scipione, was creating a series of pleasure pavilions now incorporated into the grounds of the **palazzo Pallavicini Rospigliosi**, where the tempestuous beauty Maria Mancini, wife of Prince Lorenzo Onofrio Colonna, once lived. Here, in 1605, immediately after the election of Paul V, Cardinal Scipione commissioned Flaminio Ponzio to build a set of 'hanging gardens' for formal and informal celebrations, banquets and conversations. Two of these pavilions survive; one of them, the *loggia delle Muse*, contains frescoes by Orazio Gentileschi (1565–1647) and Agostino Tassi, with *Muses* and a *Concert*; that pavilion is now enclosed in the courtyard of the *Ninfeo* or nymphaeum of the palace, with a huge stage-set fountain with river gods. Frescoes from the third pavilion, demolished for the construction of the via Nazionale, are in the Museo di Roma: these are by Cigoli and depict the story of *Cupid and Psyche*.

The most famous of the cardinal's pavilions is now called the **Casino dell'Aurora**. This is reached by a little staircase to the left of the main driveway inside the main gate and is set in its hanging garden, built over remains of the ancient Baths of Constantine; it was completed, like the palazzina of the Villa Borghese, by Giovanni Vasanzio, and here the veneer-like cladding of ancient reliefs is still intact. Ancient sculptures vie for attention with the expected Borghese dragons and eagles. The façade reliefs all refer to resurrection, hence to Scipione Borghese as an Apollo resurrecting the arts. Inside, on the ceiling of the main room, from January to August 1614, Guido Reni painted his celebrated fresco of *Aurora scattering flowers before the chariot of Apollo*. Apollo, once again a metaphor for the cardinal, is bringing daylight to the world, preceded by the beautiful figure of Aurora, the dawn. Reni was a great proponent of a Raphael-like style and palette, and was contrasted with his contemporary Caravaggio, also admired by Scipione. Where Caravaggio was dark and painted in dramatic darkness, Reni was said to be beautiful and painted in bright colours. Reni was, famously, virginal – Caravaggio, by contrast, was scandalously linked with several prostitutes and controversy rages over his sexuality.

The cardinal also had a residence in the Borgo, close to the Vatican, which once held his collection of art: this severe and beautiful late fifteenth-century palace, now **palazzo Giraud Torlonia** (never open) on the via della Conciliazione, was sold by Scipione, apparently out of boredom, in favour of palazzo Borghese. Eventually it fell into the hands of the Torlonia family, princes of Fucino, the rich and detested landlords of much of Rome; they live here still. Before the construction of the via della Conciliazione, which eviscerated the medieval neighbourhood of the Borgo, palazzo Giraud Torlonia stood on piazza Scossacavalli, whose strange name refers to the horses which, according to legend, balked at that point when the pillaging Goths riding them approached the tomb of the apostle. The piazza's new fountain, also spouting water from Paul V's new aqueduct, was removed during the construction of the via della Conciliazione and now stands as the fountain of **piazza Sant' Andrea della Valle**. This elegant fountain occupies a commanding position in front of the great church of St Andrew at the junction of corso Rinascimento and corso Vittorio Emanuele II, and is decorated with Borghese emblems. A similar fountain, once in piazza del Popolo, is now the **fountain of piazza Nicosia**, not far from palazzo Borghese, where it was moved after the piazza was redesigned in the early nineteenth century at the command of Paolina Borghese's brother Napoleon.

The church of **San Gregorio Magno** (open 9–12, 16–18; for admission ring at the porter's lodge at the right-hand side of the atrium) on the Celian hill has its origins in the monastery which Pope Gregory I (590–604, a benevolent reign that brought him sanctification as St Gregory the Great), of the ancient noble Anicii clan, converted from his family mansion. Paul V made his nephew Cardinal Scipione the commendatory abbot of the richly endowed Camaldolese monastery here. During the pontificate of Urban VIII Barberini (1623–44), Cardinal Scipione desired to make a public act of generosity. In 1633 he commissioned Giovanni Battista Soria to build a more substantial front for the medieval church. Soria produced a sober, classical façade, including staircase, front elevation and atrium, in front of the original church. On the ground level, three arches surmounted by the Borghese emblems with their wings triumphantly outstretched admit visitors into the atrium, which is filled with Renaissance and Baroque funerary monuments, among which is the tomb of Sir Edward Carne, an envoy of Henry VIII and Mary I, who was recalled to England by Elizabeth I but remained in Rome for reasons of faith – and to keep his head on his shoulders.

The interior of the church was thoroughly reconstructed in 1725–34 but outside, to the left of the façade, through a gate and up some steps, is a group of three little chapels, the left-hand and central ones both dating from the Middle Ages, and the right-hand one built as a pendant in 1603. All three chapels were renovated under the patronage of the great Counter-Reformation church historian Cardinal Cesare Baronio from 1602 to 1606, and the works were completed by Cardinal Scipione Borghese in 1606–8. Though the frescoes in the left-hand chapel, that of Santa Barbara, were made in 1602 by Antonio Viviani (1560–1620), most of the frescoes inside the other two chapels date from 1608–9 and were made by Cardinal Scipione's artists: in the central chapel, the **oratorio di Sant' Andrea**, Domenichino painted the *Flagellation of St Andrew* and Guido Reni the *St Andrew brought to the torture*, while in the right-hand chapel, the **oratorio di Santa Silvia**, mother of St Gregory the Great, Reni and an assistant frescoed a *Concert of angels*. Outside the complex, to the left up the narrow ancient street called the Clivo di Scauro, there is a Baroque portal with Cardinal Scipione's name and devices above it: this leads to an ancient and never finished building, unroofed now, called the Library of Agapetus after the pope of 535–6, whose efforts to build a great university at Rome were thwarted by the terrible wars between the Gothic rulers of Italy and the Byzantine Empire, bent on reconquest of the West. The portal was a secondary entrance to the group of three chapels.

Outside the city walls, on the via Appia, the great ancient basilica of **San Sebastiano** (open 9–12, 16.30–18) also received a thorough renovation under Cardinal Scipione. This was a major pilgrimage church, originally dedicated to the saints Peter and Paul, whose remains were said to have been kept here during the persecutions of AD 258. Thirty years after that the soldier-saint Sebastian was said to have been martyred and his remains buried here; the church took his name as early as the ninth century. Sebastian was one of Rome's popular saints, though he came from Narbonne in France, and part of his cult here involved a visit to the catacombs under the church and its surrounding territory. This ancient subterranean cemetery was one of the few visited constantly throughout the centuries, and the original basilica, built by the Emperor Constantine, was probably mainly funerary in character, perhaps not even covered with a roof, but merely an enclosure with graves. Substantial remains of the original ambulatory survive, but between 1608 and 1613 the main church was rebuilt by Flaminio Ponzio and his assistant Giovanni Vasanzio, like the palazzina of the Villa Borghese. The simple façade reuses the columns of the original basilica and inside, the wooden ceiling, by Vasanzio, has the crest of the cardinal as well as a somewhat lurid representation of the martyrdom of St Sebastian. Cardinal Scipione commissioned the altarpiece and canopy, but the most striking piece of work in the church, the *Dead St Sebastian*, is the masterpiece, from 1671–2, of a student of Bernini's, Antonio Giorgetti (d. 1672).

Within the great Dominican church of **Santa Maria sopra Minerva** (open 9–19) various works reflect the interests of Cardinal Scipione; among his responsibilities was the protectorship of the Dominican order. He also used this church to commemorate his father's family, the Caffarelli. The first two chapels on the right aisle, by the door, were remade by him immediately after his elevation to the cardinalate; the first, a baptistery, was subsequently redesigned, but the second, the **Caffarelli chapel**, is much as he made it, with paintings by the Cavalier d'Arpino, Gaspare Celio (1571–1640), who also did work in the Galleria Borghese, and one of Bernini's principal followers, il Baciccia (Giovanni Battista Gaulli, 1639–1709). The church's organs, in two large lofts in the transepts, were also the gift of Cardinal Scipione. These beautiful instruments, which are still used, date from *c*.1620; they sport two dragons on each side of the composition and an eagle at the apex.

Another church of the cardinal's deserves mention: **Santa Maria della Vittoria** (open 9–12, 16–18.30), built by Carlo Maderno in 1608–20, for the Discalced Carmelite order of monks. During the building works, undertaken by the not very wealthy order on its own behalf, the famous *Hermaphrodite* was discovered, perhaps a decoration from the ancient gardens of Sallust. Cardinal Scipione acquired the piece for his collection in 1608 and in exchange arranged for his architect Giovanni Battista Soria to build the façade at his expense, though work only began in 1624 and was finished two years later: at that time Cardinal Scipione was very interested in sponsoring prominent public works in order to deflect criticism, to which, as a cardinal nephew of a by then dead pope, he was very prone. The Borghese eagles decorating Soria's façade express his patronage.

The little church of **Santa Maria del Carmine** (rarely open), round the corner from the Torre Colonna in a tiny cul-de-sac, was built at the order of Cardinal Scipione in 1624, though his sponsorship is uncredited; the high altar is decorated with a painting by Gaspare Celio. Two other minor churches received significant Borghese patronage, and their relative proximity to palazzo Borghese indicates the local power the family exercised in the *rione* Campo Marzio. The little church of **Santa Lucia della Tinta** (open for prayer, Thursdays at 16.30, with a tour of the church offered after the service) on via di Monte Brianzo had previously served a small parish of seventy-two families living nearby; after its parish withered, it was given to the Coachmen's Guild, but in the early seventeenth century it fell under Borghese patronage. Prince Marcantonio II reconstructed it in 1628 and a large plaque in the entrance corridor records his generosity. A little further north on via Vittoria is the now ex-church of **Santa Orsola** (open for performances only), founded in the late seventeenth century by the pious Princess Camilla Orsini Borghese for a community of Ursuline Augustinian nuns. Now it is the auditorium of the national music conservatory of Santa Cecilia, but in its day its annexed convent housed the sisters of Louis XVI, no less, who fled here from France during the Revolution.

Intermezzo:
the seventeenth century

After the death of Paul V in 1621, a Bolognese cardinal, Alessandro Ludovisi, was elected pope, taking the name of **Gregory XV** (1621–3). Though his pontificate was brief, his nepotism was intense and the Ludovisi family was able to amass a significant fortune. The papal nephew Ludovico Ludovisi was a principal sponsor of the Jesuits, whose second main church in Rome, Sant' Ignazio, was built by him. The Ludovisi quickly became one of Rome's most important and wealthiest families, and Ludovico built a large suburban villa just inside the city walls by the Villa Borghese, which the family sold in lots in the late nineteenth century to form today's Ludovisi district, the via Veneto and its neighbouring streets.

The glorious Villa Ludovisi in the eighteenth century. The gardens are long gone, but this building, the Casino Grande, still stands as an annexe to the late nineteenth-century palazzo Margherita, now the American Embassy. The villa's statuary was partly acquired by the Italian state, and partly sold abroad, to great outcry.

The Borghese had established a clear precedent in their creation of the family complex around piazza Borghese. Though subsequent seventeenth-century papal families varied the Borghese plan, they all wanted a display space that would function as the setting for their family courts. As each pope was monarch of the Papal States, his family was royal for the duration of their relative's pontificate. Palace, family church, piazza, outbuildings and villa all became important and increasingly interrelated ways of expressing a family's new social significance.

6   The Barberini

The Barberini came from the Florentine territory of the Val d'Elsa, where the castle of Barberino gave them their surname; their original patronymic, Tafani, means 'horsefly' and their emblem was made up of those not very picturesque insects, which were later transformed, with the disappearance of the Tafani name, into bees.

The Barberini first made their fortune from the sale of cloth, specifically canvas. This unromantic material provided them with enough wealth to buy a good deal of property, and one of their earliest public acts of patronage was to build a church and a hospital in Barberino. They intermarried with some of the most prominent Florentine mercantile families, such as the Bardi and the Rucellai, and their funerary chapel in Florence was in the great noble sacrarium of the church of Santa Croce. *Francesco di Antonio Barberini* (1469–1527) built the family's Florentine palace in piazza Santa Croce; Francesco, a great expander of the family wealth, organised trade with the East, through Ragusa (Dubrovnik) and Ancona, and in 1515 opened a branch office of the family cloth business in Pera, near Istanbul. However, the Barberini were not helped by their enmity against the Medici, who dominated Florence for most of the fifteenth century, and Francesco's sons, *Nicolò* (1492–1574) and *Antonio Barberini* (1494–1559), fled the city: Nicolò went to the family business office at Ancona and opened new branches in Pesaro and, later, Antwerp, while Antonio went to Rome. He was a close associate of the chief Medici enemy, Piero Strozzi, and his death in 1559 was commissioned by the Florentine ambassador: he died of stab wounds in a Roman street. The Barberini wisely decided to reconcile with the Medici regime; the admission of one of Antonio's nephews into the Order of San Stefano, founded by the Medici grand duke, was proof of their success.

Another of Antonio's nephews, *Francesco di Carlo Barberini* (1528–1600), embarked on a career in the church, which was to transform the family fortunes. He was made papal treasurer and apostolic protonotary (an important legal functionary), and through these offices became wealthy, attaining the rank of monsignor, a title just beneath cardinal. He bequeathed his fortune to his nephew, *Maffeo Barberini* (1568–1644), and from the 1580s onwards vigorously promoted Maffeo's ecclesiastical career: in time, he would become pope. At nearly the same time Maffeo's older brother, *Carlo Barberini* (1562–1630), moved to Rome with his family, converting the rather modest Barberini property into a large palace. He devoted himself to consolidating the family business, selling the Ancona branch and accumulating capital.

POPE URBAN VIII (1623–44)

Maffeo grew up in the household of his uncle, Monsignor Francesco, and studied at the new Jesuit school, the Collegio Romano. He obtained a law degree in Pisa in 1588 and began to rise in the ecclesiastical hierarchy. For his posting as papal nuncio to the court of Henri IV of France in 1604–7 he received a cardinal's hat from Paul V Borghese. His bishopric of Spoleto was then his principal source of income, though he renounced it in 1617 as it became clear that his career was to be at the papal court. From 1611 to 1614 he was papal legate or governor of Bologna, a post generally given to the most skilful administrators and widely seen as a proving ground for future popes.

Even as a junior member of the papal court, Maffeo Barberini developed his interests as a patron and poet. He had his portrait painted by the young Caravaggio in 1598 and five years later commissioned another painting from him, while his nunciature in Paris brought him an enduring appreciation for French art and culture. The French court also taught him the propaganda value of the arts, which, under Henri IV, strongly upheld the glory of the king. Maffeo perhaps perceived that a career as patron could compensate for the relative humility of his lineage. He consciously cultivated a poetic image, adding Apollo's laurel and sun to his emblems, and replacing the inglorious Tafani horseflies on his family crest with bees, which reflected one of Horace's odes (IV.ii):

Urban VIII's patronage of art and architecture enriched Rome even as it emptied the pontifical coffers.

> . . . but I, very much in the manner
> of a Matine bee
> laboriously harvesting thyme
> from numerous groves and the banks of many-
> streamed Tibur, inconspicuously accrete
> my intricate verses.

With income from his bishopric of Spoleto, Maffeo could act in earnest as a patron. He began with his family property near the Campo de' Fiori, the Casa Grande ai Giubbonari, which, with his brother Carlo, he enlarged to reflect his new status as a cardinal. Maffeo sponsored his family chapel in Sant' Andrea della Valle, and began to gather together a library and a collection of early and mid sixteenth-century paintings, including works by Correggio and Andrea del Sarto. Cardinal Maffeo was a serious poet, whose poems encompassed both religious and pastoral subjects, and his circle included other poets and writers. He provided moralising verses for the base of Bernini's *Apollo and Daphne* group, made for his friend Scipione Borghese and for the same artist's fountain of the Barcaccia in piazza di Spagna. From 1620 his poems were published, in more and more elaborate editions, in the major centres for printing in Catholic Europe; one edition was illustrated by Bernini and another had a frontispiece by Peter Paul Rubens.

Upon the death of Gregory XV Ludovisi in 1623, the college of cardinals was split between adherents of the last two papal nephews, Ludovico Ludovisi and Scipione Borghese. In the sweltering heat of the Roman summer the conclave was at first uncomfortable, then deadly, as malaria struck the gathering; in the end, eight cardinals of the fifty-four present would die of the illness. There was pressure on the conclave to elect. The name of Maffeo Barberini came up as a compromise and though Scipione Borghese was initially hesitant, he withdrew his objections and, in the first secret ballot in a papal conclave, Barberini was elected pope. However, only fifty-three ballots were accounted for: Barberini insisted on a new vote, to prevent questions of his legitimacy and thus, as his early biographers pointed out, he was the only pope ever to be elected twice.

Maffeo Barberini, a cultivated poet and an experienced diplomat, appeared an excellent choice, though, at fifty-five, a rather young man for the job. His sympathies with the French were likely to prevent too close an attachment to the Spanish interest, which otherwise dominated the Italian peninsula. Indeed, the policies of the new Barberini pope, who was elected on 6 August 1623 as Urban VIII, were strongly in favour of the independence of the States of the Church from Spanish influence. This aspect of his policy can be seen in St Peter's, where he caused the body of the Countess Matilda of Tuscany to be reburied in 1634, with an imposing monument by Bernini. Matilda of Tuscany embodied the submission of the temporal power to the spiritual, as she, an early medieval ruler of vast wealth, left her lands and money to the pope; it was near her castle at Canossa that Pope Gregory VII forced the Holy Roman Emperor Henry IV to submit to his power in 1077, leaving the emperor on his knees for three days in the snow waiting for papal absolution. This message of the pope's supreme temporal authority resonated loudly through most of Urban VIII's actions.

His court was one of the most brilliant and glittering of any age. Urban VIII's three emblems, the bee, the sun and the laurel, were all reinterpreted in Christian terms: the bee was seen as wise and chaste, attributes of Christ, while the sun again referred to the blaze of wisdom that was Christ and the laurel represented eternal life, achieved through poetic skill. The bee itself was reinterpreted not only as an image of poetic industry, as in Horace, but also, according to the ancient tradition that bees were immortal, as symbols of the soul and of resurrection, following Virgil, who in his *Georgics* (IV.226–7) wrote that for bees

> There is no room for death: alive they fly
> To join the stars and mount aloft to heaven.

These lines were written on the temporary triumphal arch erected on the Capitoline hill upon Urban's election. The emblems of bee, sun and laurel thread their way dramatically through nearly all the monuments of this busy pope. The preponderance of the bee, in particular, provoked the hostile remark that a swarm had invaded the Papal States; one contemporary counted 10,000 painted or carved examples of the insect. That number attests to Urban VIII's exuberant outlay of money on decoration and building. The Baroque winged into Rome on the backs of the Barberini bees.

The marshal at the front of this artistic onslaught was the pope's close friend Gianlorenzo Bernini. Though Bernini had begun life as a protégé of Cardinal Scipione Borghese, he developed a genuine friendship with the aspiring poet-priest Maffeo Barberini, an ardent admirer of his work. Upon his election, Urban VIII reportedly told Bernini, 'It is your good fortune to see Maffeo Barberini elected pope; but it is our great good fortune to have the Cavalier Bernini living during our pontificate.' Bernini had extraordinary privileges, even to the extent of having the right to enter the pope's private chambers unannounced, a right not possessed even by close members of the pope's family. Under Urban VIII, Bernini achieved a dominance over the Roman artistic and architectural scene that could hardly be exaggerated. His workshop expanded to include some of the most talented artists of his generation and became the principal disseminator of the Baroque style, which, as it excellently expressed the authority of princes and the glory of God, soon spread across Italy and the rest of Catholic Europe.

Bernini was also made architect of the Fabbrica of St Peter's, the agency responsible for the completion of the great basilica, and determined much of the basilica's interior design, particularly the *baldacchino* (canopy) over the high altar beneath the dome, which he made from 1623 to 1634, from bronze taken from the portico of the Pantheon. To compensate, perhaps, for this theft, the artist built two bell towers on to the sides of the Pantheon's portico, which were immediately labelled 'the ass-ears of Bernini'. Bernini had no luck, either, with a more prominent pair of bell towers: his project for the façade of St Peter's included two towers on either side of Maderno's front elevation, but owing to the instability of the ground, the one tower that he built there began to crack off and had to be demolished, to the great detriment of his reputation. He also came under attack for hollowing out four huge niches in the piers supporting the central dome of St Peter's, provoking fears that the fifty-year-old dome would simply collapse like the bell tower. Within the basilica, Bernini also made the tomb of the pope himself (1628–47), in the tribune behind the high altar. On it and in balance with the tomb of Paul III Farnese across the tribune, Urban VIII appears in the papal tiara, the emblem of the pope's worldly and spiritual authority, while the Barberini bees seem to escape from the sarcophagus.

The pope was also interested in other churches, particularly of early Christian martyrs; one of his first commissions was for Bernini to rebuild the church of Santa Bibiana (1624–6), following the discovery of the body of the virgin martyr. Other constructions at the pope's behest took place at Santi Cosma e Damiano, Sant' Anastasia and Santi Luca e Martina, all older churches of great traditional importance. His interest in promoting the advance of Catholicism encouraged him to open up missionary activity in the Far East, which had previously been restricted to the Jesuits, to other monastic orders, and in Rome this led to the construction of the College of the Propagation of the Faith on piazza di Spagna and the much smaller Neophyte College in the Monti region. In general, his church-building programme took place in two areas, the first in and around the ancient Forum and the second surrounding his new family palace above the renamed piazza Barberini, whose expensive construction took up a massive and prominent corner of the Quirinal hill.

The pope was not a great street builder, nor a constructor of aqueducts, and his hand cannot be found marking a particular district as Paul V's had done in the Monti and Trastevere. The principal street he created – or, rather, straightened – was the via Urbana, also in the Monti region, which he set at right angles to Sixtus V's *strada Felice*, the extension of the via delle Quattro Fontane which bordered on his new palace. However, Urban VIII did undertake one major public work: the fortifications on the Janiculan hill south of the Vatican, which enclosed the hill and joined the two separate walled settlements on the western side of the Tiber, Trastevere and the Borgo. He also built a granary, now vanished, near his palace at the Quattro Fontane and elaborated the fortifications of the Castel Sant' Angelo, testifying to his concern for the city.

As a politician, Urban VIII had to deal with a Europe embroiled in agonising, protracted religious conflict. The Thirty Years War, which pitted the Catholic south of Europe against the Protestant north, raged throughout his reign, and Urban had to find an uneasy path between supporting the great Catholic bulwarks of Austria and Spain, under the Habsburgs, and his own preference for the French, whose leader, Cardinal Richelieu, was funding the Protestants against the emperor. France helped to maintain papal independence from Spain, whose king dominated both northern and southern Italy. Urban successfully induced the aged Duke of Urbino, Francesco Maria II della Rovere, to will Urbino to the Papal States, thereby bringing about the final enlargement of the pope's domains.

The interest he had shown in intellectual activity as cardinal was tempered by his keen support of orthodoxy as pope. As cardinal he had been a friend and supporter of Galileo Galilei, the astronomer, whose revolutionary discoveries about the movement of the planets overthrew the Church-supported theory that the sun revolved round the earth. After Urban's accession, Galileo had six interviews with him on the subject of his discoveries, but in 1632 their patron–client relationship was irrevocably broken when Galileo published his *Dialogue Concerning the Two Chief Systems of the World*, in which the astronomer put the argument in favour of divine omnipotence (a subject of discussion between pope and scientist in 1623) in the mouth of the foolish traditionalist Simplicio. This personal insult was perhaps behind Urban's refusal to pardon Galileo, who was forced to recant his findings by the Inquisition: he did so, denying that the earth moved round the sun, but as he left the court he famously muttered '*Eppur si muove*' (Nonetheless, it moves).

Urban's domestic policy met with one very serious reverse at the end of his reign, and that was closely tied to his nepotism. On a visit to Rome in 1639, Odoardo Farnese, Duke of Parma and Piacenza, refused to acknowledge Don Taddeo Barberini as prefect of Rome, as protocol would require Odoardo to cede precedence to him; the duke also snubbed Donna Anna, Taddeo's wife and a member of the great Colonna family. Duke Odoardo seems to have travelled to Rome with the intention of insulting the Barberini: he even strode unannounced into Urban's bedchamber at the Vatican to berate the still reclining pope for what he saw as the insolence of his nephews. By 1641 Urban had had enough. To punish the duke, he forbade the sale of grain from the Farnese duchy of Castro to the rest of the pope's territory. As a result, the duke could not repay his debts to the papal Camera, and Urban, in the role of bailiff, moved 10,000 troops, under the command of his nephew Taddeo, into the duchy of Castro. The city of Castro capitulated on 13 October and a papal victory seemed assured. The pope issued a *bando* (decree of outlawry) against Duke Odoardo and seemed prepared to push his troops even further north; rumours that he intended to capture Parma for the Barberini electrified European politics.

The result of this aggressive action was that the north-central Italian states of Tuscany, Venice and Mantua formed an alliance against the pope and, with their support, Duke Odoardo's cavalry pushed south suddenly into the Papal States, trouncing Taddeo Barberini and decimating the papal army. The ruinous campaign ended in early 1644 when France brokered a humiliating peace, in which the pope was forced to reinstate the Farnese in all their privileges. This first war of Castro (a second would be fought by the following pope, Innocent X) destroyed Urban's much-desired reputation as a peacemaker once and for all, and pushed the papacy towards bankruptcy. The pope had to institute a new tax duty, the *gabella*, on salt and other products, in order to make good the losses, as well as creating no less than nine extraordinary jubilees, in addition to the normal one in 1625, to attract pilgrims with the promise of remission of sins. Of this cynical money grubbing, Pasquino said acidulously:

> *Urbano ottavo dalla barba bella,*
> *Finito il giubileo, impone la gabella.*
> (Urban VIII, whose beard is a beauty,
> Once the jubilee's over, imposes a duty.)

The failure of the first war of Castro was the turning point for Barberini ambitions. The pope died on 19 July 1644, not long after this crushing blow to his pride and his family's honour.

THE *NIPOTI* OF URBAN VIII

In the area of nepotism, the Barberini pope outdid all his predecessors. An astonishing deluge of wealth and titles poured over the papal family, prompting many satires and much bitter criticism. Indeed, one author wrote that all the preceding pontifical nepotists 'were only the vigil: the true feast day of nepotism began in Rome under Urban VIII'.

Unlike Paul V Borghese, who poured money into only one ecclesiastic nephew and one secular nephew, Urban VIII gave fantastic riches to four of his relatives, who were widely satirised, for each failed to give satisfaction in his own way. In fact, the pope himself was heard to describe Cardinal Francesco the Elder as a saint without miracles, Cardinal Antonio the Elder as a friar without patience, Cardinal Antonio the Younger as an orator without eloquence and Prince Taddeo as a general without swordsmanship. Taddeo was a more dedicated trencherman than soldier, and the diarist Giacinto Gigli records that the pope decreed Taddeo should receive the choicest cuts of all the large fish caught in his territories.

FRANCISCVS EPVS OSTIEN·SACRI COL· DE CANVS CARD·BARBERINVS S·R·E· VICE·CANC·ET SVMMISTA ARCHIPBER·BASIL·S·PETRI FLOR·II·OCT·MDCXXIII·

Cultured and intellectual, Urban VIII's nephew Cardinal Francesco the Elder lived to a respected old age.

Urban VIII was not the eldest of his family: his brother *Carlo* (1562–1630), six years his senior, became the head of the secular wing and his marriage to Costanza Magalotti, a Florentine aristocrat, was the basis for the Barberini succession. The pope's younger brother *Antonio the Elder* (1569–1646) was a Capuchin friar and soon took his place by the pope's side as patron of art on his order's behalf, constructing, decorating and endowing the austere new church and convent of Santa Maria della Concezione just across piazza Barberini from the family's palace. However, Cardinal Antonio the Elder remained largely apart from the rest of his family, as his ascetic faith required him to do.

The austere impulse entirely deserted both the other family cardinals, Carlo's sons *Francesco the Elder* (1597–1679) and his brother *Antonio the Younger* (1608–1671). Francesco took his place as Urban VIII's secretary of state, a true cardinal nephew, while Antonio was a sort of understudy for his older brothers and was kept from taking major orders until after the second brother, *Taddeo* (1603–47), had produced offspring: the family line needed to be protected and it would not have been difficult to dispense Antonio of his vows if Taddeo had died prematurely. The three brothers were intensely jealous of each other and argued endlessly over their respective precedences. No wonder Cardinal Antonio the Elder preferred the company of his Capuchin brethren.

Cardinal Francesco received vast benefices, becoming commendatory (absentee) abbot of the richest abbeys in the Papal States, Farfa, San Salvatore and Grottaferrata. After the early death in 1632 of the previous cardinal nephew, Ludovico Ludovisi, he became papal vice-chancellor and moved into the Cancelleria: he was to spend the rest of his life surrounded by frescoes celebrating the triumph of his family's enemies, the Farnese. Following the death of Cardinal Scipione Borghese in 1633, Francesco became Archpriest of St Peter's, which brought with it a significant income from pilgrim donations. He spent his money with an enlightened interest in the arts and sciences: he founded the family tapestry works in the palazzo Barberini and chose Giovan Francesco Romanelli (1610–62), a pupil of Pietro da Cortona, as his court painter. In 1627 Francesco was made prefect of the Vatican Library, though he ceded the task to his uncle Antonio nine years later and instead created a vast library of his own in the palazzo Barberini, filling it with a court of scholars, including the great antiquarians Lucas Holste (known as Holstenius) and the cardinal's cupbearer, Cassiano dal Pozzo.

Cardinal Antonio the Younger was kept in the shade by his elder brother Francesco, but in compensation he was made almost equally rich, and he distracted himself with colossal festivals and displays of wealth. The abbeys of Tre Fontane and Nonantola fell into his hands, and the pope unified three benefices in Malta and made Antonio the Prior, much to the displeasure of the order of the Knights of Malta. Antonio was the principal link between the papacy and the traditional Barberini alliance with the French, and when he was sent to Bologna as legate (governor) in 1629 he was accompanied by the young Giulio Mazzarino, who as Jules Mazarin was soon to become the successor to the powerful Cardinal Richelieu as prime minister of France. In 1633 he became nuncio to Avignon, a papally ruled enclave in the south of France; this, too, was a sinecure, with minimal duties and maximum income. He became co-protector of France at the papal court in 1637, along with the Cardinal of Savoy, and in the following year he was made papal chamberlain. His love of luxury was famous, and his principal court painter was Andrea Sacchi (1600–1661), whose masterwork was the ceiling fresco called the *Divine Wisdom* in the Princess Anna apartment of palazzo Barberini. Sacchi and Pietro da Cortona were famously at odds about what constituted good painting, but this did not prevent Antonio from sponsoring Cortona as architect of a great new Barberini theatre. Antonio's summer residence was near Viterbo, in what is today known as the villa Lante at Bagnaia, but his principal home was palazzo Barberini, of which he was the main occupant.

Taddeo Barberini, the dynast of the family, started life as a rather mild and modest young man, and diplomats of the time of Urban's accession commented on his sweet nature, but this was quickly to change as the pope heaped wealth, power and rank upon him. In 1626 he was made lieutenant-general of the Church, and in the following year his marriage to Anna Colonna linked him with the oldest and most representative of Roman noble houses. In 1629 the pope bought him the fief of Palestrina, a traditional Colonna property, and made him prince; in 1630 Taddeo's father Carlo died and Taddeo inherited all his offices: general of the Church, governor of the Borgo and Civitavecchia, castellan of the Castel Sant'Angelo and captain of the papal guards.

The imperious expression of Taddeo Barberini, prince of Palestrina and prefect of Rome, in a contemporary engraving, hints at his pride, which could result in violence.

These posts brought large stipends and soon Taddeo was extraordinarily rich. The last great plum was the office of prefect of Rome, a position traditionally held by the della Rovere dukes of Urbino: but when the last duke of Urbino ceded his domain to the Church and died, the position became vacant. It was the highest secular post to be had in the Papal States and brought extraordinary privileges, ranking above even the most important ambassadors. Moreover, it was hereditary, and for it to fall into the hands of Urban's family was a guarantee that the Barberini would have enduring primacy.

All this turned the modest Taddeo into a monster of arrogance and it was not long before trouble started. Giacinto Gigli commented:

> The office of the Prefecture, conferred on the person of the pope's nephew, gave cause for much disgust among the kings and great princes. Because, this being the highest rank of office in Rome, even though Don Taddeo was prince of Palestrina, General of the Church and nephew of the pope, it did not seem to them, even with all this, that he was a prince to be compared with the deceased Duke of Urbino, who had this office, and, therefore, not one of the kings and rulers wanted to order that their ambassadors have to give precedence to him.

The Duke of Urbino had rarely appeared at the papal court and therefore had caused little embarrassment; moreover, the della Rovere had enjoyed a century and a half of prominence and the family was considered worthy of dignity. For the kings of Europe to allow their ambassadors to cede precedence to this young Barberini upstart would be to grant that Taddeo had a higher rank than the kings themselves and this they were unwilling to do: as a result, the ambassadors of France and Venice for a time withdrew from the papal court. Taddeo himself fanned the flames by creating a ridiculous controversy over the precedence of coaches. As prefect of Rome, he claimed the extraordinary right to have every coach in the street not merely give his coach right of way, but to stop entirely until he passed. As his retinue could contain as many as sixty or seventy carriages, this was no trivial inconvenience. A coachman of the Venetian ambassador was bribed by Taddeo to drop his hat as if by accident and stop to retrieve it, when Taddeo's carriage passed that of the ambassador, but this ploy worked only once. The coachman was forced to flee the wrath of the Venetian, who figured out what was going on, but the ambassador's assassins caught up with him in Paliano (a fief of the Colonna, Taddeo's wife's family) and the coachman paid for his breach of protocol with his life.

The despoliation of the Papal States by the Barberini provoked much criticism. Perhaps to forestall a posthumous audit, Urban VIII called a commission of inquiry in 1643 to determine whether he had not, perhaps, been a little more generous to his nephews than he ought. The commission obediently returned an answer of 'no' and the pope's conscience was eased. However, after his death the next pope, Innocent X, who as Giambattista Pamphilj had been raised to the cardinalate by Urban, did not let the matter lie. His own inquest, conducted during a period in which popular hatred and rage against the recently disempowered Barberini were at their height, discovered a startling fact: during the pontificate of Urban VIII the Barberini family had accumulated, in lands and cash, the staggering amount of 30 million ducats, more or less twelve times the annual income of the entire Papal States.

The Barberini seemed to have only one course open to them: flight. The most flamboyant of them, Cardinal Antonio the Younger, escaped to France in September 1645, dressed as a workman. His brothers, Cardinal Francesco and Prince Taddeo, with Taddeo's children, joined him in January 1646. The diarist Gigli described the flight:

> They left dressed as huntsmen, and the four children, three sons and a daughter, were all dressed as pages. Don Taddeo and his children left the house [the Casa Grande] on foot, with his wife Donna Anna Colonna

carrying their youngest son in her arms, and they reached the Campo de' Fiori, where carriages with guards and many vassals of the house of Colonna were waiting, and Donna Anna returned to the house, telling the children that they needed to go to the *vigna* [perhaps the family villa behind the palazzo Barberini, or the other Barberini villa on the Janiculan hill] where she would join them shortly. But the youngest son said to her: 'My lady mother, it is now night-time, and we are not going to the *vigna*, but are fleeing.'

Only Princess Anna and the unworldly Cardinal Antonio the Elder remained to tend to the family's interests, which were in grave disarray, especially when Innocent X sequestered all Barberini properties and threatened to strip the family of them entirely. Cardinal Antonio the Elder died in September of the same year, 1646. His funeral was widely attended and Gigli remarks with approval that despite the great hatred in which the Barberini were then held, no one could find anything ill to say of him. His will left all he had to the College of the Propagation of the Faith in piazza di Spagna, which his brother Urban VIII had founded, and he left nothing whatsoever to his relatives, which excited a good deal of surprised praise.

In France, the family's assiduous cultivation of Cardinal Richelieu and his protégé Mazarin soon bore fruit. French troops threatened Spanish positions on the Tuscan coast and the Spanish-aligned Pamphilj pope, intimidated, not long afterwards forgave the Barberini, and returned their properties and privileges to them. In February 1647, Cardinal Francesco returned to Rome. Prince Taddeo died in exile in that year, but his second son and heir *Maffeo* (1631–85) married a relative of Innocent X's, Olimpiuccia Giustiniani, in 1653. Scandal followed the start of this marriage, as the bride refused to let the groom lay a finger on her: naturally, as the pomp of the family required that nearly every private event was lived in full public view, the bride's reluctance was quickly communicated to the world. Luckily she changed her mind after about a month. In celebration of the alliance between the Barberini and the Pamphilj, Taddeo's eldest son *Carlo* (1630–1706) received the cardinal's hat, completing the rehabilitation of the family.

Cardinal Antonio the Younger came back to Rome in the same year and continued to rise in wealth, through his assiduous cultivation of his French connection, achieving the prestigious archbishopric of Reims. Cardinal Francesco sponsored great works like the guild church of the artists of Rome, Santi Luca e Martina, near the Roman Forum, and other churches around Rome; he was a reformer of religious institutions, especially houses for women, and he occupied himself with works in his family palace, his tapestry factory, his gardens and his academy of intellectuals until his death in 1679, eight years after that of his younger brother Antonio.

THE BARBERINI SUCCESSION

Maffeo's son *Francesco the Younger* (1662–1738) was the family's last important cardinal and his son *Urbano* (1664–1722) was the last prince of Palestrina of the pure Barberini line. His daughter *Cornelia Costanza* (1716–97) was his only heiress and she married a Colonna, Giulio Cesare Colonna di Sciarra, Prince of Carbognano, in 1728. By papal dispensation, the family was able to continue: the first-born son of the union took the Colonna di Sciarra name and the Carbognano title, and the second-born took the Barberini name, titles and properties. This line, called the Colonna Barberini, continued until the middle of the twentieth century when the last princess, Maria Colonna Barberini, died in 1955. Her husband, Luigi Sacchetti, was another Roman prince and by a royal decree he took the Barberini name: their descendants still hold the titles and what remains of the Barberini patrimony. However, by the mid twentieth century the family wealth had been dispersed by these multitudes of family divisions, and by bad management and misfortune. The family were constrained to sell their art collections in 1934 and Palazzo Barberini to the Italian state in 1949; around the same time they sold the greater part of their palace in Palestrina, retaining only a small area. The current Barberini princes live by the back corner of the palace of their extinct familial enemies, the Farnese, in a small house on the via Giulia, where the Barberini arms, now quartered with the Colonna column, are the last remaining vestige of the family's old taste for display.

BARBERINI ITINERARY

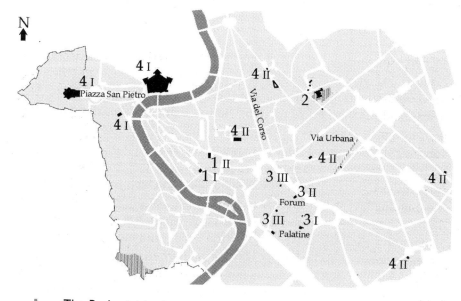

N

The Barberini presence in Rome is overwhelming, even today. The monuments of the family are so numerous that even with the destruction of some principal sites, the swarm of carved bees that contemporaries noted still hovers over the city. This itinerary takes in only the most important sites, roughly grouped into three areas. The first comprises Barberini property off the eastern end of the Campo de' Fiori, including the family palace on the via dei Giubbonari and the old family chapel in Sant' Andrea della Valle. The second part covers an area surrounding the piazza Barberini and the more famous palazzo, the most splendid family palace in Rome, as well as the main family church of Santa Maria della Concezione. The third, perhaps the most surprising, occupies the centre of the ancient city, the Roman Forum and the Capitoline and the Palatine hills, where the Barberini were patrons of several churches, expressing the family interest in early Christian martyr-saints, and where they had a *vigna* (rustic retreat).

All over Rome the alliance with the Colonna recurs in crests, signalling the joining of the new papal family to the medieval clan. With the Barberini, the visitor can explore fully the courtly and aristocratic life of the seventeenth century, with its splendour and its rigid formality. The great ceiling of the salone of palazzo Barberini celebrated the triumph of Divine Providence above, while the family savoured the triumph of earthly protocol below.

▌ The Barberini in the centre of town: the Casa Grande and the cappella Barberini

| THE CASA GRANDE AI GIUBBONARI
Via dei Giubbonari 41 and piazza del Monte di Pietà. Admission from the piazza into the vestibule and courtyard alone

Though the family gained their greatest fame from their palace on the outskirts of seventeenth-century Rome, the Barberini had a longer history in the area close to the Campo de' Fiori, in the densely built area of *rione* Regola. Our first certain record of a Barberini house here dates from 1581, when Monsignor Francesco Barberini bought the nucleus of the **Casa Grande** on via dei Giubbonari, slowly enlarging the house over the following years. In 1584 his nephew Maffeo Barberini moved in with him, on an upper floor of the house, and after the Monsignor's death in 1600, Maffeo brought his elder brother Carlo, his wife Costanza and their three young children to live here, as well as his widowed mother. The 'Great House' soon proved to be far too small for such a large family and their retainers, and by 1622 the Barberini palace had begun to stretch all the way across its city block.

When Maffeo became Pope Urban VIII in 1623 the building grew even

Barberini sites
near the Campo de' Fiori, from
the Nolli map of 1748

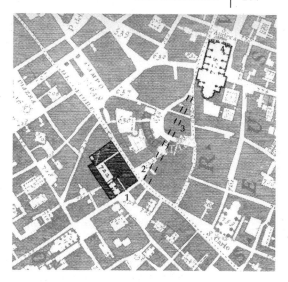

Key:
1 Casa Grande ai Giubbonari
2 largo dei Librari
3 unbuilt street joining Casa
  Grande with Sant' Andrea della
  Valle
4 Barberini chapel, Sant' Andrea
  della Valle

more dramatically, although as pope he left the palace to his brother Carlo. Though construction continued at a frantic pace, it was insufficient to house both the ecclesiastical and the secular wings of the family, let alone their household staff: a sign of the decay of Orsini fortunes was that their great palace across the road, palazzo Pio Righetti, was rented out to the Barberini for use by their retainers in 1627. When Carlo's son Taddeo, born in the palace in 1603, married Anna Colonna in 1627, another series of renovations took place. They used different architects: Flaminio Ponzio, the Borghese architect, was in charge at one point, and Carlo Maderno also worked here.

At a time when a structure was given dignity through its visual separateness from its surroundings (like palazzo Farnese), the Casa Grande remained side by side with its neighbours, which were small shops and humble dwellings, and even rented out its ground floor as shop space, which it continues to do today. As a result, this vast palace makes almost no impression from the street. If you look carefully along the mezzanine level of windows (the small set of windows directly above the ground floor) on the via dei Giubbonari side of the Casa Grande, you will see that they vary in size and placement, though the *piano nobile* floor above is entirely regular: this variation of windows stems from the buildings on the spot previously, which were not so much demolished and replaced as modified and engulfed. The Casa Grande is a perfect example of the cannibalistic tendency of Roman palaces.

Prince Taddeo Barberini became prefect of Rome in 1631, the city's chief nobleman, and the narrowness of the palace's entrance was unseemly and inconvenient for his carriage train. In 1634 a fire providentially destroyed some houses diagonally opposite the eastern corner of the palace. These had faced on to a tiny piazza in front of the church of Santa Barbara dei Librai (St Barbara of the Booksellers). Taddeo had the ruined houses demolished and the piazza enlarged, to give light and prominence to the corner of his residence, which even today sports the Barberini bees. Indeed, a whole new street was projected, cutting along the right-hand side of the little church of Santa Barbara, and through two other city blocks to reach the side of Sant' Andrea della Valle and, from there, the via Papalis. This Barberini avenue was never constructed, however, though the largo dei Librari remains to hint at what might have been. In 1639 an even grander scheme was put into motion, with the demolition of a block of houses separating the Casa Grande from the piazza del Monte di Pietà, creating a much larger piazza; at the same time the old Santacroce palace housing the Monte, the papal pawnbrokers, was enlarged as well.

Prince Taddeo lived in the Casa Grande until his flight to France, where he died. The family, when it returned, lived in the other palazzo Barberini and in 1734 they relinquished the palace, donating it to the Discalced Carmelite monks of St Theresa, who used it as their Curia Generale or main administrative seat. The main entrance's atrium on via dell'Arco del Monte was stripped of its granite columns (which were sent to decorate the Vatican Museums) and turned into a chapel. This was the beginning of three centuries of decline, which was hastened by the palace's conversion in the second half of the eighteenth century as an annexe of the Monte di Pietà, when a bridge was built to join the two buildings, the so-called Arco del Monte. The Carmelites' chapel was taken out and plaster columns replaced in the atrium, which became a theatre in the early twentieth century. Today, badly mistreated and neglected, the palace is given over to a number of different bodies, including the local health authority office, the neighbourhood's Socialist Party headquarters, two separate schools and a number of other concerns. The atrium houses a print shop.

You can walk round the building on two sides. From the via dei Giubbonari, the Casa Grande appears, or, rather, coalesces from the street level with its multitude of shops into a rather austere building, pinkish in colour, with a high *altana* or summer dining room on the top, obscured by a grim, prison-like fence that surmounts the whole cornice. An extremely peculiar arched entrance on the right-hand end of the palace, towards the Campo, is a later insertion. On the corner of the building where it intersects with via dell'Arco del Monte, the Barberini bees can be seen, the only element of decoration in the otherwise very plain building. The largo dei Librari, however, which narrows as it moves further from the via dei Giubbonari, is very appealing, especially the little church of Santa Barbara dei Librai with its late seventeenth-century façade.

Round the corner, the entrance hall and adjoining atrium that opens from the piazza del Monte di Pietà are accessible today. The entrance hall still has a plaster frieze with the family bees, and the atrium opens to the left. An elegant room, even stripped of its granite columns, it alone hints at the grandeur of the building under the Barberini. It is strikingly reminiscent of a church, with its space measured out by columns, and one can easily see how it could have been adapted as a chapel and a theatre in the past. From just beyond the piazza del Monte di Pietà a door opens into the base of a great spiral staircase, possibly the work of Maderno, which leads to the school upstairs: a vigilant porter will make sure you go no further, but the entrance space is beautiful and above one of the doors is written '*Qui si piglia oro e argento*' (here you pick up gold and silver), a memory of its life as part of the Monte di Pietà. Of the palace's interior decoration little or nothing appears to have survived; on the other hand perhaps it simply awaits some loving restoration to peel off layers of whitewash.

II   CAPPELLA BARBERINI, SANT' ANDREA DELLA VALLE
Entrance from piazza Sant' Andrea della Valle (intersection of corso Vittorio Emanuele II and corso Rinascimento. Open 9–12, 16.30–18). Chapel generally closed, but entirely visible through the grille

The vast church of **Sant' Andrea della Valle** interrupts the old papal procession route, forcing it to go round the side and front of the building; the front is now on the nineteenth-century corso Vittorio Emanuele II but its position has, if anything, been made more prominent with the placement of the fountain of piazza Scossacavalli (as we have seen, a Borghese fountain, now beautifully restored and well lit at night) in the fascist-era piazza in front of it. However, even without such emphasis, the church has always been a significant monument, the result, like the Gesù not far away, of Counter-Reformation spirituality.

Like the Gesù, Sant' Andrea della Valle is the mother church of a religious order, in this case the Theatine order. The Theatines had their origins in a circle of educated clerics who sought a spiritual refuge in the midst of the worldly sink-hole of Rome of the 1520s. Under the leadership of Gaetano Thiene and the iron Gian Pietro Carafa, the future Paul IV, it formed itself into the 'Congregation of Divine Providence' and obtained official approval from Clement VII de' Medici in early 1524. The Congregation was swept up in the affairs of Italy in its early years, its members fleeing from Rome to Venice after the Sack of Rome in 1527 and only returning piecemeal in the following decade. But the austere urge that lay behind the creation of the Congregation was well suited to the piety of the period of the Council of Trent and in 1591 an old church on this site, dedicated to St Sebastian, was replaced by a massive new structure dedicated to St Andrew 'of the Valley', which referred in equal parts to the slight dip (now vanished) caused by the former presence of an ornamental lake in the ancient gardens of Agrippa and to the powerful family of the della Valle, whose two large palaces still stand on the opposite corner of the piazza.

This church was the biggest new piece of construction in the vicinity of the Casa Grande ai Giubbonari, where Maffeo Barberini, the future Urban VIII, was living in the last decade of the sixteenth century. Maffeo was probably motivated to commission a family chapel in the church more because of its closeness to his family house, and because it promised to rival the Gesù in its size and magnificence, than because of any spiritual kinship with the Theatines. It was the perfect opportunity for an up-and-coming prelate to display his family's wealth and his own taste. He might have been encouraged by other Florentine families, like the Rucellai and the Strozzi, who also sponsored chapels in the church.

The building went through several different phases and met with a series of financial obstacles, but in 1608 its patronage was finally taken up by the great Cardinal Alessandro Peretti Montalto, who paid for its completion, leaving only the façade unfinished at his death. The front was finally completed at the expense of Alexander VII Chigi in 1656–65 by Carlo Rainaldi, though it still lacks one of the two angels that were intended to replace the traditional volutes easing the transition between the two levels of the façade. The story, totally unsubstantiated but popular, goes that the pope objected to the way one of the wings of the extant angel had been carved and suggested that the same method not be used in the second angel's wings, at which point the sculptor (Ercole Ferrata, a very able pupil of Bernini's) downed tools and refused the commission to complete the second one: 'If you think you can do better, do it yourself!'

The **interior** resembles the Gesù, at least in its arrangement of space: as in the Jesuit church, there are no side aisles. The nave ceiling, painted in the early twentieth century, does not have the elaborate illusionism of that of the Gesù, and the whole building is decorated in a sober classicism of gold and white. The drama of the Baroque begins to burst through only in the mornings, when sunlight pierces the yellow-tinted windows of the dome's drum and the dome frescoes by Giovanni Lanfranco are illuminated. These represent the *Glory of Paradise* and were made in 1625–8. The pendentives beneath the dome were painted by Domenichino in 1621–8, in a sort of talent competition with Lanfranco. Domenichino also made the frescoes depicting episodes in the life of St Andrew which are in the half-dome of the apse. Of

Domenichino's paintings in this church, Stendhal wrote in his *Roman Journal* of 1828, 'There are days when it seems to me that painting can go no further.' Completing this spectacular ensemble are three frescoes of the crucifixion, martyrdom and burial of the saint by Mattia Preti (1613–99) made in 1650–1 at the behest of the great power broker of the next pontificate, Donna Olimpia Maidalchini.

None of these works was in place when Carlo Barberini and his brother Monsignor Maffeo Barberini (as he was then) commissioned the **family chapel**, the first on the left-hand side, in 1604. In fact, the whole church was not consecrated until 1650, long after the death of Urban VIII, though the chapel was consecrated in 1616; Maffeo's cardinal's hat is a prominent feature above the Barberini crest. Its architect was the minor Matteo Castelli (active *c.*1604–26), but the sculptures are by the best sculptors of the period just before Gianlorenzo Bernini: his father Pietro contributed a *San Giovanni Battista* and Francesco Mochi (1580–1654), across the floor of the chapel, a fine *Santa Marta*. Here, too, are the tombs of Maffeo's benefactor, his uncle Monsignor Francesco Barberini and, in the connecting passage to the right, the two memorials to Maffeo's parents, rarely visible in the darkness. The marbles are all spoils from ancient buildings in the Forum, and the frescoes in the upper register of the chapel are by Domenico Cresti, Il Passignano (whom we have already met as the author of a fresco in the baptistery of Santa Maria Maggiore for Maffeo's friend Cardinal Scipione Borghese). There he painted an *Assumption of the Virgin*, a subject he reprised for the altarpiece in this chapel. Yet there is a strange flaccidness to both the painting and the sculpture, typical of the period just before the first surge of the Baroque.

This is the chapel where, traditionally, the first act of Puccini's opera *Tosca* is set, though of course in the opera it is given to a different, fictional, family. It reminds us that under the papal administration, the right of sanctuary was still respected and criminals escaping from prison often made their way straight to a church, as Angelotti does in the opera. Perhaps to protect the chapels from such unwelcome occupants, each one in this church is closed off with a stout grille.

2 The Barberini on the edge of town: palazzo and piazza Barberini

Palazzo Barberini, Galleria Nazionale d'Arte Antica; entrance from via Barberini 18. Open Tuesday–Sunday 9–19, open until 22 on Friday and Saturday. Admission €6.03, reduced for students €3.53

The Barberini on the edge of town

Key:
1 palazzo Barberini
2 cortile della Cavallerizza
3 teatro Barberini
4 houses for servants
5 gardens
6 San Carlino alle Quattro Fontane
7 Santa Maria della Concezione and Capuchin monastery

The most prominent monuments of the Barberini are undoubtedly their great palazzo on a crest of the Quirinal, and its nearby piazza in the valley between the Quirinal and Pincian hills. The palace, most magnificent of Roman noble houses, is an eloquent expression of the Baroque in secular architecture and even in its somewhat dilapidated condition has the capacity to impress. The palace rears up above its piazza, behind a row of lesser buildings, dominating its slope of the Quirinal hill. Though much altered, the complex remains one of Rome's most impressive princely court structures and has a unique double nature, at once a city palace and a suburban villa. It is visible from as far away as the Janiculan hill across the Tiber and has two very different and distinctive façades: one, on the north, resembles a traditional Roman palace front, centrally planned with a *portone*, and the other, the west front, is an exuberant flourish of arcades on three storeys, resembling the Villa Farnesina built a century previously by Agostino Chigi (for which see the Chigi itinerary).

I THE PALACE AND ITS DEVELOPMENT

The splendid site of the palace made it a natural location for a suburban villa in the sixteenth century. Cardinal Rodolfo Pio da Carpi bought a small

The main façade of palazzo Barberini (centre left), overlooked the cortile della Cavallerizza. The now-demolished teatro Barberini is shown at right angles to the main façade, on the left.

casina (villa building) here from the Cesi family in 1549, which was praised by the sixteenth-century antiquarian Ulisse Aldovrandi as a place of delight, uniting nature with the cultivated pleasure of a sculpture collection; the same cardinal later sold it to the della Rovere family, from whom it passed by inheritance into the hands of a branch of the Farnese, the Sforza of Santa Fiora. They sold it in 1625 to Cardinal Francesco Barberini, who soon transferred legal title of it to his secular brother Taddeo. The former pleasure grounds of Cardinal Pio da Carpi turned into a vast construction site, with work continuing until 1633.

The neighbourhood was still semi-rural. The nearest built-up part of Rome lay to the north, towards the Pincio hill and piazza di Spagna. South and east the area was full of gardens and farms, while to the west lay monasteries and nunneries, set in their own gardens. Palazzo Sforza stood in this area like a cuckoo in the nest, a town palace with no town around it. The palace was an odd shape, a brick of a building, not set round a courtyard but simply a long thin structure three windows deep, whose *piano nobile* backed on to the gardens at the higher ground level.

Urban VIII and his nephews changed the building almost completely. Their chief architect, the ageing Carlo Maderno, first considered a traditional square palace design set round a central courtyard, but chose a radically different design in the shape of an H, with the existing Sforza palace forming one of the long sides and the short crossbar taking on the appearance of a series of loggias. Maderno died only four years into the project, in 1629, but he had already introduced two architects into his workshop who were to prove decisive for the formation of the Roman Baroque. After Maderno's death, Gianlorenzo Bernini, thirty-one years old, was appointed head of the building works, with only one architectural project, the church of Santa Bibiana, in his past.

The second great architect was Maderno's own relative, a young mason and stuccoist from the Ticino region in the north, Francesco Borromini (1599–1667). His early years were spent learning the building trade in Milan and when he came to Rome in 1619 he was already well versed in the practicalities. He was given some decorative work in Maderno's *cantiere* (building site) at St Peter's and because of his excellent draughtsmanship he soon became the older architect's right-hand man.

It has become customary to contrast the characters and careers of Bernini and Borromini. Bernini, after all, was a consummate courtier, friendly, charming, increasingly rich and almost without interruption successful, while Borromini was withdrawn, unsociable, neurotic, almost paranoid, indifferent to wealth and often acted as his own worst enemy, withdrawing from commissions in anger or being fired for his delays. Yet Borromini was by far the more inventive architect and the one who inspires the most admiration today. Bernini's architectural style was accomplished, sculptural and modestly innovative, but for the most part his passion was for classicism in form, matched with lavishness in material. Borromini, on the other hand, employed a classical vocabulary without a strict attachment to its rules and preferred to use a complicated geometry to express his ideas, keeping colour and costly materials to a minimum.

In palazzo Barberini the two architects worked in a slightly uneasy alliance. Bernini was responsible for the design of the great salon, which takes up two storeys of the central block, and the oval room behind it, as well as the square-plan staircase that today leads to the Galleria Nazionale (for which see below). However, it is likely that he relied a good deal on the experience of Borromini, to whom other features have been ascribed, including perhaps the palace's most beautiful architectural feature, the staircase in the south block, a single helix on an oval plan. Cardinal Francesco Barberini, who was in a position to know, ascribed the greater part of the palace to Borromini. That the north wing was the main front also determined that the main staircase would be there: designed by Bernini along lines set by Maderno (one recognises echoes of Maderno's main staircase in palazzo Mattei di Giove), it brought visitors up into a vestibule that gave on to the great salone where Pietro da Cortona's famous fresco was the main decorative element.

The **palace exterior** is a complex organism arranged on several levels. The principal entrance was originally from piazza Barberini, through a great arch that opened more or less where the mouth of the modern via Barberini now gapes at the back of the piazza: it led via a ramp into the great lower court, the **cortile della Cavallerizza** (Courtyard of the Riding School). Today this survives only as a strip of cobbled terrace between the palace and a wing of modern buildings, but in the seventeenth century it was the site of some of the most splendid displays of pageantry and fireworks ever held in Rome, often featured in paintings and engravings. At the eastern end of the cortile is a modern building that incorporates stone details like the entrance *portone* and window frames from Pietro da Cortona's great **Teatro Barberini**, commissioned by Cardinal Antonio the Younger in 1640. Seating 3000, it was one of the principal centres for Baroque opera and other forms of music, and formed the setting for much lavish spectacle. Mussolini demolished it to open the ugly via Barberini. The west façade, with its porticoes, was at a higher level and could be reached from via delle Quattro Fontane. The vast gardens, today much reduced, were originally only reached via the noble apartments, as *giardini segreti* along the lines of those in the villa Borghese, but in the later seventeenth century a ramp was cut from the middle of the west façade, behind Borromini's great carriage vestibule, through to the back of the palace, making it a more accessible area. Of the formerly splendid gardens little remains, though the grounds-man still breeds tame rabbits that hop about free, a last trace of the palace's almost rural original setting. At the back of the grounds is the one remaining garden statue from the seventeenth century, the *Apollo Barberini*, an Apollo of the lyre-playing type, much restored. Round the side of the palace Bernini built a broken bridge or **ponte rotto**, perhaps Europe's first false ruin, the broken part made whole with a wooden bridge leading to the cardinals' garden, now part of the Armed Forces Club grounds.

The palace was meant as a showpiece, the setting for a glittering court, but it also had to house two different aspects of the family: the secular side, the princes of Palestrina beginning with Taddeo Barberini, and the ecclesiastical side. As they had specific and differing roles and status, the palace was constructed in an H to give them separate parts of the building. The princes of Palestrina had the north (ex-Sforza) wing, while the cardinals possessed the south. As we will see, this division is still clearly indicated in the interior of palazzo Barberini.

II THE INTERIOR OF THE PALACE

The palazzo Barberini is a splendid guide to the basic module of every noble palace in Rome: the apartment. The expression of status had a living component in the etiquette of the Roman aristocracy, which had come to be among Europe's most complex. It was outlined in different handbooks, so a family's major-domo could consult an authoritative text. Offering insult and doing honour, two sides of the same coin, could have serious consequences. Rank was paramount: in Rome, of course, churchmen outranked laymen and this was reflected in etiquette. There were other gradations, too: elder members of a family outranked younger, older families outranked newer ones, and ambassadors of more powerful nations outranked those of weaker ones. This rank was also expressed in different ways. The size of one's retinue was a certain indicator of status (larger was better), but the most telling sign was the way one was treated by other nobles. Palazzo Barberini was constructed to allow the largest possible variation of politeness.

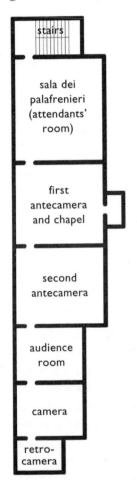

Particularly respected guests would be greeted by the host upon arrival, but that was a supreme honour, seldom granted. Guests could be met at the top of the stairs, in the first room in the suite, or, depending on the gradations of rank of both guest and host, at almost any point between the stairs and the audience room. The more important the guest, the more the host moved forwards to greet him (and it was usually a 'him'). The noble apartment was designed for this human chess game.

A guest would climb the stairs to the *piano nobile*, usually the floor above ground level, and if he had not already been met at ground level by the *palafrenieri* (attendants) of the host, he would be met either at the top of the stairs or at the door to the big main room of the apartment, the *sala dei palafrenieri*, where the host's attendants would

The noble apartment, a schematic diagram for seventeenth-century Roman palaces (after P. Waddy). The rooms progressed, via an enfilade – a series of aligned doorways – from larger to smaller and from more public to more private.

gather. This room had a *baldacchino* in it, to one side, with a piece of furniture called a credenza beneath it which stored the dishes for banquets: these dishes were sometimes displayed on top of the credenza. The furnishing was quite minimal, with only benches for the attendants, and chests lining the walls that contained bedding for the night staff who slept here, in case their master required anything.

The next set of rooms in the suite were the antecamere ('before-rooms'), which preceded the main audience room (*camera d'udienza*). In the sixteenth century there was seldom more than one antecamera, but in the seventeenth it was customary to have at least two, and sometimes more. In some particularly elaborate palaces, like palazzo Barberini, there would be side chambers branching off the antecamera that served as waiting rooms if the host were already occupied. The first antecamera had another *baldacchino* in it, if the host were a cardinal: when he was not there, the chair was turned to the wall. A chapel generally opened off this room; though it was not, as a rule, particularly large, it was so located as to permit the whole antecamera to be used as a subsidiary chapel space if the connecting doors were open. Quite often the chapel had a window into it from a more private room in the suite, so the host could hear Mass in isolation.

The last public room was the audience room, generally of moderate size. It too was strongly tied to representing the power and courtesy of the host, and here too gradations of rank were observed: a curtain called a *portiera* separated the audience room from the second antecamera, which could be left raised or half lowered, or lowered completely, depending on the prestige of the guest being given the audience. The position of the chairs of guest and host was also an important determiner of rank, since that facing the entrance door was more prestigious; the Barberini courtier Cassiano dal Pozzo described a visit of the Grand Duke of Tuscany to Cardinal Francesco Barberini in which both the Grand Duke's chair and the cardinal's were positioned so as to have their sides facing the door, though the Grand Duke, 'through an excess of goodness and modesty', adjusted the position of his chair on two occasions to show deference to the cardinal. Cardinal Francesco, not to be outdone, moved his own chair accordingly to restore the balance of politeness. In palazzo Barberini this audience room was furnished with yet another *baldacchino*, whose tapestried ceiling can now be seen in the Museo di Roma.

After the audience room was the host's bedroom, the camera, where on certain occasions, to avoid a mistake in courtesy, he might retire, claiming illness, until he could determine the proper degree of courtesy to be offered an unexpected guest. By the end of the seventeenth century, the bedroom, too, had taken on a state function and an official bed or *zampanaro* could be used for a public retiring ceremony at night: the noble occupant would be escorted into his or her state bed, perhaps receiving more visitors at the same time; then, after the visitors and attendants left, he or she would go to the real bedroom not far away in the private suite. Behind the bedroom was a smaller room, the retrocamera, the most private in the suite, which could be used as a study, a gallery or a library. There was no fixed dining room, though generally meals were set up in the first antecamera, and banquets in the *sala dei palafrenieri*, due to its size. Rituals connected with dining were also laboured and governed by etiquette: when the host drank, for example, the attendants all had to doff their hats. It was thought notable that Cardinal Antonio Barberini the Elder ate alone and simply, with his table turned to the wall. Separate bathrooms were rare and nobles bathed in portable tubs in their private rooms; chamberpots and *chaises percées* were used for the bodily necessities.

Palazzo Barberini was constructed to suit the demands of rigid seventeenth-century etiquette. The linear sequence of rooms left over from the old Sforza palace needed little adaptation for the elaborate dance of formality. However, other complications had to be addressed. Not only did the ecclesiastical and the secular parts of the family need distinct areas but the two Barberini cardinals required apartments that were both completely separate and reflected their different ranks, with Antonio the Younger subtly less important. On the secular side, both Taddeo Barberini, Prince of Palestrina, and his wife Anna Colonna had to have separate apartments. And on top of that, all of these personages needed a summer and a winter apartment. These requirements imposed a vast size on palazzo Barberini.

The palace's north wing, where the Galleria Nazionale is presently arranged, was given over to the secular side, and its rather conventional façade with *portone* did, indeed, serve as a traditional family palace entrance. However, there were two noble floors in the north wing, since the ground floor on the west façade level corresponded with the first floor from the piazza Barberini–cortile della Cavallerizza level. This floor, which we will call for convenience the first noble floor, was designated for the use of Prince Taddeo, the family's principal dynast, Prince of Palestrina and prefect of Rome. Yet the main apartment was reserved not for the Barberini prince but for his wife, Anna Colonna Barberini.

The reason for this extraordinary and at first glance puzzling arrangement is interesting. Anna Colonna represented many things to the Barberini. To begin with she was a link with the ancient family of the Colonna, and thereby brought legitimate Roman nobility to their new and foreign (Tuscan) family. She also provided continuity between the old rulers of Palestrina, which Urban VIII bought for Taddeo in 1624 from the

Colonna, and the new. But perhaps most important, she was the pope's closest female relative and as such had to function in a sense as his state consort, a hostess for diplomatic ceremonies. As a pure-blood Roman noblewoman she was excellently suited for the task and consequently she received the palace's greatest apartment, whose *sala dei palafrenieri* was the huge salone of Pietro da Cortona.

The Galleria Nazionale is slowly closing and renovating different parts, and thus it is not possible to describe a room-by-room visit to the north wing, while the south wing, with the exception of the Princess Cornelia Costanza apartment on the second floor, has never been open to the public. The Galleria Nazionale is presently arranged in some of the rooms of Princess Anna's apartment; if plans to expand into both wings of the palace on both noble floors ever come to pass, a visit to the Prince Taddeo apartment and the cardinalate apartments will also be possible. However, some general outlines may help to make the decoration of the palace more understandable, both to visitors and to readers interested in Barberini pictorial self-glorification.

The north wing was the more lavishly decorated. Taddeo and Anna took up residence there in 1632: by then, building works must have finished, as it would be impossible for the couple to perform their state functions in rooms that were still under scaffolding. The decoration of Prince Taddeo's suite on the first noble floor was elegant and entirely classical in theme. A visitor, arriving at the front door, would enter a hall (today's ticket hall for the Galleria Nazionale) and proceed, as gallery visitors do now, up the staircase directly opposite the front door. However, at the top of the stairs the seventeenth-century visitor would turn left into Taddeo's *sala dei palafrenieri*. At the moment this is the entrance room to the Circolo delle Forze Armate, the Army Officers' Club, and therefore not accessible. From the *sala* Taddeo's guest would proceed through no less than three antecamere before reaching the audience chamber; a chapel opened off the second antecamera and an even more private oratory for the use of the prince alone was set beside it, frescoed with an image of Taddeo's guardian angel. The audience hall itself had a ceiling fresco depicting *Parnassus*, the mythical gathering of the muses with Apollo on the top of Mount Parnassus that represented the arts in glory. Other frescoes in the apartment represented the legend of Orpheus and the room preceding the audience hall was frescoed with an image of Hercules.

Here, of course, the idea was to connect the attributes of Apollo with Urban VIII himself, with the pope's nephew Taddeo standing in as Hercules, a most useful hero for Roman families, representing strength and heroic virtue. The four private rooms of Prince Taddeo's suite in palazzo Barberini occupied the north-west of the palace's H shape and were directly beneath those of Anna, linked by a private spiral staircase.

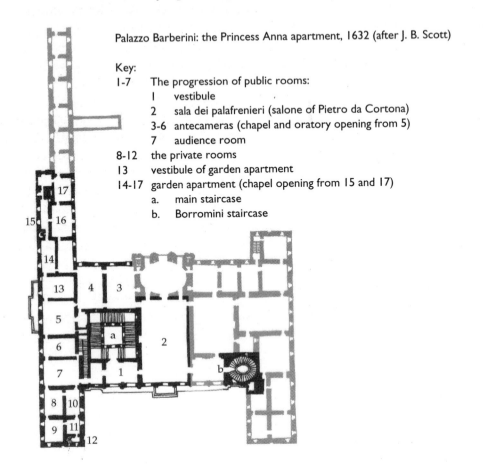

Palazzo Barberini: the Princess Anna apartment, 1632 (after J. B. Scott)

Key:

1-7	The progression of public rooms:
1	vestibule
2	sala dei palafrenieri (salone of Pietro da Cortona)
3-6	antecameras (chapel and oratory opening from 5)
7	audience room
8-12	the private rooms
13	vestibule of garden apartment
14-17	garden apartment (chapel opening from 15 and 17)
a.	main staircase
b.	Borromini staircase

Upstairs, the great rooms of **the Princess Anna apartment** can generally be visited, as they contain the collection of the Galleria Nazionale. The way in is under the west loggia, to the entrance at the foot of the **Great Staircase**. The effect of this colossal space is somewhat damaged by the insertion of an elevator, but the wide, shallow steps designed by Bernini (perfect for the skirts of noblewomen and prelates alike) seem to sweep visitors up towards each corner landing, where a statue faces out from a niche. The bases of these statues are all covered with Barberini emblems, not simply the bee, but the sun and laurel of Apollo. At the entrance to the upper noble floor an antique statue of a lion stands guard beside the doorway, under the gaze of a statue of Apollo himself.

The **entrance vestibule** is decorated with portrait busts by Bernini:

Antonio the Elder and Urban VIII by the right-hand door, and a similar Urban VIII and the sixteenth-century Antonio Barberini assassinated by Medici agents, also by Bernini, on the other side. The portals are signposts to the parts of the palace on either side. Above the gallery entrance is the marital crest of Anna Colonna Barberini (the Barberini bees on the left, the papal keys and parasol in the middle and the Colonna column on the right), while the opposite door, which leads into the salone, has nothing but the Barberini crest: the salone was shared space, the *sala dei palafrenieri* of both Princess Anna and her brothers-in-law the cardinals, the other door being private, leading into the Princess Anna apartment alone. This door now forms the main entrance to the Galleria Nazionale.

Visitors in the seventeenth century would be led to the left, where the **great salone** of Pietro da Cortona waits to stupefy the guest. This vast room, whose walls are now a rather gloomy grey, once blazed with tapestries from the Barberini tapestry works. However, it was a public space – anyone could enter – and was sparsely furnished, as were all rooms of this type: though it resembles a ballroom, in fact it was purpose built as a waiting room for attendants. It was shared by the cardinals' apartment on the far side, but was principally considered part of the Princess Anna suite. It was lit by the windows in the east and west fronts, and heated by a vast fireplace set into the north wall.

Though Carlo Maderno had made similar rooms, this was certainly the largest *sala* in a Roman palace and its huge vault, unencumbered by inserted windows or a visible framework in stucco, was used by Pietro da Cortona as a canvas for a gigantic ceiling fresco whose ambition and skill were not to be surpassed. Cortona was hired by the pope himself, with the support of Cardinal Francesco, and carried it out from 1632 to 1639. This long duration is explained by the fact that the artist was dissatisfied with much of the work when it was finished and remade it. His absences from the palace prompted a revolt from among his assistants, who intrigued to supplant their boss, with the active support of Prince Taddeo. However, these plans were thwarted by the pope and Cortona returned to finish the fresco to great acclaim. Less than a year after its completion the attendant responsible for the room found it worthwhile to publish a small pamphlet explaining the fresco to the hordes of visitors who had already begun to frequent what was to be one of Rome's main tourist sites for 200 years.

Cortona's fresco, *The Triumph of Divine Providence*, provides a complex allegory of the election and policies of Urban VIII. Apart from its propagandistic meaning, however, it is one of the supreme masterpieces of Baroque art, a fantastical and magical irruption of the supernatural into the real world of the palace, with its violent motion and powerful visual thrust upwards. From a point in front of the central window of the salone, looking into the room, the figure of Divine Providence rears up on a bank of cloud. Divine Providence, the force that allowed Urban to be elected by secret ballot not once but twice, rules over the present and the future: accordingly, Time, in the form of the god Saturn, is represented below her throne, and beside him are the Fates, representing the future. Round the central figure others are grouped in the background, among them Justice, Mercy, Eternity and Truth. Divine Providence is commanding Immortality, the figure flying up to the left bearing a diadem of stars, to crown the Barberini coat of arms, remarkably depicted as a set of three colossal bees flying skywards and occupying as real a space as the other figures. The bees are surrounded by laurel branches held by the figures of Faith and Hope at the sides and Charity at the bottom, the three principal theological virtues. Religion holds the papal keys above the crest and above her is the goddess Rome, holding the tiara. A cherub to the left holds another laurel wreath, signifying the poetic skill of the pope.

The idea of Divine Providence was strongly linked to the fatal conclave in which Urban VIII was elected. The unexpected success of Maffeo Barberini was much celebrated as an act expressing the unknowable will of God, through the medium of the new secret balloting process instituted by a bull of the previous pope, Gregory XV. A contemporary wrote:

> The election could with reason be called surprising not only because of the circumstance of Gregory's new bull, but also because of the great number of old and meritorious cardinals and the disunion of the heads of the two opposed factions. No less worthy of admiration is Divine Providence, which, after having restored to the electors their freedom of choice by means of secret voting, with no less gentleness made them know how to conduct themselves in this election so that the majority of them confessed to not being able in this conclave to elect as pope anyone other than Cardinal Barberini.

A sign of Divine Providence, witnessed before the election, entered Barberini family legend: during the conclave a swarm of bees coming from the direction of Tuscany, where the family originated, was said to have alighted on the exterior wall of the future pope's cell. Nothing could have been more propitious, or more remarked-upon, and this may have been part of the genesis of this vast fresco.

Around this central scene four others are displayed: clockwise from the back wall (the wall facing the west façade with its three windows), the subjects are *Minerva overthrowing the Giants*, a metaphor about Wisdom defending attacks upon the Church; *Moral Knowledge being lifted Heavenwards* by the figure of Divine Assistance, flanked on both sides by scenes of peacetime; *Temporal Government* (above the western wall) as represented by Authority carrying the ancient Roman symbol of office, the fasces, and Abundance with her cornucopia, while Hercules casts out the Harpies, representing the chastisement of temporal monarchs. These figures allude to the three papal nephews, Authority being Cardinal Francesco as vice-chancellor, Abundance being Cardinal Antonio the Younger as papal chamberlain (in charge of alms giving) and Hercules, as we have seen before, standing in for Prince Taddeo. The fourth side painting, above the entrance wall, represents *Dignity* in the sense of 'rank', probably personifying the papacy, whose rank was supreme. Dignity is looking into a mirror offered by Prudence, while Power is carrying orders to lock the doors of the Temple of Janus, which are being closed by Peace. Though the walls are now generally bare, they once were covered with large tapestries, each in its own way elaborating the theme of family virtue. This colossal room was an eloquent assertion of Barberini authority and its trumpet blasts were assertive precisely to deafen critics of the family's modest origins.

From here it is occasionally possible to pass through the first rooms of the cardinals' suite, through the door directly opposite the one from the staircase vestibule. Note that the crests above the doors in this part of the palace have a cardinal's hat over them. At the end of the enfilade, the long line of doorways, a door opens on to the **oval staircase** of Borromini, also accessible from the west-front ground-floor loggia. This extraordinary staircase reaches all the way to the old Barberini library room, whose former contents now swell the Vatican collections; this was the principal service staircase for the cardinals' wing. Its design provides for a slow, measured ascent or descent, along the outside wall, or a rapid one towards the centre of the wall. The column capitals are simple, each adorned with a bee, but they all conform to a segment of an oval, rather than being awkward rectangles.

From the back of the salone, a door (usually closed) gives on to the **oval salon**, which was part of the cardinals' apartment and was used by Cardinal Francesco's court intellectuals, who held meetings and conferences there. The room, designed by Bernini, was soon to be echoed in Bernini's oval design for the church of Sant' Andrea al Quirinale, not far away. Today it can best be seen from the back of the palace, where great french doors open on to the rear terrace. Currently used as a dining room for the Armed Forces Club, it has been provided with very peculiar blond-wood furniture, a gift of the Spanish dictator Francisco Franco to Mussolini, for the two of them plotted the Spanish Civil War together in this room. The chairs have Franco's arrow emblem on the backrests. The rooms to the right, also in the cardinals' suite, are sometimes open for exhibitions and contain a series of ancient statues as well as a few seventeenth-century pieces belonging to the Barberini.

From the salone, the seventeenth-century visitor visiting the Princess Anna apartment would pass through the eastern door in the north wall and through two large antecamere which are not open to the public. For us to rejoin the sequence, we need to enter the Galleria Nazionale and go to the room (number 5 on the plan above) which was known as the **salotto** (lesser drawing room). This once served as a first audience hall for Princess Anna and as a main traffic intersection for the palace's different sets of rooms: a door in the centre of the southern wall gives into the **chapel**, containing a *Crucifixion* over the altar by Pietro da Cortona, and ceiling vault frescoes by Cortona and his circle. A door in the western corner, now walled up, once opened into Princess Anna's private oratory.

The *salotto* contains, as its ceiling fresco, the masterwork of another Baroque artist, Andrea Sacchi, the *Divine Wisdom,* painted in 1629–30. It has much in common with the later salone fresco of *Divine Providence,* though more austere. Both involve an illusionistic sky populated with allegorical figures. From its ideal viewpoint near the central window, the fresco rears up in its full *trompe-l'oeil* glory. Its programme is to praise Wisdom, the ruler of the world, the female figure at the centre of the painting, with the sun blazing from her heart. She is directing her spear bearers, above her, to aim at the earth below. One of them, riding a lion, is Love, and the other, seated on a hare, is Fear. Other figures to the left represent Divinity with Beneficence sitting below, Suavity holding a lyre, Strength holding the club of Hercules (Hercules again, which we by now easily recognise as an allusion to Prince Taddeo), Eternity with her mirror, Virtue holding a crown of stars, and Justice with scales. The group to the right of Divine Wisdom represents Holiness and Purity, with Perspicacity and Beauty below.

But what does it all mean? One of the most interesting things about this fresco is that it places the sun in the centre of the picture, with the earth in a subordinate position: it seems to express a Galilean view of the solar system, the very thing that was to be condemned by the Inquisition under Urban VIII's direction only two years after the fresco was completed. A clue is provided by a contemporary commentator, who wrote: 'Such a painting is appropriate to the majestic edifice of the Barberini family in order that it be understood that since that happy family was born and elected to rule the Church in the place of God, it governs with Divine Wisdom, equally loved and revered.' Divine Wisdom has many of the attributes of the Virgin Mary and the message is that wisdom can be attained in part through contemplation of the virtues that surround her. The room served as an antechamber for the chapel, where the household could gather to hear Mass. Divine Wisdom takes her place directly above the entrance to the chapel, indicating that prayer is the route to wisdom. It can also be interpreted as an expression of the just rule of the Barberini family. As well as a chapel antechamber, the chamber served as a reception room for greeting the visiting princes of Europe. Particularly important guests might be presented by Princess Anna with an easel copy of the fresco on the ceiling. In the corners a familiar emblem can be seen: the Colonna Siren, last seen on the entrance to the Villa Colonna.

The gilt stars in the ceiling fresco point towards another curiosity of the work: it expresses Urban VIII's interest in astrology. The pope had the somewhat disagreeable habit of having his cardinals' horoscopes cast, including their predicted deaths; when the tables were turned on Urban and his own death was forecast, he responded by forbidding astrological predictions and particularly those relative to popes. However, he remained a devoted believer and spent many hours with Tommaso Campanella, his court astrologer, whom he later silenced with a trial before the Inquisition. The *Divine Wisdom* represents the horoscope on the day of Urban's election, and certain elements of the fresco, like the hare, the lion, the eagle and the scales held by Justice, refer directly to the pope's fate as foretold by the stars.

The following room (6) acted as a **vestibule** to the princess's audience chamber (7). Its ceiling has a graceful fresco by Andrea Camassei (1602–49), one of Cortona's pupils, depicting the *Creation of the Angels*. The central figure of God the Father, derived from Michelangelo's Sistine Chapel ceiling, floats in a nimbus of light, surrounded by the hierarchy of angels, each with different attributes according to his rank, from the humble angels at the bottom through nine levels to the seraphim at the top. Not only does this reiterate the Barberini interest in rank, but it asserts the family's belief in angels as God's ministers and protectors of humanity (we have already noted that Taddeo's private oratory downstairs was frescoed with an image of his guardian angel).

The **audience chamber** (7) was redecorated in 1774 by the French painter Laurent Pécheux (1729–1821), after the original ceiling was damaged in a fire caused by lightning striking the rooms above, though along roughly similar lines to the original: it, too, has a Christian theme, the *Division of the Elements*, another part of the creation myth following on from the creation of the angels. From this room – which is, confusingly, the first room entered in the modern Galleria Nazionale – two doors opened on to the **private suite** (8–12), arranged in a square, where Anna Colonna Barberini had her bedroom (10), dressing rooms and private study, as well as the spiral stair (now blocked) that linked her private rooms to those of her husband. These are all frescoed with rather beautiful works by Antonio Viviani (1560–1620), an artist we have already met in the chapels at San Gregorio Magno decorated under Scipione Borghese; these frescoes are left over from the old Sforza palace and are of Old Testament scenes: clockwise from the south-eastern room (10), in narrative order, they are *The Flood, Noah and his Sons, Abraham with the Angels* and *Abraham with God.*

From the *salotto*, we can sometimes enter the vestibule of the **garden suite** (13–18), which also served as a waiting room for guests. Princess Anna used these rooms in the summer and the main room (16) had a door which gave on to a private garden with a fountain in it. The decorations in the main rooms have a lighter, summery theme, like a villa retreat for Anna Colonna to use for more intimate occasions, with her children. It, too, conserves frescoes left over from the Sforza occupancy, as well as some new landscapes depicting Barberini properties.

Upstairs on the second floor is the **Princess Cornelia Costanza apartment** (access, sometimes from the oval staircase, included in ticket for Galleria Nazionale; timed entry with Italian guide only). Decorated in 1750–70 in a rather debased Rococo style, this apartment expresses a completely different idea of how nobles should live. Where opulence was signified in the seventeenth century by living with a great crowd of attendants in huge sumptuous public rooms, in the eighteenth century the idea of privacy became paramount. Thus where there are no real corridors in the Princess Anna apartment, in the Princess Cornelia Costanza apartment a series of passages runs behind the walls for servants to scurry through, neither seen nor heard; cupboards often conceal doors to these corridors. These rooms are much smaller, though their decoration is no less thorough.

The principal room is the **salone delle battaglie** (hall of battles), whose two long sides are painted with scenes celebrating another union between the Colonna and Barberini families, when the last Barberini heiress, Cornelia Costanza (1716–97), married Giulio Cesare Colonna di Sciarra, Prince of Carbognano, in 1728, at the age of twelve. The histories of both families are represented, including the only portrait in Rome of the beatified Margherita Colonna. Other rooms here include an interesting **chinoiserie hall**, complete with a bizarre piece of Rococo furniture, half-mirror and half-sofa, a **chapel** that could be turned into a drawing room with the closing of shutters round the altar, a room with walls of painted silk representing scenes from the New World, a state bedroom, another chapel, **a room of seascapes**, which functioned as a men's smoking room, a dining room with secret doors for the servants and the **hall of desks**, where seventeenth-century *écritoires* of elaborate inlay line the walls. These rooms preserve little of their original furniture, apart from an elaborate cradle and a few other effects; the remainder come from a bequest by a noblewoman, Edith Dusmet, in 1950.

III· THE BARBERINI COLLECTIONS IN THE GALLERIA NAZIONALE

Urban VIII placed his family's collection of art under a *fidecommesso*, a legal act that forbade listed works to be sold or given away. This did not, however, include some pieces of extraordinary worth: the famous ancient glass vessel known as the Portland Vase, in the British Museum, was bought by Cardinal Francesco Barberini in 1627 and sold by Princess Cornelia Costanza in 1780 to pay her gambling debts. On her death in 1797 the old collections were equally divided between her first-born son, who took the Colonna di Sciarra name, and her second-born, who took that of Barberini. The Sciarra collection was broken up and sold in the late nineteenth century. At the end of the eighteenth century two daughters of Prince Carlo Barberini married into the Corsini family and took three-eighths of the collection to Florence. What remained was finally dispersed in 1934 when a special law broke the *fidecommesso* for good. The Italian state received one-third of the collection, a second third was thus freed for sale by the family without tax and the final third remained in the hands of the Barberini, subject to the normal laws of sale. Among the masterpieces sold in 1934 were works by Caravaggio and Poussin. In the Galleria Nazionale, added to the works received in 1934 are a further 112 sold by the Barberini family to the Italian state in 1952, in a continuing haemorrhage of the family wealth.

Among the fifteenth- and sixteenth-century works are a wonderful, almost Flemish *Nativity with Saints Lawrence and Andrew* by Antoniazzo Romano (*c.*1452–*c.*1512), a famous work by Andrea del Sarto (1486–1530), the *Holy Family*, which came from the original collection of Urban VIII, a beautiful *Madonna and Child with St John the Baptist* by Domenico Beccafumi (1486–1551), and Raphael's great *Fornarina* of *c.*1520, which may have hung in this palace when it was the property of the Sforza of Santa Fiora before passing into the hands of the Barberini in around 1642. The works reflect the predominantly Tuscan taste of the family.

Works by contemporary artists comprise the majority of the remaining Barberini collection. These include three paintings by Guido Reni. One, the *Sleeping Putto*, has a story attached to it, told by Bernini: Reni, who felt himself out of practice in fresco, used this as a practice piece. He had a small stucco panel prepared and then, in the presence of Cardinal Francesco Barberini, painted this putto so rapidly that the plaster had not dried by the time the work was done. Another Reni work, the St Mary Magdalene of 1633, was commissioned by Cardinal Antonio Santacroce and presented by his heir to Cardinal Antonio Barberini. A third is the Beatrice Cenci, whose subject and author have both frequently come into question. For several centuries, this was one of the most famous paintings in Rome: Nathaniel Hawthorne called it 'the saddest picture ever painted or conceived' and Herman Melville 'that sweetest, most touching, but most awful of feminine heads'. Another interesting work is Giovanni Lanfranco's painting of Venus playing the harp, painted for the court harpist, Marco Marazzuoli, who bequeathed it to Cardinal Antonio. The harp in the painting is the famous Arpa Barberini, now the centrepiece of Rome's Museo Nazionale degli Strumenti Musicali. It evokes the enormous musical output of the Barberini court, which produced pieces from chamber music to full operas.

Two paintings by Simon Vouet (1590–1649) show the lingering influence of Caravaggio: the Fortuneteller of 1617 and the Mary Magdalene. The latter shows a move to the Raphael-influenced classicism that was supplanting Caravaggism in Roman taste in the 1620s. An Allegory of Peace, painted by an enigmatic artist known only as 'the brother of the Cavalier Muti', also seems to have come from a member of Vouet's circle. The last major works are the huge cartoons made by Pietro da Cortona for the Barberini tapestry works. These are drawings on paper representing episodes from the life of the Emperor Constantine, and were commissioned by Cardinal Francesco in order to complete a tapestry cycle designed by Rubens and given to the cardinal by Louis XIII of France.

IV   THE PALACE IN HISTORY

The north wing was occupied by Prince Taddeo and his wife Anna for only two years. In early October of 1634 they moved back to the Casa Grande ai Giubbonari. The official reason was that the princess found the air on the Quirinal hill disagreeable, and the palace itself was very humid and damp. The real reason was that the superstitious Anna was pregnant and wanted to give birth to a boy: her two previous boys had been born in the Casa Grande, while in the palazzo Barberini she had borne a daughter. Not long afterwards, in 1635, the Princess Anna apartment was occupied by Cardinal Antonio the Younger. Here he held many sumptuous pageants, and sponsored operas specially written for his theatre, in the cortile della Cavallerizza.

During the period of the Barberini's disgrace (1645–7) the palazzo was threatened with expropriation by Innocent X. However, the family, in exile, managed to make sequestration impossible by lending it to the French ambassador. In the turbulent social environment an embassy was a focus for discontent and even armed activity, both as an emblem of some hated foreign power and because the ambassador's own men could easily issue out of the embassy and engage in hand-to-hand combat. The traditional hostility between France and Spain made the French occupancy of palazzo Barberini rather eventful: at one point in the summer of 1650, when Roman youths in piazza San Silvestro started throwing stones at the Spanish troops who were press-ganging Romans into the Spanish fleets, the French ambassador sent his men-at-arms out of the palazzo to help the stone throwers. Swift action by the pope's troops prevented an all-out anti-Spanish and anti-papal riot, but the episode showed how the palace was still one of the city's hot spots even in the Barberini's absence.

The family continued to occupy the palace until not long ago, but the main apartments fell out of fashion and were leased to different occupants. In the early nineteenth century the sculptor Bertel Thorvaldsen (1770–1844) rented the teatro Barberini as a studio and later another sculptor, the American William Wetmore Story, rented the Princess Anna apartment. He was closely linked with the literary and artistic world of nineteenth-century Rome. Henry James, his biographer, tells the story of a memorable children's party held there in 1854, where Hans Christian Andersen read out one of his stories, 'The Ugly Duckling', and Robert Browning read 'The Pied Piper', which, as James recounts, 'led to the formation of a grand march through the spacious Barberini apartment, with Story doing his best on a flute in lieu of bagpipes'. In 1949 the palace was sold to the Italian state, though the family occupied the Princess Cornelia Costanza apartment until the 1960s. In 1953 it played the role of an embassy once again, in the movie *Roman Holiday*, from which the young princess played by Audrey Hepburn escaped for a brief day and night of adventure: the palace, built to glorify its creators, became a gilded cage, keeping a free spirit away from the modern world.

V   PIAZZA BARBERINI AND ITS FOUNTAINS

The busy, traffic-ridden piazza Barberini has completely lost its former semi-rural appearance. With the construction of the via del Tritone in 1911–25, the sleepy piazza became the centre of a grand node of streets.

Originally the piazza was simply an adjunct to the former main street of the area, the *strada Felice* of Sixtus V that extends across the bottom of the piazza, changing its name from via Sistina to via delle Quattro Fontane as it does so. The palazzo Barberini does not dominate the piazza as it once did, either. With the demolition of Cardinal Antonio's theatre and the reduction

Piazza Barberini and the Triton fountain, by Vasi. The palace both dominates and withdraws from the piazza; the buildings at its foot housed Barberini family retainers.

of the cortile della Cavallerizza, the old formal entrance to the palace was masked behind an ugly row of low buildings, one of which today contains a cinema. The buildings on the corner of the piazza with via delle Quattro Fontane, backing on to the palace, once contained servants' lodgings. Today the piazza is home to one of modern Rome's ugliest twentieth-century buildings, the Hotel Bernini Bristol, and the principal sight, Bernini's great **fountain of the Triton**, is nearly inaccessible in the centre of a colossal traffic roundabout.

This fountain was one of Bernini's last commissions from Urban VIII and dates from 1642–3. Four dolphins bear on their tails a huge open shell, on the hinge of which sits a powerfully built merman or triton, who blows a conch-shell horn from which a plume of water rises skywards. It owes its water to Sixtus V's Acqua Felice, which it still displays today. Old engravings show it with much greater force to the water: when the neighbourhood was built up in the early twentieth century the water pressure suffered.

A more modest fountain by Bernini now stands on the corner of the piazza towards the via Veneto. This **fountain of the bees** shows three of the family's armorial insects bending to drink at three small spouts of water; another large scallop shell forms a backdrop for an inscription which when originally carved proclaimed that the fountain was placed by Urban VIII for the use of persons and their animals, in the twenty-second year of his pontificate. The superstitious Romans noted that the inscription anticipated the actual arrival of Urban's twenty-second regnal year: one pasquinade remarked that Bernini must be 'more blind than I thought!' and another said bitterly that 'now that the Barberini have drained the whole world dry, they want to drain time itself'. Cardinal Francesco nervously ordered the extra 'I' to be taken from the 'XXII' of the inscription (no trace of it can now be seen), but it was too late: bad luck had already been decreed for the pope. Sure enough, Urban VIII died only eight days before his twenty-second year as pope would have begun. The fountain used to stand on the corner with the via Sistina, but it was removed as an obstacle to traffic in 1887 and placed in its current position in 1919. Its original character as a wall fountain is clearly indicated by the rough blocks at its back.

VI   SANTA MARIA DELLA CONCEZIONE AND THE CAPUCHIN CRYPT

Via Veneto at piazza Barberini. Open 9–12, 16–18. Crypt open at same time, offering required for admission

The spiritual renewal which provoked the foundation of new orders like the Theatines in the early sixteenth century also inspired the reform of existing orders. The Capuchins are a reformed Franciscan order, which strove to rid itself of the curse of property. In 1528 three Franciscan friars, who wore a pointed brown hood or *cappuccio* over their habits, in imitation of the costume St Francis was depicted as having worn, won permission from Clement VII de' Medici to live according to their own precepts, freeing them from censure by their superiors. Other Franciscans joined this new reformed group, which utterly rejected property in the personal sense and sternly restricted property held in common, which was, in any case, to remain in the hands of a benefactor or of the town where it stood. No more land was to be taken for monasteries than that which was strictly necessary for the building itself; the monasteries were meant to be extremely humble and if possible built of wattle and mud, while the churches were to be small and narrow. 'The friars are to bear in mind the admonition of St Francis', said the original constitution of the order, 'that their churches and houses must be such as to proclaim that those who dwell in them are but pilgrims and strangers on the earth.' Initially no more than twelve monks were to live together in their monasteries, which were called hermitages, though this inevitably changed as the order grew more popular.

The Capuchins were at the forefront of Franciscan extremism and their best preacher, Bernardino Ochino, was so popular that in the churches where he spoke, people sat in the rafters to hear him. The devout Marchioness of Pescara, Vittoria Colonna, was one of the order's protectors. In 1542 her intervention saved it when Ochino, the General, fled Rome for Protestant territory, fearing the oppression of the newly established Roman Inquisition. Though the order survived, it remained on the very edge of orthodoxy, practising an aggressive self-mortification.

This was the order that Urban VIII's younger brother, the future Cardinal Antonio the Elder, joined before his brother became pope. Even though he reluctantly had to take on worldly responsibilities, Cardinal Antonio remained faithful to Capuchin precepts. By Urban's accession the Capuchins possessed a small convent on the lower slope of the Quirinal hill (today's church of Santa Croce e San Bonaventura ai Lucchesi, given to the citizens of Lucca by Urban VIII in 1631), but he and Urban agreed that this was not large enough for the size of the community, which was transferred to a new church and monastery, **Santa Maria della Concezione**. These were built in 1626–30, on the far side of piazza Barberini, to the plans of the architect Antonio Casoni (1559–1634), who was already working for the Irish Franciscans at Sant' Isidoro nearby.

Before the opening of the via Veneto the church possessed a dominant position in a piazza of its own, piazza dei Cappuccini, adjoining piazza Barberini in extensive grounds belonging to the ostensibly property-free order. Piazza dei Cappuccini was famous for its *olmata* (elm grove), a double row of trees in the space before the church. When the via Veneto was cut through in 1886–9 the piazza and convent were destroyed, the ground level was lowered and all that remains of the original urban design are two minor streets, via dei Cappuccini and its cross-street, via della Purificazione. A new convent was built to the right of the church's austere façade in 1926, 'on the seventh centenary of the transit of St Francis' as it says in an inscription on the front. A double staircase was built to adapt the church to the new lower ground level, and the burial crypt of the Capuchin brothers, formerly underground, found itself floating well above ground level. A door on the right-hand landing of the stairs to the church now gives admission; most visitors to Rome visit the crypt and ignore the church.

The church's dark **interior** at first seems to conform with the requirements of humility. Five chapels on either side of a nave lead up to the presbytery or main altar space. When it was first built the church was the tallest structure in the area and was full of light, not being dwarfed by high-rises as it is today.

Santa Maria della Concezione is remarkable for having nearly all its chapels simultaneously sponsored by different members of the Barberini family, making it, more than any other church, an expression of the artistic

The austere façade of Santa Maria della Concezione dominated its own piazza until the creation of the via Veneto. Vasi leaves out the *olmata* or elm grove in the piazza, which must have contributed greatly to this church's semi-rural setting.

and spiritual interests of the family. There is no overarching decorative or religious theme, probably because different Barberini patrons were interested in different religious episodes and styles. The **first chapel** on the right has, as its altarpiece, a 1636 painting by Guido Reni, the *Archangel Michael*. Cardinal Antonio the Elder was the commissioning patron and his choice of subject reflects the family devotion to the cult of angels. The archangel is depicted defeating the devil, who turns wrathfully towards him: the devil's face is said to be a malicious portrait of Giambattista Pamphilj, the future Pope Innocent X, who was no friend of Reni's, arguing with the artist over the interior decoration of St Peter's. Cardinal Pamphilj confronted the artist about his depiction as the devil and Reni retorted that he had striven to depict a face of pure evil: if the cardinal resembled it, that was a defect of the cardinal's physiognomy, not of Reni's art. Not too surprisingly, Reni never got any commissions from Pamphilj.

The **second chapel** has an altarpiece commissioned by Prince Taddeo for the family chapel in Sant' Andrea della Valle, but which ended up here instead: it is a *Transfiguration* by Mario Balassi (1605–67) and is loosely based on the more famous *Transfiguration* of Raphael now in the Vatican Museums. On a side wall is a *Nativity* by Giovanni Lanfranco, commissioned in 1631, perhaps the original altarpiece. The **third chapel** has as its altarpiece an *Ecstasy of St Francis* by Domenichino, which the artist painted just before his departure for Naples in 1630: he painted it as an *ex voto* in gratitude for having been cured of a dangerous illness and it once decorated the presbytery of the church. Another Domenichino painting, a fresco saved from the old convent when it was demolished, hangs on the left-hand wall, depicting the same subject. The **fourth chapel** has a painting by an older artist, Baccio Ciarpi (1574–1654), the *Oration of Jesus in the Garden*, commissioned by Cardinal Francesco, perhaps on the recommendation of Pietro da Cortona. The last chapel on the right-hand side, the **fifth chapel**, has an altarpiece showing *St Anthony of Padua raising a dead man*: it was made by Andrea Sacchi from 1631 to 1636 at the order of Cardinal Antonio the Younger. The **high altar** is somewhat disappointing, as it is an eighteenth-century copy of an original by Lanfranco, which was badly damaged in a fire. From the fifth chapel, access is given to the back of the church area, including two saints' rooms, a truly hideous statue of the new Capuchin saint, Padre Pio, and the lovely **Choir** which contains more art of the early seventeenth century.

Across the nave the **fifth chapel on the left** has another Sacchi altarpiece (mostly painted by assistants), *St Bonaventure adores the Virgin*, which was commissioned by the patient Cardinal Antonio the Younger in 1631 but not executed until 1635–6. The next chapel towards the main entrance sports a nineteenth-century image of the Virgin, but the **third chapel on the left** has a rather beautiful *Pietà* from 1631 by Andrea Camassei. The altarpiece in the **second chapel on the left** depicts *San Felice da Cantalice receiving the Holy Infant from the Virgin*. One of the first paintings in the new church, it was made in 1629–30, probably for Cardinal Antonio the Elder, by Alessandro Turchi, called L'Orbetto (1578–1650). The subject, the first Capuchin saint, was beatified by Urban VIII in 1625. Finally, the **first chapel on the left** has a beautiful altarpiece by Pietro da Cortona, *St Paul healed by Ananias*, made in 1631 at the order of Cardinal Francesco. The decoration of the church shows a restrained classicism, as well as the enduring though fading influence of Caravaggio, one of whose paintings, a *St Francis*, used to hang here before being moved to the state collections. In the centre of the nave, before the high altar, is the unpretentious tomb of Cardinal Antonio the Elder: 'HIC JACET PULVIS, CINIS, ET NIHIL' (here lies dust, ashes and nothing). This indifference towards the body, embracing what St Francis called 'sister bodily death', is taken to an extreme in the crypt below.

In the **Capuchin crypt**, more than 4000 separate skeletons of Capuchin monks and their lay admirers were used, from the late seventeenth century onwards, to decorate the five chapels. A chapel in the middle of the sequence, the only one with no bones visible in it, contains tomb monuments of different Roman aristocrats, including the great-niece of Pope Sixtus V, attesting to the power of the order to attract the wealthy patrons it needed. In the last chapel, furthest from the entrance, the centrepiece is a whole skeleton of a child on the ceiling, representing Death with a sickle and the scales of justice. These are the remains of an eighteenth-century Barberini princess who died young.

VII SAN CARLO ALLE QUATTRO FONTANE
Via del Quirinale, corner with via delle Quattro Fontane. Open 9–13, 16–19

In 1599 Clement VIII Aldobrandini approved a constitution or *regola* that reformed the medieval order of the Trinitarians, bringing them back to the principles established by their founder, San Giovanni de Matha, in 1198. This created the branch called the Discalced or 'shoeless' Trinitarians, the name reflecting their commitment to personal poverty; its unreformed and 'shod' brother order, the Trinitari Calzi, died out in the nineteenth century. In 1609 four Spanish brothers of the order came to Rome, to find a site for their mother house. The site at the Quattro Fontane seemed ideal: on the edge of the built-up section of the city, it nonetheless nearly adjoined the pope's summer palace at the Quirinal and was well supplied with water from Sixtus V's fountains. They bought a house there in 1611 and developed it into a tiny monastic community, converting a room into a chapel, which they dedicated to the Trinity and to San Carlo Borromeo, the Milanese aristocrat and papal nephew of Pius IV, recently canonised.

The building was too small to be useful, but the poverty-stricken order could not afford a great building or a famous architect. Accordingly, in 1634 they chose the relatively unknown Francesco Borromini to redesign the site to include a church and monastery, with maximum density on their tiny plot of land. Borromini, fresh from work at the palazzo Barberini a block away, offered his services as an act of faith, for free. The order was without rich sponsors, but one of their number, Juan de la Anunciación, was the private confessor of Cardinal Francesco Barberini, and the cardinal made a donation of 1000 scudi. Expensive materials were out of the question: the Trinitarian brothers had difficulty even paying the builders to put brick upon brick. The complex, in plain stucco and brick, was finished in just seven years, the church itself in an extraordinary three (1638–41). The result is one of the most beautiful Baroque spaces in Rome, a fluid sequence of well-designed areas maximising the small available area while maintaining an air of monastic contemplation.

The **interior**, in white with gilded details, has been recently restored to its original Borrominian appearance. Its floor plan is designed on two triangles set base to base, and the theme of threes, implying the Trinity, repeats again and again. The high altar, by Pierre Mignard (1612–95), depicts the *Holy Trinity with the Founders of the Trinitarian Order*, but the principal ornament of the church is undoubtedly the dome, a large oval whose coffers are suffused with light from partially concealed windows. To the left of the high altar is the **Barberini chapel**, with an altarpiece by Romanelli, a *Rest on the Flight to Egypt*. In the ceiling is a discreet inscription commemorating the patronage of Cardinal Francesco Barberini and a crest with the familiar bees. Borromini intended this church as his burial place and perhaps the unadorned but visually arresting side chapel in the **crypt** (accessible by a corridor behind the high altar) was to be his; in the event, he was buried in San Giovanni dei Fiorentini near his relative, Carlo Maderno.

3 The Barberini in the centre of ancient Rome

This nineteenth-century view of the Forum (from the Orti Farnesiani) shows livestock grazing among the mounds of earth which concealed the ruins. By then, the Forum had been almost entirely surrounded by monastic buildings like those of Sant' Adriano, the former Senate House, to the right. Behind is the Barberini church of Santi Luca e Martina.

The old heart of the Roman republic and the empire, the Forum, was a neglected backwater in the early seventeenth century. Repeated floods had brought with them the typical alluvial silt which gave the Tiber its distinctive yellow-brown colour, and the ancient ground level had vanished to depths perhaps as great as 4–6 metres below the present surface. The Forum had become slowly enclosed with residential structures, churches and monasteries, while the work of the papally sanctioned *scavatori* (stone robbers) continued to demolish what remained of the ancient structures. These were thoroughly despoiled in the sixteenth century, particularly, as we have seen, under Paul III Farnese. The Roman Forum itself remained an open space, a sort of no man's land where Roman youths from different *rioni* could engage in bloody rock-throwing battles, and it was still used as a pasture, from which its old common name, the *Campo Vaccino* (cow field), was derived. Paul III had tidied up the stretch of the via Papalis that passed in front of the Orti Farnesiani. But until the first archaeological excavations in the eighteenth century the Forum was a melancholy place composed of mud and bushes, with only a few columns and the arch of Septimius Severus poking up from the earth to indicate what once had stood there.

Over the centuries, churches slowly found a place here. It seems unlikely that the Barberini family undertook a concerted programme: instead, a series of different impulses motivated various family members to undertake works involving nearly every church in the area.

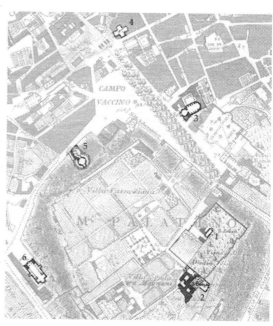

The Barberini in the centre of ancient Rome

Key:
1   San Sebastiano in Pallara
2   San Bonaventura
3   Santi Cosma e Damiano
4   Santi Luca e Martina
5   San Teodoro
6   Sant' Anastasia

THE PALATINE: SAN SEBASTIANO AND SAN BONAVENTURA
Via di San Bonaventura (access from the via Sacra, entrance from
piazza del Colosseo). San Sebastiano open Monday–Saturday,
9–12.30, 15.30–19, closed Sunday; San Bonaventura 9–18 every day

Running up the Palatine hill, accessible to the public without admission to
the Palatine archaeological area, is the little country lane called the via di San
Bonaventura. It leads to the top of the hill and on its way it passes the first
and the last sites sponsored by the Barberini in this area.

In 1631 the pope purchased a *vigna* (vineyard) from the Capranica family,
surrounding the church of San Sebastiano on the Palatine hill. The *vigna
Barberini* continues to exist as a shape on the surface of the hill, but before
we reach its gate we arrive at the church of **San Sebastiano al Palatino**,
also known as **San Sebastiano in Pallara**. For admission during the stated
opening hours ring at the gate.

This corner of the Palatine was artificially built up, very likely to support
a series of gardens called the Adonea (Gardens of Adonis), and was rebuilt
under the Emperor Commodus (AD 180–92) as the precinct for a temple.
The church on this site dates back to the tenth century and was important
during the high Middle Ages. However, the site had been abandoned by the
fourteenth century.

In 1624 the recently elected Urban VIII decided to return the church to
use. Urban had a strong interest in early Christian martyr-saints and of these
perhaps the third most important in Rome (after St Lawrence and St
Stephen) was St Sebastian, the Roman soldier shot with arrows for not
taking his oath on the Emperor Diocletian's godhead. Sebastian survived to
be martyred a second time, as a kindly Roman woman named Irene healed
his wounds, only for him to be bound up anew and clubbed to death by the
same military squad that had botched the arrow execution. This time they
were luckier and Sebastian received his crown of martyrdom.

The cult of St Sebastian was celebrated here, because it was thought that
on the steps of the temple of Elagabalus (*gradus Helagabali* or *Heliocabulli*)
the saint was martyred. The battle in northern Europe between Catholic
and Protestant was raging in the pontificate of Urban VIII, and the pope
wanted to underline the political message that Catholicism was worth dying
for. He commissioned Luigi Arrigucci (1575–c.1644), who was to become an
architect of the circle of Cardinal Francesco Barberini, to rebuild the church,
retaining only the tenth-century apse, which conserves a remarkable fresco
(c.970) of *Christ between Saints Sebastian and Zoticus with Saints Stephen and
Lawrence* and, below it, *The Lamb of God with the twelve sheep*. The rest of the
church was brought thoroughly up to date by Arrigucci, who produced a

graceful façade decorated with the Barberini crest, and a simple interior enlivened by new fresco work by Bernardino Gagliardi (1609–60) in the apse half-dome and pendentives. In 1633 Andrea Camassei contributed an altarpiece on the left-hand wall, the *Martyrdom of St Sebastian*. In the same year Urban VIII converted the lands of the old Capranica property, which he had bought two years before, into an endowment connected with the church, which he converted into a bailiwick of the Knights of Malta, with the proviso that the title holder should always be a Barberini. Accordingly, eight consecutive Barberini Knights of Malta had their seat here in the monastic buildings; it was purchased by the state in 1909. Today, the remains of the old Benedictine monastery can be seen and the large remnants of ancient wall which form part of the entrance gate come from the old temple enclosure. It is hard to imagine a more pleasant spot than this peaceful enclave, covered with climbing vines and with the vast ruins of the Colosseum in the valley below visible across a large empty field.

Further up the via di San Bonaventura, past a set of eighteenth-century *Stations of the Via Crucis* by Antonio Bicchierai (1688–1766), is the last family commission in the area, the church of **San Bonaventura al Palatino**.

This church was founded by Cardinal Francesco the Younger (1662–1738) in 1675, with an attached Franciscan convent, over ancient cisterns once serving the baths of the imperial palaces. It was consecrated in 1689 and today is popular for weddings. The interior was remade in a pallid, unconvincing neoclassical style in 1839–40 by the Torlonia family. The altarpieces, however, remain as Cardinal Barberini ordered them: it is worth a hike up the Palatine to see the most beautiful of them. The high altarpiece and the second altarpiece on the right-hand wall are mediocre works, but the remaining three altarpieces, all by Giovanni Battista Benaschi (1636–88), are highly skilled. The *Crucifixion* (first altarpiece on the right) stands out particularly, a quotation of the famous painting of the same subject by Guido Reni in the church of San Lorenzo in Lucina. The first altarpiece on the left, Benaschi's *Archangel Michael*, is a direct reference to Reni's painting of the same subject in Santa Maria della Concezione, another Franciscan church: the Barberini dedication to the cult of angels seems to have persisted through the seventeenth century. The little monastery attached to the church still hosts a small but active community of Franciscan monks.

II THE FORUM: SANTI COSMA E DAMIANO AND SANTI LUCA E MARTINA
Santi Cosma e Damiano: entrance from via dei Fori Imperiali, 9–12, 16–18, closed Sundays; Santi Luca e Martina, façade accessible from Clivo Argentario. Open only upon special request to the Accademia di San Luca, tel. 06 679 8850

The oldest Christian church in the Forum area is that of the medical saints Cosmas and Damian. It stands back from its fascist-era street, the via dei Fori Imperiali, in an urban environment completely different from that which it had when it was first built. Santi Cosma e Damiano is an older church than the Pantheon, in an older building than the Pantheon. When it was first built, it formed part of the Temple of Peace, a large open-air enclosure built by the Emperor Vespasian in AD 71–5 to celebrate the suppression of the Jewish revolt. It functioned as a sort of art museum, with statues from different parts of the empire placed on distinctive pedestals in rows in the open part of the space. Recent excavations have uncovered the pedestals and their inscriptions, which indicate the presence of famous works by ancient artists like Praxiteles. None of these, alas, remains to be seen.

At the eastern end of the enclosure, near where the great vaults of the basilica of Maxentius now soar, were the roofed altar area and four large halls, two on either side of the altar area. In the southernmost of these (towards the Forum), the Emperor Maxentius put an audience hall and built a domed vestibule, widely known today as the 'temple of Romulus'. This hall was converted into a church dedicated to the Syrian martyrs Cosmas and Damian by Pope Felix IV (526–30), who received it in donation from the Gothic rulers of Italy, Theodoric and Amalasuntha. Felix inserted a great mosaic into the apse, describing the *Parousia*, the last appearance of Christ on earth, part of the Apocalypse. The side walls were decorated with inlaid marble panels, and the ensemble must have been a dazzling Christian response to the enduring paganism of the Forum area and particularly to the similar medical cult of Castor and Pollux in a temple not far away.

By the seventeenth century, however, the church was in severe decline and two different monastic communities dependent on it were also in danger of disappearance. The monks made an unusual deal with Urban VIII in 1626 to save their church: in return for a thorough rebuilding, they offered the pope all the stone from the east wall of the church, to be replaced in brick. As Urban was looking for material to build palazzo Barberini, he readily agreed, and the east wall was accordingly demolished and reconstructed. By 1632, when this took place, the floor level of the church was well below the level of the via Papalis outside and this problem, too, needed to be addressed. Urban commissioned Luigi Arrigucci, his architect for San Sebastiano al Palatino, to run the building work, though the designs for the restoration were made by Orazio Torriani (c.1601–c.57), the architect of the church of San Lorenzo in Miranda next door.

Arrigucci inserted a new floor level 7 metres above the old surface, transforming the lower half of the hall into a crypt or lower church (now visible only upon special request – it contains little of interest, though remnants of a pre-Cosmatesque floor can be seen, as well as an altar of precious *pavonazzetto* marble and various interments) and filling in the sides of the upper church with chapels. During this restoration the apse mosaic, now remarkably disproportionate to the remaining space, was also mended and the triumphal arch in front was severely cropped. A cloister, to the west, formed the centre of the new monastery.

Entering from the via dei Fori Imperiali, the visitor first sees a large stone wall of ancient date, which forms one side of the entrance passage. Here, too, is the door of the parish office, where one may request to see the lower church. This entrance space opens into the **cloister**, with a little fountain in the centre. A room to the right contains a fantastical eighteenth-century Neapolitan crèche scene, a *presepio*. At the back of the cloister a door to the left opens into the church, in pure Counter-Reformation style, with a central nave flanked by three chapels on either side. A large glass wall separates this from the **vestibule**, the so-called 'Temple of Romulus' whose original doors remain *in situ* and which is now an archaeological area. Traces of frecoes have been found in niches in the vestibule, not easily visible, but dating from the ninth or tenth century. The vestibule has been returned to its original ground level: across from the level of the current church, a whitewashed rectangle indicates the location of the door in Urban VIII's time. The dome, too, had a Baroque lantern, and the inscription around the oculus gives the date 1638, when the work was completed.

Inside the church proper, the dominant feature is the spectacular **mosaic** of Christ standing on the clouds of dawn, with Peter and Paul presenting Cosmas and Damian to him. This central group is flanked by Felix IV, the founder of the church and patron of the mosaic, and on the other side the warrior saint, Theodore. The **high altar** was designed by the architect Domenico Castelli (d. 1658), probably the brother of the Matteo Castelli who designed the Barberini chapel in Sant' Andrea della Valle; Domenico Castelli is often given credit for the design of the cloister as well. Of the Barberini works in the church, the most impressive is the central chapel on the right-hand side, with Caravaggesque oil paintings by Caravaggio's biographer and enemy Giovanni Baglione (1566–1644) from 1638, depicting the Madonna with St John. The **ceiling**, too, is a fine

Barberini production, with beautiful grey and gold decorations, though slightly marred by an inferior central panel, the *Glory of Saints Cosmas and Damian* by Marco Tullio Montagna from 1632.

Further along the via dei Fori Imperiali, past the back of the Senate House, the imposing bulk of the huge church of **Santi Luca e Martina** appears. It is now rarely open (though it is possible to make an appointment with the Accademia di San Luca to see it), but it is one of the most spectacular pieces of Barberini patronage and if it were regularly accessible it would be widely known as one of the most impressive Baroque churches in Rome.

The old church of St Martina had been built by Pope Honorius I (625–38) and given to the Accademia di San Luca, the artists' guild, by Sixtus V in 1588, at which point it became known as 'San Luca in San Martina'. Plans for its demolition and reconstruction were in place as early as 1623, but nothing happened until Cardinal Francesco Barberini became protector of the Academy in 1627. He appointed Pietro da Cortona, now *principe* or head of the Academy, as architect. Work began in 1635 and continued until 1664, with many pauses. Cortona obtained consent to excavate his own family mortuary chapel under the high altar, with the unexpressed hope of discovering the body of the martyr-saint Martina whose church this was: when a similar project, the restoration of the church of Santa Bibiana (for which see below), had been undertaken for the jubilee of 1625, the discovery of the martyr's body prompted a thorough rebuilding of the church. Cortona's hopes were more than fulfilled. He found not only the body of St Martina, but those of the saints Concordius and Epiphanius, as well as that of another unidentified saint. Urban VIII immediately earmarked a significant amount of money for the rebuilding of the church, to honour both St Luke the Apostle, patron of the Academy, and St Martina the martyr. This resulted in a greater importance for the crypt, which became a lower church of its own.

As the church's original context has been shorn away, with the demolition of the surrounding neighbourhood and the buildings of the Academy which once surrounded it, the importance of its alignment on the via Papalis has vanished, as the street itself has; it stands isolated and alone, with its back to the main road of the via dei Fori Imperiali, overlooking the Forum, to which it is no longer connected. The **façade** has a strong verticality and the ribbed dome has a distinctive scalloped edge, created by strange shapes set above the windows of the drum. Inside, the **interior** takes the form of a Greek cross. It is a large, dignified volume in white and grey, with colour only in selected areas, in the altarpieces and tombs; most of the decoration is relief work from the later seventeenth and eighteenth centuries. A stair leads to the **lower church**, with Cortona's tomb.

III   LESSER SITES AROUND THE FORUM: THE CAPITOLINE AND
       THE FOOT OF THE PALATINE

The Barberini interest in the Franciscan order extended to the great civic church on the Capitoline, **Santa Maria in Aracoeli**. Here, in 1636, Urban VIII's crest was set above a magnificent new pulpit in carved wood, probably the design of Bernini. At the same time a colossal **commemorative inscription** celebrating the Barberini pope was inserted into the inside of the church's façade.

Also on the Capitoline, Urban VIII is evoked in a large marble statue by Bernini from 1635–9 in the Sala degli Orazi e Curiazi, the first room in the Conservators' Apartment of the **Capitoline Museums**. This is the classic representation of the Barberini pope, with his small beard and the pursed, discerning lips of the connoisseur. In the next room, the Hall of the Captains, where we have previously observed the statues of Marcantonio Colonna and Alessandro Farnese, is the statue of Urban's brother *Carlo Barberini* (1630), against the left-hand wall from the entrance. The torso of the statue is ancient, a general's statue which had been deprived of head and limbs; the limbs were replaced by Alessandro Algardi and the head by Bernini, an excellent example of the reuse and 'improving' of ancient statues which is strongly visible elsewhere in the Capitoline Museums. The next room, the Hall of Triumphs, displays two works of Urban's pontificate, Pietro da Cortona's *Victory of Alexander the Great over Darius* (1635) and Cortona's pupil Giovan Francesco Romanelli's *Santa Francesca Romana* of 1638. Upstairs in the Pinacoteca, Room VI is dedicated to the works of Pietro da Cortona, including several masterpieces like the *Rape of the Sabines* (1629) and the *Sacrifice of Polyxena* (1620), as well as a portrait of Urban VIII. Many of these works came from the collection of the Sacchetti, clients or dependants of the Barberini family. In the twentieth century a Sacchetti prince married the last Barberini Colonna di Sciarra princess to keep the family going.

Not far away, in the ancient Velabrum district, between the Capitoline and Palatine hills, two other churches were altered by the Barberini. One of them, the ancient church of **San Teodoro** (via di San Teodoro; open 8–12, 16–18, converted into a Greek Orthodox church by special papal grant in 2004), now restored to a semblance of its early Christian appearance, is an interesting round church dedicated to the same soldier-saint we have seen in the apse mosaic of Santi Cosma e Damiano. More significantly, further along the same street, which skirts the slope of the Palatine, a small piazza opens towards the hill: this is the forecourt of the church of **Sant' Anastasia**.

In early Christian Rome, Sant' Anastasia held one of the most exalted positions of any Roman church, ranking third behind San Giovanni in Laterano and Santa Maria Maggiore. Dating from as early as the fourth century AD, it took its name from the *titulus Anastasiae*, a house belonging to a certain Anastasia, wife of Publius. This was used as a cult centre perhaps even before the legalisation of Christianity and it came to be associated, as was often the case with ancient *tituli* or cult centres, with a saint of the same name, martyred at Sirmium in AD 304, and a popular cult at Constantinople. Throughout the early Middle Ages the church was connected with the imperial viceroy, who lived in the palaces above. It went through many rebuildings and received attention from Urban VIII, in part through his interest in restoring and updating churches of the early Christian martyrs and in part through necessity. The façade of 1618 was destroyed in 1634 by a tornado and Urban charged Luigi Arrigucci, his preferred architect for this area, with remaking it. The result is a modest but elegant façade of brick, flanked on either side by bell towers which extend the front rather in the manner of St Peter's. The interior does not bear any trace of the Barberini, as it was redecorated in the eighteenth century. Underneath the church (special permit required), no hint of the *titulus Anastasiae* has been found, but an ancient road has been excavated, with large shops on either side: this was part of the mercantile district next to the Circus Maximus, whose vast outline can still be traced in the park nearby.

4   Other Barberini sites in Rome

I   AROUND THE VATICAN: ST PETER'S, THE VILLA BARBERINI
AND THE FORTIFICATIONS OF THE JANICULAN HILL

Urban VIII is best recalled, perhaps, in **St Peter's**. The great basilica, the work of more than a century and hundreds of artists, was finally brought to substantial completion under the Barberini pope and it was his protégé Bernini, appointed as chief architect after the death of Carlo Maderno in 1629, whose efforts made it what it is today. The idea was to complete the decoration for the jubilee of 1650; as early as 18 November 1626, Urban solemnly consecrated the new basilica, 1300 years, it was calculated, from the original date of consecration.

The marble cladding of the floor and walls all serve to force the visitor's attention towards the crossing. There, the huge dome sits on top of piers, which were carefully scooped out by Bernini to provide four great niches for statues representing the four saints whose relics were preserved in the reliquaries above: the spearhead of St Longinus, a piece of the True Cross, found by St Helena, the mother of the Emperor Constantine, the kerchief of St Veronica with its miraculous representation of Christ's face, and the head of St Andrew the Apostle. Bernini himself made the statue of *San Longino*, which seems to burst out of its niche with arms outstretched in revelation; François Duquesnoy's *Sant' Andrea* is a beautiful piece, and Francesco Mochi's *Santa Veronica* is delicately carved, though the figure, depicted in some unexplained motion, as if she were rushing towards someone to display the miraculous cloth, came in for some criticism during the eighteenth century. This confusion was, in fact, due to a change in the design of the central feature of the crossing, the *baldacchino*: it was originally intended to have a figure of the risen Christ as its pinnacle and all the statues in the niches around are reacting to this invisible figure, St Longinus stretching his arms out in awe, St Veronica bringing her kerchief to show him, St Andrew a figure of proud fortitude and St Helena showing Christ her discovery, the True Cross. If we imagine this figure of Christ (finally too heavy to be feasible) at the top of the *baldacchino*, the statues in the piers make more sense.

Bernini's great **baldacchino** rises over the site of Peter's grave. Dedicated by Urban VIII on 28 June 1633, it is made of bronze from the beams of the porch roof of the Pantheon, prompting the most famous of pasquinades, '*Quod non fecerunt barbari fecerunt Barberini*' (what the barbarians didn't do, the Barberini did). However, never was an ancient monument sacrificed to better effect: the *baldacchino* unites the colossal scale of the basilica with its focal point, the tomb of St Peter, centred precisely under the highest point of the dome. It was a colossal feat of bronze casting, its components huge in size yet delicate in detail. The *baldacchino* sports four peculiar twisting columns, a memory of the eight that decorated the iconostasis or screen surrounding the main altar of Old St Peter's, which were said to have come from the temple of Solomon (they didn't). Some of the original columns were reused by Bernini in the reliquaries, and to replace them in their approximate original area (though not in their original configuration) he copied them on a monster scale.

Bernini's son Domenico later wrote that his father had 'to leave behind the rules of art' to make the *baldacchino* visually important in the vast area under Michelangelo's dome: he did this by combining the traditional form of the ciborium, a four-columned enclosure round an altar, with a canopy, which was a mark, as we have seen, of noble rank, but hitherto had not borne a religious meaning. Barberini bees buzz merrily over the whole thing and above the tops of the columns the Apollonian sun emblem of Urban

VIII is displayed. On the bases of the columns Barberini crests face outwards and part of the crests' elaborate frames are female faces. The face atop each crest seems to have a different grimace, while one is not of a woman but of a serene cherub. This probably commemorates his nephew's wife, Anna Colonna, who had just come through a difficult childbirth: the cherub signifies the happy ending. The crests themselves, seen in profile, have a feminine shape, with the familial bees apparently decorating key points of the female anatomy; some have detected that the swell of the 'belly' grows with each successive crest until the final one, which is flat. Also notable, though close to invisible, is Bernini's private offering to St Peter: on the top of the pedestal of the rear left-hand column he sculpted a set of rosary beads, draped casually over the base of the pillar as if he had left it there in homage.

The **tomb of Urban VIII** in the apse, also by Bernini, took twenty years to make (1627–47) and went through several redesigns. Conceived as a pendant to the tomb of Paul III, it has a pyramidal design, with a portrait of the pope at the top, splendid in his pontifical robes and tiara. The pope's portrait is flanked by the two marble figures of Charity, who is barely holding a fat baby, and Justice, who is staring despondently into space. Death himself, in the form of a bronze skeleton, sits below the papal effigy, inscribing Urban's virtues on a bronze plaque, while bees, the immortal bees of Virgil's *Georgics*, fly to the heavens from various points on the monument.

The **monument to Countess Matilda of Tuscany** stands by the second pier to the right of the nave of St Peter's. Built by Bernini to coincide with the interment of the countess's remains here in 1635 (though she died in 1115), it expresses Urban VIII's interest in asserting, somewhat anachronistically, the temporal power of the papacy. The relief on the sarcophagus depicts the humbling of the Emperor Henry IV at Canossa; the features of the pope concerned, Gregory VII, are similar to those of Urban himself. Another monument, the tomb of **Cardinal Francesco Barberini**, can be found in the passage from the basilica to the Museo del Tesoro: made in 1679–80 at the behest of the cardinal's nephews Cardinal Carlo Barberini and Prince Maffeo, it shows a strong Berninian influence, with a striking portrait bust surrounded by energetic angels.

Not far from the colonnade of St Peter's, and directly above the porta Santo Spirito through which we have passed when looking at the works of Paul III Farnese, is what remains of the **villa Barberini**. Today it is part of the Jesuit complex on the corner of via dei Penitenzieri and borgo Santo Spirito (for access, contact the Istituto Storico della Società di Gesù, tel. 06 687 5214). Constructed in 1670 by Prince Maffeo Barberini, the son of Taddeo, its grounds once stretched across the whole northern end of the

Janiculan hill. The villa building, much altered, retains a little Baroque façade and two of its rooms have original ceilings from the time of Maffeo's son, Prince Urbano Barberini (1664–1722), one of which displays Barberini ducal and cardinalate crests and emblems, quartered with the Pamphilj and Giustiniani crests to commemorate Maffeo's wife Olimpiuccia Giustiniani, the great-niece of Innocent X Pamphilj. The villa's position on top of the bastion of Paul III makes it nearly invisible, but it commands wonderful views over Rome in one direction and St Peter's in the other.

Urban VIII took care to ensure that Rome was provided with up-to-date fortifications. He made some alterations to the **Castel Sant'Angelo** (as testimony, the great fireplace in the Hall of Clement VIII has Anna Colonna Barberini's crest on it, and other decorations all over the castle bear the familiar bees). More impressively, however, he also undertook to extend the great stretch of the **city walls** all along the rear of the Janiculan hill. This massive public work, one of the last undertaken by the pope (1642–4), sought to prevent a sack similar to the one that devastated the city in 1527, by closing off the commanding hilltop position and thereby protecting the rather luxurious district of the via della Lungara below, towards the river. The new walls, canted outwards to repel cannon fire, run all the way from the porta Cavalleggeri behind the Vatican to the point where they meet the old Aurelianic circuit at the porta San Pancrazio (which Urban rebuilt, though what we see there today is a later rebuilding by Pius IX). They then bend towards the river to reach porta Portese, today home to a great fleamarket. Near the porta San Pancrazio a visitor may be interested to explore yet another Barberini villa, the **Villa Sciarra**, which was bought by the Barberini Colonna di Sciarra in the eighteenth century, now, since 1930, a pleasant public park overlooking the city.

II   A MISCELLANY

The area around Termini train station today is sometimes called *Roma piemontese*, due to its resemblance to Turin. This resemblance is intended: the area was redeveloped in the late nineteenth century as a residential district for the officials of the Piedmontese monarchy that had come to rule all of Italy. The station, which brought immigrants and merchandise and noise into the city, scuppered the well-intentioned plans for this suburb; today, still dirty and traffic-ridden, though it is undergoing a new gentrification, its multi-ethnic society makes it one of the most interesting parts of modern Rome. Buried in the area, however, are traces of an older zone of churches and noble villas, and of these perhaps the worst served by the modern world is the little church of **Santa Bibiana** (via Giolitti, corner with via di Santa Bibiana; open 7.30–11, 16.30–19.30, tel. 06 446 1021). Choked by traffic, it huddles against the side of the station, easily missed by nervous visitors.

A church has stood here since ancient times. St Bibiana, or Vivian, was thought to have lived on this site, in a house surrounded by the gardens of the third-century Emperor Gallienus, with her father Flavian, her mother Daphrosa and her sister Demetria. The whole family was exterminated in the terrible anti-Christian persecution of the Emperor Julian the Apostate between AD 361, and 363, and a centre of worship was said to have been set up here almost immediately after the death of the emperor in 363, by the pious matron Olympina. The real foundation was probably later, during the reign of Pope Simplicius (468–83). Though the church had been restored in the thirteenth century, by the seventeenth it was a ruin. The newly elected Urban VIII, who saw in the suffering of St Vivian a reflection of the troubles facing Catholics in the Europe of the Thirty Years War, was interested in restoring the church for the jubilee of 1625 and he charged the twenty-six-year-old Gianlorenzo Bernini with the task. Restoration began in 1624, but the discovery of the relics of the slaughtered family of the saint prompted a more thorough job, a complete rebuilding. The young Bernini thus received his first commission as solo architect.

The result was an elegant building, completed in 1626, only two years after work began, though after the jubilee that was its intended target. The façade is severe and almost undecorated, though originally it featured the Barberini crest. From a small forecourt the visitor passes through a portico before entering the church itself. The interior has a nave and two side aisles, unusual for a seventeenth-century Roman church, but probably deriving from its early Christian predecessor. Certainly the eight columns are ancient spoils. On the walls are frescoes depicting scenes from the life of the saint: those on the left are virtuoso works by Agostino Ciampelli (1565–1630), at that point *principe* of the Academy of San Luca and at the height of his success, and on the right by the young and unknown Pietro da Cortona. Cortona's frescoes here are of remarkable grace and beauty; though he was paid less than half of what Ciampelli got, these frescoes informed Rome that a new talent had arrived. The statue above the high altar, of *Santa Bibiana*, is by Bernini (made 1624–6). At the end of the aisles are two chapels: to the right the altarpiece of *Santa Dafrosa* is by Cortona, while the corresponding altarpiece in the left-hand chapel, *Santa Demetria*, is by Ciampelli. The relics of the saints are kept in an ancient container under the high altar.

In the piazza di Spagna are two monuments of Urban VIII. The first, and most central, is the **fountain of the Barcaccia**, constructed at the pope's command in 1629, to the design of Pietro Bernini and his son Gianlorenzo.

It resembles a sinking ship, a *barcaccia* or rotten boat; the story goes that it was placed here to commemorate the great Tiber flood of 1598 that left a small boat deposited in this piazza when it receded. Whether or not this is true, the fountain was certainly intended as a visual endpoint for the via Condotti, the main stretch of Paul III's *via Trinitatis*. The Spanish Steps behind were constructed later, in 1723–6: during the reign of Urban VIII, the fountain was set against a background of trees scattered on a steep and muddy hill. The Barcaccia is set slightly below ground level, to make the most of the weak water pressure from the Acqua Vergine aqueduct that feeds it even today. It is decorated with the familiar bee crest and Apollonian suns.

At the south-eastern end of the piazza, beyond the nineteenth-century Column of the Immaculate Conception, is the **Palazzo della Propaganda Fide**, the palace of the Propagation of the Faith. This was a religious college dedicated to missionary work, founded by Gregory XV Ludovisi in 1622 and transferred here in 1633. Bernini designed the piazza façade, an unusually simple and modest construction in brick, in 1644. The palazzo is, however, most distinguished by its front on via di Propaganda, designed by Francesco Borromini in 1666, one of his last works: it makes the most of its awkward situation by drawing the eye up its vertiginous lines. Borromini also designed the chapel of the **Re Magi** inside, at the same time, after destroying Bernini's oval chapel of 1634.

The ancient baptistery of the cathedral of Rome, **San Giovanni in Laterano** (baptistery open 8–12, 16–19), was also in a grievous condition when Urban VIII was elected. This edifice, dating perhaps from the reign of Pope Sixtus III (AD 432–40), was thoroughly restored by the architect Domenico Castelli and redecorated in 1637 by the Barberini artists; it underwent a further restoration under Alexander VII Chigi twenty years later. The walls have frescoes by Andrea Camassei, Giacinto Gimignani (1606–81) and Carlo Maratta (1625–1713), while in the central drum the frescoes are copies after Andrea Sacchi depicting the *Acts of St John the Baptist*, the originals now being conserved in the Lateran Palace next door. The column capitals were altered, with the addition of a heraldic bee in place of the more traditional central flower, though the eight porphyry columns themselves are original.

In the quiet zone of *rione* Monti hides the ancient church of **Sant' Agata dei Goti** (open 8–12, 16–18): its front gate on via del Mazzarino is never open and though its venerable brick apse can be seen from the via dei Serpenti behind, its entrance, on the side, is through a modest arch on the via Panisperna. Notices of this church exist from as early as AD 460, when Ricimer, the German head of the Roman army in the city (d. 473), had the apse decorated in mosaic. After the fall of the Western empire in 476, the Goths who ruled Italy chose this church as theirs: they were followers of the schismatic Bishop Arius and thus heretics, as far as the Catholics were concerned; after the fall of the Gothic kingdom Pope Gregory the Great (590–604) reconsecrated the church for Catholicism.

Saint Agatha was a particularly good example of a martyr-saint who suffered for her faith. Her breasts were cut off with hot scissor-like pincers; she is today the patroness of breast cancer victims. When, in 1633, the church was in need of repair, it fitted the Barberini programme of sponsoring the restoration of early Christian sites. Cardinal Antonio the Younger chose Sant' Agata dei Goti as his project. The walls were mended and the apse mosaic, or what remained of it (once mosaic starts to decay, it is hard to prevent the whole thing from crumbling off the wall), was erased and replaced in 1633–6 by a large fresco of *St Agatha in Glory* by Paolo Gismondi (1612–85). The **interior** is quite simple, apart from the fresco: sixteen ancient columns separate the apse from its aisles, and the ciborium over the high altar is twelfth or thirteenth century, from the workshops of the Cosmati family. From the nave, through doors that are usually closed, it is possible to enter the small **forecourt**. Though the street façade and the buildings surrounding the forecourt are eighteenth century, the court preserves a faint memory of its ancient form. The name of Cardinal Antonio is inscribed over the main door, and set into the wall opposite, below the double staircase leading up to street level, is the cardinal's crest, with the distinctive cross of Malta set behind.

Not far away, on the little via Urbana, stands the inconspicuous church of **San Lorenzo in Fonte**, also known as **San Lorenzo ed Ippolito** (rarely open). This sixteenth-century building was the church of the papal pageboys and was renovated at the command of Urban VIII in 1630 by Domenico Castelli, whom we have already met in Santi Cosma e Damiano and the Lateran baptistery. The church commemorates that most Roman of martyr-saints, Lawrence, who was said to have been kept in a well on this site, in punishment for teasing the urban prefect: the prefect had ordered Lawrence to turn over the riches of the church, to which the saintly deacon responded by gathering up a mass of the poor and presenting them to the official. While in his watery prison, Lawrence took the opportunity to splash his jailer, Hippolytus, which constituted a baptism. The soldier was converted on the spot and, not too surprisingly, was executed soon afterwards. This episode is depicted in the church's main altarpiece, by Andrea Camassei. The site of the well is also visible, through a hole in the left-hand wall.

Cardinal Antonio the Younger sponsored the new **sacristy** in **Santa**

Maria sopra Minerva (open 8–19). This great church had been under the patronage of Cardinal Scipione Borghese until his death, when Antonio Barberini took over as protector of the Dominican order which has its seat in the church and adjacent monastery. His court artist Andrea Sacchi, in 1635–7, designed and built the sacristy and the chapel of St Catherine of Siena which lies behind it, containing frescoes detached from the walls of the room where the saint died. Sacchi painted the altarpiece of the sacristy, a *Crucifixion*, and did some of the decoration, though the central panel in the ceiling, the *Glory of St Dominic*, was made by Giuseppe Puglia (c.1600–36). The sacristy contains rather beautiful walnut cabinets, perhaps designed by Sacchi, which, of course, sport the omnipresent Barberini bees. On the façade of the church itself a number of plaques commemorate the Tiber floods: the terrible inundation of 1598, under Clement VIII Aldobrandini, which was recorded by the Barcaccia fountain, and the hardly less damaging flood of 1637, during the reign of the Barberini pope himself.

7 The Pamphilj

THE CONCLAVE OF 1644

The death of Urban VIII in 1644 sent tremors through the city of Rome and into the rest of Europe. When the conclave gathered on 9 August 1644 it was immediately convulsed by factional rivalry. Outside, in the streets, Rome lay under the hand of rioters, as was common during the *sede vacante*, the period between popes. French mercenaries under the nominal command of Taddeo Barberini, prefect of Rome, menaced Romans and cardinals alike. In order to 'guarantee the freedom of the conclave', the Grand Duke of Tuscany and the Viceroy of Naples both massed troops on their borders with the Papal States. The French and Spanish factions could not agree on a candidate, and the cardinals cast around for a compromise. The choice soon fell upon Giambattista Pamphilj, who had been made cardinal by Urban VIII. Pamphilj had spent long periods in Spain and Spanish Naples, but funded by his strong-willed sister-in-law Olimpia Maidalchini, so he was not financially indebted either to the Barberini party or to the Spanish.

Don Taddeo Barberini warned his brothers Francesco and Antonio against Pamphilj, who had spoken out strongly against the nepotism of Urban VIII, while Pasquino cautioned against the cardinal's sister-in-law Olimpia:

> *Se sarà Panfili papa,*
> *Io vi giuro, o Barberini,*
> *che la nostra Maidalchini*
> *vi farà del capo rapa.*
> (If Pamphilj will be pope,
> I promise you, o Barberini,
> That our Maidalchini
> Will give your heads a good drubbing.)

Giambattista Pamphilj was elected on 15 September and took the name of Innocent X. His pontificate soon showed his pro-Spanish sympathies and proved Pasquino's predictions. After a year of grace, the Barberini were set to flight. Marforio, the river god statue now on the Capitol, asked Pasquino:

'What kind of a man is the new pope?' Pasquino, thinking of the Barberini's heraldic bee emblem, replied, 'He's not a man, he's a fly-swatter!'

THE PAMPHILJ FAMILY

The Pamphilj came from Gubbio in Umbria, claiming descent from one Amanzio Pamphilj, a ninth-century follower of Charlemagne; they asserted that its coat of arms, a dove with an olive branch in its beak and three fleurs-de-lis, was granted by that emperor. The Pamphilj were perhaps nobles of Gubbio by 1150, when one Pamphilio appears in the city archival records.

The rise from minor nobility to a respectable height began with *Antonio Pamphilj* (d. 1485), a friend of Sixtus IV della Rovere who appointed him Procurator Fiscal for the Papal States, a position of trust and respect, and of significant income. He obtained the hand of a Roman noblewoman for his son *Angelo Benedetto* (c.1469–c.1501). The first Pamphilj cardinal, *Girolamo* (1545–1610), was created in 1604. Angelo's son *Pamphilio* (1495–1563) married Orazia Mattei, a granddaughter of Isabella Borgia, one of the lesser illegitimate children of the infamous Pope Alexander VI. Their son *Camillo* (1539–1610) was the father of *Giambattista Pamphilj* (1574–1655), the future Innocent X. Camillo wed Maria del Bufalo, whose family's palaces stood between the Trevi fountain and piazza di Spagna. All these marriages indicate precisely where the Pamphilj stood in the Roman order: eligible for marriage with members of the declining baronial aristocracy, unimpeachably noble, but unextraordinary. That was soon, and suddenly, to change.

POPE INNOCENT X (1644–55)

Giambattista Pamphilj was born in Rome on 7 May 1574. He took a degree in law at the Jesuit Collegio Romano, graduating at the age of twenty. His first patron, Clement VIII Aldobrandini, appointed him as a consistorial lawyer and an auditor of the Rota, placing him firmly within the legal and financial framework of the Vatican hierarchy. There he remained throughout the pontificate of Paul V Borghese. Paul's successor Gregory XV Ludovisi appointed Pamphilj as ambassador to Naples and Urban VIII made him datary, a high office of the papal chancery, and sent him to accompany his nephew Francesco, when legate to France and Spain. Urban made Pamphilj titular Patriarch of Antioch, an empty title but one which brought with it a certain pre-eminence.

His long association with the Spanish vice regency of Naples resulted in his being made nuncio to Spain itself. Urban VIII created him Cardinal-

Innocent X, after Velázquez. 'Hearing that Pamphilj had been made pope,' wrote Gigli, 'the people stayed still and did not make great celebrations, because he was taken to be a severe man, not very generous.'

Priest of San Eusebio on 30 August 1626, and for most of the Barberini pontificate Cardinal Pamphilj functioned as mediator between the pope and the crown of Spain. At no time, however, did he hold a bishopric and his ecclesiastical career was accordingly under-written by his rich sister-in-law, *Olimpia Maidalchini* (c.1591–1657). She and her husband, Giambattista's elder brother *Pamphilio* (1563–1639), followed the cardinal to Naples during his residency there. Unpleasant rumours already accused the strong-willed Olimpia of having an undue influence over her husband's brother. The family returned to Rome, to their property on the south-west corner of piazza Navona next to the family palace of their cousins the Mellini, and lavished money on their house to convey the dignity of a cardinal.

Pamphilj, one of the few members of the court to disagree in public with Urban VIII, was hostile to the first war of Castro, considering it a vain attempt to enlarge Barberini wealth and power. This resistance won him a reputation for uprightness within the College of Cardinals, and he was unquestionably a strict and fair administrator. But his taciturnity and strictness counted against him: in Paris, he had been known as 'Monseigneur On-ne-peut-pas' (Monsignor One-Can't). He was slow to trust and prone to bouts of furious bad temper.

Soon after his election, Innocent chose as his secretary of state a minor cardinal, Giovanni Panciroli (d. 1651). Donna Olimpia's son *Camillo* (1622–66) was made captain-general of the papal armies, putting Taddeo Barberini out of a job, and Donna Olimpia planned to marry her son to a Barberini princess. But Innocent halted her plans, making Camillo a cardinal, although relying on Panciroli and Donna Olimpia for political advice. In 1647 Camillo put aside his ecclesiastical authority and wed, instead, the beautiful and wealthy widow of Paolo Borghese, *Olimpia Aldobrandini* (1623–81). Innocent decided, rather unfortunately, to elevate Donna

Olimpia's seventeen-year-old nephew Francesco Maidalchini to the cardinalate, to assist the ageing Panciroli, but the experiment was a failure due to Francesco's youth.

In 1650 Innocent gave another relative of Donna Olimpia a cardinal's hat. This was *Camillo Astalli* (1619–63), charming and urbane, and from an old Roman baronial family. Cardinal Astalli successfully got rid of Cardinal Panciroli, but soon showed his own incompetence; after ignoring the pope's order not to visit the Spanish ambassador, to whom he had revealed secrets of state, he was deprived of his income and dismissed to the village of Sambuci. In 1651, at last, the pope looked outside Donna Olimpia's family and selected Fabio Chigi (1599–1667), a practised diplomat and sincerely pious, as his secretary of state. The Oratorian Virgilio Spada (1596–1662), a friend of the pope's, became Private Almoner and took over practical control over papal patronage of art. He favoured Francesco Borromini: Bernini, associated with the hated Barberini, slowly returned to favour late in Innocent's reign.

Innocent's career as pontiff was characterised by an increasing awareness of the papacy's impotence in European politics: his power decayed in Europe, and at home the national debt had risen astronomically, and flood and disease threatened. The account books of the papacy were sinking into a mire of mismanagement and graft. Under threat of French invasion, Innocent rehabilitated the Barberini and this betrayal of the Romans, combined with his family's greed, caused him to be hated throughout Rome. Innocent taxed food heavily to pay for his family's building programme: grain prices soared and a new penny tax on salt and meat during lean years in Rome provoked outrage. A desperate graffito found scribbled near palazzo Pamphilj while the Fountain of the Four Rivers was being built declared:

> *Noi volemo altro che guglie e fontane:*
> *Pane volemo, pane, pane, pane!*
> (We want other than obelisk and fountainhead:
> It's bread we want, just bread, bread, bread!)

The principal issue to be settled in the Papal States was the vexed problem of the Farnese duchy of Castro, in default of its loans to the Camera. Innocent sent a large force of papal troops to Castro, successfully besieged it and razed it to the ground; he confiscated the entire duchy of Castro to make up the duke's debt. The population survived to found a successor town, Ischia di Castro, not far from the original. However, nothing remained above ground of the beautiful Renaissance town built for Paul III Farnese until excavations in 1960–70 unearthed the basic ground plan and the cathedral foundations. Nothing, that is, but a column, erected by Innocent's engineers, with the iron-throated inscription '*Qui fu Castro*' (Here was Castro). It was a message of a pope's authority over his territories.

Donna Olimpia, the pope's embarrassing sister-in-law, had been exiled to her country estates in 1650. In 1651 the pope was reconciled with his nephew Camillo and his wife. The princess soon took the place of the other Olimpia in power and position, acting as the pope's chief female representative. She, too, was open to bribery, but in the spring of 1653 the pope arranged for the return of his sister-in-law, and the two Olimpias made a public reconciliation. It is likely that the pope was simply lonely: his friend Cardinal Panciroli had died and he lacked confidantes. At the reconciliation banquet came another, more humiliating, reconciliation. Innocent announced that Maffeo Barberini was to marry Donna Olimpia's granddaughter Olimpiuccia Giustiniani. Maffeo's elder brother Carlo Barberini was raised to the cardinalate in 1653, leaving Maffeo to inherit the title and lands of the Prince of Palestrina. Cardinal Carlo Barberini retained the title of prefect of Rome, which he had inherited from his contentious father, Don Taddeo; after Carlo's death, the title was not revived and the obnoxious issue of the title's precedence faded away.

In the spring of 1654 Innocent X reached his eightieth birthday. He became increasingly senile, disliked and under the thumb of Donna Olimpia. He finally died on 7 January 1655. Cardinal Camillo Astalli, back from his internal exile, turned up at the requiem mass in St Peter's without bothering with the traditional mourning robes. Perhaps Innocent had simply been too difficult a personality to love: the pope's other relatives showed a similar indifference. Donna Olimpia, Prince Camillo Pamphilj and Prince Nicolò Ludovisi all refused to pay for a funeral, and at last his body was buried with minimal pomp in the family crypt at Sant' Agnese in Agone, in the piazza which he had starved his people to construct.

OLIMPIA MAIDALCHINI PAMPHILJ (c.1592–1657)

Olimpia Maidalchini was born in 1591, 1592, or 1594, in Viterbo, near the old Farnese dominions in the north of Lazio. At eighteen she married a wealthy merchant of Viterbo, Paolo Nini. Three years later she had buried her husband and an infant son, and gained a vast fortune. On a pilgrimage to Loreto, in the Marches, she stayed overnight at an inn in Borghetto, on the great highway of the via Flaminia, where she met a Roman aristocrat, Pamphilio Pamphilj. They married in 1612, as each had what the other desired: Pamphilio wanted Olimpia's wealth and Olimpia longed to escape from the narrow confines of Viterbese life. At twenty-one she had succeeded in marrying into the minor Roman aristocracy. Her husband, more than twice her age, was able to pursue an honourable career in the Capitoline administration with the money she provided.

In Rome, Donna Olimpia moved into the unprepossessing Pamphilj family residence at the southern end of piazza Navona. She had three children: two daughters, Maria and Costanza, and a son, Camillo. Pamphilio's younger brother, the up-and-coming cleric Giambattista, also lived in the old palazzo Pamphilj. She took her young family to Naples when Giambattista became papal nuncio there (Camillo was born in Naples) and her wealth kept the family in style. Giambattista was said to have returned from his nunciature in Spain 'with sacks full of money' – but he never forgot that it had been Olimpia's money that maintained his Neapolitan embassy and she, for her part, took easily to Roman high society, attending Barberini festivities without her increasingly aged husband, as companion to her brother-in-law. Needless to say, tongues wagged. When Pamphilio died in 1639, Olimpia 'covered herself in mourning and had many masses said in different churches for his good soul', as one commentator remarked. Many doubted the sincerity of these pious gestures.

Olimpia was a satirist's dream: a tough, rich, bossy woman with a reputation for avidity. A commentator described her as '*di nauseante ingordigia*' (sickeningly greedy). The morning after Innocent's election a painting appeared at the base of the mutilated statue of Pasquino, showing a hand carrying the papal tiara covered with a widow's veil, and the legend: 'I'm bearing a gift from the new pope to Donna Olimpia.' Satires throughout Innocent's ten-year reign portrayed him as a tool of his sister-in-law, who was referred to as *la dominante,* or *la papessa* (she-pope). Her name also took on the negative suffix *accia*, which means something like 'rotten' or 'nasty', becoming 'Olimpiaccia'. It was easy to associate her with the brassy Pimpa, the shameless heroine of a seventeenth-century play, and she was transformed in the popular imagination into 'La Pimpaccia'.

Pasquinades clearly, if not eloquently, indicate that the Roman people considered Donna Olimpia to be the only gatekeeper to the pope's favour and a corrupt one at that. This neatly puns on *porta* (door) and *portare* (to carry or bring):

PASQUINO: *Dov'è la porta di Donna Olimpia?*
MARFORIO: *Chi porta vede la porta;*
               chi non porta non vede la porta.
(PASQUINO: Where is the door of Donna Olimpia?
MARFORIO: If you bring a gift you see the door;
               If you don't, you don't.)

Every unpopular decision of the pope's was laid immediately at her door. There was, perhaps, more than a tinge of sexism in the hostility, because in effect she took over the role of cardinal nephew, although for a time her own son Camillo nominally had that position. Whether or not the accusations of venality were true, Donna Olimpia possessed a power that was deemed inappropriate, in seventeenth-century eyes, for a woman. As Pasquino remarked:

> Chi dice donna dice danno.
> Chi dice femmina dice malanno.
> Chi dice Olimpia Maidalchini
> Dice donna, danno, e rovina.
> (Who says 'lady' says harm.
> Who says 'woman' says misfortune.
> Who says Olimpia Maidalchini
> Says lady, harm, and ruin.)

Her influence over the pope came principally from his gratitude for her support during his years of poverty. However, the Romans, and indeed the rest of Europe, could only understand her power in sexual terms, all the more sinister because she was not what would generally be considered alluring. The satires written against her display none of the jokey mockery of even the harshest criticisms of the Barberini, but a real and vicious hatred. As the palazzo Pamphilj backed directly on piazza di Pasquino, she could hardly avoid noticing the daily attacks on her. She responded proudly by not modifying her behaviour in the slightest. This toughness of character was seen as yet more evidence of her monstrous unwomanliness.

She was often criticised for corruption and during the jubilee of 1650 it was acidly noted that the gold medals traditionally walled up in the Holy Doors of the four great basilicas of San Pietro, San Paolo fuori le Mura, San Giovanni in Laterano and Santa Maria Maggiore vanished and reappeared, as if by magic, in the hands of Donna Olimpia. But she, in her position as the pope's principal female relative, received the whole of Roman high society in her salon in piazza Navona with her head held high. She was rarely frightened: once, when her carriage was stopped and insulted by the Roman mob, she quoted a proverb with characteristic sang-froid: 'The coat of the mistreated horse is glossier', or, in other words, that adversity only made her healthier.

Her critics grew louder and the jubilee medals scandal was one of the reasons that Innocent sent her back to San Martino again in 1650. Another reason was a serious breach in family unity caused by her son Camillo's departure from the cardinalate in 1647 and his marriage to Olimpia Aldobrandini. This represented a major rebellion of son against mother and matters were further complicated by the fact that the Olimpias loathed each other. At first Innocent tried to solve the problem by sending the newly-weds to Frascati. However, Camillo returned to Rome in the jubilee year of 1650, taking up residence in his wife's colossal palace on the Corso, palazzo Santoro-Aldobrandini, which is today known as palazzo Doria-Pamphilj. Relations within the family were at an all-time low; the palazzo Pamphilj in piazza Navona was a battleground between mother and son, daughter-in-law and mother-in-

A nineteenth-century representation of Donna Olimpia Maidalchini under attack by the mob. 'It is known that she will be the Dominatrix in this pontificate,' wrote Gigli in his diary.

law, and, increasingly, between the pope and Donna Olimpia. When, to ease matters Innocent exiled Donna Olimpia to San Martino her reputation in Rome was so bad, with pasquinades appearing every day against her avarice, that her absence was politically necessary.

She was also becoming an international embarrassment. As far away as London a masqued entertainment was mounted to amuse the Lord Protector, Oliver Cromwell, called *The Marriage of the Pope*, in which Innocent was represented as proposing to Donna Olimpia. In the masque she refused him until he offered her not just the keys to heaven but to hell as well, to protect her against his eventual abandonment. News of this heretical entertainment was not at all pleasing to the real pope, whose sense of personal dignity was extreme. It was three years before he allowed her to return to her palace in piazza Navona. Once again, however, adversity had merely made her stronger, and it was not long before the old accusations of corruption and misbehaviour swirled around her. Pasquino's cruellest and cleverest cut was a simple pun on her name: '*Olim pia, nunc impia*' (Once pious, now impious).

In the last years of Innocent's pontificate Donna Olimpia's authority increased as her brother-in-law's mental faculties declined. She prepared for Innocent's apparently imminent death in December 1654 by fleeing her palace in piazza Navona by night, audibly sighing 'So soon!' – she took refuge in palazzo Barberini alle Quattro Fontane where her granddaughter was safely installed as the wife of Prince Maffeo Barberini. However, the pope's health rallied and she returned home.

When Innocent X finally died on 7 December 1655, Donna Olimpia was widely rumoured to have stolen two strongboxes full of gold coins from under the pope's bed, which he had destined to pay for his funeral. This ultimate act of avarice was compounded by her refusal to finance his burial: Donna Olimpia claimed she was simply a poor widow and could not support such an expense. Innocent's corpse was moved to a shed, where a guard was employed to keep the rats from eating it, then buried humbly in the family church of Sant' Agnese, as we have seen. Only much later did a subsequent Pamphilj erect a monument to the family pope.

At Innocent's death the city celebrated with an explosion of joy, mixed with hatred:

> Finita è la foia
> di questa poltrona
> di piazza Navona:
> chiamatele il boia.
> Finita è la foia.
> È morto il pastore,
> la vacca ci resta:
> Facciam'le la festa,
> cavatele il core.
> È morto il pastore.
> (The madness is over
> of this idle woman
> of piazza Navona:
> Let's call the executioner for her.
> The madness is over.   -
> The pastor is dead,
> But the cow still remains:
> Let's make merry with her,
> let's tear out her heart for her.
> The pastor is dead.)

The next pope, Alexander VII Chigi, Innocent's former secretary of state, almost immediately exiled her for life to her little principality of San Martino al Cimino and her days of power in Rome were over. Donna Olimpia Maidalchini passed the last two years of her life ruling over San Martino and spending a surprising amount of money on charitable activities there. Lawsuits against her proliferated in Rome and accusations similar to those against the Barberini *nipoti* were levelled against her: however, she evaded even these charges in the end, by the simple expedient of dying. In 1657 the plague came to San Martino, and she died suddenly and alone. Her lavish floor monument is one of the principal ornaments of the abbey church of San Martino. She left a fortune of 2 million gold scudi in cash, an astonishing amount of liquid wealth, to her heir Camillo.

Donna Olimpia's memory remained, blurrily, as that of a famous harlot, and 'Olimpia' became a popular prostitute's pseudonym for centuries, visible even in Manet's famous nineteenth-century portrait of a female nude, *Olympia*. She is one of Rome's few ghosts. On nights of the full moon, it is said that a black carriage can be seen leaving the small riverside property in Trastevere once known as 'the baths of Donna Olimpia', being pulled at breakneck speed along the river bank by jet-black horses with eyes of flame, crossing the river at the ponte Sisto (one source says the carriage plunged into the Tiber from the bridge) and rolling through the streets to disappear into the gate of palazzo Pamphilj in piazza Navona. Chests of money have been spied strapped to the roof of the coach and a menacing black shape is said to be visible inside it. La Pimpaccia rides again.

CAMILLO PAMPHILJ (1622–66)

With such a strong-willed mother, Camillo Pamphilj was destined for a near lifelong struggle for independence. He was born in Naples and grew up in the Pamphilj house on piazza di Pasquino: he had a modest education and was of commensurate gifts. Though his abandonment of the cardinalate and wedding in 1647 angered his mother, he had made an excellent choice of wife for an up-and-coming Roman nobleman. The Princess of Rossano, Olimpia Aldobrandini, was both wealthy and beautiful, from a papal family. A brief honeymoon in Caprarola and Frascati, waiting for the storms in Rome to subside, came to an end in 1651 when Camillo and the Princess of Rossano were allowed to return to the city and his uncle's good graces.

Camillo was the family's first major collector and commissioner of art. His projects included their vast suburban villa, today's Villa Doria-Pamphilj, the renovation of his wife's palace, palazzo Santoro-Aldobrandini (Doria-Pamphilj), and a good amount of church building. In these projects he was concerned to enhance the prestige of his family, including faking an ancient tomb 'of the *gens* Pamphylia', conveniently located in the little necropolis in the Villa Pamphilj, and doing his best to accentuate his imaginary descent from the legendary king of Rome, Numa Pompilius (which he strove to depict as a variant of 'Pamphylius').

CAMILLVS PAMPHILIVS
PRINCEPS ROMANVS

Don Camillo Pamphilj, cardinal and prince,
after a portrait by Baciccia.

Like his mother, he was no intellectual and he inherited her taste for riding. His patronage of artists was enlightened but sabotaged by his meanness: the art critic Passeri, writing not long after Camillo's death, commented that 'though he, more than anyone of his time, gave opportunities to painters and sculptors, he was always having trouble with them over questions of money'. The painter Pierfrancesco Mola (1612–66) made frescoes for the prince in his palace at Valmontone but, on dissatisfaction with the meagre payment, had some of them obliterated after a lawsuit. They were replaced by new frescoes, this time by Donna Olimpia's client painter, Mattia Preti.

Francesco Baratta, best known as one of the sculptors of the Fountain of the Four Rivers in piazza Navona, and Ercole Ferrata were both forced to seek satisfaction in the courts for unpaid work they did for Camillo. This meanness made him an unsatisfactory patron and many of the works he commissioned were, perhaps not coincidentally, less than inspired.

His wife Olimpia Aldobrandini brought Camillo not only her fortune, but also her family's extraordinary collection of art. Already a widow by 1646, when her husband Paolo Borghese died at twenty-two, the Princess of Rossano was constrained by a rigid inheritance law, a *fidecommesso*, instituted by Clement VIII and ratified by subsequent popes: her wealth was kept separate from her husband's and a special papal decree was necessary in order to unite her art collection with Camillo's. She was, unfortunately, a schemer like her mother-in-law; her ambitions were, however, thwarted by the pope, who never quite took to her. As a patron of art and architecture she was conservative, completing her husband's commissions but not venturing far from his taste.

THE PAMPHILJ SUCCESSION

The Pamphilj family tree was cut short, since within three generations Camillo's direct male line died out and his daughter *Anna Pamphilj* (1652–1728) became the main family dynast. Camillo's two sons, *Giovanni Battista* (1649–1709) and *Benedetto* (1653–1730), devoted themselves to completing their father's architectural projects and Benedetto, who had a career as cardinal, became a distinguished collector of landscapes and still-life canvases, and was a friend of Handel, Scarlatti and Corelli. The Aldobrandini *fidecommesso* was revived in the generation of Giovanni Battista's children. Thus his eldest son, *Innocenzo* (1673–95), was expected to take on the family title of Prince of San Martino al Cimino (a legacy of Donna Olimpia), while Innocenzo's younger brother Camillo Filippo (1675–1747) became known as *Camillo Pamphilj Aldobrandini*, the rebuilder of much of palazzo Doria-Pamphilj. This Camillo inherited the responsibilities of his elder brother after the latter's death in 1695, but Camillo had no children to take on either the Aldobrandini or the Pamphilj names and the titles passed to the third brother, *Girolamo* (1678–1760). Girolamo's son *Benedetto* (1709–56) predeceased his father and had no children. The vast inheritance of the Pamphilj went to the descendants of Anna Pamphilj, who had married into the Genoese family of the Doria Landi.

The Doria were among the most prominent families of the maritime republic of Genoa, and had supplied the state with many doges and generals, the most important being the famous *Andrea Doria* (1466–1560), admiral of the Holy Roman Emperor Charles V and indefatigable pirate hunter. The branch into which Anna Pamphilj married had already merged with another family, the Landi, of similar prominence. It was Anna's grandson *Giovanni Andrea IV Doria Landi* (1705–64) who moved his family to Rome to take up the Pamphilj inheritance. However, an ugly three-way lawsuit was to ensue concerning the inheritance, claimed by both the Colonna family (who wanted the Pamphilj name and properties) and the Borghese (who claimed, with eventual success, the Aldobrandini bequests). Eventually a deal was struck that let the Doria Landi keep the Pamphilj names and titles, the palazzo on the via del Corso and the art collection. In 1763 Giovanni Andrea IV Doria Landi's son *Andrea IV* (1747–1820) won the right to assume the name Pamphilj. His two younger brothers, *Antonio* (1749–1821) and *Giuseppe* (1751–1816), both had successful ecclesiastical careers and served as loyal counsellors to Pius VI Braschi (1775–99), during the difficult Napoleonic era.

Remarkably, since 1839 each Doria-Pamphilj spouse has been English, making the family more English than Italian. In that year Prince *Filippo Andrea V* (1813–76) wed Mary Talbot, daughter of the Earl of Shrewsbury and sister of Gwendolen Talbot who had married Prince Borghese. Filippo Andrea V was the deputy mayor of Rome after its unification to the kingdom of Italy in 1870. His younger brother *Domenico* (1815–72) founded a hospital for the chronically ill poor in Trastevere, on the site of the old *bagni di Donna Olimpia* on the bank of the river.

Perhaps the most remarkable Doria-Pamphilj of the twentieth century was *Filippo Andrea VI* (1886–1958), whose vocal opposition to the fascist regime, at great personal risk, was rewarded with the post of mayor of Rome after the Second World War. His daughter, *Orietta Doria-Pamphilj Landi* (1922–2000), was the last blood relation of Innocent X to hold the family patrimony. She married an English soldier, Frank Podgson, and they adopted two children from an English orphanage. The current head, *Jonathan Paul Andrew Doria-Pamphilj Landi* (b. 1963), Prince of San Martino, is dedicated to protecting the heritage of his adoptive family, modernising and expanding accessibility to the Doria-Pamphilj gallery.

PAMPHILJ ITINERARY

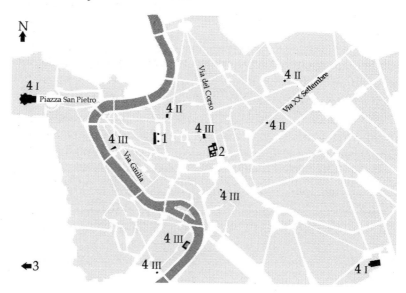

N

With the Pamphilj we find a family strongly identified with one place, piazza Navona, in a manner at first reminiscent of the residential patterns of medieval and early Renaissance nobles. Yet the Pamphilj *isola* in piazza Navona is very different from that of their relatives the Mattei, for example: in the Pamphilj buildings there is a grandeur, coherence and splendour that no medieval family could have created. This is due in part to the massive wealth available to a papal family of the seventeenth century, but there is also a deeper shift at work, away from a cluster of dwellings that served as a fortress or a show of family strength towards a triumphant expression of family authority using open spaces rather than walls.

Innocent X was conservative, in the sense that he preferred tradition to innovation (with Borromini his one exception), and indeed reactionary, as he began his reign by rejecting the two masters preferred by his Barberini predecessor, Pietro da Cortona and Gianlorenzo Bernini. Both artists, however, returned to papal favour in the latter part of Innocent's reign and both have major works in piazza Navona. Innocent preferred the talent of Bernini's great peer Alessandro Algardi (1598–1654) in sculpture, while in architecture he combined the efforts of the Rainaldi family, father and son, whose work we have already met in the *Orti Farnesiani* and the Villa Borghese, with the more revolutionary work of Francesco Borromini. His construction of new prisons on the via Giulia, with Antonio Del Grande as architect, served multiple purposes but primarily represents a new interest in the humanitarian care of prisoners. Donna Olimpia Maidalchini's patronage is visible in piazza Navona, for it was perhaps through her efforts that Bernini received the commission for the Fountain of the Four Rivers, but otherwise her taste is difficult for the visitor to discern, as the fresco cycle she commissioned in palazzo Pamphilj is generally closed. The apse frescoes of Sant' Andrea della Valle, which we have already visited in connection with the Barberini, are the only clear examples in Rome of her taste in painting.

Her son Prince Camillo's tastes in large part reflect the preferences of his uncle the Pope. For Camillo, Algardi built the main palazzina of the colossal Villa Pamphilj (today's Villa Doria-Pamphilj). Del Grande, architect of the New Prisons, was employed by Camillo for one of the façades of Camillo's own palace, today's palazzo Doria-Pamphilj. He shared with his contemporary, Prince Lorenzo Onofrio Colonna, a taste for landscapes, and his preference for Gaspard Dughet and Claude Lorrain is still visible in the family's art collection, the Galleria Doria-Pamphilj. Camillo was a major church builder: in 1654 he constructed the church of San Nicola da Tolentino in the area of piazza Barberini. He also sponsored the reconstruction of Sant' Agnese in Agone, the family church, by Girolamo Rainaldi and Borromini, during his uncle's lifetime, and afterwards he helped to sustain the incredible expense of Bernini's oval church of Sant' Andrea al Quirinale, his one unequivocally lavish act of patronage.

Later Doria-Pamphilj princes were less prolific in their sponsorship, contenting themselves with completing and renovating the main family palace and the Villa Doria-Pamphilj. Prince Filippo Andrea V, in the nineteenth century, expanded his family villa and relandscaped it in the

English style, at the same time transforming the productive part of the villa into a modern farm, once again along English lines. The same prince and his son Prince Alfonso were major collectors of fourteenth- and fifteenth-century paintings.

▌ Piazza Navona and the Pamphilj

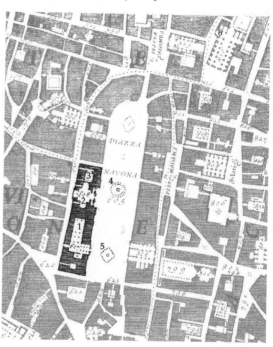

The Pamphilj in and near piazza Navona, from the Nolli map of 1748

Key:
1 palazzo Pamphilj
2 Sant' Agnese in Agone
3 Collegio Innocenziano
4 fontana dei Quattro Fiumi
5 fontana del Moro
6 Pamphilj chapel of San Tommaso di Villanova in Sant' Agostino

Sleepy **piazza Navona** had been, until the pontificate of Innocent X, a somewhat rusticated and irregular place. Early seventeenth-century engravings show its edge crowded with small houses like those that still exist on the Campo de' Fiori nearby. The Pamphilj were to change this large and undisciplined space, previously noteworthy mainly for its market, into the very centre of papal Rome. It remains, in a real sense, the heart of Rome today.

The piazza had been an open space since ancient times. Domitian (AD 81–96) constructed a stadium on the site for a new series of games in the Greek style, including running, javelin throwing and wrestling, and in Greek fashion they were held in the nude. The Romans, prudish about nudity, did not take to this form of competition and in fact the main pious legend about the piazza (for which see below, Sant' Agnese in Agone) involves a miraculous concealment of a nude person. The piazza's name also derives from the sports competitions held here, the *ludi agonales* ('*agonales*' from the Greek word for struggle), which became the 'platea in Agone' and then 'piazza N'agone' and finally Navona.

Under Urban VIII, palazzo Barberini's cortile della Cavallerizza had been the site of the city's most splendid festivals and ceremonies, but with Innocent X the scene shifted to piazza Navona, beginning with the celebrations surrounding the pope's *possesso* or accession to power as ruler of the States of the Church. Huge firework displays were set off in the piazza, including one exploded from a papier mâché Noah's Ark on top of a temporary Mount Ararat in front of the Spanish national church of San Giacomo across from palazzo Pamphilj. The English diarist John Evelyn wrote: 'Thus were the streetes this night as light as day, full of Bonfires, Canon roaring Musique playing, fountaines running Wine in all excesse of joy and Triumph.'

I PALAZZO PAMPHILJ AND ITS DEVELOPMENT
Piazza Navona 14. No admission

Since the 1480s the Pamphilj had possessed a house in the block at the south-west corner of the piazza, facing outwards to piazza Pasquino instead of into piazza Navona. This was the house in which Giambattista Pamphilj was born in 1574. Donna Olimpia, on behalf of her cardinal brother-in-law, started to expand it into a palace by buying up the properties inside the block and constructing a large building with ten windows looking on to piazza Navona.

Almost as soon as Pamphilj was made pope, Donna Olimpia and her son Camillo began buying up the properties to the north of the Pamphilj cardinalate palace, as far as the site of the current church of Sant' Agnese. At the time this area was mostly occupied by a palazzo of the locally important old nobles, the Mellini, and smaller houses. The architect, Girolamo Rainaldi, left the houses intact and simply unified them behind a single façade, something which we have already noted in the Barberini's Casa Grande ai Giubbonari. In the spring of 1646 the palace was extended further. At that point, and following the suggestion of the pope's almoner Virgilio Spada, the architect Francesco Borromini was called in to consult about the plans. After Donna Olimpia's disgrace the palace was temporarily in the hands of Cardinal Camillo Astalli-Pamphilj, though when he, too, was sent packing, the palace stood empty until *la papessa* returned.

Borromini's influence is confined to the interior, where his plans included a great *sala dei palafrenieri* similar in size to that of palazzo

Barberini. To him, too, are ascribed some of the stucco decorations of the main floor; but his more adventurous plans for the palace, including a beautiful *altana* or open-air loggia for which plans survive, never came to fruition. The palace was meant to be completed by the great jubilee year of 1650 and it was, at least on the outside; the interior was decorated only later. The most significant Borrominian addition was the great gallery, which stretched the whole way across the city block from one façade to the other. This gallery, flooded with light from huge Serlian windows (composed of a central arched opening flanked by two smaller rectangular apertures) at both ends, was meant as a further audience hall referring back to the grand rooms in palazzo Farnese and palazzo Mattei di Giove.

As it stands, the palace extends round a courtyard, with two façades: a nineteenth-century façade, on piazza Pasquino and via Santa Maria dell'Anima, clads the old nucleus of the palace, and a much grander, papal front on piazza Navona. The main state rooms stretch across the piazza Navona front and are gracefully decorated with frescoes. By now, the stigma attached to the previous pontificate had lessened and some of the artists decorating the interior were former Barberini clients, for example, Giacinto Gimignani, Andrea Camassei and Herman van Swanevelt (*c.*1600–65), a Dutch contemporary of Claude. The aged Agostino Tassi contributed a room of seascapes and Gaspard Dughet a room of landscapes. The most important commission, however, was the ceiling of the new gallery, which was obtained in December 1651 by Pietro da Cortona. The commissioner may have been Donna Olimpia, who was eager to signal her interest in allying her family with that of the Barberini, or, on the other hand, perhaps Camillo and the Princess of Rossano, both of whom were far more cultivated than Donna Olimpia (whose recreational preference was for the hunt).

The ceiling fresco took more than three years to paint. Its subject is the adventures of the Latin hero Aeneas, an allegory for the fortunes of the Pamphilj family and the virtues of Innocent X. The long, relatively narrow room was not suitable for a single scene as in palazzo Barberini, so Cortona broke the space into several different scenes, which centre upon the main image of the *Apotheosis of Aeneas*, in which the hero is received in heaven by the Olympian gods, including Venus with a dove, Minerva with the olive branch and Juno with a fleur-de-lis – the family emblems. The whole work is decorated with painted festoons that resemble Carracci's work in the Farnese gallery, and the effect is made lighter and more playful through the use of a paler and more delicate palette of colours than Carracci's.

The palazzo Pamphilj had a short life as the main family palace. Prince Camillo did not live here after his marriage in 1647 and his wife's frosty relationship with his mother ensured that the couple did no more than visit

Donna Olimpia in her vast suite of reception rooms. Indeed, there is a good chance that Camillo met the Princess of Rossano here, at one of his mother's society gatherings. The marriage between Camillo Pamphilj and Olimpia Aldobrandini was a true love match, and perhaps it began here, even during the lifetime of the princess's first husband, the youthful Paolo Borghese.

Thus, with the Pamphilj, we find a family that speedily abandons its own most glorious stage set. The palazzo Pamphilj was a prestigious rental property for centuries and housed Rome's Musical Society for a time; in 1960 the family finally sold it to the Republic of Brazil, as its embassy, which it remains today. Now not even the courtyard can be visited and it joins the palazzo Farnese as one of Rome's legendary hidden treasures. However, the embassy does turn the lights on in the great gallery on most evenings, so strollers in piazza Navona can catch a glimpse of the Baroque beauty of Pietro da Cortona's frescoed ceiling.

II SANT' AGNESE IN AGONE
Piazza Navona, next to palazzo Pamphilj. Open 9–12, 16–18, though opening hours are subject to change

The great church which dominates the centre of the Pamphilj block in piazza Navona occupies the site of the old palazzo Mellini, which was bought by Innocent X and demolished in order to build a family church as a monument to Pamphilj piety and taste. As it turned out, it stands perhaps more as a testimonial to their ongoing intrigues and strife, and as with any broth in which too many cooks have had a hand, the end result is a bit of a jumble, though a spectacular one.

A tiny church stood on a fraction of the present site, with its apse towards the piazza and its entrance on via di Santa Maria dell'Anima. It commemorated one of Rome's favourite martyrs, the fourteen-year-old Agnes. According to her legend, upon refusing to wed one of the friends of the Emperor Diocletian (a familiar theme for virgin saints, who all tended to roll their eyes heavenwards, citing a prior commitment to a divine bridegroom), Agnes was stripped naked by the emperor's soldiers and put on public display in this stadium. The saint's hair purportedly grew at a miraculous rate to conceal her nudity, at which point she was tossed into a brothel, occupying the site of the old church. In fact, the spaces under stadiums were often rented out as brothels, so much so that the euphemism 'going to the vaults' was used in Latin to refer to visiting a house of prostitution. As the Latin word for this kind of vault was *fornix*, the word which has come down to us reflects the old euphemism: 'fornicate'. In any case, Agnes's virginity was defended by fiery angels and, in exasperation,

Diocletian executed her, though even the execution was difficult: a pyre somehow failed to burn, so her head was cut off. She was buried on the via Nomentana, where her catacomb and great medieval basilica stand today; when her servant Emerentiana visited her tomb, she too was stoned to death by the Roman mob, at which point servant and mistress were united in the same tomb. After her death, Agnes became the object of one of Rome's most important saint cults. Through a punnish quirk – 'Agnes' resembles the Latin word *agnus* (lamb') – it is at her via Nomentana basilica that the papal lambs are shaved to make the wool for the pallium, the consecrated cloth strips that are given to new bishops.

In 1651 the old church of St Agnes in piazza Navona was measured by an architect. The site of the old palazzo Mellini was cleared and building work was entrusted to Girolamo Rainaldi, the architect of the Farnese and Borghese, and his son Carlo, the same duo who had done most of the work on palazzo Pamphilj. They were particular favourites of Prince Camillo Pamphilj, who as the pope's secular heir was the most appropriate supervisor for the project. Girolamo Rainaldi, by this time an old man, was less and less involved in the designing, and it was his son Carlo who suggested a concave plan for the façade, after a central plan for the church had been rejected, reducing the main axis of the church (front to back) and extending the secondary one (side to side). In the summer of 1653 the pope had one of his occasional rages over the slow progress of construction and, perhaps as a result, or more likely due to the rehabilitation of Donna Olimpia in late summer 1653, the Rainaldi were dismissed and after a time Francesco Borromini was appointed to take over.

Borromini's plans to alter Carlo Rainaldi's designs included making the façade more curved and lowering the bell towers on either side, but these came to naught and very little of the church today reflects a Borrominian design. Work was slow and eventually Prince Camillo did away with Borromini completely, in 1657, in favour of his preferred architect, Carlo Rainaldi. The final indignity for Borromini took place after Don Camillo's death, when the Princess of Rossano appointed Bernini to complete the façade, in the course of which Bernini substituted a simple triangular pediment in his usual classicising style for the more complex one Borromini had intended. On the inside, too, the decoration of the church fell into Bernini's gift and his protégé Giovanni Battista Gaulli, known as il Baciccia, received the commission to fresco the pendentives, the triangular spaces on the piers just below the dome. Apart from a little relief-work altarpiece in the lower church, by the papal favourite Algardi, the interior of the church was entirely decorated after the death of Innocent X, and reflects the patronage of Don Camillo and his heirs.

The concave **façade** and the convex dome form a visual unity that some have seen as a mid seventeenth-century critique of the façade of St Peter's, where the great dome recedes behind the front of the basilica as the viewer approaches. Here, on the contrary, the dome is the crown of the visual composition, matched by the two bell towers completed by Carlo Rainaldi and Antonio Del Grande in a trinity of skyscraping points. The Pamphilj emblem of the dove and olive branch decorate the railing, and appear at several spots across the façade: the viewer is meant to be in no doubt that this is a family church. Indeed, until recently, when the Doria-Pamphilj gave the church into the care of a corporate body, the Pamphilj princes had the privilege of being greeted with incense when they visited Sant' Agnese.

The **interior** is surprisingly airy and large. Almost immediately the visitor is beneath the dome and the sumptuous decoration pulls the eye upwards towards the fresco in the cupola, Ciro Ferri's *Glory of Paradise*, from 1689: this was the artist's last work and in fact he died just before it was completed. The *Cardinal Virtues* in the pendentives are, as we have noted, by Gaulli. The eight precious columns of *cottanello* red marble carry colour across the pale fields of the sculptural altarpieces. These are seven in number, the most successful of which, in terms of composition and finishing, is the one on the pier to the left of the high altar, Antonio Raggi's *Martyrdom of St Cecilia*. Also interesting are the statue above the altar in the right transept, *St Agnes on the pyre*, by Ercole Ferrata, and that above the left-hand altar towards the door, *St Eustace among the wild animals*, by Melchiorre Cafà. Cafà, a favourite of Don Camillo, received this and another major commission (in Sant' Agostino, which we will see later) from the prince, but died in a foundry accident before he could finish either of them, so they were completed by Ferrata, a gifted pupil of Algardi's. Pamphilj doves and *gigli* are festooned around the entire building. Above the main entrance is the pallid monument to Innocent X that was finally made in 1729–30 by Giovanni Battista Maini (a sculptor who also made a Santacroce family tomb in Santa Maria in Publicolis).

A door (often locked) in the right transept leads down into the tiny **underground church** of Sant'Agnese, converted from the ancient brothel set into the arches of the stadium; it has some badly conserved medieval frescoes amid much flaking nineteenth-century medieval-style fakery, some genuine ancient mosaic flooring and a lovely relief in marble by Alessandro Algardi from 1653, *The miracle of the hair of St Agnes*. Back upstairs, two other interesting relics stand in the two chapels on either side of the left transept, which features a beefcake St Sebastian by Pier Paolo Campi (active 1702–35): in the chapel on the piazza Navona side is a rough stone font from the medieval church, at which Francesca Ponziani, Santa Francesca Romana, was baptised. Across from it, in a rather bare chapel that served as a passage from the palazzo to the church, the startlingly tiny head of St Agnes is displayed in a reliquary. Beneath the high altar (no admission) is the burial crypt of the Pamphilj and their successors, the Doria-Pamphilj Landi; in the sacristy (entrance from the right transept or via di Santa Maria dell'Anima), of Borrominian design, concerts are sometimes held.

III   COLLEGIO INNOCENZIANO

Piazza Navona, angle with via di Sant' Agnese in Agone. Entrance at via dell'Anima 30. No admission

This building, a partner to the Borrominian section of the palazzo Pamphilj on the other side of Sant' Agnese, was built in 1654 in part to the designs of the great architect. It was founded by Innocent X as a college for the education of young men from Pamphilj family lands who might consider the priesthood. The large Serlian windows, mirroring those of palazzo Pamphilj's great gallery, open into the college's old library room, frescoed by Francesco Cozza (1605–82), a Calabrese artist one of whose later frescoes decorates the Pantheon. Alone of the Pamphilj properties in piazza Navona, this building remains in the hands of the family, and now in part is a smart rental property and in part houses a small community of nuns. This odd combination of neighbours is typical of Rome.

IV   THE FONTANA DEI QUATTRO FIUMI AND THE OTHER
FOUNTAINS OF PIAZZA NAVONA

The new prominence given piazza Navona, as a Pamphilj equivalent to the Barberini's cortile della Cavallerizza and the Borghese family piazza, seemed to require a monumental fountain. In the late sixteenth century, Gregory XIII Boncompagni had installed fountains at each end of the piazza, designed, as so often, by Giacomo della Porta. The centre of the piazza, an obvious location, was occupied only by a stone trough for watering livestock. Innocent X determined that the Acqua Vergine aqueduct, whose terminus was at the still unfinished Trevi fountain, would feed a new fountain here and opened a competition, inviting Francesco Borromini to submit a design.

The pope intended that the centrepiece of the fountain should be an obelisk taken from its discovery site in the villa of the Emperor Maxentius. This meant, of course, that whatever plan was put into use, the obelisk rather than the water would be the main feature. Perhaps Borromini found this requirement stifling, or maybe he was not particularly interested in fountain design. In any case his plan was rather unimaginative and was rejected. Instead, in the spring of 1647, the commission was given to the hitherto disgraced Gianlorenzo Bernini.

How this came about is the subject of two differing tales: Bernini's son Domenico says it was through the support of Donna Olimpia's son-in-law Prince Nicolò Ludovisi; Bernini made a scale model of his plan, which Ludovisi placed in a room in palazzo Pamphilj that the pope passed through regularly. The pope, catching sight of it, was said to have been enchanted and remarked, 'We must indeed employ Bernini, although there are many who would not wish it; the only way to resist him is not to see his work.' He thereby won the job. The other story, which seems somehow more plausible, was told by the ambassador of Modena: it would seem that Bernini made a model of the fountain in solid silver and presented it to Donna Olimpia, who then ensured he got the commission. It is hard to tell. Certainly no silver model exists today.

Construction began, at enormous expense and with public outcry at the misappropriation of public funds in a time of extreme privation, in 1649; in August of that year the obelisk was raised on to its tall travertine base and two years later, in June 1651, the fountain was officially unveiled. Its final cost was more than 29,000 scudi, Bernini receiving 3000 and his assistants 10,000, as their fees. Gigli, however, asserted that it cost an additional 12,000 scudi just to transport the obelisk to Rome.

The fountain is one of Rome's most iconographically complex public sculptures, open to many different interpretations. The obelisk had long been recognised as a solar symbol, *digitus solis* (the finger of the sun), and here might refer to the peaceful, sunny rule of the Pamphilj, with the family dove and olive branch perched at the top. What we see is the work of Bernini and his studio, doubtless in conference with Innocent X: the sculptures, in marble, of four over-lifesized muscular male river gods preside over a travertine landscape teeming with plants and animals. The whole thing is a metaphor for the earth, with the four river gods standing in for the four corners of the world. Atop it all is the obelisk surmounted by the Pamphilj emblem: everything under the sun is represented as under the dominion of the pope's family.

On the south side, the *Ganges* by Claude Poussin (d. 1661) represents Asia, holding an oar to indicate that the great river was navigable for most of its length, and the *Danube* by Antonio Raggi stands for Europe, holding up the papal crest as befitted the only entirely Christian continent. On the north side, the *Rio della Plata* representing the Americas, by Francesco Baratta (d. 1666), has distinctively (if inappropriately) negroid features, and a nearby scatter of gold coins to indicate the great wealth of the largely Catholic New World. A peculiar beast next to the figure of the Rio della

Piazza Navona *allagata,* flooded for the August festival. Note the fortunate few observing the spectacle from the balcony of palazzo Pamphilj, left

Plata is an armadillo, or at least a seventeenth-century idea of one: it looks like a dragon and might refer to traditional dragon symbolism, for instance, the evils and snares of the sinful world. The figure of the *Nile,* by Giacomo Antonio Fancelli (1619–71), has his head shrouded, a reference to the river's at that time undiscovered source.

The fountain may be seen as Bernini's response to his critics, who had mocked him for the débâcle of his bell towers for St Peter's: the obelisk stands, apparently suspended in thin air, above a void formed by the four pillars on which the river gods recline. Of course, the structure is perfectly sound, but it excited much anxious comment during its construction and Bernini's son Domenico said that his father, in response, tied a string to the obelisk, then to a nearby building, and walked off laughing: 'There, that should hold it.' Bernini's accomplishment was not limited to the engineering success of holding an obelisk aloft: the fountain represents the final stage in a progression from an architectural fountain, like the Great Fountain of the Ghetto, to a sculptural fountain in which water and stone combine in a unified whole, sculpture in motion.

The fountain's drain, in the shape of a sea monster, still sucks up water at a dramatic rate. It was often blocked on purpose, from the seventeenth to the nineteenth centuries, to flood piazza Navona. In the month of August, one of the hottest, the piazza would be turned into the *lago di piazza Navona,* a shallow lake, and the people who lived around it would send invitations to their friends to enjoy the evening coolness from their balconies. The coaches of the Roman aristocracy would circle, splashing, round the piazza. In 1727 the diarist Valesio recorded no less a figure than the seven-year-old Bonnie Prince Charlie, the heir of the Catholic pretender to the British throne, throwing coins from his balcony, to watch the urchins fighting over them: 'hardly decent behaviour for a king's son'. By the nineteeenth century the event had become a more populist entertainment: tents and booths were set up round the edge of the piazza, selling food and toys, and people waded out into the doubtless rather murky water. The festivities came to an end once and for all in 1867, when the pavement level was altered to create a road surface round the outside edge of the piazza, which remains today.

The two earlier fountains in the piazza by Giacomo della Porta pre-date the central one by seventy years. The southern fountain, the **Fontana del Moro**, of beautiful *portasanta* marble, has four tritons, copies of the originals which were thought to be in danger of erosion from pollution and were moved to the Villa Borghese in the nineteenth century, and in the centre a much later *Ethiopian with a dolphin* added in 1654. This was commissioned by Donna Olimpia from Bernini's workshop: the master made the original design, but the work itself was carved by his pupil Giovanni Antonio Mari (d. 1661). The basin surrounding the fountain was designed by Borromini, though executed by the studio of Bernini. The central statue, known as the Moor, is wrestling with a dolphin from whose mouth a stream of Acqua Vergine water gushes. The northernmost fountain, the **fontana di Nettuno**, is also by della Porta, though its central figure, too, was added later, by the nineteenth-century sculptors Antonio della Bitta (1807–*c.*73) and Gregorio Zappalà (1833–1908). Here Neptune, a decidedly Berninian figure, is set to spear a huge octopus, which seems to be giving as good as it gets. Two mermaids and two baby tritons complete the ensemble, all nineteenth century and all rather charming.

2 Palazzo Doria-Pamphilj and its collections

Colder and more comfortless than can possibly be imagined . . .

Nathaniel Hawthorne

Principal entrances at via del Corso 304, piazza del Collegio Romano 2. For admission to the Galleria Doria-Pamphilj see below. No admission to the rest of the palace

palazzo Doria-Pamphilj and its neighbourhood

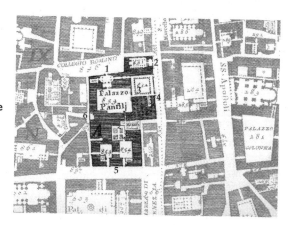

Key:
1 Del Grande façade and entrance to Galleria
2 Santa Maria in via Lata
3 Santoro courtyard (*cortile d'onore*)
4 Valvassori façade
5 Ameli façade
6 Busiri Vici façade

The colossal palazzo Doria-Pamphilj, one of Rome's largest, remains in the hands of Prince Camillo's successors, the Doria-Pamphilj Landi. It houses one of Rome's greatest private art collections, the Galleria Doria-Pamphilj, the result of the union of the Aldobrandini collection of the Princess of Rossano with the Pamphilj collection largely established by her husband, Prince Camillo. Today the palace's three chief façades dominate the end of the via del Corso, the via del Plebiscito and the piazza del Collegio Romano.

I   THE DEVELOPMENT OF THE PALACE

The nucleus of the present palace dates from 1489, when Cardinal Giovanni Fazio Santoro, canon of the nearby church of Santa Maria in via Lata, bought land and some old buildings on the western side of the via del Corso. He built his cardinalate palace there, a beautiful and elegant construction of up-to-the-minute modernity, with a classical courtyard with two levels of arcades, resting on reused ancient columns. His palace brought the cardinal no luck, exhausting him financially and earning him the unwelcome envy of Julius II who, as we have seen, described it as 'more worthy of a duke than a cardinal'. The unfortunate Santoro was required to cede the palace to the pope, who immediately gave it to his nephew, Duke Francesco Maria I della Rovere of Urbino. Until the early seventeenth century it was the city seat of

1. Collegio Romano. 2. Palazzo de Carolis. 3. Chiesa di S. Maria in Vialata. 4. Monasterio delle Monache di S. Marta.

The Pamphilj wing of palazzo Doria-Pamphilj, built for don Camillo Pamphilj by Antonio Del Grande. Atop the palace is the *altana* built by the Aldobrandini above the older part of the building.

the prefect of Rome, a hereditary title of the della Rovere until the extinction of the family. They possessed it for the rest of the sixteenth century, buying up neighbouring properties and slowly extending it, but in 1601 they sold it to Pietro Aldobrandini, cardinal nephew of the reigning pope Clement VIII. Cardinal Pietro built two wings round the great courtyard and an *altana*. It was this palace, palazzo Santoro-Aldobrandini, that Cardinal Pietro's heiress, Olimpia Aldobrandini, Princess of Rossano, received as one of the prime pieces of family property, along with a number of other buildings and the family villas at Frascati and in town at largo Magnanapoli (at the foot of today's via Nazionale), where the cardinal's famous art collection was kept.

When the palace became the main residence of Olimpia Aldobrandini and her new husband, Prince Camillo Pamphilj, the palazzo was enlarged in accordance with the division of property required by the Aldobrandini legal settlement. Prince Camillo built a new wing, today's main wing on piazza del Collegio Romano, to serve as the 'Pamphilj' part of the palace, while the 'Aldobrandini' part of the family, the couple's second son and his children, were expected to live in the old nucleus, around Cardinal Santoro's Renaissance courtyard. To build the new wing Camillo slowly acquired the houses next door, struggling with the bad-tempered clergy of Santa Maria in via Lata who did not want to sell, but having an easier time with the nuns of

Santa Marta nearby. The most important neighbour, however, was the Jesuits' Roman College, across the piazza that now bears its name. The Jesuits had received the adjacent palazzo Salviati as a bequest, and Prince Camillo purchased and demolished part of it for the construction of the 'Pamphilj' wing. Payments to the family architect, Antonio Del Grande, are recorded in the Doria-Pamphilj archive until 1671, half a decade after Camillo's death. The widowed Princess of Rossano and her sons, Prince Giovanni Battista and the future Cardinal Benedetto, completed the works. Prince Giovanni Battista lived in the Aldobrandini section of the palace on the Corso, while his younger brother Benedetto lived in the apartment facing on to the piazza del Collegio Romano.

Subsequently, however, the inheritance was divided again, between Prince Giovanni Battista's two sons. Camillo, the younger brother, commissioned another phase of significant building work, the construction of the façade on the via del Corso and a general modernisation from 1731 to 1734. The architect was Gabriele Valvassori (1683–1761), whose new Corso façade was one of the most eloquent expressions of the Rococo in Rome. Even today the façade is notable for the size and number of its windows, and the grace of its decoration. This Camillo enclosed the upper level of Cardinal Santoro's Renaissance courtyard to make a proper gallery for his family's art collection and had the new rooms thoroughly decorated, even giving the palace its own Hall of Mirrors.

When the lawsuits surrounding the Pamphilj succession were under way, Giovanni Andrea IV Doria Landi moved, with his children, into the palace in 1760. Six years later it underwent another convulsion, under the architect Francesco Nicoletti (d. 1776), who redesigned the chapel and was responsible for the conversion of the fifteenth-century courtyard into a temporary ballroom in 1769, in honour of Pietro Leopoldo I, Grand Duke of Tuscany and brother of Joseph II, the Holy Roman Emperor. The façade on via del Plebiscito was built to the designs of Paolo Ameli in 1744. In the nineteenth century, Andrea Busiri Vici (1817–1911), a prolific Roman architect and founder of a dynasty of architects, built the stable wing and the covered riding school (1848, now commercial space), and the façades on via della Gatta and piazza Grazioli. The Doria-Pamphilj family today use the state apartment in the Aldobrandini part of the palace, while the Pamphilj apartment forms part of the Galleria.

11 THE GALLERIA DORIA-PAMPHILJ

Open 10–18 daily, closed Thursday, access from piazza del Collegio Romano entrance. Admission €7.30. Website: www.doriapamphilj.it

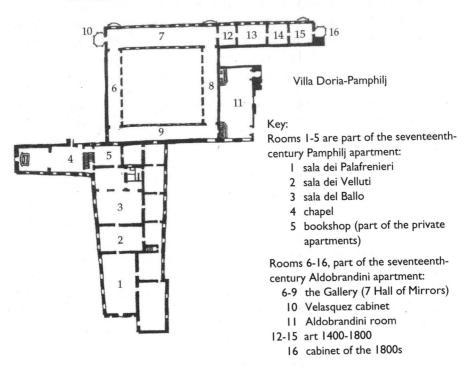

Villa Doria-Pamphilj

Key:

Rooms 1-5 are part of the seventeenth-century Pamphilj apartment:

  1 sala dei Palafrenieri
  2 sala dei Velluti
  3 sala del Ballo
  4 chapel
  5 bookshop (part of the private apartments)

Rooms 6-16, part of the seventeenth-century Aldobrandini apartment:

  6-9 the Gallery (7 Hall of Mirrors)
  10 Velasquez cabinet
  11 Aldobrandini room
12-15 art 1400-1800
  16 cabinet of the 1800s

The art collection in this palace is unquestionably the best remaining in private hands in Rome. Unlike the Colonna gallery, which is only open for half a day once a week, the Doria-Pamphilj collection is easily accessible and user-friendly, with an audioguide in English, in part narrated by the current prince himself, Don Jonathan. The discussion here will be confined to a brief description of the Pamphilj apartment, the growth of the collection, and the tastes of the family's main patrons. Tours of the private apartments are sometimes available.

The two sections of the palace open to the public are the Pamphilj apartment built by Prince Camillo, and the gallery itself. The **apartment** has been very greatly altered, especially in the nineteenth century: thus the sequence of state rooms now conforms less to the requirements of seventeenth-century protocol than does palazzo Barberini. The apartment is two rooms thick, ranged along the whole Del Grande façade. These are the principal public rooms of the suite that once housed Prince Camillo, his son Cardinal Benedetto and Camillo's grandson Prince Girolamo. Coming up the main staircase, we pass a large ante-room before coming to the richly decorated entrance to the Pamphilj apartment, surrounded by classical statuary, in part removed here from the family's villa.

The overall impression of the apartment, and indeed of the gallery as well, is one of the utmost magnificence. The main sightline is the long enfilade of aligned doorways that lead from the top of the staircase to a window in the façade on the Corso, in the distance. A nineteenth-century visitor, Nathaniel Hawthorne, experienced the palace in wintertime:

> All the rooms, halls and galleries of beautiful proportions, with vaulted roofs, some of which glow with frescoes; and all are colder and more comfortless than can possibly be imagined without having been in them. [. . .] In the whole immense range of rooms of the Palazzo Doria, I saw but a single fireplace, and that so deep in the wall that no amount of blaze would raise the atmosphere of the room ten degrees.

Though the rooms have been rearranged and improved, in at least one respect they have not changed from Hawthorne's days: they are still frigidly cold. In the winter, the unfortunate attendants have to wear hats and gloves as if outdoors.

The first room in the apartment, the *sala dei palafrenieri*, is recognisable from its dimensions alone: stretching two floors high, it forms an impressive entrance to the princely suite. Although not in excellent condition, this room is immediately notable for the paintings it houses, for unlike the *sala dei palafrenieri* in palazzo Barberini, this still contains its original canvases in something like their original positions. They are almost all by the painter we have met in palazzo Colonna, Gaspard Dughet: because he was the brother-in-law to the more famous Nicolas Poussin, this room is also sometimes known as the *Sala del Poussin*. Dughet's landscape frescoes in the church of San Martino ai Monti in 1647–51 had caught the eye of Prince Camillo. He commissioned Dughet to decorate the room, though some of the paintings are in such poor condition that their original quality is hard to determine. A door to the right leads to the throne room, akin to that which we have seen in palazzo Colonna, once again with its throne turned with its back to the room, either in protest at the fall of papal rule or, more likely, following the tradition that the chairs under the *baldacchini* of cardinals were turned to the wall when the cardinal was not in residence.

The great enfilade begins with a door leading into what had been, in the seventeenth century, the first antecamera, though the wall hangings of precious velvet which give this room its name, the *sala dei velluti*, have been replaced in restoration and the furniture here, as in the previous room, is eighteenth century. The next room, today's *sala del ballo* (ballroom), was set up in the early twentieth century, replacing the second antecamera. From here, through a little passage to the left, is the chapel, a later insertion by the architect Carlo Fontana in 1691 (the same architect also worked on palazzo Colonna, underlining once again the similarity in taste of the two families). It was altered twice, in the eighteenth and then in the nineteenth century, so it does not bear a great resemblance to its original condition, though it was always large. Its placement off the audience chamber, instead of one of the antecamere, breaks with the established pattern of a noble apartment: in compensation, the chapel has two sections, one closer to the altar, reserved for members of the family, and a more spacious antecamera for visitors and members of the household. By the entrance to the chapel antecamera is a glass case containing the body of St Theodora, to which Anna Pamphilj was so devoted that she brought it with her to Genoa upon her marriage and it only returned to the palace with the arrival of the Doria-Pamphilj. The last room is today the gallery's bookshop and bears little sign of its former role as the bedroom or study of Prince Camillo. The door leading from here into the gallery area pierces through the divide in the palace between the section reserved for the Pamphilj and that intended as the Aldobrandini apartment.

The **gallery** itself is arranged principally round the four sides of the upper level of the Santoro courtyard. A sequence of four rooms off the Hall of Mirrors is now devoted to art from 1400 to 1800 and a large hall off the Third Wing of the gallery, the Aldobrandini Room, is a repository of ancient statuary brought from the Villa Doria-Pamphilj. A somewhat controversial rehanging of the collection in 1996 brought it back to a partial simulacrum of its arrangement in the 1760s, when a detailed plan was made. The new arrangement does not, unfortunately, entirely remedy John Ruskin's complaint in the nineteenth century that he 'could not see one [picture], all in direct front lights or no lights at all'.

The first main source of the gallery's art is the Aldobrandini collection, the contribution of the Princess of Rossano, mainly formed in the first and second decades of the seventeenth century by her forebear, Cardinal Pietro Aldobrandini. His holdings were vastly enriched when the collection of the Este dukes of Ferrara was expropriated by Clement VIII, bringing many masterpieces of Ferrarese art, including the *Dido* of Dosso Dossi, and works by Mazzolino and Garofalo. The *Salome* of Titian, the *Nativity* by Parmigianino and the *Double Portrait* by Raphael also entered the Pamphilj collection through the Aldobrandini bequest. Among the most important pieces commissioned by Cardinal Pietro Aldobrandini are the famous Aldobrandini Lunettes, six semicircular paintings depicting episodes from the life of the Virgin by Annibale Carracci and his circle: Annibale perhaps completed only one or two, the *Flight into Egypt* and possibly the

Entombment, the rest being painted under the direction of his pupils. Very little of the Princess of Rossano's own taste can be detected, though her portrait bust by Giovanni Lazzoni (1617–88) commissioned near the end of her life, is of a very conservative and formal style.

The gallery's most famous painting, the *Innocent X* by Diego Velázquez (1599–1660), a penetrating and somewhat unflattering portrait – described by the pope himself as being *'troppo vero'* (too true) – was not a commission of the pope's, but a gift. Velázquez had been sent to Rome on a diplomatic mission for his master, Philip IV of Spain, and while in Rome the great painter also made portraits of other important personages, including Cardinal Camillo Astalli-Pamphilj (now in the collection of the Hispanic Society, New York City). Two portrait busts of Innocent in marble are by Bernini and Algardi: Algardi's realism contrasts with Bernini's more idealised and spiritual portrayal. Donna Olimpia's artistic taste is displayed by a painting formerly in her palace at San Martino al Cimino, Guercino's *Erminia discovering the wounded Tancred,* and by the impressive portrait bust of her by Algardi, where she looks fully as formidable as her reputation makes her.

Prince Camillo, the most important Pamphilj collector, contributed two wonderful landscapes by Claude Gelée, called Le Lorrain (*c.*1604–682), *Landscape with Dancing Figures* and *Landscape with a View of Delphi*, idealised views of the Roman Campagna and its monuments. Camillo also prized his two unusually lyrical early works by Caravaggio, the *Rest on the Flight into Egypt* and the *Penitent Magdalene*. A third, the *Gypsy Fortuneteller*, was presented to Louis XIV in 1665 by Prince Camillo and is now in the Louvre.

The nineteenth-century Prince Filippo Andrea V Doria-Pamphilj expanded the family collections with purchases of early art, medieval and fifteenth century: the most important of these acquisitions is part of a triptych by Hans Memling (active *c.*1435–94), the *Lament over the Dead Christ, with donor*. The same collector acquired the *Annunciation* by Filippo Lippi (*c.*1406–69) and other early paintings; a small cabinet at the end of the 'Art of the 1400s' room, a pendant to the one containing the Velázquez *Innocent X*, contains his bewhiskered portrait, flanked by those of his English wife Mary Talbot and her sister, the beautiful and saintly Gwendolen Talbot Borghese by Pietro Tenerani (1789–1869), one of Rome's stable of icily classicising nineteenth-century sculptors.

3 The Villa Doria-Pamphilj

Entrances from via di San Pancrazio, via Aurelia Antica (not recommended, as it is a busy street with no footpaths) and via Leone XIII. Closed at sunset. Free admission. No admission to the Casino Algardi or major buildings

At 184 hectares in area, the Villa Doria-Pamphilj is Rome's largest public park and though it enjoys less fame than does its counterpart on the other side of the river, the Villa Borghese, it is full of interest. It became the property of the city of Rome as recently as 1967, when it was expropriated in lieu of back taxes, and it was brutally cut in two by a bleak and unfriendly highway, via Leone XIII (named after the pope whose entire reign, from 1878 to 1903, was spent without leaving the Vatican Palace). One single bridge links the two parts of the villa; the far side is the less remarkable. The Casino or main building, was taken over by the Senate of the Republic of Italy as a reception space and separated from the rest of the property with a high iron fence; the villa has suffered greatly from this division and the interior of the Casino, of great interest, is not open to the public, though there has been some suggestion of converting it into a museum.

After it became a public park, the property suffered terrible vandalism, when the heads of the ancient statue collection were hacked off by thieves and the grounds sank into decay. It is only now beginning to be restored, with what remain of its statues being replaced by casts. Some of the statuary has been saved by its removal, either to the palazzo Doria-Pamphilj or elsewhere, one day perhaps to return. Indeed, a new museum, the Museo di Villa Doria-Pamphilj (tel. 06 3937 6616), is advertised as being at via Aurelia Antica 183, in the building known as the Villa Vecchia, but at the time of writing, calls were not answered and several visits to this address met with no sign, no open gate or door and, all too clearly, no museum.

The villa, in its present form, is more a reflection of the nineteenth-century Doria-Pamphilj interest in English style and land use than a pristine survival of the seventeenth century. It was divided, soon after its acquisition in 1630 and expansion in the 1640s, into three parts: the *pars urbana*, given over to formal gardens, the *pars fructuaria*, which had fruit trees and a more natural landscape, and the *pars rustica*, which was used as farmland: the Doria-Pamphilj were agricultural innovators and used their villa as a sort of laboratory, inviting their countrymen to come and learn about the English farming techniques they had imported.

I   A VISIT TO THE VILLA DORIA-PAMPHILJ PARK

Start: main entrance in largo 3 Giugno 1849, the junction of streets facing porta San Pancrazio from along via di San Pancrazio

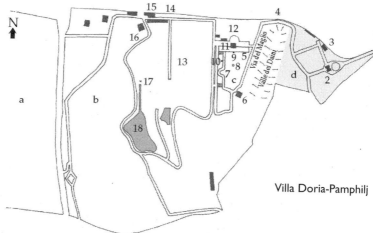

Villa Doria-Pamphilj

Key:

I   remains of the Villa del Vascello
2   arco dei Quattro Venti
3   Palazzina Corsini
4   arch of Paul V
5   giardino del teatro
6   cappella Doria-Pamphilj
7   teatro
8   Cupid Fountain
9   Fountain of Venus
10 grotto of the Satyr
11 giardino segreto

12 Casino
13 Pineta
14 monument to the French dead
15 Villa Vecchia
16 Snail Fountain
17 Giglio Fountain and cascade
18 lago del Giglio
a. *pars rustica* given over to farming
b. *pars fructuaria* with fruit trees
c. *pars urbana* with formal gardens
d. section of the villa once part of
    the Villa Corsini

Our walk begins in the part of the villa that was acquired from the Corsini heirs after the fall of the Roman Republic in 1849. On via di San Pancrazio we have already passed the signs of the French siege in the mostly ruined villa building on its north side, the Vascello. This was once the celebrated Baroque residence of the French envoy, Abbot Elpidio Benedetti, a fantastical construction of 1663–5, and it contained frescoes by Giovanni Francesco Grimaldi, Algardi's collaborator, as well as late works by Pietro da Cortona. It took the form of a large, round-ended galleon, resting on a shell. The bombardments of summer 1849 levelled this confection above the ground level and what remains was restructured in 1897 in a rather pathetic rearguard action by its last owner, Luigi Medici, who bore the title of conte del Vascello from this property.

The area of Rome directly to the south of the via di San Pancrazio is called Monteverde, the 'Green Hill', a pleasant modern suburb mostly developed from the 1920s onwards and now, like the rest of Rome, extremely expensive. Until its development it was an expanse of vineyards and villas belonging to different families, most prominent among them the Corsini, whom we will meet in greater detail in the final chapter. Cardinal Neri Corsini acquired the property in 1662 and ordered the construction of a casino at the highest point of the hilly area, which luckily rose opposite the porta San Pancrazio, the city gate. This building, the Casino dei Quattro Venti (of the Four Winds), stood on a high basement pierced with an open arch and functioned solely as a sort of viewing platform for the surrounding territory; it commanded spectacular views and no other decoration, it seemed, was necessary. The villa Corsini was largely given over to cultivation.

Entering the park, immediately to the left we pass a small building of strange appearance, partially covered in maiolica tiles. This is the old **porter's lodge** of the villa Corsini, which was given a make-over in 1881 by Andrea Busiri Vici, to look like the nineteenth-century's idea of a Swiss cottage. Through a grove of trees a path leads towards Busiri Vici's most important building here, the **Arco dei Quattro Venti**. This monumental arch was built in 1859 on the site of the old Casino of the villa Corsini and followed the ancient model of a triumphal arch, decorated with bits and pieces of the Pamphilj collection of Roman statuary. It is surmounted by four statues representing the winds, and a painted inscription describing its construction at the order of Prince Filippo Andrea V. This area was thoroughly relandscaped by Busiri Vici in the style of an English garden, with winding paths. If we take the gate to the right of the Arco and the first path branching off to the right, we will arrive at the **palazzina Corsini**, one of the few remaining buildings from the tenancy of the previous owners. It was restructured by Busiri Vici as the residence of the Doria-Pamphilj heir, so that different generations of the family could occupy different areas of the villa without impeding each other. This building is undergoing very slow restoration.

Down a hill, we rejoin the main path as it curves round the end of the **valle dei Daini**, the old boundary valley separating the Corsini from the Pamphilj property. It remains off limits as a wildlife preserve and we soon reach the northern perimeter of the villa, along the via Aurelia Antica. The wall here is made of the arches of the Acqua Paola and, as we continue along the path, we can look back to see the **arch of Paul V** that carries the aqueduct over the road, with a beautifully carved inscription and the Borghese symbols. At the end of this stretch of the path we arrive at the fence which separates the property claimed by the Senate from the public park and turn south once again.

Here we are on the one path that unquestionably remains unaltered from the seventeenth-century Villa Pamphilj. This is the **viale del Maglio**, the original entrance road: it stretches along the edge of the valle dei Daini all the way to the Cappella Doria-Pamphilj. On our way we will pass the cast of what remained of an ancient sarcophagus after the vandals got to it. The Romans are hard on their parks and few of the fountains in the villa are working, which certainly detracts from its monumental appearance.

This part of the park today looks rather strange. In the seventeenth century it was the grand monumental garden space, the *giardino del teatro*, so called from its theatrical fountains and topiary. This was destroyed and relandscaped in the nineteenth century in the English style, leaving a few of the original decorations. A restoration in the 1990s inserted an awkward-looking rose garden, with trellises meeting in a cross with four newly carved griffin-headed marble benches, copies of benches which once stood here. As we continue along the path, we find ourselves passing small copses of trees, an integral part of the English garden style. At the end of the viale del Maglio is the **Cappella Doria-Pamphilj**, a surprisingly ugly insertion in an alien neo-medieval style from 1902. It continues to be the family funerary chapel, though why anyone would choose to be buried here instead of in Sant' Agnese in Agone is an open question.

The path here turns right, to cross to the other side of the giardino del teatro, and across from the Cappella, set into the retaining wall, is a **wall fountain**, with two statues (casts) in niches, surmounted by a balustrade upon which is a cast of the **bust of Paolo Giordano Orsini** by the school of Bernini. The original is said to be in the Museo di Villa Doria-Pamphilj; Orsini, Duke of Bracciano was a cultivated and discerning friend of Prince Camillo. Further along is the **Teatro**, a semicircular exedra with niches which, one hopes, will one day contain casts of the statues that once adorned it. Already the reliefs that decorate its lower areas have been replaced with copies. A cast of the statue of **Pan**, put here in the eighteenth century, stands in the centre of the semicircle, on line with the central room of the **Teatro** which was built and decorated at the same time. Its interior (closed with a gate) is delicately decorated in stucco, with pan pipes in the middle of the ceiling referring not just to the Pan statue outside but to the water organ, destroyed in the French siege of 1849, that once stood behind the door in the back of the room.

Striking out into the centre of the *giardino del teatro* we approach the damaged **Cupid Fountain**. This nineteenth-century creation bears a close resemblance to Renaissance fountain styles; it too is only partially

Villa e Casino Pamfili detta del bel Respiro

1. Prima vista della Villa 2. Scale che portano al giardino segreto, 3. Scale che possono al secondo piano della Villa, 4. Viale del Pineto.

The Casino and *giardino segreto* of Villa Doria-Pamphilj, by Vasi. In front runs the via del Maglio, while the Pineta is visible in the background. Modern visitors find this view quite unchanged.

functioning, its central jet stilled. From here we can see the beautiful main Casino in front of us and, walking towards it, we approach the **Fountain of Venus**, of Algardian design, though altered over time, with the figure of Venus herself being a later substitution for a lost statue of higher quality. In fact, half of the current Venus is also gone – an enterprising thief has sawn her off in mid torso, leaving her legs perched on a half-shell like some cannibal's hors d'oeuvre. The stucco work here is of good quality and this fountain has been restored, so it can be seen today in an approximation of its original condition.

From here we turn left again, towards the western side of the garden and a staircase that rises ahead of us: before reaching the stairs, we will make a brief detour to look at the **Grotto of the Satyr**. This, too, was an original Algardian fountain and has also been restored, though only to a pallid version of its original self: in the seventeenth century it was surmounted by an exedra, a curved structure, on a level above, with another fountain and a statue of the river god of the Tiber. The latter remains, though in a rather denuded environment, and inside the grotto two marble tritons and two sirens keep company with a finely sculpted marble satyr. Water spurts upwards from a conch and trickles along the outside walls of the grotto to tumble picturesquely into a pool, while the arch of the grotto is held up by two vague male forms of brick and stucco, much decayed.

Returning to the stairs, I suggest going right to the top before looking back towards the Casino. From here the view over the **giardino segreto** is impressive. Low bushes are trimmed into fantastical shapes in the Italian manner. At the centre is a **bronze fountain**, a copy of the fountains in Florence's piazza della Santissima Annunziata, by Pietro Tacca (1577–1640). From here the elegant garden façade of the Casino can be seen most clearly, its stucco and marble decorations newly cleaned against a restored surface of sky-blue. Prince Camillo intended the interior and the exterior of the villa to flow together as part of a whole, and this beautiful and unusual building has a very simple design inside, of rooms grouped round a central circular hall. It contains more ancient statues, some of them restored by Algardi. Unfortunately it is closed to visitors and its front garden, with an ancient Roman necropolis, is also outside the public area.

Walking alongside the wrought-iron fence to the right, we pass, on our left, the open spaces and trees of the **Pineta**, an eighteenth-century addition, and a prime site for picnicking and the occasional game of football. Once again we find ourselves along the perimeter of the villa formed by the via Aurelia Antica and we carry on along the path named the viale del Monumento ai Caduti Francesi, passing beneath the pines and reaching the **monument to the French dead of 1849**. Behind the abundant moustaches of Prince Filippo Andrea V Doria-Pamphilj, who commissioned this monument from Busiri Vici, lurked a political reactionary of the first order and to him this monument owes its existence. One seeks in vain for a similar monument to the Roman dead of the siege; however, as if in compensation, the city authorities have named many of the surrounding paths after female heroes and revolutionaries: Filippo Andrea V must be spinning in his crypt at the knowledge that one path is named after Rosa Luxémburg, the great Communist fighter.

The viale here continues between a rather ugly concrete wall and the wrought-iron fence that encloses the garden and the building of the **Villa Vecchia**. At first this building was the centre of the *pars fructuaria* of the villa, a sort of super-farmhouse, but in the eighteenth century it was converted into an elegant Rococo residence for the servants of the prince. It is here that the Museo di Villa Doria-Pamphilj is to be arranged. We emerge into a little piazza with a drinking fountain, stone seats, and some stylish rococo fences and gates designed by Valvassori. From here it is clear that the ugly concrete wall was merely the back of the **greenhouses**, in neo-Gothic style, presently undergoing restoration, after which they are destined to house temporary exhibitions and a much-needed café. Beyond is the **giardino dei Cedri**, the cedar garden, the remaining piece of ideal landscape that Prince Camillo might have recognised. Its main monuments are two great fountains by Algardi, the **Snail fountain**, which rises further west in a field, and the **Giglio fountain**, further south, which forms the top of an **ornamental waterway**.

The waterway, an eighteenth-century reworking of the previous century's canal, is broken by three cascades. It has just been restored to its spectacular former condition. At its far end is the beautiful **lago del Giglio**, the artificial lake extant under Prince Camillo but given its present form in the early nineteenth century by the family architect Francesco Bettini. It is a serene home to wildlife, including ducks, geese and swans, as well as a large colony of turtles and fish. From the southern edge of the lake a glance back up in the direction from which we have come shows the dominance of Algardi's waterwork: not even the Villa Borghese can boast such a dramatic long view, with cascades and water jets rising up to culminate in the Giglio fountain.

Here the path branches off in two directions: to the west is the bridge to the other side of the villa, the *pars rustica*, which was expanded into a thriving farming concern by the nineteenth-century Doria-Pamphilj princes. An exploration of this will bring the visitor to the medieval farmhouse (closed) of **Casale di Giovio**, built atop an ancient Roman funerary mound. Slowly the agricultural and manufacturing buildings are coming back to life, as museum space and, one hopes, as a functional farm again. However, it is at the lake that the path branches back towards the Casino, and the eastern branch will return us eventually to the entrance to the park and the end of our visit.

4   Other Pamphilj sites in Rome

I   INNOCENT X AND THE GREAT BASILICAS

The advent of the Holy Year of 1650 spurred Innocent X and the Reverenda Fabbrica, the agency in charge of rebuilding **St Peter's**, to complete the **interior decoration** of the great basilica. It had been almost a century and a half since Julius II della Rovere had begun the demolition of the old basilica and St Peter's had swallowed up the marbles of hundreds of ancient buildings and the income of twenty-one pontificates. It was high time to finish the project.

Despite the humiliation Bernini suffered in 1645 when a commission of his fellow architects decided to demolish his bell tower, he retained his position as chief architect and it was to his studio that the interior decoration was naturally entrusted. A project to insert marble medallions into the piers of the nave met with papal favour, especially since the nave of the Constantinian basilica had borne similar portraits. Bernini's assistants made fifty-six portraits of popes from St Peter to Benedict I (575–9), with attendant putti and the picturesque Pamphilj dove perching close by, all in beautiful polychromatic marble. These were completed by 1648 and allegorical figures representing the virtues were placed above the arches of the nave. The floor of the nave, too, was adorned in a wealth of reused marbles, some, like the great porphyry disc near the main door, from the demolished basilica. Older decoration from the beginning of the century, by mid century embarrassingly out of style, was removed and replaced.

Though Bernini had control over the general appearance of the interior, individual commissions were given to complete the altars: Alessandro Algardi, who had already received the order to carve the tomb monument of Leo XI de' Medici (1605), also got one of the most desirable commissions a sculptor could ask for: a major altarpiece in St Peter's. This was the same altarpiece, above the **altar of Leo the Great**, that had previously been the subject of vitriolic discussion between the then Cardinal Pamphilj and the painter Guido Reni, prompting the vengeful portrait of Pamphilj as the devil in Santa Maria della Concezione. Algardi's subject, *The Meeting of Leo the Great and Attila*, shows the legendary moment when the pope turned the Hun away from sacking Rome. Though history suggests that the pope sent Attila away simply by telling him the truth – that Rome was then being decimated by an unstoppable plague – Algardi followed the pious legend that Leo threatened Attila with divine wrath in the form of Saints Peter and Paul, who in the relief are shown swooping down with swords in hand. Full of drama and movement, it is one of the masterpieces of the Baroque. Attila, dressed as a Roman soldier with billowing cape, is turning away in terror from the apparation of the two Roman saints boiling out of heaven to smite him. Behind the calm figure of the pope, who is pointing skywards, a crouching figure clutching his robes represents the people of the city, dependent on him for their protection.

This sculpture was not ready for the jubilee, unfortunately, so a full-sized plaster model was set up for the occasion, which won great acclaim; it was subsequently given by Alexander VII to the Oratorian order, perhaps in sign of the Oratorian Virgilio Spada's efforts as Innocent X's unofficial minister of arts. It can still be seen in the great ex-monastery of the order, in piazza della Chiesa Nuova. In fact, since the marble relief that was finally put in place in St Peter's in 1653 is often inaccessible behind a velvet rope barrier, a visit to the Oratorian monastery to see the model is a good substitute for the real thing: it also allows the visitor to enjoy one of the most complete buildings of Francesco Borromini, its principal architect.

The work on St Peter's was certainly important, but even more urgent was the restoration of Rome's cathedral, St John Lateran, **San Giovanni in**

Laterano. The basilica was in a condition of terrible decrepitude, almost about to collapse: one of its upper walls was leaning inwards at 80 centimetres out of the true. Virgilio Spada, the pope's confidant, was appointed to supervise the restoration of the cathedral in April 1646 and it was a notable sign of the times that the order went out to repair, not to demolish and rebuild, as had happened under Julius II at St Peter's. The motive was only in part a new interest in preserving early Christian churches: financial considerations also came into play.

The architect for this complex job was Borromini, and he made a detailed examination of the fabric, to see how much could be salvaged. The old columns of the medieval basilica had mostly been replaced with octagonal pillars in the fifteenth century, so later critics of Borromini who complained that he clad marble columns in unnecessary plaster bulwarks are unjust: there is no evidence that any such columns remained to be saved. His plan was revolutionary: instead of a colonnade, he fitted the nave with a wall pierced by huge arches, with aedicules set into the walls to contain statues. His desire to give the nave a vaulted roof was thwarted by the pope, who commanded that the coffered wooden ceiling of the sixteenth century be saved, so while the walls of the nave are a calm Borrominian white, the ceiling is dark and heavy, gilded and painted, creating an oppressive effect contrary to the architect's intentions. Above the niches are reliefs by different artists, including Algardi and Bernini's pupil Antonio Raggi, in inexpensive stucco. The niches were given their statues only in the eighteenth century.

Borromini was more fortunate in his reconstruction of the aisles: the inner aisle is a sequence of domed spaces separated by arches, while the outer aisle is lower and decorated with beams and flat ceilings. The outer aisles are dark, while the middle aisles are lofty and full of interesting perspectival light effects, emphasising the brightness of the nave, 'sculpting' with light to produce a lively articulation of the surfaces and spaces. Throughout, the architect's distinctive stucco work, also in white, provides a sober and graceful decoration. The great windows in the centre of the nave, as well as elsewhere in the basilica, are decorated with the papal arms: thus the two most important churches in Rome came under the sign of the Pamphilj dove.

II   THE SPLENDID PIETY OF CAMILLO PAMPHILJ

In 1653 Camillo's niece Olimpiuccia Giustiniani married the Barberini heir, Don Maffeo. The following year Camillo sponsored the near total reconstruction of the Discalced Augustinian church of **San Nicola da**

Tolentino, round the corner from palazzo Barberini, and it is hard not to see the two events as linked; by funding a church in the Barberini neighbourhood, Camillo was signalling the family alliance. Today the church flounders, lost in a grid of soulless streets behind piazza Barberini, looking sad and dirty, waiting to be taken care of. It is rarely open, but the porter of the Armenian College, whose chapel it now is, will gladly unlock it if you ask at the college entrance at piazza San Nicola da Tolentino 17 (9–12, 16–19).

The church had been built in 1599, in what was then a remote area of vineyards far from the inhabited part of Rome, and though it had undergone some modifications in 1620, Camillo ensured it was thoroughly remodelled by the studio of Algardi. The master himself had less than a year to live, so his great sculptural altarpiece (a form which, as we have seen, is practically a trademark of Pamphilj patronage), *The Vision of St Nicholas of Tolentino*, was finished by his pupils Ercole Ferrata and Domenico Guidi, whose work we have already seen in Sant' Agnese in Agone; Algardi's hand is visible in the composition, which is of a striking starkness: the kneeling St Nicholas and his vision of the Madonna and Child with Saints Augustine and Monica rise in a bare, dark niche, the visionary on the ground of the niche and the others on a dreamlike cloud further up. The sculptor Francesco Baratta, one of Bernini's assistants for the Fountain of the Four Rivers, was the architect of the church's façade in 1670, and Pietro da Cortona designed the second chapel on the left and frescoed its dome, while another of Bernini's students, Cosimo Fancelli, made the sculptural altarpiece, the *Apparition of the Virgin to the Blessed Antonio Botta*. The main dome was frescoed by Giovanni Coli and Filippo Gherardi, whom we have already met in the Galleria Colonna, with a *St Nicholas in Glory*.

In 1658, after Prince Camillo inherited his mother's millions, he was at last in a position to get some truly grandiose projects under way. He began immediately with two commissions, one relatively modest, again for the Augustinians, and one that was of stupefying extravagance. The modest project was the Pamphilj chapel in **Sant' Agostino** (piazza Sant' Agostino; open 9–12, 16.30–19), the Augustinian mother church. The immediate motivation was the canonisation of the Spanish Augustinian bishop Tomas of Villanueva that year. The **Cappella di San Tommaso da Villanova** was a joint effort, with Cortona and Baratta advising about the architecture and sculpture. The sculptor for the altarpiece was Melchiorre Cafà, whose work we have seen in Sant' Agnese. Here his figure of *San Tommaso dispensing charity* has his typical grace and fluidity, but again, as in the Sant' Agnese relief, Cafà's accidental death prevented the work's completion according to his original plan, and the figure of the woman receiving charity and the children around her are by his teacher, Ferrata. Pamphilj crests announce the prince's patronage and beneath them are sculptural panels by Andrea Bergondi from 1760.

The magnificent project was the great Jesuit church of **Sant' Andrea al Quirinale** (via del Quirinale; open 9–12, 16–19). This was the third principal church of the order in Rome, after the Gesù, which, as we have seen, was a Farnese church, and Sant' Ignazio, a more vexed project under the sponsorship of the Ludovisi family. The Jesuits' novitiate house stood and still stands here, in what once had been a context of vineyards, backing on to the ancient church of San Vitale. Complaints that the site was too cramped and the church too old and nondescript led to repeated requests to the pope to have it rebuilt; permission for this was rejected again and again, on the basis that he did not want his view from the Quirinal palace, opposite, obstructed. However, in 1656 Alexander VII endorsed the project and encouraged his court to donate money. Prince Camillo was the greatest benefactor of the new church by far, which cost an estimated 60,000 scudi, the most expensive single project of its time. Perhaps this was Camillo's attempt to curry favour with the pope, who had been making threatening noises about prosecuting Donna Olimpia for corruption before her death; certainly Camillo was also interested in promoting his family's link with the Quirinal hill, which was tied in Roman legend to the mythical king Numa Pompilius, the so-called ancestor of the Pamphilj clan.

This soon became one of Camillo's most beloved projects. When he visited the building site in 1663 and was told more funds were needed, he immediately gave 1000 scudi to the project's architect, none other than Gianlorenzo Bernini, and said to the workmen, 'You must do whatever Cavalier Bernini orders, even if all I have should go in the process.' The work continued after Camillo's death in 1666 and was faithfully funded by his son Giovanni Battista.

Outside, the simple **exterior** of Sant' Andrea has as almost its only decoration the large Pamphilj crest over the porch, coupled with the papal keys and parasol. Camillo's munificence is immediately obvious in the lavish **interior**, where a riot of coloured marbles enlivens a simple oval plan. A series of four chapels, two to each side, run round the outside of the building, with the high altar across from the entrance. Round the rim of the beautiful dome, above the windows, are a series of angels and putti, all observing and interacting with the stucco depiction by Raggi above the high altar, *St Andrew in Ecstasy*. A colossal inscription on the inside of the façade commemorates Prince Camillo, as does the Pamphilj crest in the stained-glass windows. The rest of the church is full of works by Bernini's school and though some critics have dismissed it as 'God's ballroom' it has received praise from surprising sources, including Nathaniel Hawthorne, who did not like Prince Camillo's palace: he wrote of Sant' Andrea, 'I have not seen, nor expect to see, anything else so entirely and satisfactorily finished as this small oval church; and I only wish I could pack it in a large box and send it home.'

Through the door to the right of the high altar one can gain admission to the public rooms of the **Jesuit novitiate** and the rooms of **St Stanislaus Kostka**, a Polish boy-saint of the order, whose effigy by Pierre Legros (1666–1719) is even more theatrical than a Berninian work: the saint is carved lying on his bed, in full colour.

III   MINOR SITES

The Corte Savella prison, on the via di Monserrato, was a fifteenth-century jail for malefactors who did no injury to persons, only to property. It was also used as a holding pen for prisoners on their way to execution and in that capacity it had contained the unfortunate Beatrice Cenci at the turn of the seventeenth century. However, by mid century it was in a state of decay and its owners, the Savelli family, asked permission from Innocent X to rebuild it to make it more humane and functional. Innocent commissioned a study from Antonio Del Grande in 1652, but in the end he decided to eliminate the prison altogether and thereby do away with a lingering trace of old baronial authority, for the Savelli had held the prison as a private responsibility on the pope's behalf. Instead, Innocent commissioned a completely new prison and placed it right on Julius II's great showpiece avenue, the via Giulia. The **Carceri Nuove** (via Giulia 52, no admission) were a revolution in penal architecture, giving prisoners separate cells and an exercise yard. The even newer prisons (1827) next door house a Criminological Museum. The Carceri Nuove answered the need for a modern prison building and brought down property values in the via Giulia, to the benefit of the pope's new area at piazza Navona.

Camillo's sister Costanza Pamphilj married Prince Nicolò Ludovisi, one of the city's richest nobles, and together they funded the completion of the Ludovisi family church of **Sant' Ignazio** (piazza Sant' Ignazio; open 8–12, 16–19); the interior boasts Costanza's crest, which quarters that of her husband with her own family's. A plaque commemorating her donation of 50,000 scudi towards the decoration of the interior is on the right-hand side of the Ludovisi mortuary chapel at the end of the right aisle.

The Pamphilj did not make many incursions into the civic space of the Campidoglio, unlike many of the previous families we have met. Innocent X ordered that the building of the Palazzo Nuovo, the Michelangelo project of almost a hundred years before, finally be completed. This was hard on the city government, as the pope refused to supply any funds at all. However, it was done and so at last, in 1655, the complex was finished. Inside the Conservators' Apartment is a bronze **statue of Innocent X** by Algardi (made 1645–50), facing Bernini's marble statue of Urban VIII. Innocent also completed Urban's circuit of city walls with the gate of **porta Portese**, the southernmost gate of Trastevere, whose exterior is a beautiful classical composition of columns, surmounted by the Pamphilj crest.

One final site in Trastevere deserves mention: it is the **Ospizio Doria-Pamphilj** (entrance from courtyard off the end of via Jandolo; no admission to church, ring bell for admission to hospice). This unites two different entities: the first, the tiny church of Santa Maria in Cappella, was consecrated in 1090, though it was reconstructed by the Doria-Pamphilj family architect Andrea Busiri Vici in 1880–92. The patroness of Rome, the fifteenth-century Roman noblewoman turned saint, Francesca Ponziani (Santa Francesca Romana), worked here in the small hospital her father-in-law had founded, but by the sixteenth century it had fallen into disrepair. The church and hospital were then taken into the patronage of the Guild of Barrelmakers (*cupellari*), which might explain the second part of the church's name. In the seventeenth century, however, it gained a powerful neighbour next door, the builder of the complex's second edifice: Donna Olimpia.

This was the site of the once famous *bagni di Donna Olimpia*, where the sister-in-law of Innocent X constructed a beautiful pleasure garden on the bank of the Tiber, with exotic plants, fountains, statues and green pathways leading to the river's edge, and a casino overlooking it all. Prince Camillo completed the work after his mother's death and it functioned as a sort of mini-villa for daily retreats. However, by the beginning of the eighteenth century the family had lost interest in the property, stripping it of much of its decoration and leasing it to the Seafarers' Guild. The brother of Filippo Andrea V, Domenico Doria-Pamphilj, converted the complex into a hospice for the cure of the poor, restoring the church which had been united to the property. Busiri Vici replaced the Casino with the Ospizio Doria-Pamphilj in 1857–75, which even today is a home for the chronic care of the old. The exterior has a few Pamphilj doves in the keystones of arches, and a brief inscription over the entrance announces its Doria-Pamphilj provenance (it is now owned by the national health service). From the Lungotevere, it is possible to look over the high fence at the building's garden façade, with a portico on two levels and a strangely pointy dome, which seems to serve no function. Inside, the area of the seventeenth-century garden has survived, though it bears little trace of the former Pamphilj pleasure grounds, and the site from which the ghostly carriage of Donna Olimpia once departed is now merely the melancholy residence of the Trasteverean elderly.

8 The Chigi

The Chigi originated in Siena, like the Borghese, and, like them, became more significant in Rome than in their city of origin. Different variants of the name exist; the seventeenth-century diarist Giacinto Gigli wrote not of Cardinal Chigi but of Cardinal Ghisi and the Latinised form is *Chisius*. Members of the family were noted in Siena as bankers and merchants from the end of the thirteenth century and were inscribed as nobles of that city in the fourteenth century, the counts of Ardenghesca, holders of several castles on the Tuscan coast. The family grew in political and economic strength, and also had two beatified members, *Giovanni da Lecceto* (1300–63) and *Angela Chigi* (d. 1400). Their connection with Rome began with *Agostino di Nanni Chigi* (1399–1460), a prosperous banker and the Sienese ambassador to the papal court from 1445 to 1448. His son *Mariano Chigi* (1439–1504) settled in Rome, sending his youngest son *Sigismondo Chigi* (1479–1525) back to Siena to continue the family there; this became, in effect, a separate branch, from which the family's pope was later to spring. Mariano's elder son *Agostino* (1466–1520), the most brilliant banker of his generation, brought the family to its first apex in Rome, while his lesser-known middle son *Francesco* (1469–1519) also lived in Rome, providing a second Chigi line that stayed in the background of Roman society, intermarrying with several different noble families but remaining quite distinct from the main line.

AGOSTINO CHIGI, IL MAGNIFICO (1466–1520)

Agostino Chigi began his surprising career as a member of the Ghinucci bank of Siena, but came to Rome and opened his own bank in 1487, at the age of twenty-one, in partnership with other bankers. His acumen brought the bank great success and it quickly opened branches in other major cities of Europe. Chigi bought his own port as a base for his trading operations: from the south Tuscan village of Porto Ercole his ships traversed the Mediterranean. Even the sultan in Constantinople admired him, calling him 'the great merchant of Christendom'.

In Rome Agostino's wealth made him welcome at the papal court, and in Julius II della Rovere he found a perfect patron and ally. Julius's bellicose projects required a large outlay of cash, which Agostino supplied, and for several years the banker held the papal tiara itself as surety for Julius's loans. Julius, for his part, made Agostino treasurer of the Curia and granted him the extraordinary privilege of assuming the papal family name of della Rovere and quartering the della Rovere arms with his own; hence the four fields of the Chigi crest, with the oak of Julius II side by side with the hills of the Tolfa alum-mining concession, perhaps the most successful of Agostino's ventures. Alum, a mineral necessary to the fulling of cloth, occurs very rarely in nature and before the discovery in 1461 of a deposit in the Monti della Tolfa in northern Lazio the only source of this precious commodity was in the hands of the Turks: Paul II Barbo (1464–71) issued a bull of excommunication against Christians who bought alum from the infidel, and the mines were intended by successive popes to fund a new crusade. Agostino Chigi built a town for his miners, Allumiere 'delle sante crociate' (of the holy crusades), which still produces alum today, though the monopoly was broken in the nineteenth century with the discovery of the formula for chemical alum.

Agostino, as a new arrival on the Roman social scene, was interested in using his wealth in the service of glorifying his own name. Accordingly he sponsored both artists and literary figures; among the latter were the historian Paolo Giovio, and the poets Pietro Bembo and Pietro Aretino. In 1515 he founded a press that produced the first books in Greek to be printed in Rome. His artistic patronage was even more impressive and he brought his fellow Sienese, Giovan Antonio Bazzi called Il Sodoma (1477–1549) and the Venetian painter Sebastiano del Piombo (1485–1547), to work for him in Rome, as well as the Sienese artist and architect Baldassare Peruzzi (1481–1536), a pupil of Sodoma's. However, his most famous employee was undoubtedly Rafaello Sanzio, Raphael (1483–1520), who worked on the great Villa Chigi (now the Villa Farnesina) and on other commissions in Santa Maria della Pace and Santa Maria del Popolo. Both churches were della Rovere foundations, further emphasising the link between the families of pope and banker.

Agostino married three times, though an offer to the Marquis of Mantua's daughter met with her rebuff; he was also closely linked with one of Renaissance Rome's most famous courtesans, Imperia, whose tomb (now vanished) in San Gregorio Magno, which he paid for, was said to be 'fit for a queen'. His last wife, Francesca Ardeasca, was the daughter of a Venetian grocer: Agostino had her kidnapped and brought to a convent to be educated before he moved her into his Roman house. With her he had four children, legitimised by a surprise marriage performed by Leo X in 1519;

one daughter, Margherita, married a Colonna, a tribute to the influence Agostino had at the papal court. His one surviving son, *Lorenzo Leone* (1517–73), was a disappointment. After Agostino's death in 1520 (within a few months of his painter, Raphael), Lorenzo squandered his father's wealth, estimated at a staggering 900,000 ducats. The Chigi bank was closed in 1528 and the prominence of the family seemed to have been a mere interlude; Agostino's line died out and the Sienese branch remained straightforward nobles of the Tuscan republic. The Villa Chigi on the via della Lungara was bought by the Farnese in 1581 and renamed the Villa Farnesina, and Agostino's town palace in today's Arco dei Banchi, a street once known as the cortile de' Chigi, was sold and demolished.

The family of Agostino's brother Sigismondo was well entrenched in the business and social life of Siena, and his descendants married into many of the city's most prominent houses. Sigismondo's son married Agnese Borghese Bulgarini, whose cousin Camillo soon rose to the papal throne as Paul V Borghese, but any hopes of Chigi enrichment were thwarted by the pope's determination to concentrate his nepotism on his two kinsmen Scipione and Marcantonio. *Flavio Chigi* (1548–1611) was relatively impoverished and his two sons, *Mario* (1594–1669) and *Fabio* (1599–1667), received an education commensurate with their position as nobles of a provincial city, for such Siena was, having lost its independence to Florence in 1559. Fabio, the more scholarly of the two brothers, was sickly, suffering from kidney stones and apoplexy as a child, which prevented him from attending school. Nonetheless, he achieved his doctorates of law, theology and philosophy at the university of Siena in 1626, and immediately embarked on an ecclesiastical career, which was to lead to the second Roman apex of his family fortunes and would change the face of Rome itself.

Fabio Chigi was an attractive man: slight of stature and of delicate health, he was nonetheless handsome and elegant in his manners. In his early career he wrote a history of his family in Latin and he was an accomplished author in Italian; a seventeenth-century gentleman to the core, he lacked any trace of the family's traditional mercantile ambition. After acting as vice-legate in Ferrara, the hands-on ruler of the city, he received a bishopric and the post of Inquisitor of Malta, then moved into diplomacy as nuncio to Cologne in 1639 and after that to the congress that established the treaty of Westphalia in 1648. Chigi's instructions from Innocent X were to uphold the rights of the Catholic church at any cost. But Innocent was not even consulted about the terms of the treaty of Westphalia, which ended the Thirty Years War. The treaty took as its precept the formula *cujus regio, ejus religio*, or in other words that the faith of the prince determined the state's religious affiliation. This sounded a death knell for the Catholic communities living under Protestant monarchs and neither Innocent nor Chigi could accept it. The political defeat was to haunt Chigi for the rest of his life. Innocent decided in 1651 to make Chigi his secretary of state and created him cardinal in the following year. When he entered the conclave after the death of Innocent X he was one of the newest members of the college.

THE CONCLAVE OF 1655

Sixty-six cardinals met in Rome in late January 1655, to elect a successor to the widely hated Innocent X. Innocent's nepotism had been a glaring problem, especially in his later years, with the economy of the Papal States in serious decay, and the population of Rome shrinking due to flood, famine and disease. The new pope would have to be a man of moral stature and well trained to deal with the expediencies of international diplomacy. However, the old split in the college of cardinals recurred. Once again the French party, the Barberini faction, was driven by the wishes of the absent Cardinal Mazarin, regent of France. The opposing faction, as before, was pro-Spanish. However, the cardinals created by Innocent X were, by and large, not affiliated to either faction: this gave them manoeuvring room and they were known as the *squadrone volante* (flying squadron). After the first few *scrutini* (ballot castings), one of the Barberini faction, the respected Cardinal Giulio Sacchetti, came close to winning, but the Spanish cardinals vetoed him; the French cardinals were offended and the conclave was deadlocked for weeks. The other main candidate, Cardinal Fabio Chigi, had a good reputation, but his election was blocked by Mazarin, who had been aware of his opposition to the treaty of Westphalia. Sacchetti, however, considered Chigi the best choice and indicated this in a letter to Mazarin. There were many complaints about the discomforts of the sealed chambers in the Vatican Palace where the election took place: over the six weeks it took to get Mazarin's response, several cardinals fell seriously ill and one died. Mazarin permitted Chigi's election, if it were certain that Sacchetti could not win. The exhausted cardinals duly elected Chigi almost unanimously, the dissenting vote (for Sacchetti) coming from Chigi himself. Chigi took the name Alexander, after a Sienese-born pope of the Middle Ages, and was crowned on 18 April 1655, four months after the beginning of the conclave. The papacy could hardly have had a more vivid demonstration of its lack of independence in the seventeenth century than the cardinals' total dependence on the will of Spanish and French rulers.

POPE ALEXANDER VII (1655–67)

The new pope was widely reputed to be modest and wise, and as he was just fifty-six at his election his pontificate was expected to be a long one. His humanist learning, in the Renaissance tradition, was shaped by his piety: when he was robed for the first time as pope, it was seen that he wore a hair shirt next to his skin. As pope, he reminded himself of the presence of death and the necessity of humility by keeping his future coffin with him in his bedroom – though given the indignities meted out to Innocent X's corpse, perhaps purchasing a 'pre-need' casket was merely prudent. He was profoundly affected by his study of the writings of François de Sales, especially de Sales's egalitarian ideas about the possibility of achieving grace; he beatified de Sales in 1661 and canonised him in 1665. Alexander's kindly and positive view of salvation was in direct contrast to the dark and near-Calvinist thread of Catholic thought called Jansenism, with its theory of predestination, which particularly affected the French Catholic Church throughout the seventeenth century.

For the pope's first regnal year he left his relatives languishing in Siena – bearing in mind his opposition to Innocent X's nepotism, he could hardly do otherwise. Alexander had been warned during the conclave that his ninety relatives constituted a serious impediment to his election. When two of his nieces wrote to him requesting dowries, he replied that the goods of the Church were not his to dispose of and suggested they enter convents where they would have no need of such things. All these signs pointed to a new and laudable spirit of reform. However, Alexander could not remain for long without his family: apart from the demands of affection, it was considered an affront to the dignity of the pope if his relatives were not ennobled. Alexander's solution was that of Urban VIII: he summoned a number of cardinals to discuss the matter and they soberly approved a limited role for

The refined face of Alexander VII Chigi, reflective and melancholy, concealed grandiose ambitions for the rebuilding of Rome.

the Chigi, notionally bound by an apostolic constitution, *Inter gravissimas*, with strict limitations on their capacity to accumulate wealth. The constitution was issued in early May 1656 and by 16 May the pope had already received his principal relations at Castelgandolfo, as they had travelled, as one observer recounted, '*in velocissime carrozze*' (in the fastest carriages).

The pope's brother, Don Mario Chigi, was given the titles of General of the Holy Roman Church, governor of the Borgo and prefect of the *annona* or food supply. However, his terrible first task was to contain the most vicious outbreak of bubonic plague that Rome had seen in a century, starting in May 1656. The population of the city in 1655 was 123,000, for the most part crowded into Trastevere, the Tiber bend and the *tridente*, the area south of piazza del Popolo. Word of the plague had come from afflicted Naples and in response the papal authorities took fierce action, employing a revolutionary new technique of quarantine, which soon came to be accepted as the standard. Such measures proved amazingly successful: Rome lost between 15,000 and 20,000 of its people, well-nigh miraculous in comparison with Naples, where 150,000 of a population of 300,000 died, with a similar toll in Genoa. In the same outbreak one lonely death barely went recorded in Rome: Donna Olimpia Maidalchini, Innocent X's *dominante* sister-in-law, sickened and died in her palace in San Martino al Cimino near Viterbo.

Rome's problems at the beginning of Alexander's pontificate were not confined to the plague: indeed, after it passed, an influenza epidemic further weakened the population. At the same time bad harvests made the price of grain rise and there was little the pope could do, though he imported grain from such diverse sources as Sicily and Holland. Moreover, the international situation was also tense, in part due to a fascinating if problematic guest of the pope's: the abdicated Queen Christina of Sweden.

Christina, the daughter of Protestant Europe's great military champion King Gustavus Adolphus, had been one of the participants in the Peace of Westphalia. She converted to Catholicism in 1655 and entered Rome on 22 December 1655, in great pomp, proceeding down the Corso to piazza San Marco (today's piazza Venezia), then turning towards the Vatican along the via Papalis. This route anticipated most of the urban alterations undertaken by Alexander VII over the following ten years. In Rome Christina did as she pleased, collecting art and gathering around her a court of intellectuals who would later band together formally as the Accademia dell'Arcadia. She died in 1689, in her final residence in the old palazzo Riario on the via della Lungara.

Queen Christina added a further element of international intrigue to the papal court at a time when intrigue was hardly lacking. War was raging between France and Spain during the early part of Alexander's pontificate. He made it clear that his role in European politics was that of protecting Catholic interests, and as such he was hostile to the elderly and ailing ruler of France, Cardinal Mazarin, often allied with the Protestant enemies of Spain. The position of the papacy was so weakened by this time that the pope was not even consulted before the Peace of the Pyrenees ended the Franco-Spanish war in 1659; this was particularly objectionable as one of the terms was the restitution of the duchy of Castro in the Papal States to the Farnese family. This, obviously, the pope refused.

However, the true threat to the Catholic world came not from the Protestants but the Turks. Alexander sent aid to Venice in the republic's efforts to save its possession of Candia (modern Heraklion) in Crete, under Turkish siege since 1648. The pope even sent the papal fleet to relieve the Venetians. On land, a Turkish campaign in the late 1650s had destroyed the defences of the kingdom of Hungary, which opened Europe to attack from the south-east: the Holy Roman Emperor Leopold I of Habsburg sought and received papal help in the form of money and gunpowder. Alexander sought to broker a Christian League to defend Europe from the Turks, but had only limited success, due to the conflicting interests of the different European monarchs.

A series of problems exacerbated relations between the pope and France. Mazarin died in March 1661 and in his will left a fortune to be spent on the defence of Europe against the Turkish threat, but the young King Louis XIV blocked the bequest: it was in his interest to keep the emperor weak and the pope in his place. Mazarin had already imprisoned one of his fellow cardinals, Cardinal de Retz, for his part in the civil wars known as the Fronde; de Retz now escaped and made his way to Rome, an enduring thorn in the side of papal–French relations. Diplomatic storms marked the pope's relations with the French crown.

In ecclesiastical matters Alexander was diligent, a good bishop of Rome who made regular visits to the city churches and kept Roman monasteries and nunneries to a high moral standard. His principal religious struggle was against Jansenism; a bull issued in 1665, *Regiminis apostolici*, condemned several Jansenist propositions, including that of predestination. At the same time he sought to moderate the Jesuit doctrine of probabilism, which taught that when one doubted the validity of a law, one was not obliged to obey it.

One other religious concern motivating Alexander was his devotion to the cult of the Virgin Mary. He silenced debate about her Immaculate Conception – the idea that Mary was different from other humans by being innocent of original sin – by issuing a special bull in late 1661, asserting that until a further pontifical examination it should be understood that Mary's conception had indeed been immaculate. The final word on the subject was only said in the nineteenth century, when Pius IX celebrated Mary's Immaculate Conception as an infallible doctrine of the Church.

Alexander VII was not much interested in painting or sculpture, though as cardinal in 1655 he had commissioned two paintings from Claude Lorrain, coastal scenes, one showing the *Rape of Europa* and the other a *Battle on the Bridge*; both of these are now in Moscow's Pushkin Museum. His literary interests ranged widely and his principal court intellectual, among a fairly highbrow crowd, was none other than Luca Holstenius (1596–1661), whom we have met before as the librarian of Cardinal Francesco Barberini. Holstenius joined Giulio Rospigliosi at court as a representative of the enduring taste and intellectual flourishing of the Barberini pontificate, otherwise a distant memory.

However, the pope was passionate about architecture. His desire to renovate and complete his two family chapels in Santa Maria del Popolo and Santa Maria della Pace developed into massive urban redesign schemes, expensive and grandiose. More than that, the Chigi family estate he purchased at Ariccia in the Alban Hills, with its colossal game park and new town centre by Bernini, demonstrated the arrival of the pope's family at the apex of Roman society. Above all, wherever his builders passed, Alexander emblazoned his crest and it still rises over many of his works, especially in the colonnade of piazza San Pietro. His building projects, undertaken at a time of general privation and poverty, won him no less hatred than that shown towards Innocent X, his far more venal predecessor.

The Chigi pope's patronage can be summed up in one name: Gianlorenzo Bernini. Bernini survived the wilderness years of the early reign of Innocent X to return to the highest possible favour under Alexander VII. Indeed, never had he been given such a large scope, or so much authority, even under his friend Urban VIII: he was the artistic director of the Chigi papacy and his hand can be detected in almost all of Alexander's commissions. Other contemporary masters barely got a look in, although Pietro da Cortona, it is true, received the projects that Bernini was too busy to take. Alexander actively disliked Francesco Borromini and gave him no new commissions, though Borromini remained architect of San Giovanni in Laterano and worked on Rome's university building, the Sapienza. Louis XIV, pressing his advantage, called on the pope to send Bernini to Paris in 1665, which he reluctantly did; Bernini's visit, though it produced the famous bust of the Sun King at Versailles, was otherwise not a success and the artist returned to Rome.

The other object Alexander kept in his private apartments, alongside his coffin, was a large wooden scale model of Rome, with movable parts, so he could see how different combinations of Rome's monuments, whether movable in reality or not, would look. His principal artistic passion was for architecture and, more than that, for urban design. In this he was the heir of sixteenth-century popes like Sixtus V Peretti and Pius IV de' Medici, but Alexander's ambition outstripped his predecessors'. His plans to turn the main processional routes of Rome into a glorification of the papacy and the Chigi family were bounded only by the limits of his extremely empty purse. As a result, he was a very creative problem solver: he completed other patrons' monuments and put his name all over the façades, as at Sant' Andrea della Valle, which had been languishing without a front since the death of Cardinal Alessandro Peretti much earlier in the century; he entered into financial partnerships with monasteries and private donors to get maximum control with minimal outlay, as in the twin churches of piazza del Popolo and the Jesuit novitiate church of Sant' Andrea al Quirinale. His priority, at all times, was to enlarge the dignity of his office and this could mean that his secondary purpose of glorifying his family suffered. Alexander also established shopping areas to replace the unsightly open-air markets blocking several of Rome's main squares.

In the spring of 1667, as Alexander's health, never excellent, took a turn for the worse, he prepared himself for a closer and more permanent relationship with his coffin. He called his cardinals to his deathbed and gave an accounting of his reign. He died on 22 May 1667, leaving Rome the poorer financially but immeasurably richer in buildings: not merely for his morals had he been teasingly referred to as 'un papa di grande edificazione'. Alexander VII's intellectualism and remoteness did not endear him to the Roman populace and his successor, Clement IX Rospigliosi, was more popular, abolishing some of the more hated taxes and lowering the price of bread: but few other popes have had a similar success in imposing their own will upon the physical face of Rome.

THE *NIPOTI* OF ALEXANDER VII

Mindful of the restrictions of his own decree *Inter gravissimas*, Alexander limited his enrichment of family members, though he increased his generosity as time put his decree further into distant memory. However, he rigorously excluded his relatives from the exercise of real power and supervised them carefully so their behaviour would not shame the papacy.

Three of Alexander's family received major preferments and others took on lesser charges. The principal beneficiaries were his brother, Don Mario, who took over much of the practical running of the city, and two of

FLAVIVS S.R E.PRESBITER CARD . CHISIVS SENENSIS IX.APRILIS MDCLVII.

Cardinal Flavio Chigi was given little power, but his embassy to France helped to stabilise the stormy relations between Alexander VII and Louis XIV.

his nephews. Don Mario was his brother's efficient lieutenant: a practical man, he was described by the Venetian ambassador, Nicolò Sagredo, as wise and economical with his conversation; though he was thought shrewd, he had a reputation for being grasping and when he died in 1669 he was not mourned by the Romans. His wife, Donna Berenice, was modest and retiring, hardly a menace along the lines of Donna Olimpia Maidalchini. Though not excessively interested in art, in 1659 he did intervene in a controversy that surrounded a satirical painting by Salvator Rosa (1615–73), an *Allegory of Fortune* that depicted the goddess Fortune showering wealth upon worthless animals. When this painting was exhibited in Rome, it caused such a stir for its thinly veiled attack on nepotism that one commentator observed: 'The affair assumed such proportions that the painter was on the point of having to explain the meaning of his picture in prison.' Don Mario stepped in to protect Rosa and the controversy faded.

Don Mario's son *Flavio Chigi* (1631–93) was raised in 1657 to the position of cardinal nephew. He had a limited interest in diplomacy and administration, and his powers were strictly curtailed. Flavio, whose cardinalate church was Santa Maria del Popolo, focused principally on his ceremonial duties and the accumulation of wealth for the family. With the income from his various church offices he purchased a series of fiefdoms from the declining baronial families of the Roman *campagna*, including the Orsini territories of Campagnano, Formello, Cesano and Sacrofano. (None of the family seems to have been interested in reacquiring the Villa Farnesina from the Farnese.) In the countryside, Flavio developed the family seat at Ariccia, where he kept his collection of *meraviglie* (marvels) in a special museum and also had a room full of portraits of Rome's most beautiful aristocratic women. Flavio sublimated his carnal urges into the pleasures of the hunt and the table. He had one ceiling in his Roman palace frescoed with an allegory of *Youth rescued from the Pleasures of Venus*, surely a piece of self-admonition. Flavio was a significant art patron: his collections included important fifteenth- and sixteenth-century pieces as well as contemporary works, and his preferred painters were Baciccia and Francesco Trevisani. His collection of ancient statues – 'improved' with additions and restorations in the seventeenth-century style – eventually formed the core of the great ancient-art collection of Dresden. Much of his picture collection is today in the Galleria Nazionale in palazzo Barberini. After Alexander VII's death, Cardinal Flavio was leader of the most powerful faction in the conclave and held positions of prestige for the rest of his life.

The major secular recipient of Alexander's largesse was his nephew *Agostino* (1634–1705). He was given the title of Captain of Castel Sant'Angelo and a prize bride was found for him, Maria Virginia Borghese, the daughter of the Princess of Rossano, Olimpia Aldobrandini, by her first marriage. Maria Virginia was widely expected to be the Borghese heir if her sickly brother Giovanni Battista did not have children and, even though he did, she was still a catch, bringing a dowry of 200,000 scudi to swell the family coffers. At a stroke, the Chigi were tied to three of the greatest Roman papal families: the Borghese, the Aldobrandini and, through the Princess of Rossano's second marriage, the Pamphilj. In order for his family to be able to hold their heads high in this august company, Alexander VII purchased the town of Farnese for 275,000 scudi, converted it to a principality and conferred it upon his nephew; the duchy of Ariccia soon followed and became the centrepiece of a huge Chigi patrimony. Agostino was less interested in art than was his cousin Cardinal Flavio, though he commissioned a landscape from Claude, *David at the Cave of Adullam* (now in the National Gallery, London), and owned paintings by Agostino Tassi and Salvator Rosa. With his uncle Don Mario, he bought his mother-in-law's unfinished palace on the edge of piazza Colonna and over the course of the subsequent century it became the palazzo Chigi that we see today. Agostino's brother, the brilliant young *Sigismondo* (1649–78), was made a cardinal at eighteen by the next pope, Clement IX Rospigliosi (1667–9). He served as legate, or governor, of Bologna from 1673 to 1676, but died at the age of twenty-nine.

THE CHIGI SUCCESSION

Agostino's son *Augusto Chigi* (1662–1744) inherited his father's huge estates and also took on the hereditary title of marshal of the conclave, the official in charge of the papal elections. Augusto Chigi wed Clement IX's relative Maria Eleonora Rospigliosi, and their son *Agostino II Chigi* (1710–69) married another papal relative, Giulia Albani, niece of Clement XI Albani (1700–21).

This intermarriage with papal families indicates how closed the Roman nobility was at its highest level; through a series of advantageous marriages the family accumulated wealth and connections with almost all the great papal families. Agostino II's brother *Flavio II Chigi* (1711–71) became another of the family's cardinals and dedicated himself to scholarly pursuits, particularly the enlargement of the great Chigi library now in the Vatican. Cardinal Flavio II also, belatedly, purchased a property off the via Salaria leading north-east out of Rome and built a small suburban villa there, a jewel of the Rococo, now a public park.

Agostino II's son *Sigismondo I Chigi* (1736–93) was the family black sheep, dabbling in arcane rationalist philosophy, and sponsoring musicians and poets whom he hosted in palazzo Chigi. He was accused, certainly unjustly, of having poisoned a cardinal and for a time fled the Papal States. His son *Agostino III* (1771–1855) wrote a brief diary of life in Rome between 1801 and 1855, mostly concerned with the social round of a nineteenth-century prince: lunch at one palace, dinner at another, interspersed with the occasional observation of the political scene. His son *Flavio III* (1810–85) was the last family cardinal, created in 1873 after the fall of the papal government, and his grandson *Mario Chigi* (1832–1914) married a Ukrainian princess, Antonietta Sayn Wittgenstein, the granddaughter of a great German general who had stopped Napoleon at St Petersburg. Mario's second son *Francesco Chigi* (1881–1953) was one of the founders of Rome's Zoo, which adjoins the Villa Borghese park.

The ill fortune that affected many Roman noble families at the end of the nineteenth century did not spare the Chigi. Risky investments foundered when the Bank of Italy collapsed in 1891, and much of the family land was expropriated and distributed to the peasants after the First World War. *Ludovico Chigi* (1866–1951) was constrained by economic necessity to sell his family palace to the Italian state in 1918, including the library and a large part of the family art collection. Today's Chigi family live in Rome and at their villa at Castelfusano. Though not much remains of the family patrimony, their effect on Rome continues to enrich the city.

Another branch of the Chigi family, descending from Francesco Chigi, a brother of Agostino Il Magnifico, also inserted itself into the Roman aristocracy, becoming the Chigi Patrizi Montoro Naro. The family still exists and its network of palaces stretches across Rome: a colossal edifice on via di Montoro, the so-called 'palazzo de' Prefetti' on via de' Prefetti, palazzo Naro on piazza Campo Marzio and another palace on via de' Nari near the Pantheon. These attest to the former wealth and prominence of this family, not really papal, but undoubtedly noble.

CHIGI ITINERARY

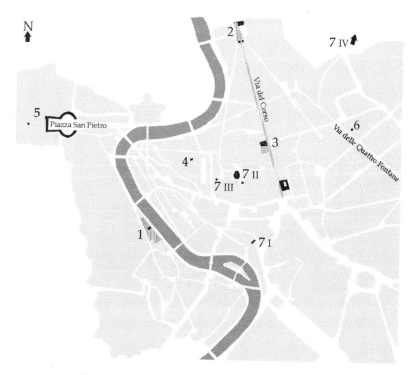

With the Chigi, the visitor is offered an entry into two very different Romes, those of the early sixteenth century and the mid seventeenth. The first phase of Chigi prominence, under Agostino Il Magnifico, encompassed great works of art by Raphael and Peruzzi, and would be significant on their own, but they are dwarfed in scale and ambition, if not skill, by the projects of Alexander VII in the 1650s and 1660s. What is perhaps most surprising is the way in which Renaissance and Baroque art combines in the places where the two phases overlap, the Chigi chapels in Santa Maria del Popolo and Santa Maria della Pace, to the benefit of at least one of those churches.

Alexander VII evolved a grandiose overall scheme for the city, rather than the development of one neighbourhood for the exaltation of one family. His interest was primarily that of a monarch, not the head of a family, and he was concerned with making Rome a fitting capital for the vicar of Christ on earth. Though he covered Rome with the Chigi crest, that was the extent of his expression of familial pride: he left family matters very much to his brother Don Mario and nephews Don Agostino and Cardinal Flavio. They, in their turn, restricted their expenditures to their new palaces, though Cardinal Flavio put his name on the Berninian renovations to his cardinalate church of Santa Maria del Popolo.

A term that recurs again and again in Alexander's own written orders for building works in Rome is 'teatro' (theatre): 'the teatro of San Pietro', 'the teatro of Santa Maria della Pace'. These and other urban spaces were conceived by Alexander as lavish stage sets, not overtly theatres for performances (though such things could certainly take place in them), but theatres for church ceremonial, or even for special buildings themselves, like St Peter's. Moreover, a teatro was a fitting backdrop for the dignified process of daily life. Lacking the funds to perform truly wide-ranging modifications to the street plan, Alexander contented himself with straightening streets, removing blockages and in a few notable places opening up a piazza where there had previously been a claustrophobic tangle of streets. His interest was in the long view, the scenographic street with something decorative at the end, and in piazze which showed energy and harmony, as in his redesign for piazza del Popolo. His devotion to Mary is evident in the number of churches he restored or built, dedicated to the Virgin.

The tastes of his cardinal nephew Flavio I are harder to discern. Santa Maria del Popolo bears every sign of being redecorated according to the pope's wishes, not Flavio's. The cardinal's former palace on piazza Santi Apostoli is inaccessible private property and his little villa, on the slope of the Quirinal, has utterly vanished, though every time you take the 64 bus to or from Termini station you cross over its site, at the corner of via Nazionale and via delle Quattro Fontane. The cardinal's principal out-of-town villa was in his fief of Formello, where he built a miniature version of Versailles, the 'villa di Versaglia', now in ruins. However, Cardinal Flavio I's art collection is one of the main sources of the state gallery in palazzo Barberini, where his eclecticism and secular interests still shine out.

▌ Agostino Chigi, Il Magnifico, and the Villa Farnesina

Via della Lungara 230, tel: 06 6880 1767. Open Monday to Saturday 9–13. Admission: €4.13; reduced €3.10

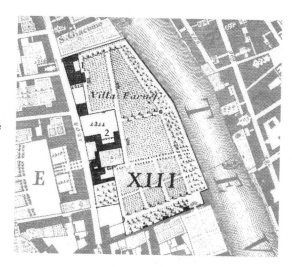

The Villa Farnesina, as it appeared in the Nolli map of 1748. Note the vast gardens

Key:
1 stable block
2 main villa building

The villa Farnesina has been badly beaten about by time. It had an auspicious beginning: *'non murato ma nato'* (not built but born) as Vasari described it. From 1505 to 1510 the great banker Agostino Chigi acquired and enlarged his properties on this site, and in 1506 construction began on the villa building itself, designed by Agostino's fellow Sienese, Baldassare Peruzzi. Most building work was completed in 1510, but additions continued to be made until Agostino's death in 1520. Its gardens were designed as an integral part of the whole, and the interpenetration of exterior and interior areas was exemplified by the two loggias on the villa's ground floor, while another loggia over the Tiber provided a further indoor–outdoor space. The main rooms inside were frescoed by the best artists in Rome, lacking only Michelangelo, who was entirely occupied by papal commissions. The villa was a byword for magnificence.

However, its heyday was brief. Sacked by the Germans, sold in 1581 by the impecunious Chigi heirs to the Farnese family who gave it their name, its gardens left to run riot, its riverside loggia a tumbledown wreck, the villa lost its prestige and was treated with indifference by its absentee Farnese and Bourbon owners. In the late nineteenth century its tenant, the Duke of Ripalta, ambassador of Spain (who bought it after 1870 from the Bourbons of Naples who had inherited it from the Farnese), reconfigured some of its rooms and inserted his crest into some of the ceilings, and the new government of the kingdom of Italy, drunk with its success in taking Rome from the pope in 1870, wreaked a terrible act of destruction-in-creation. The guidebook author Augustus Hare, writing in 1897, told the story:

> [Agostino] Chigi desired Baldassare Peruzzi so to design the Farnesina that the villa and its gardens should form one complete composition. This was nobly effected in the glorious ilex avenue, which ended in the pavilion where Chigi entertained Leo X. and all the famous men of his time. The greater part of these beautiful gardens with their avenue were wantonly destroyed by the present government in 1878–80, causing the death from grief of their owner, the Duca di Ripalda, when, in accordance with a silly scheme of Garibaldi, and to flatter the aged patriot, the course of the Tiber was changed, to the annihilation of all the beauty of this part of the city. In the spared portion of the gardens all the magnificent old trees have been cut down. The frescoes of the Farnesina have already shown signs of serious injury, and it is doubtful whether by an act of consummate folly, which has disgraced her in the eyes of the whole civilised world, Rome has not thrown away one of the most precious jewels in her possession.

Forty per cent of the villa's property, the section bordering the Tiber, was expropriated and obliterated to straighten the river and to build the embankment, which is here called the Lungotevere Raffaello Sanzio. However, Hare's epitaph for the Farnesina was written too hastily; the fortunes of the villa were to revive when it came into the hands of the state in 1927. Restoration commenced immediately, and the building and its frescoes today appear almost in their original condition. The villa is under the supervision of the Accademia dei Lincei, whose headquarters and great library are in palazzo Corsini across the street. In some ways its neglect for centuries was a blessing: it preserves for us a private space of the High Renaissance, almost miraculously opening a window into a vanished and hard to imagine time.

| A VISIT TO AGOSTINO'S VILLA
Start: corner of via della Lungara and salita del Buon Pastore

As a result of the changes and injuries of fortune, it is difficult to pay a visit to the villa as Agostino Il Magnifico would have seen it. However, if we approach it from the north, from along Julius II's great via della Lungara, we can get a sense of its original appearance. Once inside the villa building itself, though, Agostino's character and artistic taste are clear.

The wall bordering the property at the corner of via della Lungara and salita del Buon Pastore looks suspiciously like a ruined building that has been converted into a perimeter wall. It is. In fact, it was one of Rome's most sumptuous **stables**, the scene of Agostino's famous bet with the Riario brothers who lived across the road. Raffaelle Riario was Julius II's cousin, the powerful vice-chancellor of the church, and his family's palace here was the last word in luxury; only a few palaces, the Vatican, palazzo Venezia, Riario's new Cancelleria itself and palazzo Borgia Sforza could compare. Agostino, a nouveau riche even by the standards of a city that rarely sneered at new money, decided to take on the Riario: he made a bet with the brothers that he could make his mere stables more opulent than the main reception rooms of palazzo Riario. The Riario, only a generation older in their wealth, scoffed at this. Agostino chose to construct a large building at this corner of his property. It had three storeys and seems to have resembled the Cancelleria in the disposition of its planes and pilasters, though all in brick. Today only part of the first storey survives, the rest having being pulled down in the nineteenth century as unsafe.

This enormous building played host to one of Rome's most famous banquets. The date was 30 April, 1518. Chigi had, as his guest, no less a person than the pope himself, Leo X de' Medici, and a selection of cardinals, including, no doubt, the Riario. The foods were so sumptuous, the music so exquisite, the wall hangings of cloth of gold so beautiful, that the pope, a genial man, exclaimed to Agostino, 'But my friend, why do you not treat me with more familiarity?'

'Your Holiness,' replied the banker, 'perhaps I have treated you with too much familiarity rather than too little. For I have invited you to a banquet in my stables!' He made a gesture and all the hangings fell to the ground, revealing the stalls and mangers of the stables. This theatrical trick won him both the admiration of the guests and his bet with the Riario.

As we walk south along the edge of the Farnesina property, a gate offers a glimpse of part of the much-reduced **gardens**. After centuries of neglect and half-hearted renovation (it is unlikely that Augustus Hare's avenue of ilexes dated from Agostino's time), the gardens were brutally bulldozed in order to build the Tiber embankment. During the course of the works the ruins of an ancient villa were discovered, perhaps the villa of Julia, the daughter of the Emperor Augustus, decorated with Egyptian motifs to celebrate her marriage with the general Agrippa; these ruins were demolished and the frescoes were taken to the National Roman Museum.

The gardens in Agostino's time were large and richly decorated with ancient statuary as well as exotic plants: the archetypal *villa suburbana* which was to be elaborated throughout the sixteenth century, culminating in the great villas of the Borghese and Pamphilj.

The most impressive of the villa's features was the loggia over the Tiber, which lay above a sort of grotto containing a fish pool whose waters were joined with those of the river. This was the site of the second of Agostino's famous banquets, only a few months after the first, on 10 August 1518. Here the food was served in dishes of gold and silver, which the servants then flung over the balustrade into the river. Naturally, Agostino had no wish to lose these precious objects, so his servants had prepared a submerged net below, where the dishes were caught. This was also a cunning security measure, for even the most high-ranking guest might have been tempted to tuck a goblet or two into his tunic.

As we continue towards the second gate, we can see the villa building rearing up behind the wall. In Agostino's day we would have entered by the first gate or from a landing on the river bank and through the garden porch, the Loggia of Cupid and Psyche. As it is, we use the back door. The second gate admits us and we can see the **villa building** clearly for the first time. It is in the shape of a shallow squared U, with the garden loggia in the inner centre, and though it seems at first to have only two storeys, in fact it also has two mezzanine storeys and a roof loggia which has been in part demolished and in part bricked in to make a fifth floor. It is thus rather larger than it appears. The villa building, one of Peruzzi's earliest architectural gems, is built according to strict guidelines set down by the ancient author Vitruvius and has a very pure classicising decoration, a simple series of pilasters, with a terracotta frieze of putti and garlands along the top. Originally, part of the façade was decorated with monochrome frescoes, but almost all traces have vanished.

The gardens are pallid reflections of the original. None of it remains from Agostino's time, and the gravel drive and box hedges have an incongruous English country house quality. A small courtyard attached to the later building across from the entrance contains a dry and ruined fountain with a familiar *giglio* on it, one of the few indications of Farnese tenancy.

We can leave these disappointments behind as we enter the villa. The **interior** contains five principal rooms for us to visit. Once through the entrance halls, redesigned by the Duke of Ripalta in the 1860s on the site of Agostino's dining room, we enter the first important room, the **loggia of Galatea**. This was enclosed in the seventeenth century, when landscapes rather in the manner of Gaspard Dughet were inserted into the spaces of the former openings. The decoration progressed from the top down: Peruzzi painted the vault frescoes in 1512, while Sebastiano del Piombo decorated the lunettes and painted the *Polyphemus* in 1512–13, and Raphael made the *Galatea*, which gave the room its name, in 1513.

The ceiling elaborately expounds the horoscope of Agostino Il Magnifico. His birth records in Siena give the date of 29 November 1466 and the ceiling expresses this: Jupiter appears in the sign of Aries, the moon is in Virgo, Mars in the Lyre, Mercury in Scorpio, the sun in Sagittarius, Venus in Capricorn and Saturn in Pisces. Peruzzi's frescoes are subtle and allusive, depending on the Renaissance viewers' deep knowledge of ancient mythology. The stars in the two main octagonal frescoes in the top of the vault allude to constellations. The first octagon, *Perseus with the Gorgon*, has an angel trumpeting the fame of the Chigi family. The second, right-hand, octagon represents the *Nymph Callisto*, the lover of Jupiter who was turned into a great bear, *Ursa Major,* and placed in the sky to preserve her from the wrath of Juno. More decorations allude to figures from the myths that produced the signs of the Zodiac and other constellations.

The lunettes, the half-circular paintings directly below the vault, were painted by Sebastiano Luciani, known as del Piombo. They too depict episodes from ancient stories, this time from Ovid's *Metamorphoses.* Sebastiano, a Venetian pupil of the great Giorgione, came to Rome at Agostino's request and his beautiful palette, bright and joyful in the Venetian tradition, caused a sensation in Rome. Particularly delicate is the *Fall of Phaethon*, though the golden-tressed women of the two lunettes on the end wall closest to the door have a brilliant grace and liveliness. The last lunette on the end wall opposite is different again, a study of a colossal male head by Peruzzi. Its presence interrupts the Ovidian scheme and surely indicates the will of the patron himself. All sorts of stories proliferated about it, the most common one being that the head was sketched there in charcoal by Michelangelo, who happened to be passing, in order to reproach Raphael for the small scale of his fresco. Unfortunately for the legend, the work is a fresco, not a charcoal sketch, and bears Peruzzi's initials. It is, however, a striking virtuoso display.

The wall frescoes are, for the most part, the landscapes from c.1650 put there by the Farnese. The two exceptions are, however, impressive: the first is Sebastiano's *Polyphemus*, in which the one-eyed giant is sitting, lost in contemplation of the beautiful Galatea, the nymph whom he loves, though hopelessly. Some scholars see in this work an ironical reference to Agostino's refused proposal of marriage to the daughter of the Marquis of Mantua. As a clever double-bluff, anticipating and defusing snobbish mockery of his insufficiently impressive origins with an erudite joke against himself, it expresses Agostino's sophistication rather than humility. The next panel is the famous *Galatea* of Raphael. The sea nymph is riding on her shell-chariot with a whole court of nymphs and tritons. The nineteenth century adored it, while modern visitors are sometimes less impressed. Raphael himself was covered with praise for it. Baldassare Castiglione, the author of the manual called *The Courtier*, wrote to Raphael of its beauty, and the artist's response was modest:

> Where the Galatea is concerned, I would consider myself a great master if it contained half the things your Lordship writes me. But I see in your words the love you hold for me, and I tell you that in order to paint one beauty I need to see a number of beauties, on condition that your Lordship is with me to make the choice. But as there is a dearth both of good judges and of beautiful women, I am using an idea which has come into my head. I do not know whether it is graced with any artistic excellence.

Raphael himself was, however, a connoisseur of beautiful women and in order to keep him at work in the villa, Agostino had to bring his lover *la Fornarina*, whose portrait is in the palazzo Barberini, to stay there, because otherwise Raphael would forever be nipping down the street to her house just inside the porta Settimiana.

The door at the far end of the loggia of Galatea opens into the old entrance portico, the **loggia of Cupid and Psyche**. Its recent restoration has brought it back to something closely resembling its original appearance, and new windows in the arches have helped to restore a relationship between the loggia and the gardens. The walls were painted during the Farnese tenancy with faux round niches containing faux bases for non-existent busts, and the floor was inserted by the Italian state in the early twentieth century (its design was inspired by intarsia, inlaid cut stone decoration, discovered in Nero's palace on the Palatine). However, the principal attraction here is the cycle retelling the legend of Cupid and Psyche, taken from Apuleius's novel *The Golden Ass*. Raphael made the drawings and some of the figures in 1517, and his studio, particularly Raffaelino del Colle, Giulio Romano and Francesco Penni did the rest. Giovanni da Udine was the author of the lavish floral festoons; a close look at the lush tumble of plants, fruits and vegetables will reveal some sly sexual innuendoes in the form of zucchini and open pomegranates, as well as some flora of the New World. The whole loggia was conceived by Raphael as a sort of pergola, with cloths stretched across to form the ceiling (the two central panels, the *Council of the Gods* and the *Wedding Banquet of Cupid and Psyche*, were painted as if they were tapestries). Agostino's motive here seems to have been to display his learning and taste, and the loggia became an archetype for the Renaissance villa, both because of its decoration and because of its role as an intermediate space between outdoor and indoor. We have seen other loggias elsewhere, perhaps most impressively at palazzo Barberini, whose debt to the villa Farnesina is clear enough. The figures in these frescoes were copied and diffused throughout Europe via engraving, and even in the period of the villa's decadence, this loggia and the loggia of Galatea were much visited. In the late seventeenth century Carlo Maratta undertook a restoration, at the command of the Duke of Parma, and though he was scrupulous, his alterations, particularly to the background of the loggia frescoes, were irreversible, so today we do not really see Raphael's blue, but merely a trace of it.

The third room on this floor is the **room of the frieze**, so called because of its painted wall decoration, just below the ceiling, by Peruzzi, also depicting mythological scenes from Ovid.

Back through the loggia and past the *Galatea* and the entrance hall, we climb the grand staircase (modified by the Duke of Ripalta in the nineteenth century). Note, just before the landing, the secret door on the left that opens into the first mezzanine floor (no admission). At the top of the stairs is the magisterial **room of the perspectives**. This was frescoed by Peruzzi in 1518–19 and is now, after heavy alterations in 1863, back in a condition approximating its original. It comprises false loggias with views over different scenes: one shows a view of Roman buildings, rather oddly jumbled together but many recognisable, while its pendant across the room shows a Lazio country scene, perhaps the countryside around the Chigi towns of Tolfa or Allumiere. Above the fireplace is a fresco of *Vulcan's Forge*, a theme repeated in the next room.

This room hosted the third of Agostino's famous banquets, on 28 August 1519, St Augustine's Day. At this banquet, in the presence of Leo X and twelve cardinals, the lavish feast was served to the guests on silver plates emblazoned with the guests' own coats of arms. At the end of the banquet Agostino prevailed upon the pope to marry him to his mistress, the beautiful Francesca Ardeasca, who had already borne him four children. However, the couple only enjoyed marital bliss for less than a year: on 11 April 1520 Agostino died. In the subsequent misfortunes that befell the villa a chilling trace was left. This is a graffito of the German occupiers during the Sack of Rome, written on the sky of the Roman streetscape fresco: 'AD 1528. *Was sol ich Schreibers . . . nd nit lachen di Landsknecht haben den Babst lauffen machen*' (Why should I who write not laugh – the Landsknechts have set the pope on the run).

The final room to visit is Agostino's nuptial bedroom, the **room of Alexander and Roxana**. The painter was Giovanni Antonio Bazzi, known to history as Il Sodoma: unusually for his time, he was quite open about his homosexuality and Vasari commented that 'since he always had about him boys and beardless youths, whom he loved beyond the usual [*fuor di modo*], he acquired the nickname of Sodoma; and in this name, far from taking umbrage or offence, he used to glory, writing songs and verses about it'. Indeed, the main fresco here prominently depicts not just Alexander, gesticulating to his new Persian bride Roxana, but Alexander's lover Hephaestion, the beautiful male nude to the right, who is making a graceful gesture of renunciation. Two bands of putti tumble across the picture, apparently unnoticed by the other figures. The composition draws heavily on ancient written accounts of a famous depiction of the subject by the painter Aethion, another compliment to Agostino's erudition. On the wall to the right of the Roxana fresco is the other main Sodoma commission, *Alexander receives the homage of the Persian Queen Mother*. Once again the episode features Hephaestion: the Queen Mother kneels before the tallest and most handsome of the men among Alexander's court, and is mortified to discover that the man next to him is Alexander. She has knelt to Hephaestion instead, but Alexander raises her up, saying affectionately, 'Have no fear. He too is Alexander.' The celebration of homosexual love in this bridal chamber may seem odd, but meant little more to the staunchly heterosexual Agostino than a classical reference and an opportunity for the artist to display his skill at painting the male form.

The figure of the Queen Mother is rather crudely painted, provoking speculation that Sodoma was not being paid to his satisfaction: Vasari recorded that his 'brush danced to the sound of coins'. But the three putti underneath, forming part of the lower-level decorative scheme representing *Vulcan's forge*, have a liveliness and charm that the fresco above lacks. The fresco on the entrance wall, *Alexander and Bucephalus*, from later in the sixteenth century, occupies the space which, in the original plan of the room, the bedhead would have concealed. Unlike later suburban villas, this was a building to be slept in and this bedroom once had a Latin verse written round the tops of the walls, saying, 'Be happy and sleep; for sleep is rest. For half their lives happy souls are no different from unhappy ones.' Even the prospect of nightmares was excluded from this beautiful place.

2 The Chigi *teatri*, I: piazza del Popolo

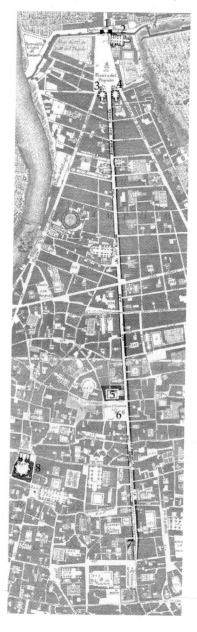

The Chigi *teatri* of piazza del Popolo, via del Corso, and piazza Colonna

Key:
1 porta del Popolo
2 Chigi chapel, Santa Maria del Popolo
3 Santa Maria in Montesanto
4 Santa Maria dei Miracoli
5 palazzo Chigi
6 piazza Colonna
7 Santa Maria in Lata
8 Pantheon

The great piazza del Popolo, in the mid seventeenth century, had not changed very much for almost a hundred years, not since Sixtus V Peretti planted the great obelisk at the visual confluence of the *tridente*, the trident of streets branching south from the piazza. Though Paul V Borghese had replaced an earlier fountain with a more graceful version (today in piazza Nicosia), the piazza remained unkempt and almost wild. During the reign of Urban VIII, ruffians setting upon a traveller here were startled off by an irate monk who roared towards them with a stick in his hand: this was the pope's brother Cardinal Antonio Barberini the Elder. The whole eastern half of the modern piazza was taken up with Sixtus IV's large monastery and grounds of the Augustinian friars of Santa Maria del Popolo, while to the west narrow roads straggled towards the Tiber. The old city gate, the porta del Popolo, had been adorned with a new exterior façade by Nanni di Baccio Bigio in the later sixteenth century, but the interior was stark brick and stone. The front of Santa Maria del Popolo, the first great church that visitors from the land routes to the north would encounter, was hopelessly old-fashioned and the interior similarly drab, contrary to all the canons of Baroque religious representation.

Piazza del Popolo was to undergo a subsequent renovation in the early nineteenth century, under the great landscape architect Giuseppe Valadier (1762–1839), who transformed it into its present vast oval. In the seventeenth century the main visual thrust of the piazza was towards the *tridente* and the first time the problem of the piazza's appearance impressed itself upon Alexander VII was at the ceremonial entry of Queen Christina of Sweden. However, he had been at work there even before his rise to the throne: the Chigi had a long-established presence in Santa Maria del Popolo and it was to this church that Alexander first turned his attention.

I THE CHIGI IN SANTA MARIA DEL POPOLO

Santa Maria del Popolo, piazza del Popolo. Open 9–12, 16–19. Chigi chapel open with church

This church, whose earlier history belongs to the della Rovere family, was a prestigious site for a family chapel: it contained a multitude of chapels housing the tombs of the della Rovere relatives of the church's rebuilder Sixtus IV, which gave it social cachet, and it was the first church inside the walls of Rome for most visitors. Thus it offered an unparalleled opportunity to make a strong impression of familial wealth and power.

Agostino Chigi, Il Magnifico, endowed a chapel here in 1513–14 and received permission from the Augustinians to construct a new physical container for the chapel, which made it entirely distinct from the church's other lateral chapels. The architect Chigi chose was Raphael, whose design included a tall rectangular space surmounted by a Pantheon-style coffered dome covered in mosaics executed by Luigi da Pace. The chapel, second on the left, employs an almost Baroque sensibility, completely original for its time, in drawing the viewer into the space. Agostino's chapel was and is much brighter than those on either side, and its decoration in multicoloured marbles (plundered, of course, from ancient buildings) also marked it as strikingly different from the serene grey and white of the rest of the church. However, above the entrance to the chapel is a bronze lamp in the shape of a crown being borne aloft by two putti. If the viewer keeps his or her eye on the lamp while approaching the chapel, it seems to surge upwards, drawing the eye in and up.

Agostino chose the chapel's dedication to the Virgin Mary and the original altarpiece was intended to depict the Assumption. It seems that the crown lamp refers to the original plan, as part of the apparatus of the coronation of the Virgin. This plan was changed, however, and the present altarpiece, painted on black stone, portrays the *Nativity of the Virgin*. We will return to this painting in a moment. As we step into the chapel itself we look up into the dome, where the perspectivally drawn figure of God the Father welcomes us into the chapel and the Virgin into heaven. The mosaics below depict the creation of the heavens and the seven planets, each given an angel as its prime mover, according to an idea of the medieval poet Dante. The mosaics therefore express motion, not only upwards, which is the course of the Virgin's ascension and of our curious eyes, but laterally with the planets. This movement across space is much more traditionally Baroque than Renaissance and expresses a surprising avant-garde sensibility for 1514.

The sculptor Lorenzetto, who was head of the building works, contributed both the relief on the altar, *Jesus and the Woman of Samaria,* and the two statues now placed diagonally across from each other in the niche to the left of the altar and the right of the entrance. His masterpiece here is the statue beside the altar, *Jonah and the Whale,* from 1520, in which the Old Testament prophet is modelled upon the figure of the ancient Antinous, the favourite of the Emperor Hadrian. His other niche statue, *Elijah,* was completed by the not very skilled Raffaele da Montelupo (c.1505–57). The two tomb monuments are to Agostino Chigi and his brother Sigismondo, founder of the branch which produced Alexander VII.

The chapel was left unfinished at Agostino's death in 1520 and it was up to the Chigi heirs to complete it. The altarpiece of the *Nativity of the Virgin* by Sebastiano del Piombo is quite dark and difficult to see. Sebastiano was hired in 1530 by the Chigi heirs and they modified the original subject to make the chapel more specifically dedicated to the Virgin of Loreto, where the cult of Mary focused around her house, which was miraculously transported there from the Holy Land by angels. The painting was unfinished in 1547 when the painter died and his son Giulio inexpertly tried to finish it but was replaced by the talented Francesco Salviati. Salviati was the author of the heavenly figures at the top of the picture, as well as the scenes from the Old Testament that run round the drum of the dome, depicting episodes from the Book of Genesis. Salviati finished his work in about 1550–3, when he was one of the most sought-after painters in Rome. Even after the collapse of Agostino's fortune, the Chigi were still concerned enough with their prestige to hire one of the city's most modish artists.

In 1652 the up-and-coming prelate Fabio Chigi decided to finish the chapel. He commissioned Bernini to complete the decoration, including oval relief portraits of Agostino and Sigismondo and sixteenth-century-style Latin epitaphs, composed by Fabio himself, on the tomb monuments. Bernini's work intensified when Chigi became pope in 1655 and he was hired to make the two remaining statues of prophets for the empty niches. In fact, Bernini was initially only asked to make one of the statues, the other being intended for his great rival Algardi. Algardi's early death put paid to that plan and Bernini got both commissions.

The two Lorenzetto statues originally flanked the altar, but Bernini moved the *Elijah* to its present position so he could tell a story across the chapel with his two pieces. His statue of *Daniel in the Lions' Den*, from 1655 to 1657, shows off his virtuoso style in making a 'painted' surface with his chisel: the prophet's skin has a different texture from that of the lion's face, which is different again from the lion's tongue as it reaches out to lick Daniel's foot. Daniel is praying to heaven to be delivered: he is locked in the lions' den and starving along with the lions, which have been miraculously pacified. Across the chapel, to the right of the altar, *The Prophet Habakkuk*, of 1656–61, shows the response to Daniel's prayer: Habakkuk, about to sit down with his lunch in a basket, is approached by an angel who proposes to carry him, by two locks of Habakkuk's hair, to the land where Daniel is being held, in order to give him some food. The angel points towards Daniel with a look of serene delight, while Habakkuk not unnaturally looks startled and dismayed at the prospect of air travel and the deprivation of his lunch. Bernini's final intervention was in the centre of the floor, where he replaced the grille closing off the Chigi sepulchre with an intarsia plug depicting a skeleton, emblem of death, carrying the Chigi shield up to heaven, in perspectival parallel with the figure of God the Father in the dome above. The legend below the skeleton, 'MORS AD CAELOS' (death [leads] to the heavens), cleverly includes the date MDCL, 1650, the most recent jubilee year. Bernini transformed the meaning of the chapel from an incomplete meditation on the Assumption of the Virgin to an expression of the universal passage from the earthly realm, through death, to the heavenly sphere above. All around this journey up quivers the movement of prophets and pyramids and planets, until the eye arrives, once again, at the welcoming figure of God the Father.

Having made a good start on his family mortuary chapel, Alexander expanded his redecoration scheme to the rest of the church. The result is less successful. The simplicity of the fifteenth-century church was distorted to support a new cornice round the top of the arched nave, above which figures of saints cling precariously, made by the industrious school of Bernini. The two transept altars were reworked and given angelic accompaniment, this time at the expense of Cardinal Flavio Chigi whose titular church this was; the angels here are obviously relatives of those to be placed on the Castel Sant'Angelo bridge under the next two pontificates. Alexander also ordered a colossal organ above the right transept: this has the Chigi–della Rovere oak tree clambering over it, rather beautifully, in gilded bronze. He relaid the floor, and had the dome reconstructed and painted with extremely indifferent frescoes by Francesco Vanni, a Sienese artist, whose father had been the pope's godfather. Alexander replaced the rose window in the façade and caused Bernini to put a pair of new and fashionable broken-pediment volutes on either side of the upper storey of the nave, as well as a three-sided stairway to the front entrances.

The Chigi family continued to use this chapel as their mortuary and in 1771 the pilaster to the left of the Chigi chapel was decorated with one of the most lavish late Baroque tombs, that of Maria Flaminia Odescalchi Chigi, the wife of Sigismondo I Chigi, Prince of Farnese and Duke of Ariccia. The princess died in childbirth at the age of only twenty and her grieving husband commissioned this tomb from the Colonna family architect Paolo Posi. It is less a tribute to the virtues of the deceased than a celebration of the armorial imagery of both the Chigi and the Odescalchi, with the Chigi–della Rovere oak supporting a cloth on which is a medallion portrait of the princess, who sports a truly superb Roman nose. Below, the Odescalchi lamp emblem is transformed into a censer from which incense billows, and an Odescalchi lion roars beside it, its paw on the Chigi *monti*.

II THE PORTA DEL POPOLO, THE TRANSFORMATION OF THE
PIAZZA, AND THE TWIN CHURCHES
Santa Maria dei Miracoli, open 8–13, 17–19.30; Santa Maria in
Montesanto, open in winter 16–19 and Sunday mornings; closed July
and August

Starting in the late spring of 1656, the renovations that were altering the appearance of Santa Maria del Popolo spread to the porta del Popolo just outside the church. Gianlorenzo Bernini was commissioned to replace the dreary medieval gateway with a grand and simple arch. The work was meant to commemorate the entrance of Queen Christina of Sweden in

December 1655. It comprises a classically proportioned triumphal arch (the two lower arches on either side are nineteenth-century additions) with a strong cornice, above which rises an attic storey with an inscription, 'FELICI FAUSTO QUI INGRESSUI, MDCLV' (To a happy and fortunate entry, 1655). Above that, in compliment to Christina, a garland incorporating the wheatsheaf emblem of her family, the Vasa, hangs between a stylish broken gable enclosing the Chigi *monti* and star.

Alexander's ambition lured him into an even more expensive project. His architects submitted plans to regularise the piazza, shaping it into a sort of reverse funnel that was meant to suck the visitor from the gate and across the piazza to one of the three streets of the *tridente*. The piazza was altered accordingly, but a new scheme was brewing that would give its city side the appearance of a monumental entrance: the two blocks between the streets of the *tridente* were to be faced with matching porticoes. This soon developed even more ambitiously into a pair of churches, both dedicated to Mary like the original church of Santa Maria del Popolo, consecrating the whole space to the Virgin.

As early as April 1657, Alexander commissioned Carlo Rainaldi, the son of that old workhorse of the Farnese and Borghese, Girolamo Rainaldi, to design the twin churches. His plan was finally approved in 1661 and the cornerstone of the right-hand church, Santa Maria dei Miracoli, was accordingly laid a few weeks later: Alexander was not taking the chance of delaying and seeing his plans fail. The chance of that happening was quite high, because the papal treasury, already emptying fast on other projects of the pope, had nothing to contribute. Alexander entered into a partnership with two religious communities to pay for the construction: the left-hand church, Santa Maria di Montesanto, was to house a Sicilian group of Discalced Carmelites, while the right-hand church, dedicated to Mary of the Miracles, replaced an earlier and smaller church roughly on the same site, dedicated to St Ursula and belonging to a little community of French Franciscan tertiaries. However, work on the churches stalled at Alexander's death.

You can feel the classicising influence of Bernini in the changes of design that make the buildings as they are today different from the plans submitted to the pope: surely it is no coincidence that the entrance porches are similar to those of the colonnade of piazza San Pietro, which were being constructed at the same time. The churches have different footprints, on different-shaped sites: Santa Maria dei Miracoli has a circular plan, while Santa Maria di Montesanto has an oval dome. Their construction history continued until the eighteenth century and they would not have been completed in their current forms at all were it not for the intervention of a new patron, Cardinal Girolamo Gastaldi.

Piazza del Popolo after the interventions of Alexander VII. The long wall in the middle background encloses the large Augustinian monastery of Santa Maria del Popolo, demolished in the early nineteenth century by Valadier to create the oval piazza.

Gastaldi was from an important noble family in the territory of Genoa. He came to Rome and held various posts in the papal government under Innocent X. Alexander VII made him Commissary of Public Health during the 1656–7 plague and Gastaldi later wrote a book, *Tractatus de avertenda et profliganda peste*, published at Bologna in 1684, which became a standard text for the treatment of the disease. He was made cardinal in 1673 and legate to Bologna for three years in 1678. Upon receiving his cardinal's hat, he looked around for a way to commemorate himself in Rome: with one eye on his future appointment as legate, he made an offer to rebuild the Roman church of the Bolognese community, San Petronio, next to palazzo Farnese, but he was rebuffed when the church committee realised the cardinal wanted his name all over the façade. Thwarted, he approached the still struggling religious communities on the southern edge of piazza del Popolo in 1673. They accepted his partnership eagerly: construction on their churches had been halted for more than five years, since Alexander's death. With Gastaldi's money, the buildings surged to completion and instead of the Chigi emblem, the façades of the twin churches bore the name of Cardinal Gastaldi. The cardinal was buried in Santa Maria dei Miracoli, along with his brother, the Marchese Benedetto Gastaldi.

Of the two churches, **Santa Maria di Montesanto** is the more interesting and the less accessible: closed in the summer months, it serves for the rest of the year as the artists' church, and its Sunday services are known for their music and for the fame of some of their participants and readers. Access can sometimes be obtained through the sacristy, at via del Babuino 198. The façade is topped by statues of Carmelite saints. The twelve-sided dome here was conceived by Bernini to suit the irregular space, and built by Carlo Fontana to Bernini's designs. The generous volume of the central space creates an impression of airy light, and the colourful side chapels, though in some cases decorated with rather ugly modern art, contrast well with the grey and white of the marble floor. The presbytery is decorated, rather strangely, with six busts of the popes under whom Gastaldi served, with a little text on each plinth explaining Gastaldi's position during each pontificate, a sort of résumé in coloured marble and bronze. The plinth labelled 'Alexander VII', however, has a bust of Urban VIII on it. The other twin, **Santa Maria dei Miracoli**, is built on a round plan with an octagonal dome, but it shares the same serene colour scheme and on its façade are statues of Franciscan saints. The most beautiful objects inside are the tombs of the Gastaldi brothers in the presbytery by Antonio Raggi, where allegorical female figures recline below a portrait of the deceased.

3 The Chigi *teatri*, II: a walk down the via del Corso and in piazza Colonna
Start: via del Corso, at piazza del Popolo

If we follow the Corso, the central street of the *tridente*, we are retracing part of the ceremonial entry of Queen Christina of Sweden. At the beginning of Alexander's pontificate the street was irregular in width, with porches sticking out into it and many buildings of one or two storeys between the unfinished churches and palaces; by the end of his reign the street had been straightened, properties pushed back or pulled forwards to a uniform line. An ancient Roman arch, called the Arco di Portogallo after the residence of an old Portuguese cardinal nearby, narrowed the Corso, at via della Vite, from 9.6 to 5.5 metres: Alexander, with some misgivings, demolished it. An inscription, composed by the pope himself, on a plaque at the corner of the Corso and via della Vite asserts that through his efforts, 'via Lata [the old name for the Corso], the racecourse of the city on festive days, deformed by intervening structures and protruding buildings, has been freed and straightened for public convenience and beauty'. Widening streets not only made for a more ample sightline, but responded to the perennial problem of coach traffic, which was infesting the pedestrian streets in the seventeenth century much as car traffic invaded in the twentieth.

Further along the Corso, the huge Milanese national church of **San Carlo al Corso** (open 8–12, 16–19) had been languishing unfinished. Its reconstruction on the site of an earlier church to St Ambrose had been begun in 1612 by the architect Onorio Longhi and continued by his son Martino. However, lack of funds and planning obstacles prevented its completion until Alexander VII intervened late in his reign, in 1665, to permit the demolition of houses behind the church in order to build the apse. Three years later the old and ailing Pietro da Cortona was given charge of the building works, and it is to him that the church owes its distinctive cupola and ambulatory round the apse, a feature of Lombard churches rarely found in Rome. It was to be the aged artist's last architectural commission. Inside, the decor must count among Rome's most overblown and ugly efforts, one of those which convince visitors that the Baroque was a disastrous artistic malaise; but the view of Cortona's dome from piazza Augusto Imperatore, behind the church, is still beautiful.

A little more than halfway down the via del Corso from piazza del Popolo the visitor is confronted with a large square opening to the right. This is **piazza Colonna**, where the first great monument of ancient Rome, the column of Marcus Aurelius, can be seen. Its second-century AD reliefs (180–93) depict the philosopher-emperor's battles in Germany against the Marcomanni, Quadi and Sarmatians.

In 1655, at Alexander's accession, the piazza was in a sorry condition. An irregular cluster of buildings occluded its northern half, while the rear contained a ramshackle church and monastery belonging to the Barnabite order. On the southern side the palazzo del Bufalo (today's palazzo Ferrajuoli) had demeaning shops set into the façade, and next to it was one of Rome's scanty social services, a madhouse. On the northern periphery of the square was the unfinished palazzo Aldobrandini, property of the Princess of Rossano, but she and her husband Don Camillo Pamphilj lived further down the Corso, and this palazzo went through phases of standing empty alternating with short-term tenancies. As early as 1657, the pope's commissioners, the *maestri delle strade*, undertook a survey of this indecorous public space. And now familial interests began to play a part in the fortunes of the piazza.

Don Mario Chigi and his nephew Don Agostino, the secular heads of the family, were looking for a site for their family palace. There were rumours in February 1658 that they were considering making an offer for palazzo del Bufalo, but soon afterwards they turned to the palazzo Aldobrandini on the other side of the piazza. In September 1659, the Princess of Rossano agreed

Piazza Colonna, with palazzo Chigi to the right, dominating the piazza. The nondescript palace at centre, behind the column, occupies the space once suggested for a Chigi palace and fountain, but it became household lodgings for the Ludovisi at palazzo Montecitorio.

to the sale: after all, she had just given her daughter Maria Virginia Borghese in marriage to Don Agostino, so it would be staying in the family. The princess accepted a bargain price, and work on palace and square was at last able to begin in earnest. Demolition of the houses in the centre of the piazza had already begun that February.

As in piazza del Popolo, Alexander's plans grew more and more ambitious as the project continued, and the idea of 'squaring off' the piazza by chopping off the front of the Barnabite convent at the western end began to look appealing. Here he had some room to manoeuvre, as the Barnabites were struggling in a court case relating to their other convent, at San Carlo ai Catinari. The pope resolved the case in favour of the Barnabites, on condition that they leave their monastery on piazza Colonna. The fathers agreed and suddenly the Chigi were offered another whole site upon which to construct an entirely new palace, if they wished to.

That they did not do so was perhaps due to lack of funds, or the urgent need for appropriate accommodation; in any case, a beautiful design for a palace by Pietro da Cortona, incorporating a colossal fountain in the façade, never got off the drawing board. The two Chigi princes were content with palazzo Aldobrandini. Instead, the pope sold the Barnabite site to the Chigi's new neighbour, Prince Nicolò Ludovisi, whom we have met as the husband of Costanza Pamphilj. The Ludovisi prince, whose family palace of

Montecitorio was next door to palazzo Chigi, built a palace there for his household instead: thoroughly overhauled in the nineteenth century, this is the modern palazzo Wedekind. After a chequered history as seat of the papal post office and a magnate's residence, it became in turn the headquarters of the Fascist Party under Mussolini and then, after the Second World War, the offices of a right-wing newspaper, *Il Tempo*.

Alexander's plans to build a great fountain here and make it the terminus of the Acqua Vergine also came to nothing. The piazza was cleared and the column, which is sited off the north–south centre of the piazza, was at least made to stand in the centre of it from east to west. The existing fountain, another product of Giacomo della Porta who made the north and south fountains of piazza Navona, was allowed to stay. But piazza Colonna was not destined to become another piazza Navona, a testament to familial power. In fact, Chigi emblems are few and insignificant.

Today the piazza has more or less regained its pristine seventeenth-century appearance: though the two buildings on the east and west sides are nineteenth and twentieth century in their present aspects, the palaces on its north and south sides have been beautifully restored. Yet piazza Colonna is strangely lifeless, a large sterile space without trees or cafés, and likely to remain thus for ever for security reasons. The old palazzo Chigi, centre of Roman social life in the second half of the Seicento, is now the headquarters of the Italian prime minister, and the piazza plays host not to glittering socialites but to police vans and the occasional political demonstration.

The history of **palazzo Chigi** (piazza Colonna 370, no admission) is long and complicated. It was the original Roman home of the Aldobrandini family and its nucleus was built after 1578 by the consistorial lawyer Pietro, brother of the family pope Clement VIII. The family house started as one of a row on via del Corso and Aldobrandini gradually acquired the houses that separated the original building from the piazza. Giacomo della Porta contributed to the design of the palace, as did Carlo Maderno. Olimpia Aldobrandini the Younger, Princess of Rossano, was the last Aldobrandini to own it.

When the two Chigi princes bought the palace in 1659, they put Felice della Greca (1626–77) in charge of finishing the building. He completed the overall appearance of the palace and built the grand staircase, which was much admired. The interior was richly decorated, with art by Baciccia, Johann Paul Schor and Adrien Manglard, a Dutch artist who contributed a room of seascapes. One of the great suite of reception rooms, the *Salone d'Oro*, was redecorated to celebrate the marriage of Sigismondo II Chigi to Maria Flaminia Odescalchi, whose tomb in Santa Maria del Popolo we have already seen. Unfortunately, all this luxury is closed to the public.

Further south along the via del Corso, Alexander's projects included the completion of the church of **Santa Maria in via Lata**. This ancient church was rebuilt internally for the 1650 jubilee by the great Neapolitan designer Cosimo Fanzago, but it lacked a façade until 1658, when Pietro da Cortona, already at work for Alexander VII on the great *teatro* of Santa Maria della Pace – which we shall be visiting next – was hired by one of the church's canons, Anastasio Ridolfi, to complete the front facing the Corso. Quite soon, however, the payments for the work were taken over by the pope himself.

The church's façade is a quiet masterpiece of classical elements grouped together to form a dynamic composition: a portico on the ground floor with two pairs of columns is matched above by a loggia whose main element is a Serliana window, a central arch flanked by two rectangular windows, evoking echoes of the great window of Borromini's gallery in palazzo Pamphilj in piazza Navona. The large, shadowy spaces of portico and loggia make the façade a dramatic play of light and dark, and the ensemble seems to rise upwards, far higher, in fact, than the rest of the church. The interior was woefully modified by Pius IX in 1863, but still retains some of its Baroque decorations. The ancient church, in five rooms of a late antique building, was also remodelled under Cortona, but this is no longer accessible due to a rise in the water table. The Chigi crest, visible in some engravings of the church, was removed in compliment to the Pamphilj princes next door.

Directly across the Corso from the church stands the Corso front of **palazzo Odescalchi**, whose main façade is on piazza Santi Apostoli behind and which we have already mentioned in conjunction with the Colonna who had possessed it previously. During the Chigi pontificate Cardinal Flavio I Chigi, the cardinal nephew, lived here. Now all has vanished under the brutal neo-Florentine Renaissance façade for palazzo Odescalchi, made by Rafaelle Ojetti (1845–1924) in 1887.

4 The Chigi *teatri*, III: Santa Maria della Pace

Entrance from piazza Santa Maria della Pace. Open Tuesday to Friday 10–12.45, Monday and Saturday 16.30–17.50, irregularly

Sixtus IV's little church dedicated to the Virgin of Peace, commemorating the end of his sordid adventure into assassination with the conspiracy of the Pazzi family in Florence as well as a general Italian peace, sits in a densely built-up area to the west of piazza Navona. Agostino Chigi, Il Magnifico, sponsored a chapel here, not very far from his own palace near the Castel

Sant'Angelo bridge and once again the guiding spirit was that of Raphael. The Chigi chapel is first on the right-hand side of the strange short nave. Its original appearance is hard to determine, as it was remade under Alexander VII, but the Raphael frescoes remain on the nave wall, over the arched niche of the chapel. They comprise four *Sibyls*, the Cumaean, Persian, Phrygian and Tiburtine, who were thought to have foretold the coming of Christ. Their monumental size and grandeur owe a debt to the sibyls of the Sistine Chapel ceiling, which had been unveiled when Raphael painted these, probably in 1511–12, though possibly as late as 1514. He also designed the frescoes on the level above, which were painted by one of his fellow artists from Urbino, Timoteo Viti (1469–1525), depicting four prophets, three of which are the same as those in Agostino's other chapel in Santa Maria del Popolo: David and Daniel, with Habakkuk and Jonah. The chapel was left unfinished at Agostino's death.

Over a century later, in 1628, the young priest Fabio Chigi undertook to repair and complete the decaying chapel, which was set in an equally decaying context: the church suffered perennial problems with ground water and the foundations kept shifting slightly. In 1655–6 the same man, now Alexander VII, was in a position to make a real improvement. As Bernini was, for once, too busy (with piazza San Pietro, as we will see), the commission went to Pietro da Cortona. The pope had more than familial motives, too: the dedication to the Virgin of Peace was most appropriate, as Alexander was trying to broker a peace between France and Spain at the time. The work here was achieved rapidly, ending in 1659. By that point, however, the entire appearance of the church and the neighbourhood around it had greatly changed. The result was one of the summit achievements of Baroque urban planning.

The situation of the church was a problem in itself. It was approached at an oblique angle by the via della Pace, which was relatively narrow and widened only at the church's façade to branch into two asymmetrical alleys, one of which, the narrower of the two, passed directly along the side of the church. The law courts, located in palazzo Nardini on via del Governo Vecchio not far away, let out at noon and Santa Maria della Pace had the privilege of holding Mass after that time, which made it a popular destination for judges, lawyers and laymen alike. However, coaches could neither linger nor turn in the ungenerous space in front of the church. Solving this became one of the principal problems facing the architect. At first the answer seemed to be a new road cut through from one street over; this would involve the costly expropriation of two houses belonging to the German confraternity of Santa Maria dell'Anima, the church whose apse uncomfortably butted up practically against the right side of Santa Maria della Pace. Cortona suggested an alternative – rather than make a new little street, why not carve out a little piazza from the properties on either side of the church?

Though this was an even more expensive proposition, Alexander gave his assent and by early autumn of 1656 Cortona presented him with the plans for the façade more or less as it appears today. It is a startlingly modern piece of design. The church itself occupies only the central part of the façade, with a convex porch that swells out into the new five-sided piazza, its space measured out with pairs of simple columns, while above the porch the upper level of the front bulges out as well, as if the wall were pushing against the columns and pilasters. A large central arched window barely corresponds with the smaller fifteenth-century opening inside; further up, a broken pediment surges upwards to become a curve, enclosing the papal crest (today erased). This is interesting enough. But the real brilliance of the plan is in the side wings of the façade, which in their relation to the centre bear a superficial resemblance to the lower level of other churches with low aisles and high nave (like Santa Maria del Popolo, for instance): there are even little curved volutes that seem to connect the sides with the higher centre. However, this is an illusion, because behind the sides quite different things are happening.

To the right of the convex porch, what at first appears to be a shaded doorway gives on to the old alley running between Santa Maria della Pace and Santa Maria dell'Anima. Cortona's solution, having a street running through the façade, is utterly revolutionary. The whole right-hand side in fact covers the back of the German confraternity's church, and the large arched window above actually corresponds to one of the apse windows of the Anima church.

The left-hand side, too, cleverly arranges a series of diverse elements. First, the pre-existing monastery with its cloister by Bramante was to be left untouched, so the street running off the piazza to the left had to remain. Second, the monastery required a new formal entrance. These two matters were elegantly resolved with a rectangular opening through which the street runs and the monastery's entrance is a match for the alley opening on the other side. The large arched window is a dummy. The façade of this church ties the whole square together and the secular buildings round it have all been given uniform fronts that refer to the church's façade while being subordinate to it. A plaque next to the street opening to the left announces that, by papal command, the piazza should not ever be altered. The overt theatricality of the design, as with many in this period, draws much of its inspiration from stage sets (which all the major Roman architects and artists designed in this period, even when at the peak of their

Vasi's engraving of Santa Maria della Pace makes the piazza much bigger than it really is, but shows the revolutionary aspects of the façade's design: to the right, figures are emerging from the shadowy alley as if from a door, while to the left, light comes in from the alley leading along the side of the old monastery.

fame) and entirely justifies Alexander's own description of the piazza as the 'teatro della Pace'.

The church's **interior** was also thoroughly updated. Cortona remade the Chigi chapel with a sculptural altarpiece by Ercole Ferrata and Cosimo Fancelli inside a Baroque aedicule, flanked by reliefs depicting the instruments of the Passion. Decorations include a pair of angels above the nave arch holding the Chigi crest. Further inside, the dome was restructured by Cortona and given a stucco surface of ribs and coffers, a trademark of Cortona's style though one soon to be copied by Bernini, with whom the artist had a healthy rivalry ('tell the major-domo that Bernini must not see the drawings of Pietro da Cortona, and vice versa,' was Alexander's instruction). The overall effect of Cortona's renovations resulted in a greater overall visual coherence, and, unlike in Santa Maria del Popolo, the seventeenth-century make-over here integrates well with the fifteenth-century structure.

5 The Chigi *teatri*, IV: piazza San Pietro, Scala Regia and Cathedra Petri

Piazza San Pietro and the basilica
under Alexander VII

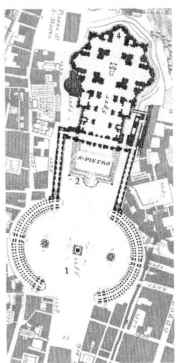

Key:
1 the oval piazza and its colonnades
2 piazza retta
3 Scala Regia
4 Cathedra Petri

The masterpiece of Alexander VII's building programme is at the Vatican, in what he always called his *teatro di San Pietro*. Though the basilica of St Peter's itself was finally more or less finished, in 1655 the piazza in front of Maderno's façade was still irregular and unimpressive. A series of low buildings and offices closed it on the south and east sides, and a corridor with a clock tower at the end of it, built during the reign of Paul V, jutted out from the right-hand side of the façade, serving as the formal entrance to the Vatican palace. Further down, the *borgo* which lay between St Peter's and the river was made up of two rather narrow main streets, the Borgo Vecchio and the Borgo Nuovo, with a series of buildings, the *spina di Borgo*, rising between the two. The result was underwhelming at best. Alexander, with his eye for aesthetics, was not slow to take action.

On 31 July 1656 he summoned the Reverenda Fabbrica di San Pietro, the agency in charge of building works, and the Fabbrica decided to ask Bernini for his suggestions about arranging the piazza and making it more monumental. Bernini had to consider several obstacles, the most obtrusive of which was the unmovable obelisk in the centre, set there by Sixtus V in a difficult engineering operation. The piazza also had to serve a number of purposes: it should be uniform, to please the eye; it should harmonise with the façade of the basilica (which had already been criticised for being too wide for its height, after Bernini's bell towers had been demolished by Innocent X); it should be able to hold a large number of people; it should provide for a dignified entrance to the Vatican palace; and it should not block the views from the pope's windows.

Bernini submitted a number of different plans. They all involved two parts: a square or trapezoidal piazza directly in front of the façade, and a larger open space round the obelisk. The final shape was suggested by the pope himself, to whom Bernini gave the credit in his report to the Fabbrica: Alexander, 'with a more than human judgement, resolved to make it in oval form, something that astounded the said Architect grown old in this profession'. An oval would allow the best use of the available space, stretching right to the Leonine wall and the *passetto*, the private corridor linking the palace to the Castel Sant'Angelo, and it would not block the view from the Vatican. It would also resemble an amphitheatre and specifically that greatest of legendary Christian martyr sites, the Colosseum. The part of the piazza in front of the façade itself would be a trapezoid, opening outwards close to the basilica in order to emphasise the height of the church front; and a new entrance to the Vatican palace was to be incorporated into the colonnade.

The final form of the piazza – Doric columns in four ranks, enclosing a wide, vaulted central corridor and two flat-ceilinged, narrower side corridors in two curves, north and south of the piazza – only emerged in 1659. The colonnade was not to serve as a base for offices or dormitories, but simply to ornament the space in front of the Apostle's basilica. An Ionic entablature, running broad and unbroken along the entire length of each arm of the colonnade, helped to unify the massive composition. If you stand on the lateral axis, say halfway between one of the fountains and the obelisk, the band of the entablature above the colonnade will seem to be on the same scale as the upper level of the façade of the basilica itself, creating a smooth visual flow round the piazza. This is all the more remarkable because the façade is vastly taller than the colonnade.

The piazza was designed on a complex mathematical foundation, depending on the axes of the obelisk; two circles drawn side by side, with their centres marked by the fountains, placed on the lateral axis, formed the basis for the oval. The arms of the colonnade had a finishing point, too, that was dictated by the point of intersection of the northern, right-hand colonnade with the sightline drawn out from the entrance to the Vatican palace at the *Portone di Bronzo* (Bronze Door) to the property line of the

Basilica di S. Pietro in Vaticano
1 Palazzo Pontificio, 2 Anfiteatro ornato con 320 colonne, e 136 statue, il tutto ... con il Tempio Laurato a scarpello nel duro travertino

A *pissoir* for dogs? Piazza San Pietro was the most extravagant papal project since the completion of the basilica. Alexander VII was forcefully criticised for the design's vanity and grandiosity.

Borgo Nuovo. This important line was entirely done away with when the big pylons of the piazza Pio XII were built for the jubilee year of 1950 and the Borgo Nuovo itself has vanished under the broad via della Conciliazione, opened in the 1930s. Bernini's original plans also included a third wing of the colonnade, the *terzo braccio*, that was meant to be set in the wide gap between the two main arms, turning the piazza into something self-contained, which would, in Bernini's words, 'embrace Catholics to reinforce their belief, heretics to reunite them with the Church and agnostics to enlighten them with true faith'. This was not built, however, for financial reasons: if it had been, perhaps Mussolini might have spared the Borgo its evisceration.

Foundations for the colonnade were laid in August 1657 and by the end of July 1658, forty-seven columns of the inmost ring had been raised. Such large quantities of travertine were transported for the columns that a temporary port was constructed on the river at the hospital of Santo Spirito. The northern colonnade was completed in 1662, but at Alexander's death in 1667 the southern one had only been begun. A close look at the interior coffering of the southern colonnade will show the stage it had reached by the pope's death. At both ends the coffers of the outer aisles have the Chigi *monti* and star in them, but the symbols vanish in the coffers of the curve, although Alexander's successors did allow his crest to be carved on the front of the southern colonnade. At the pope's death, about half of the ninety-six statues adorning the attic of the colonnades had been carved, also of travertine, by Bernini's studio to his designs.

The great simplicity of the colonnade, with its plain shapes and colossal air of weight and stability, is somewhat leavened by the statues on top, which give it a Baroque flourish. Inside the central aisle, in the half-circular spaces at each end below the vault, Alexander placed inscriptions: one claims his authorship of the piazza and the other three are apposite biblical quotations; one of them, from Isaiah, says 'Come, let us ascend the hill [*montem*] of our Lord, let us pray in his holy temple', alluding not only to the Vatican hill but also, of course, to the Chigi *monti* on the huge papal crests.

The massive expenditure on this project was the primary source of popular dislike for Alexander. Indeed, it was criticised from all sides: the uselessness of the colonnades, for instance, made them a waste of space. One pamphleteer wrote of Alexander that he 'creates glory through stones, through the colonnade of St Peter's where he spends a fortune on a dive for footpads and a *pissoir* for dogs'. A more balanced observer, the Venetian ambassador Nicolò Sagredo, wrote in 1661 that

> the building of the colonnades which encircle the piazza di San Pietro will be an achievement to recall the greatness of ancient Rome . . . It is true that Rome is getting more and more buildings and fewer and fewer inhabitants. This decrease is very striking and obvious to everyone, and in the Corso and in the busiest streets one sees nothing but empty houses and the sign *To Let*.

His successor, writing more savagely around the time of Alexander's death, commented:

> The erection of the porticoes at St Peter's is without any conceivable advantage. There are obvious weaknesses in the architecture for which Bernini has been blamed. The three hundred columns, arranged in an oval plan, merely serve as an architectural precinct for the marvellous church of the Prince of the Apostles. But they will make the Leonine city permanently uninhabitable, cause the Vatican to be abandoned and perhaps make it impossible to hold the conclave there. For the razing of houses, the increase of water for fountains and the extinction of fires will lead to malaria. All this confirms the worst rumours that over a million scudi have been spent on a series of catastrophic mistakes.

The building was, however, defensible as a make-work project for the Roman poor: Pallavicino, the pope's biographer, said Alexander 'deemed it wrong to support with alms the able-bodied'. It was true that the colonnades impoverished the papal treasury, and the million-scudi figure given above was accurate. It is thought that by Alexander's death, the public debt had risen to 50 million scudi, on an annual income of less than 2 million. The system of public loans, called *monti*, were perhaps also unintentionally evoked by the Chigi crest.

A good deal of money was lavished, too, on the remodelled entrance to the Vatican palace, at the end of the northern colonnade: this entrance is today often referred to as the *Portone di Bronzo* and it included one of Bernini's most ingenious architectural solutions, the great staircase called the Royal Stair, the **Scala Regia**. In designing the staircase, which was made of wide, shallow steps because it had to be negotiable by the pope's chair bearers, Bernini came up against a number of difficulties. The staircase had to link to the Vatican's main reception hall, the Sala Regia, yet also needed to function as a ceremonial link between basilica and palace; thus it made a U-turn part-way up. The lower part of the stairs ran along a retaining wall holding back the Vatican hill behind, and the upper part had to skirt the exterior wall of the Sistine chapel. The lower flight actually had to run underneath the Sala Regia. In order to accommodate this difficult site, Bernini resorted to illusion: he created a series of columns running up the sides of the lower staircase, which diminish in height as they draw closer to the top and pull closer in towards the side walls, which helps to regulate the space and make it all appear the same from below. Halfway up, a light well interrupts the vault, breaking up the otherwise monotonous length. The solution was theatrical in the extreme, and it was all surmounted by the Chigi crest and two figures of Fame above the vault at the first landing, where Bernini's own statue of *The Conversion of Constantine* was placed against a stucco drapery, the light of divine revelation sent down from a hidden window. This statue had been commissioned by Innocent X for a different situation in St Peter's, but here it took pride of place. It was unveiled in 1670, four years after the completion of the staircase.

Inside St Peter's the main decoration of the basilica was completed with the installation of the great reliquary shrine in the apse, the **Cathedra Petri** (Chair of Peter). This was a ninth-century seat given to Pope John VIII by the Carolingian emperor Charles the Bald around 875. As time passed, it became known as the chair of St Peter itself and it thus had a powerful symbolic value that Alexander VII wanted to use. The idea of making the Cathedra the ultimate focus, and the iconography of its setting, were both personal projects. In a world where his authority was continually denied, by Protestants, Jansenists and the kings of France and Spain alike, Alexander's concern in his principal church was to make a strong statement of the supremacy of the popes as successors to St Peter.

Even before the redesign of the piazza had been decided on, Bernini had been commissioned to work on the Cathedra: work on both took place simultaneously and it is interesting to consider them as part of the same project, a building up of theatre, from the rather austere grandeur of the colonnade to the exuberant burst of gilded bronze, viewed through Bernini's *baldacchino*, of the Cathedra. The creation of the monument took a long time and it was not unveiled until 17 January 1666. The difficulties included casting the four Fathers of the Church who, in the final composition, are supporting the Chair with ribbons. These were the largest bronze statues cast since antiquity, and some trial and error was necessary before the method was perfected: in the end, it was considered wisest to bury the moulds in the ground before pouring in the bronze, to avoid cracking them.

A visitor to St Peter's should not, as most tourists do, immediately turn to their right upon entry to visit the *Pietà* of Michelangelo, but should stand on the porphyry disc in front of the central doors and look down the nave at the Cathedra, framed by the *baldacchino*. It looks different at different times of day as the passage of light makes the statues seem almost to move. As we draw closer to the apse, the vivid, painterly quality of the Cathedra becomes even more impressive. On the lowest level of the composition are the Fathers of the Church, two Greek Fathers and two Latin Fathers, part of worldly existence, dark bronze and gold in colour. The eye passes easily from left to right, from St Ambrose and St Athanasius, along the ribbons supporting the bronze throne, before continuing to St John Chrysostom and St Augustine on the right. Further up, the throne hovers, apparently weightless, with a relief of Christ and his flock, by Bernini himself, on the back of the chair. The progress to the other-worldly continues further up, as bronze angels gather round the oval stained-glass window bursting with bronze rays of light, at the centre of which is the dove of the Holy Spirit. This powerful assertion of papal authority radiates a joyous solemnity that expresses Alexander VII's own cheerful theology.

On the left-hand wall of the basilica, behind the pier supporting the dome and quite close to Algardi's gigantic relief altarpiece of Leo the Great, is the **tomb of Alexander VII**. This had originally been intended for Santa Maria Maggiore. Bernini was commissioned relatively early in the pope's reign and the two had discussed some of the details – for instance, the pope was to be depicted bareheaded, not wearing the tiara – but the project was only begun in earnest after Alexander's death and stretched from 1671 to 1678, paid for by his nephew Cardinal Flavio. It is a very personal meditation on death, reflecting the thoughts of both patron and artist. The inconvenient requirement of incorporating a door into the monument became a positive feature, as Bernini made it the fulcrum of the composition: the pope, kneeling in prayer, with his tiara, symbol of his authority, at his side, humbly awaits divine mercy. Around him four Virtues are gathered. The two in the rear are barely visible in the dark, but the two in the front are portrayed in full, with Charity on the left rushing towards the pope and Truth on the right holding a sun symbol, reminiscent of one of Urban VIII's emblems. They extend themselves across a large sculpted cloth of Sicilian jasper from the folds of which, ominously, a skeletal hand holding an hourglass juts out from below. This is the hand of Death, warning us all that our time is finite, and his bony form looms out from the doorway, which has been transformed by Bernini into the passageway between this life and the next, in an elaboration of the same theme he had treated years earlier in the Chigi chapel in Santa Maria del Popolo. It can be quite disconcerting to see ordinary people, the custodians of the basilica for example, strolling through the door in the pope's tomb when it is open, so powerful is Bernini's illusion.

6 The Chigi art collection in the Galleria Nazionale, palazzo Barberini

When Don Ludovico Chigi Albani della Rovere sold his family palace to the Italian state in 1918, the package included many pieces of art and important furniture: 164 artworks entered the Galleria Nazionale in palazzo Barberini from the Chigi collection and many are visible today. Some of the Chigi art had already been part of a 1902 donation and still others were sold to the gallery in 1951.

The earliest significant piece from the collection of the principal Chigi collector, Cardinal Flavio I, is the *Rape of the Sabine Women* from the first or second decade of the sixteenth century, by Il Sodoma, the painter of the bedroom frescoes in the villa Farnesina for Agostino Il Magnifico. Flavio also owned a pair of paintings from Ferrara: the *Ascension of the Virgin* by Garofalo from c.1519 and Dosso Dossi's *Saints John and Bartholomew*. A later work connected with the same city is Guercino's *Flagellation of Christ* of 1657–8, commissioned by Cardinal Lorenzo Imperiali, legate to Ferrara, and given to Alexander VII. The pope's own taste is represented by a rare painting by Bernini of *David with the Head of Goliath* from c.1630, which was in the family collections by 1658, and by one of the pope's few commissions, the *Guardian Angel* of 1656 by Pietro da Cortona, which is full of dramatic light effects. An important Tintoretto, *Christ and the Woman Taken in*

Adultery of *c.*1545–50, was noted in an inventory of the Chigi collection in 1666. Two Poussins, both *Bacchanals with Putti* from *c.*1626, were noted in the same inventory, but they later passed by inheritance to the family of the Incisa della Rocchetta, who donated these canvases to the gallery in 1979.

Cardinal Flavio was very interested in secular art, as shown by his collection of portraits of beautiful noblewomen, now at the palazzo Chigi in Ariccia. Even in religious paintings he liked scenes where ordinary life intruded: thus the *Rest on the Flight into Egypt* by Angelo Caroselli (1585–1652) includes the presence of the midwife, offering the baby Jesus a flower, and a shepherdess with her flock. One of the paintings probably commissioned by Flavio himself, the *Allegory of Time* by the southern German painter Johann Heinrich Schönfeld (1609–83), shows Eros presenting his clipped wings to Old Father Time; it seems quite likely that this was a specific reference to Cardinal Flavio's not entirely contented chastity, which was strictly overseen by his uncle the pope. The cardinal also commissioned a *Pietà* from Baciccia in 1667, a beautiful and stately work which once hung in his audience room. Francesco Trevisani's *Allegories of the Continents* are the only representatives in the Galleria Nazionale of the work of this talented artist, favoured by the cardinal. The Sienese painter Bernardino Mei (1612–76) was one of Cardinal Flavio's preferred artists; his *Allegory of Fortune* from the 1660s depicts a philosopher scorning the riches offered to him, philosophy placing him above the vicissitudes of fortune. Perhaps this is a commentary on the earlier painting of the same subject by Salvator Rosa that caused controversy for its apparent attack on papal nepotism: here there is no trace of any such barb.

7 Other Chigi sites in Rome

I PIAZZA CAMPITELLI AND SANTA MARIA IN CAMPITELLI
Church entrance in piazza Campitelli. Open 8–12, 16–19

The church of Santa Maria in Campitelli owes its present condition to Alexander VII and to the plague of 1656–7. It contains a miraculous image, said to have been a divine present to a Roman noblewoman named Galla Patritia in AD 524, whose palace had a wing in it consecrated as a church by Pope John I. This was supposedly in part of the old Portico of Octavia, so the church was called Santa Maria in Portico. The image of the Virgin, a tiny picture in gold on a background of precious blue stone, was said to offer a cure for the plague, and its many devotees attested to the miracles it produced. The icon was said to be supernaturally linked to its church, as several different attempts to steal, loot, or move it had resulted in its magical return. This church, however, was located in a depressed region of the city further downriver. It was inconveniently close to the plague hospital on the Tiber Island in 1656 and, despite public outcry, the church was closed.

On 8 December 1656 the entire city government came to the church, and read a vow to improve the placement and situation of the holy image; from that day forwards it seemed that the plague began to abate. By March of the following spring the church had been reopened, 'with much rejoicing and celebration of the populace, as if Heaven itself had opened', according to a contemporary account. However, Alexander VII had visited the church in January and had already decided to move the image to a more salubrious location not far away, at Santa Maria in Campitelli. Santa Maria in Portico was in a poor quarter, but Santa Maria in Campitelli was surrounded by the palaces of Roman nobles, although both churches belonged to the same order, the Congregation of the Mother of God. Despite loud protests against the proposed move, the pope insisted that this was the only way for the city government to fulfil its vow. This was finally done, under cover of night, on 14 January 1662. Santa Maria in Portico was stripped and reconsecrated as Santa Galla, and eventually fell to Mussolini's demolition men. Santa Maria in Campitelli, for its part, had already been chosen for a massive reconstruction.

The old church of Santa Maria in Campitelli had been constructed in 1618–19 and enlarged in 1642–8, but Alexander's plans to enhance the dignity of the icon demanded that a new church be built. The palaces of the Capizucchi, Albertoni and Serlupi families surrounding the piazza not only added prestige to the new location, but also suggested possible donors for the new church. Alexander's coffers were emptier than ever by September 1662 when the first stone was laid, so the new church incorporated some of the structure of the old, in the nave, which was extended into a Greek cross. The architect was Carlo Rainaldi, *architetto del Popolo Romano*, the official civic chief of architecture, and he created a beautiful structure, with a high and complex façade that included the double tympanum (a curved one enclosed by a triangular one) made fashionable at Santa Maria della Pace by Pietro da Cortona. The Chigi arms decorated the tympanum until the eighteenth century, when they were replaced by those of the Capitoline government of Rome, whose parish church this was. Inside, the church's neighbours donated chapels. The Capizucchi chapel (second to the left) was intended as a rich monument to the posterity of that family, which was dying out. Beside it (first to the left) the Albertoni–Altieri chapel was paid for by the up-and-coming family formed by the merger of two families in the

Chiesa di S. Maria in Campitelli
: Casa de Chierici Regolari della Madre di Dio, a, Palacci dei Sig.i Serlupi, Fabrici, Paulucci, e Caporucchi. 3. Strada verso Piazza Montanara.

Santa Maria in Campitelli. The Servite monks abandoned Alexander VII's grand plan to build two symmetrical residences either side of the church façade, constructing the relatively humble monastery to the right.

district, the head of which, Emilio Altieri, ascended the papal throne in 1671 as Clement X. The Albertoni–Altieri chapel, in contrast to the Capizucchi, is without bombastic inscriptions: indeed, the tombs to either side are simply inscribed, with modish modesty, 'Shadow' and 'Nothing'. The shadows, of marble, and the nothing, of gold, speak more eloquently of the family's wealth and power than any inscription.

II THE PANTHEON AND PIAZZA DELLA MINERVA
Pantheon, Santa Maria ad Martyres, open 9–19 every day. Entrance in piazza della Rotonda

In the 1650s the Pantheon was in a bad way. Houses were attached to its great brick drum, while the ground level had risen above the level of the portico floor. Two columns were missing from the left of the portico and both sides were bricked up, with vendors' stalls backing against them. The piazza and the Pantheon itself were regularly flooded by the river and a faulty sewage system.

This situation did not accord with Alexander VII's idea of the dignity of the ancient church. In June 1656 the pope decided to move the market out of the square: in 1662, as the market was surprisingly persistent, he had the vendors forcibly removed to piazza di Pietra. Nine months later they were

Phœnx. Clauon. inuen.   S. Maria Rotunda.   Philipp. Gall. excud.   1.

A sixteenth-century view of the piazza in front of the Pantheon, showing buildings butted up against the Pantheon's portico, and with the persistent vendors at their trestle tables. Alexander VII struggled against them, but market forces prevailed.

back again. Alexander had the canons' house attached to the left-hand side of the Pantheon demolished, though the canons were permitted to rebuild it and to leave ground-floor space for shops, as long as the new building was set back from the piazza. This house was finally demolished only after Rome became capital of the kingdom of Italy. The pope also graded the piazza to one step below the floor of the portico, giving the façade 'majesty cleansed of sordidness', as he proclaimed in a medal commemorating the action. Alexander ordered the two missing columns to be replaced with ones that had fortuitously been discovered in the ruins of the Baths of Nero not far away, with recarved capitals that featured the Chigi star emblem.

Alexander also had ambitious plans for the interior of the ancient church, envisioning not just its cleaning and restoration but also its conversion into a monument to himself and his family. Plans exist among the Chigi documents (now in the Vatican Library) that show a new decorative scheme: a glazed lantern was to replace the open oculus in the dome, while the band round the oculus was to be given a large inscription bearing the pope's name, and the coffers of the dome decorated with the Chigi emblems of the *monti* and star amid rosettes. Only the pope's death prevented this appalling scheme from being carried out; even Bernini refused to be a part of it and the task of designing it devolved upon Carlo Fontana, whom we have met in the building of the gallery of palazzo Colonna.

Behind the Pantheon and to the left is the **piazza della Minerva**. In 1665 the Dominican fathers of the convent attached to Santa Maria sopra Minerva discovered a small obelisk buried in their garden, a relic of the old temple to Isis and Serapis. The following year Alexander VII considered different proposals for a monument incorporating the obelisk: one of the Dominican fathers, Domenico Paglia, suggested a design including his order's symbol of the dog ('*Domini canes*' means 'hounds of the Lord' in Latin), but Alexander rejected it in favour of an old plan Bernini had created, perhaps for the Barberini gardens, of an elephant supporting the obelisk. This was a conceit derived from an old favourite of Renaissance literature, the *Hypnerotomachia Poliphili*, which described a similar vision of a stone elephant bearing an obelisk.

The elephant, which was carved by Ercole Ferrata to Bernini's design, bears the Chigi arms on his saddlecloth, and the base of the statue contains inscriptions explaining that 'a strong mind is needed to support a solid knowledge', among other things. The elephant, an emblem of wisdom, was also a tribute to the wisdom of the pope. The author of the rejected scheme, Father Paglia, expressed alarm that the four legs of the statue would be separate and that the weight of the obelisk would not be supported directly from beneath: Bernini, a past master of the open void in sculpture, as in his fountain in piazza Navona, ridiculed this objection, but the aged and ill pope agreed that the legs should be carved in relief and the saddlecloth extended to conceal the stone behind. It is said that, in revenge, Bernini caused the elephant to be positioned with its rear end saluting the Dominican convent.

III   SANT' IVO AND THE SAPIENZA

Corso del Rinascimento 40. Sant' Ivo open 10–16 Monday–Saturday, closed July–August

The old university of Rome, the Studium Urbis founded by Boniface VIII Caetani in the early fourteenth century, had gone through many alterations, especially in the sixteenth century when the palace that housed it was rebuilt under Pius IV de' Medici. The works were carried on under Gregory XIII Boncompagni by Giacomo della Porta. Urban VIII gave the responsibility of completing the palace to Francesco Borromini, who designed the college chapel of Sant' Ivo in 1632, on a floor plan reportedly based on the proportions of the Barberini bee emblem. However, the works dragged on and it was only under Alexander VII that the complex was finished.

Sant' Ivo is perhaps Borromini's chief architectural work. Set at the back of the large palace courtyard, it perfectly dominates its own self-contained *teatro*, and its fantastical spiral lantern soars above one of the most elaborate of the city's domes. The front of the church, a simple but strong concave of brick, is surmounted by the Chigi *monti* and star at either end, in three dimensions. The interior, a tour de force of Baroque architecture, is dominated by the great dome, of alternating concave and convex, curved and cornered ribs, covered in white plaster, which also bear the Chigi arms, including the *monti* banded with three crowns corresponding to those of the papal tiara. The rear façade of the university building, on piazza di San Eustachio, was completed by Borromini during Alexander's pontificate. It presents a typical Borrominian series of inventions and contrasts, in a muted key: the flat surface of the palace façade is a base for the extravagant invention of the dome, which swells upwards and outwards above.

IV   THE VILLA CHIGI ALLA SALARIA
Entrance from via di Villa Chigi. Admission to park only

In 1763, for the cost of 3000 scudi, Cardinal Flavio II Chigi (1711–71), the grand-nephew of Alexander VII's *cardinal nipote*, acquired a vineyard and building to the north-east of Rome, off the ancient road called the via Salaria, 'in the place called Monte delle Gioie, and the street called of the Crucifix', an irregular and rather small property. The cardinal had the building enlarged by the architects Tommaso Bianchi and Pietro Camporese the Elder (1726–81), between 1763 and 1766, and had it furnished at the same time, finishing in 1771. As was the case in grander villas like that of the Borghese, this villa, too, was divided into different areas: one, alongside the villa building itself, was given over to formal gardens, while a second, on one side of a grand avenue, was left as an open field, and a third, on the other side, was used for the cultivation of olives. The villa was richly decorated and the interior, which is undergoing a lengthy restoration (the building is private property), still contains some of its original furniture as well as its wall and ceiling decoration. The property is accessible, though today it appears as a relatively undistinguished neighbourhood park, surrounded by the comfortable homes of the Salario district rather than, as in the eighteenth century, a pleasant country landscape.

Epilogue
The abolition of nepotism

Pontifical finances, already in decline due to diminishing revenues as early as the 1630s, continued to suffer with successive pontificates. The 900,000 scudi that Alexander VII transferred to his family during his reign was overshadowed two popes later by **Clement X Altieri** (1670–6), who gave his relatives, the Albertoni–Altieri, a startling 1,200,000 scudi during a relatively brief pontificate: his cardinal nephew was so concerned that the ailing pope would die before the massive reconstruction of palazzo Altieri on piazza del Gesù was complete that he had workmen building it round the clock, by torchlight during the dark hours. **Alexander VIII Ottoboni** (1689–91) managed to transfer 700,000 scudi of papal money to his nephews in only sixteen months and with little to show for it in terms of benefit to Rome, either artistically or architecturally.

The election of Antonio Pignatelli, a Neapolitan, as **Innocent XII** (1691–1700) marked a turning point in this increasingly sordid story. The kindly Innocent was not expected to upset the status quo, but to Rome's astonishment he issued a bull on 22 June 1692 abolishing the practice of papal nepotism. The bull forbade popes to transfer wealth to their relatives, even if they were needy, and it eliminated some of the more venal offices of state like that of captain-general of the Roman Church, the traditional preserve of the pope's chief secular relative, while strictly curtailing the salaries of other posts. Popes were only to create cardinals from among their relatives if the candidates showed particular merit and holiness, and their income was capped at 12,000 scudi, hitherto an amount sufficient for table expenses alone. Innocent XII also showed concern for the poor in his completion of the great poor hospital of San Michele a Ripa (today's ministry of cultural property), a veritable city in miniature containing trade schools, orphanages and even a women's prison. 'My true nephews are the poor,' said the pope.

Nepotism was not so easily suppressed and, despite these restrictions, the election of Lorenzo Corsini as **Clement XII** (1730–40) brought back a semblance of the good old days of patronage. The pope's nephew, Neri Corsini (1685–1770), was created cardinal immediately and six years later bought the old palazzo Riario, to begin its transformation into a huge Versailles-like family palace. The family chapel in San Giovanni in Laterano, the first such chapel in over a century, was one of Rome's first Neoclassical pieces of architecture: its designer, the pope's fellow Florentine Alessandro Galilei (1691–1737), had travelled in England and had been impressed by the writings of the Earl of Shaftesbury, who had argued in favour of a return to classical simplicity and formality. Galilei also designed the façade of San Giovanni in Laterano, the first construction in Rome to be paid for from the proceeds of the new state lottery, and put a front on the Florentine national church, San Giovanni dei Fiorentini at the end of the via Giulia. The pope's favourite architect, however, was another Florentine, Ferdinando Fuga (1699–1781). He received a number of major commissions during Clement's pontificate, including the palazzo della Consulta, the papal supreme court, on piazza del Quirinale, and the new façade of Santa Maria Maggiore: these were not Neoclassical at all, but rather Rococo. Finally Clement XII began to construct the long-delayed Trevi fountain to the designs of Nicola Salvi (1697–1751), a task which was to last throughout most of the subsequent two pontificates.

The last great palace to be built with the fruits of papal nepotism was palazzo Braschi (piazza San Pantaleo 10), during the reign of **Pius VI Braschi** (1775–99). Built on the site of an important Orsini palace that had undergone several reconstructions, it was given to the pope's nephew, Duke Luigi Onesti-Braschi (1745–1816), on the occasion of his marriage to Costanza Falconieri in 1780. The duke did not enjoy his colossal new palace, the work of the architect Cosimo Morelli of Imola (1732–1812), for very long. In 1798 the French occupied Rome and the pope was taken prisoner: he died in exile in France in 1799. Duke Luigi was also arrested and his palace expropriated, the statues removed to Paris, the furniture sold. After his release, Luigi was made provisional mayor during the occupation and he completed the palace, but it bankrupted him and when his heirs put the palace up for auction the papal government blocked the sale, reserving the palace for the use of visiting cardinals. At last, following the fall of the popes' temporal power in 1870, the Braschi creditors sold the palace to the Italian state. It served as the Ministry of the Interior, then, under the fascists, as the headquarters of the Rome Fascist Federation; during the post-war period it was occupied and damaged by squatters who inserted extra floors into the high-ceilinged rooms. Today, after a long restoration, it contains the Museo di Roma, which is still being arranged in the rooms at the time of writing. Its collections hold many interesting traces of Rome's noble families.

The last great family in Rome to sponsor art in the grand manner was the upstart immigrant family of **Torlonia**, Rome's Rothschilds. From humble beginnings in France, the family were cloth merchants and tailors in piazza di Spagna in the late eighteenth century and founded a modest bank. This bank was parlayed into a powerful force by the real founder of the

Torlonia fortunes, Giovanni Torlonia (1754–1829). In the aftermath of the French occupation the old Roman nobility was suffering from severe financial problems; the Torlonia bank offered them loans, upon non-payment of which many old properties swiftly fell into Torlonia hands. Title after title and villa after villa were the rewards of this clever banker's industry; his were the factories supplying the papal armies, his the agency which sold bread to the Roman poor.

The family quickly married into the Roman nobility whose properties it had already collected. In its first period of prominence the Torlonia family was keen to be seen to do the right thing with its wealth and founded orphanages, poor hospitals and schools, as well as refurbishing many churches. They gave the façade of San Pantaleo, next to the palazzo Braschi, a new Neoclassical look in 1806 by Giuseppe Valadier, the redesigner of piazza del Popolo, and in the subsequent decade the family redecorated the interior of the old Barberini church of San Bonaventura al Palatino. The palazzo Giraud in the Borgo, once the home of Cardinal Scipione Borghese, became a family seat, which it remains today, though another great palace, the palazzo Frangipane Bolognetti in piazza Venezia, was the real showpiece; it fell to Mussolini's demolition men when he expanded the piazza, though some of its painted decoration and furniture is now in the Museo di Roma. The last family chapel in Rome, the Torlonia chapel in San Giovanni in Laterano, dates from 1830–50, in the family's trademark Neoclassical style.

The Torlonia lost their charitable impulse once they had attained the social heights they sought; their schools are closed, their orphanages derelict. They rented their family villa, on the via Nomentana, to Mussolini as his own residence: it was there, on the very site of an ancient Jewish catacomb, that the dictator declared that 'the Jews have no historic place on Italian soil'. The villa, expropriated by the city government after years of post-war abandonment, is now slowly undergoing restoration. The richest of the modern Roman aristocrats, the Torlonia family witnessed the final years of noble power in Rome.

Chronology 1191–1878

Papal names in *ITALICS* are members of the principal families mentioned in this book. Important events both in Rome and abroad are noted during the relevant pontificates.

CELESTINE III (1191–8), *Giacinto Bobone Orsini*, Roman noble

INNOCENT III (1198–1216), Lotario de' Conti di Segni
   The pontificate of Innocent III is the high point of papal authority in the Middle Ages. This pope builds Rome's Tor de' Conti near the Forum.

HONORIUS III (1216–27), *Cencio Savelli*, Roman noble

GREGORY IX (1227–41), Ugolino, de' Conti di Segni, Roman noble

CELESTINE IV (October–November 1241), Goffredo Castiglioni

INNOCENT IV (1243–54), Sinibaldo de' Fieschi

ALEXANDER IV (1254–61), Rinaldo di Ienne

URBAN IV (1261–4), Jacques Pantaléon

CLEMENT IV (1265–8), Guy Foulques

GREGORY X (1271–6), Tebaldo Visconti

INNOCENT V (February–June 1276), Pierre de Tarentaise

ADRIAN V (July–August 1276), Ottobono Fieschi

JOHN XXI (1276–7), Petrus Juliani (Petrus Hispanus)

NICHOLAS III (1277–80), *Giovanni Gaetano Orsini*, Roman noble

MARTIN IV (1281–5), Simon de Brion

HONORIUS IV (1285–7), *Giacomo Savelli*, Roman noble

NICHOLAS IV (1288–92), Girolamo Masci

CELESTINE V (August–December 1294), Pietro da Morone

BONIFACE VIII (1294–1303), *Benedetto Caetani*, Roman noble
   This pope institutes the first jubilee year in 1300. His humiliation at Anagni at the hands of the French king and the Roman noble Sciarra Colonna represents the crash of the papacy's temporal power.

BENEDICT XI (1303–4), Niccolò Boccasini

CLEMENT V (1305–14), Bertrand de Got
   The papacy moves to Avignon in 1309, under the protection and control of the French crown. Until 1378, only Frenchmen are elected pope.

JOHN XXII (1316–34), Jacques d'Euse

BENEDICT XII (1334–42), Jacques Fournier
CLEMENT VI (1342–52), Pierre Roger
INNOCENT VI (1352–62), Stephen Aubert
URBAN V (1362–70), Guillaume de Grimoard
GREGORY XI (1370–8), Pierre Roger de Beaufort
> This pope returns the papacy to Rome in 1377 but dies soon afterwards.

URBAN VI (1378–89), Bartolomeo Prignano
> 1378, beginning of Great Schism. A rival papacy is established at
> Avignon; the last Avignonese antipope is deposed in 1430, while the
> legitimate succession remains at Rome.

BONIFACE IX (1389–1404), Piero Tomacelli
INNOCENT VII (1404–6), Cosimo de' Migliorati
GREGORY XII (1406–15), Angelo Correr
> To end the Great Schism, a church council is convened at Pisa in 1409,
> but this results merely in a third pope, 'John XXIII'. Only with Gregory
> XII's death and the removal of the council to Constance are the other
> popes deposed, whereupon Martin V is elected by the council.

MARTIN V (1417–31), Oddone Colonna, Roman noble
> This pope re-establishes the reunified papacy at Rome.

EUGENIUS IV (1431–47), Gabriel Condulmer
NICHOLAS V (1447–55), Tommaso Parentucelli
> Constantinople falls to the Turks in 1453, bringing the Byzantine
> Empire, the last vestige of the ancient Roman Empire, to an end;
> monks and scholars flee to Rome.

CALLIXTUS III (1455–8), Alfonso de Borja (Borgia)
PIUS II (1458–64), Enea Silvio Piccolomini
PAUL II (1464–71), Pietro Barbo
SIXTUS IV (1471–84), Francesco della Rovere
INNOCENT VIII (1484–92), Giovanni Battista Cibò
ALEXANDER VI (1492–1503), Rodrigo Borgia
> The Italian Wars begin in 1492 when Charles VIII of France invades
> Italy, with the intention of taking the crown of Naples. War on Italian
> soil between France and the Habsburg empire (the Holy Roman
> Empire and Spain) will continue until the mid sixteenth century, when
> Spanish dominance of the peninsula is established, controlling the
> duchy of Milan in the north and the kingdom of Naples in the south.

PIUS III (October 1503), Francesco Todeschini Piccolomini
JULIUS II (1503–13), Giuliano della Rovere, Roman noble
LEO X (1513–21), Giovanni de' Medici
ADRIAN VI (1522–3), Adrian Florenz
CLEMENT VII (1523–34), Giulio de' Medici

6–7 May 1527, Rome's defences are breached by Imperial troops, beginning the Sack of Rome, which will last for a year.

PAUL III (1534–49), Alessandro Farnese, Roman noble

JULIUS III (1550–5), Giovanni Maria Ciocci del Monte

MARCELLUS II (April–May 1555), Marcello Cervini

PAUL IV (1555–9), Gian Pietro Carafa

PIUS IV (1559–65), Giovan Angelo de' Medici

The French wars of religion begin in 1562, to be resolved only in 1598 with the edict of Nantes which guarantees religious toleration; this will be revoked by Louis XIV in 1685.

PIUS V (1566–72), Antonio Ghislieri

The sea battle of Lepanto in 1571 reassures Europe that the Turks can be defeated.

GREGORY XIII (1572–85), Ugo Buoncampagni

SIXTUS V (1585–90), Felice Peretti

URBAN VII (September 1590), Giovanni Battista Castagna

GREGORY XIV (1590–1), Niccolò Sfondrati

INNOCENT IX (November–December 1591), Giovan Antonio Facchinetti

CLEMENT VIII (1592–1605), Ippolito Aldobrandini

LEO XI (April 1605), Alessandro de' Medici

PAUL V (1605–21), Camillo Borghese, Roman noble

The terrible Thirty Years War begins in 1618, the final series of great European religious wars.

GREGORY XV (1621–3), Alessandro Ludovisi

URBAN VIII (1623–44), Maffeo Barberini

Louis XIII dies in 1643 and the Barberini protégé Giulio Mazzarino, Jules Mazarin, is regent for the young Louis XIV.

INNOCENT X (1644–55), Giambattista Pamphilj, Roman noble

The treaty of Westphalia is signed in October 1648, ending the Thirty Years War.

ALEXANDER VII (1655–67), Fabio Chigi

In 1661, the young king of France, Louis XIV (d. 1715), takes the reins of government following the death of his chief minister Cardinal Mazarin. This opens a new phase of French domination in European politics.

CLEMENT IX (1667–9), Giulio Rospigliosi

CLEMENT X (1670–6), Emilio Altieri, Roman noble

INNOCENT XI (1676–89), Benedetto Odescalchi

ALEXANDER VIII (1689–91), Pietro Ottoboni

INNOCENT XII (1691–1700), Antonio Pignatelli

CLEMENT XI (1700–21), Giovanni Francesco Albani

INNOCENT XIII (1721–4), Michelangelo de' Conti, Roman noble

BENEDICT XIII (1724–30), Pietro Francesco Orsini, Roman noble

CLEMENT XII (1730–40), Lorenzo Corsini

BENEDICT XIV (1740–58), Prospero Lorenzo Lambertini

CLEMENT XIII (1758–69), Carlo Rezzonico

CLEMENT XIV (1769–74), Giovanni Vincenzo Antonio Ganganelli

PIUS VI (1775–1799), Gianangelo Braschi

> In 1798, French troops under the command of Napoleon Bonaparte enter Rome and the city is declared a republic. Pius VI is taken to France in exile and dies there.

PIUS VII (1800–23), Barnaba Chiaramonti

> Napoleon is finally defeated at Waterloo in 1815 and the Congress of Vienna restores the old regime across Europe. Pius VII re-establishes papal rule in Rome.

LEO XII (1823–9), Annibale della Genga

PIUS VIII (1829–30), Francesco Saverio Castiglioni

GREGORY XVI (1831–46), Bartolomeo Alberto Cappellari

PIUS IX (1846–78), Giovanni Maria Mastai Ferretti

> In 1870, Rome falls to the new kingdom of Italy and Pius IX, the last pope-king, retreats to the Vatican; his successors are self-imprisoned there until a 1929 concordat, the *conciliazione*, creates the Vatican City as an independent state.

Family trees

COLONNA FAMILY TREE

a)   ORIGINS

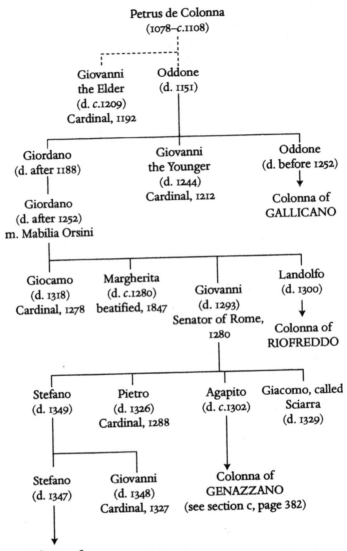

Petrus de Colonna
(1078–c.1108)

Giovanni
the Elder
(d. c.1209)
Cardinal, 1192

Oddone
(d. 1151)

Giordano
(d. after 1188)

Giovanni
the Younger
(d. 1244)
Cardinal, 1212

Oddone
(d. before 1252)

Colonna of
GALLICANO

Giordano
(d. after 1252)
m. Mabilia Orsini

Giocamo
(d. 1318)
Cardinal, 1278

Margherita
(d. c.1280)
beatified, 1847

Giovanni
(d. 1293)
Senator of Rome,
1280

Landolfo
(d. 1300)

Colonna of
RIOFREDDO

Stefano
(d. 1349)

Pietro
(d. 1326)
Cardinal, 1288

Agapito
(d. c.1302)

Giacomo, called
Sciarra
(d. 1329)

Colonna of
GENAZZANO
(see section c, page 382)

Stefano
(d. 1347)

Giovanni
(d. 1348)
Cardinal, 1327

Colonna of
PALESTRINA-CARBOGNANO
(see section b, page 381)

COLONNA FAMILY TREE

b)   COLONNA OF PALESTRINA-CARBOGNANO (Colonna di Sciarra)

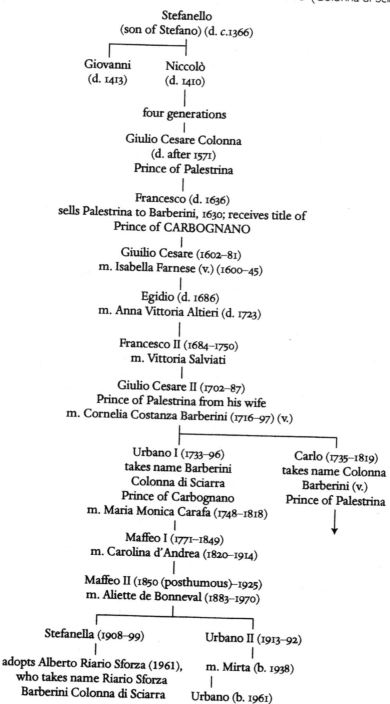

Stefanello
(son of Stefano) (d. *c*.1366)

Giovanni   Niccolò
(d. 1413)   (d. 1410)

four generations

Giulio Cesare Colonna
(d. after 1571)
Prince of Palestrina

Francesco (d. 1636)
sells Palestrina to Barberini, 1630; receives title of
Prince of CARBOGNANO

Giuilio Cesare (1602–81)
m. Isabella Farnese (v.) (1600–45)

Egidio (d. 1686)
m. Anna Vittoria Altieri (d. 1723)

Francesco II (1684–1750)
m. Vittoria Salviati

Giulio Cesare II (1702–87)
Prince of Palestrina from his wife
m. Cornelia Costanza Barberini (1716–97) (v.)

Urbano I (1733–96)   Carlo (1735–1819)
takes name Barberini   takes name Colonna
Colonna di Sciarra   Barberini (v.)
Prince of Carbognano   Prince of Palestrina
m. Maria Monica Carafa (1748–1818)

Maffeo I (1771–1849)
m. Carolina d'Andrea (1820–1914)

Maffeo II (1850 (posthumous)–1925)
m. Aliette de Bonneval (1883–1970)

Stefanella (1908–99)   Urbano II (1913–92)

adopts Alberto Riario Sforza (1961),   m. Mirta (b. 1938)
who takes name Riario Sforza
Barberini Colonna di Sciarra   Urbano (b. 1961)

COLONNA FAMILY TREE

c) COLONNA OF GENAZZANO, ZAGAROLO, AND PALIANO

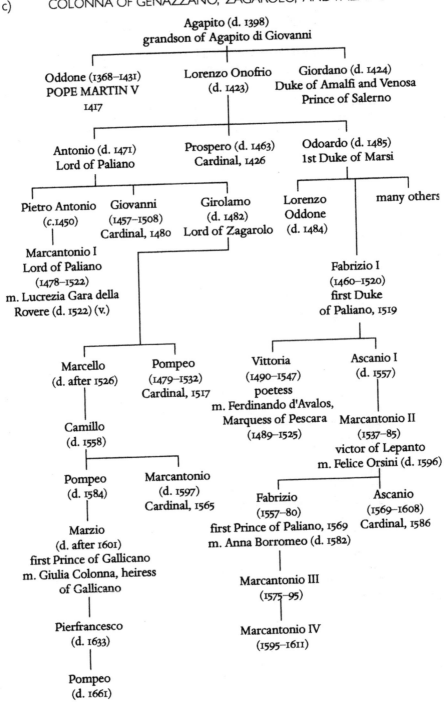

Agapito (d. 1398)
grandson of Agapito di Giovanni

Oddone (1368–1431)
POPE MARTIN V
1417

Lorenzo Onofrio
(d. 1423)

Giordano (d. 1424)
Duke of Amalfi and Venosa
Prince of Salerno

Antonio (d. 1471)
Lord of Paliano

Prospero (d. 1463)
Cardinal, 1426

Odoardo (d. 1485)
1st Duke of Marsi

Pietro Antonio
(c.1450)

Giovanni
(1457–1508)
Cardinal, 1480

Girolamo
(d. 1482)
Lord of Zagarolo

Lorenzo
Oddone
(d. 1484)

many others

Marcantonio I
Lord of Paliano
(1478–1522)
m. Lucrezia Gara della
Rovere (d. 1522) (v.)

Fabrizio I
(1460–1520)
first Duke
of Paliano, 1519

Marcello
(d. after 1526)

Pompeo
(1479–1532)
Cardinal, 1517

Vittoria
(1490–1547)
poetess
m. Ferdinando d'Avalos,
Marquess of Pescara
(1489–1525)

Ascanio I
(d. 1557)

Camillo
(d. 1558)

Marcantonio II
(1537–85)
victor of Lepanto
m. Felice Orsini (d. 1596)

Pompeo
(d. 1584)

Marcantonio
(d. 1597)
Cardinal, 1565

Fabrizio
(1557–80)
first Prince of Paliano, 1569
m. Anna Borromeo (d. 1582)

Ascanio
(1569–1608)
Cardinal, 1586

Marzio
(d. after 1601)
first Prince of Gallicano
m. Giulia Colonna, heiress
of Gallicano

Marcantonio III
(1575–95)

Pierfrancesco
(d. 1633)

Marcantonio IV
(1595–1611)

Pompeo
(d. 1661)

COLONNA FAMILY TREE

c)   COLONNA OF GENAZZANO, ZAGAROLO, AND PALIANO (cont'd)

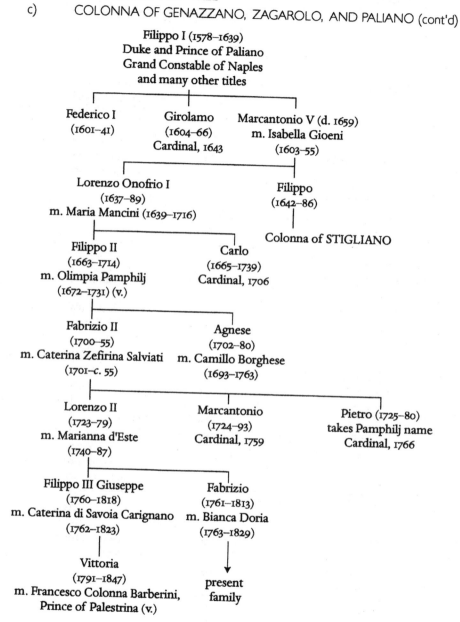

Filippo I (1578–1639)
Duke and Prince of Paliano
Grand Constable of Naples
and many other titles

Federico I
(1601–41)

Girolamo
(1604–66)
Cardinal, 1643

Marcantonio V (d. 1659)
m. Isabella Gioeni
(1603–55)

Lorenzo Onofrio I
(1637–89)
m. Maria Mancini (1639–1716)

Filippo
(1642–86)

Colonna of STIGLIANO

Filippo II
(1663–1714)
m. Olimpia Pamphilj
(1672–1731) (v.)

Carlo
(1665–1739)
Cardinal, 1706

Fabrizio II
(1700–55)
m. Caterina Zefirina Salviati
(1701–c. 55)

Agnese
(1702–80)
m. Camillo Borghese
(1693–1763)

Lorenzo II
(1723–79)
m. Marianna d'Este
(1740–87)

Marcantonio
(1724–93)
Cardinal, 1759

Pietro (1725–80)
takes Pamphilj name
Cardinal, 1766

Filippo III Giuseppe
(1760–1818)
m. Caterina di Savoia Carignano
(1762–1823)

Fabrizio
(1761–1813)
m. Bianca Doria
(1763–1829)

Vittoria
(1791–1847)
m. Francesco Colonna Barberini,
Prince of Palestrina (v.)

present
family

DELLA ROVERE/RIARIO FAMILY TREE

a) THE FAMILY OF SIXTUS IV

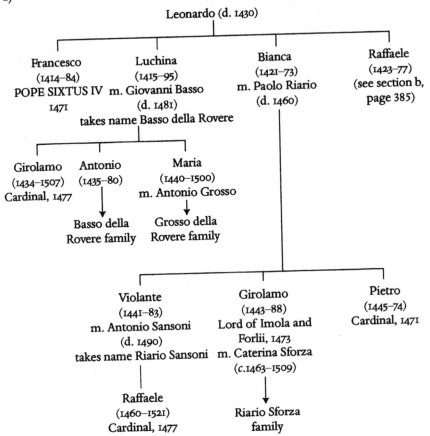

Leonardo (d. 1430)

Francesco
(1414–84)
POPE SIXTUS IV
1471

Luchina
(1415–95)
m. Giovanni Basso
(d. 1481)
takes name Basso della Rovere

Bianca
(1421–73)
m. Paolo Riario
(d. 1460)

Raffaele
(1423–77)
(see section b,
page 385)

Girolamo
(1434–1507)
Cardinal, 1477

Antonio
(1435–80)

Maria
(1440–1500)
m. Antonio Grosso

Basso della
Rovere family

Grosso della
Rovere family

Violante
(1441–83)
m. Antonio Sansoni
(d. 1490)
takes name Riario Sansoni

Girolamo
(1443–88)
Lord of Imola and
Forlii, 1473
m. Caterina Sforza
(c.1463–1509)

Pietro
(1445–74)
Cardinal, 1471

Raffaele
(1460–1521)
Cardinal, 1477

Riario Sforza
family

DELLA ROVERE/RIARIO FAMILY TREE

b)   THE FAMILY OF JULIUS II

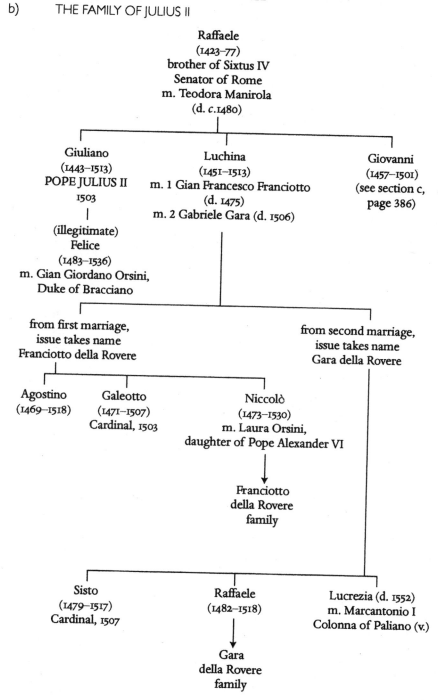

Raffaele
(1423–77)
brother of Sixtus IV
Senator of Rome
m. Teodora Manirola
(d. c.1480)

Giuliano
(1443–1513)
POPE JULIUS II
1503

(illegitimate)
Felice
(1483–1536)
m. Gian Giordano Orsini,
Duke of Bracciano

Luchina
(1451–1513)
m. 1 Gian Francesco Franciotto
(d. 1475)
m. 2 Gabriele Gara (d. 1506)

Giovanni
(1457–1501)
(see section c,
page 386)

from first marriage,
issue takes name
Franciotto della Rovere

from second marriage,
issue takes name
Gara della Rovere

Agostino
(1469–1518)

Galeotto
(1471–1507)
Cardinal, 1503

Niccolò
(1473–1530)
m. Laura Orsini,
daughter of Pope Alexander VI

Franciotto
della Rovere
family

Sisto
(1479–1517)
Cardinal, 1507

Raffaele
(1482–1518)

Gara
della Rovere
family

Lucrezia (d. 1552)
m. Marcantonio I
Colonna of Paliano (v.)

DELLA ROVERE/RIARIO FAMILY TREE

c) THE DELLA ROVERE DUKES OF URBINO

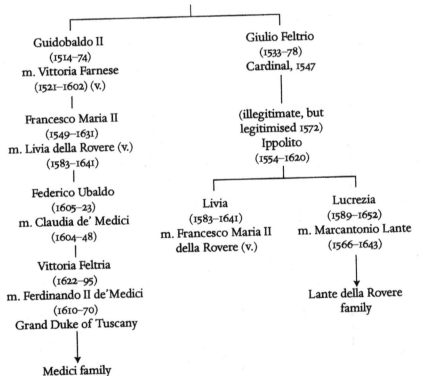

Giovanni
(1457–1501)
brother of Julius II
Prefect of Rome, 1475
m. Giovanna di Montefeltro
(1463–1514)
daughter of Guidobaldo I, Duke of Urbino

Francesco Maria I (1490–1538)
Duke of Urbino and Gubbio, 1513;
stripped of duchy by Leo X in 1516,
restored in 1523
m. Eleonora Gonzaga
(1493–1550)

Guidobaldo II
(1514–74)
m. Vittoria Farnese
(1521–1602) (v.)

Francesco Maria II
(1549–1631)
m. Livia della Rovere (v.)
(1583–1641)

Federico Ubaldo
(1605–23)
m. Claudia de' Medici
(1604–48)

Vittoria Feltria
(1622–95)
m. Ferdinando II de'Medici
(1610–70)
Grand Duke of Tuscany

Medici family

Giulio Feltrio
(1533–78)
Cardinal, 1547

(illegitimate, but
legitimised 1572)
Ippolito
(1554–1620)

Livia
(1583–1641)
m. Francesco Maria II
della Rovere (v.)

Lucrezia
(1589–1652)
m. Marcantonio Lante
(1566–1643)

Lante della Rovere
family

FARNESE FAMILY TREE

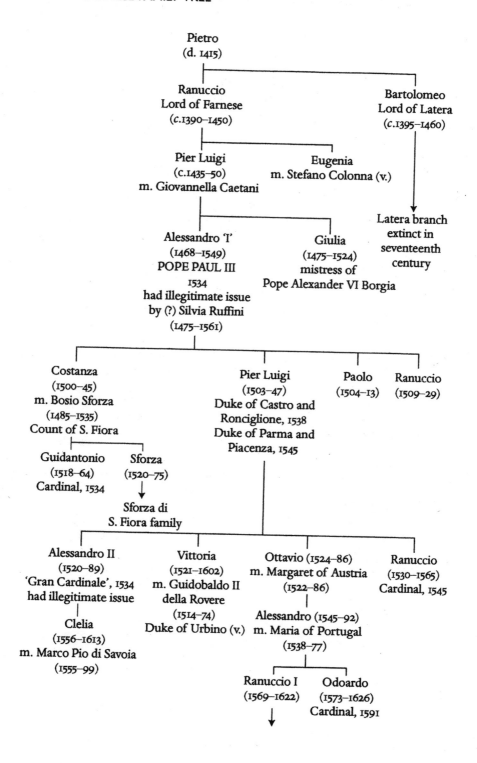

FARNESE FAMILY TREE

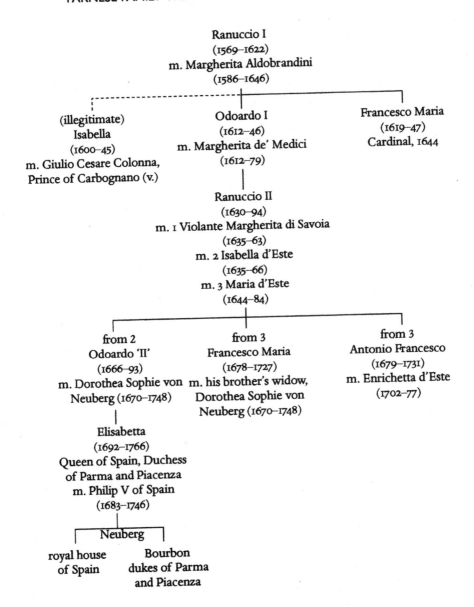

Ranuccio I
(1569–1622)
m. Margherita Aldobrandini
(1586–1646)

(illegitimate)
Isabella
(1600–45)
m. Giulio Cesare Colonna,
Prince of Carbognano (v.)

Odoardo I
(1612–46)
m. Margherita de' Medici
(1612–79)

Francesco Maria
(1619–47)
Cardinal, 1644

Ranuccio II
(1630–94)
m. 1 Violante Margherita di Savoia
(1635–63)
m. 2 Isabella d'Este
(1635–66)
m. 3 Maria d'Este
(1644–84)

from 2
Odoardo 'II'
(1666–93)
m. Dorothea Sophie von
Neuberg (1670–1748)

from 3
Francesco Maria
(1678–1727)
m. his brother's widow,
Dorothea Sophie von
Neuberg (1670–1748)

from 3
Antonio Francesco
(1679–1731)
m. Enrichetta d'Este
(1702–77)

Elisabetta
(1692–1766)
Queen of Spain, Duchess
of Parma and Piacenza
m. Philip V of Spain
(1683–1746)

Neuberg

royal house
of Spain

Bourbon
dukes of Parma
and Piacenza

BORGHESE FAMILY TREE

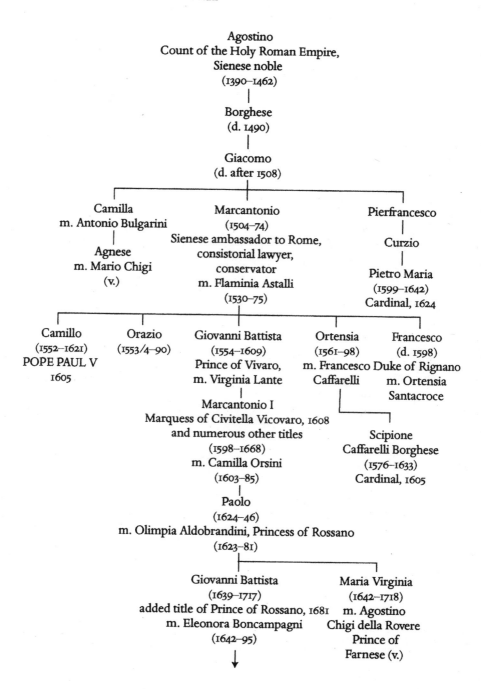

Agostino
Count of the Holy Roman Empire,
Sienese noble
(1390–1462)

Borghese
(d. 1490)

Giacomo
(d. after 1508)

Camilla
m. Antonio Bulgarini

Agnese
m. Mario Chigi
(v.)

Marcantonio
(1504–74)
Sienese ambassador to Rome,
consistorial lawyer,
conservator
m. Flaminia Astalli
(1530–75)

Pierfrancesco

Curzio

Pietro Maria
(1599–1642)
Cardinal, 1624

Camillo
(1552–1621)
POPE PAUL V
1605

Orazio
(1553/4–90)

Giovanni Battista
(1554–1609)
Prince of Vivaro,
m. Virginia Lante

Ortensia
(1561–98)
m. Francesco
Caffarelli

Francesco
(d. 1598)
Duke of Rignano
m. Ortensia
Santacroce

Marcantonio I
Marquess of Civitella Vicovaro, 1608
and numerous other titles
(1598–1668)
m. Camilla Orsini
(1603–85)

Scipione
Caffarelli Borghese
(1576–1633)
Cardinal, 1605

Paolo
(1624–46)
m. Olimpia Aldobrandini, Princess of Rossano
(1623–81)

Giovanni Battista
(1639–1717)
added title of Prince of Rossano, 1681
m. Eleonora Boncampagni
(1642–95)
↓

Maria Virginia
(1642–1718)
m. Agostino
Chigi della Rovere
Prince of
Farnese (v.)

BORGHESE FAMILY TREE

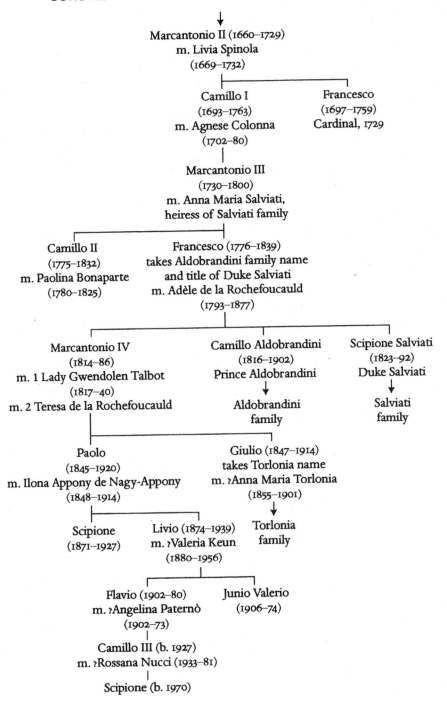

↓

Marcantonio II (1660–1729)
m. Livia Spinola
(1669–1732)

Camillo I
(1693–1763)
m. Agnese Colonna
(1702–80)

Francesco
(1697–1759)
Cardinal, 1729

Marcantonio III
(1730–1800)
m. Anna Maria Salviati,
heiress of Salviati family

Camillo II
(1775–1832)
m. Paolina Bonaparte
(1780–1825)

Francesco (1776–1839)
takes Aldobrandini family name
and title of Duke Salviati
m. Adèle de la Rochefoucauld
(1793–1877)

Marcantonio IV
(1814–86)
m. 1 Lady Gwendolen Talbot
(1817–40)
m. 2 Teresa de la Rochefoucauld

Camillo Aldobrandini
(1816–1902)
Prince Aldobrandini
↓
Aldobrandini
family

Scipione Salviati
(1823–92)
Duke Salviati
↓
Salviati
family

Paolo
(1845–1920)
m. Ilona Appony de Nagy-Appony
(1848–1914)

Giulio (1847–1914)
takes Torlonia name
m. ?Anna Maria Torlonia
(1855–1901)

Scipione
(1871–1927)

Livio (1874–1939)
m. ?Valeria Keun
(1880–1956)

Torlonia
family

Flavio (1902–80)
m. ?Angelina Paternò
(1902–73)

Junio Valerio
(1906–74)

Camillo III (b. 1927)
m. ?Rossana Nucci (1933–81)

Scipione (b. 1970)

BARBERINI FAMILY TREE

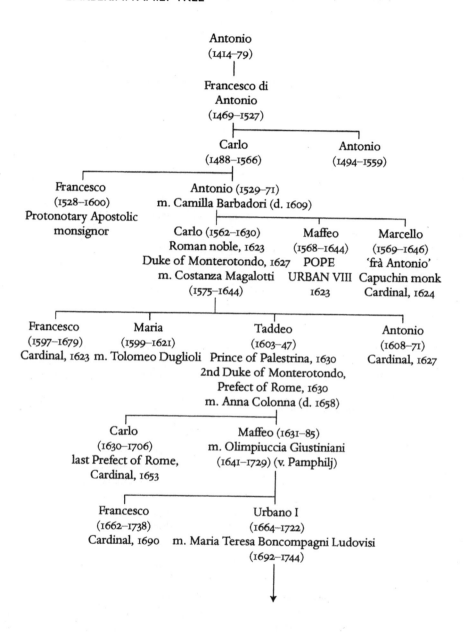

Antonio
(1414–79)

Francesco di
Antonio
(1469–1527)

Carlo
(1488–1566)

Antonio
(1494–1559)

Francesco
(1528–1600)
Protonotary Apostolic
monsignor

Antonio (1529–71)
m. Camilla Barbadori (d. 1609)

Carlo (1562–1630)
Roman noble, 1623
Duke of Monterotondo, 1627
m. Costanza Magalotti
(1575–1644)

Maffeo
(1568–1644)
POPE
URBAN VIII
1623

Marcello
(1569–1646)
'frà Antonio'
Capuchin monk
Cardinal, 1624

Francesco
(1597–1679)
Cardinal, 1623

Maria
(1599–1621)
m. Tolomeo Duglioli

Taddeo
(1603–47)
Prince of Palestrina, 1630
2nd Duke of Monterotondo,
Prefect of Rome, 1630
m. Anna Colonna (d. 1658)

Antonio
(1608–71)
Cardinal, 1627

Carlo
(1630–1706)
last Prefect of Rome,
Cardinal, 1653

Maffeo (1631–85)
m. Olimpiuccia Giustiniani
(1641–1729) (v. Pamphilj)

Francesco
(1662–1738)
Cardinal, 1690

Urbano I
(1664–1722)
m. Maria Teresa Boncompagni Ludovisi
(1692–1744)

BARBERINI FAMILY TREE

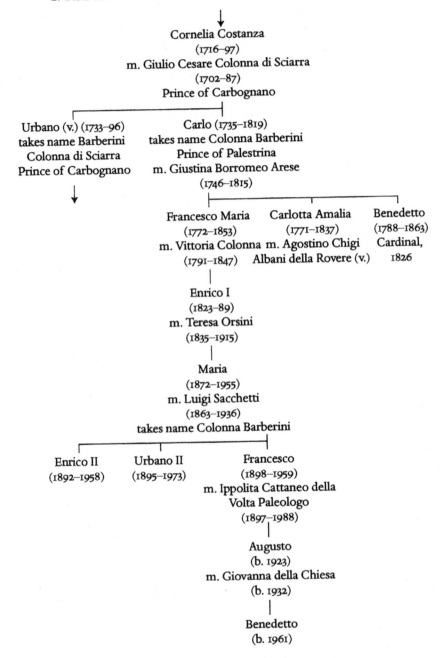

↓

Cornelia Costanza
(1716–97)
m. Giulio Cesare Colonna di Sciarra
(1702–87)
Prince of Carbognano

Urbano (v.) (1733–96)
takes name Barberini
Colonna di Sciarra
Prince of Carbognano

↓

Carlo (1735–1819)
takes name Colonna Barberini
Prince of Palestrina
m. Giustina Borromeo Arese
(1746–1815)

Francesco Maria
(1772–1853)
m. Vittoria Colonna
(1791–1847)

Carlotta Amalia
(1771–1837)
m. Agostino Chigi
Albani della Rovere (v.)

Benedetto
(1788–1863)
Cardinal,
1826

Enrico I
(1823–89)
m. Teresa Orsini
(1835–1915)

Maria
(1872–1955)
m. Luigi Sacchetti
(1863–1936)
takes name Colonna Barberini

Enrico II
(1892–1958)

Urbano II
(1895–1973)

Francesco
(1898–1959)
m. Ippolita Cattaneo della
Volta Paleologo
(1897–1988)

Augusto
(b. 1923)
m. Giovanna della Chiesa
(b. 1932)

Benedetto
(b. 1961)

PAMPHILJ AND DORIA-PAMPHILJ LANDI FAMILY TREE

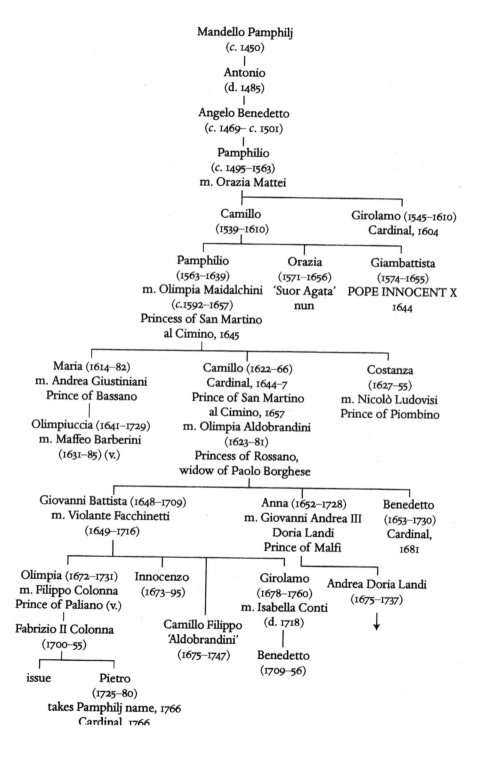

Mandello Pamphilj
(c. 1450)

Antonio
(d. 1485)

Angelo Benedetto
(c. 1469– c. 1501)

Pamphilio
(c. 1495–1563)
m. Orazia Mattei

Camillo
(1539–1610)

Girolamo (1545–1610)
Cardinal, 1604

Pamphilio
(1563–1639)
m. Olimpia Maidalchini
(c.1592–1657)
Princess of San Martino
al Cimino, 1645

Orazia
(1571–1656)
'Suor Agata'
nun

Giambattista
(1574–1655)
POPE INNOCENT X
1644

Maria (1614–82)
m. Andrea Giustiniani
Prince of Bassano

Olimpiuccia (1641–1729)
m. Maffeo Barberini
(1631–85) (v.)

Camillo (1622–66)
Cardinal, 1644-7
Prince of San Martino
al Cimino, 1657
m. Olimpia Aldobrandini
(1623–81)
Princess of Rossano,
widow of Paolo Borghese

Costanza
(1627–55)
m. Nicolò Ludovisi
Prince of Piombino

Giovanni Battista (1648–1709)
m. Violante Facchinetti
(1649–1716)

Anna (1652–1728)
m. Giovanni Andrea III
Doria Landi
Prince of Malfi

Benedetto
(1653–1730)
Cardinal,
1681

Olimpia (1672–1731)
m. Filippo Colonna
Prince of Paliano (v.)

Fabrizio II Colonna
(1700–55)

Innocenzo
(1673–95)

Girolamo
(1678–1760)
m. Isabella Conti
(d. 1718)

Andrea Doria Landi
(1675–1737)

↓

Camillo Filippo
'Aldobrandini'
(1675–1747)

Benedetto
(1709–56)

issue

Pietro
(1725–80)
takes Pamphilj name, 1766
Cardinal 1766

PAMPHILJ AND DORIA-PAMPHILJ LANDI FAMILY TREE

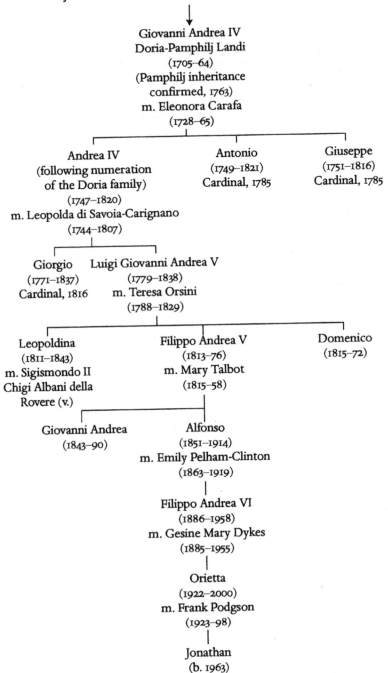

Giovanni Andrea IV
Doria-Pamphilj Landi
(1705–64)
(Pamphilj inheritance
confirmed, 1763)
m. Eleonora Carafa
(1728–65)

Andrea IV
(following numeration
of the Doria family)
(1747–1820)
m. Leopolda di Savoia-Carignano
(1744–1807)

Antonio
(1749–1821)
Cardinal, 1785

Giuseppe
(1751–1816)
Cardinal, 1785

Giorgio
(1771–1837)
Cardinal, 1816

Luigi Giovanni Andrea V
(1779–1838)
m. Teresa Orsini
(1788–1829)

Leopoldina
(1811–1843)
m. Sigismondo II
Chigi Albani della
Rovere (v.)

Filippo Andrea V
(1813–76)
m. Mary Talbot
(1815–58)

Domenico
(1815–72)

Giovanni Andrea
(1843–90)

Alfonso
(1851–1914)
m. Emily Pelham-Clinton
(1863–1919)

Filippo Andrea VI
(1886–1958)
m. Gesine Mary Dykes
(1885–1955)

Orietta
(1922–2000)
m. Frank Podgson
(1923–98)

Jonathan
(b. 1963)

CHIGI FAMILY TREE

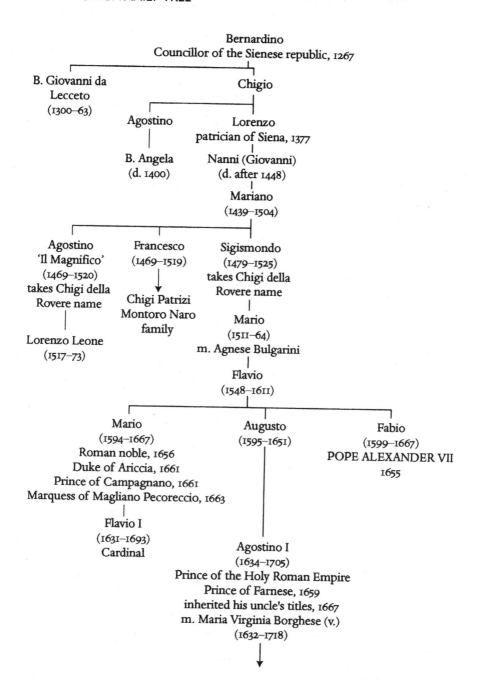

Bernardino
Councillor of the Sienese republic, 1267

B. Giovanni da
Leccerto
(1300–63)

Chigio

Agostino

Lorenzo
patrician of Siena, 1377

B. Angela
(d. 1400)

Nanni (Giovanni)
(d. after 1448)

Mariano
(1439–1504)

Agostino
'Il Magnifico'
(1469–1520)
takes Chigi della
Rovere name

Lorenzo Leone
(1517–73)

Francesco
(1469–1519)

Chigi Patrizi
Montoro Naro
family

Sigismondo
(1479–1525)
takes Chigi della
Rovere name

Mario
(1511–64)
m. Agnese Bulgarini

Flavio
(1548–1611)

Mario
(1594–1667)
Roman noble, 1656
Duke of Ariccia, 1661
Prince of Campagnano, 1661
Marquess of Magliano Pecoreccio, 1663

Flavio I
(1631–1693)
Cardinal

Augusto
(1595–1651)

Fabio
(1599–1667)
POPE ALEXANDER VII
1655

Agostino I
(1634–1705)
Prince of the Holy Roman Empire
Prince of Farnese, 1659
inherited his uncle's titles, 1667
m. Maria Virginia Borghese (v.)
(1632–1718)

CHIGI FAMILY TREE

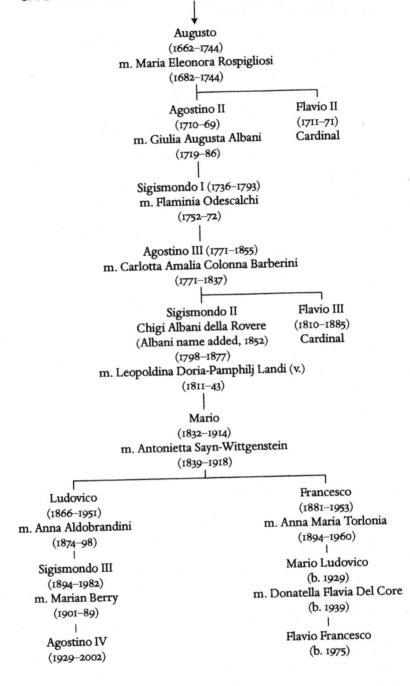

Augusto
(1662–1744)
m. Maria Eleonora Rospigliosi
(1682–1744)

Agostino II
(1710–69)
m. Giulia Augusta Albani
(1719–86)

Flavio II
(1711–71)
Cardinal

Sigismondo I (1736–1793)
m. Flaminia Odescalchi
(1752–72)

Agostino III (1771–1855)
m. Carlotta Amalia Colonna Barberini
(1771–1837)

Sigismondo II
Chigi Albani della Rovere
(Albani name added, 1852)
(1798–1877)
m. Leopoldina Doria-Pamphilj Landi (v.)
(1811–43)

Flavio III
(1810–1885)
Cardinal

Mario
(1832–1914)
m. Antonietta Sayn-Wittgenstein
(1839–1918)

Ludovico
(1866–1951)
m. Anna Aldobrandini
(1874–98)

Sigismondo III
(1894–1982)
m. Marian Berry
(1901–89)

Agostino IV
(1929–2002)

Francesco
(1881–1953)
m. Anna Maria Torlonia
(1894–1960)

Mario Ludovico
(b. 1929)
m. Donatella Flavia Del Core
(b. 1939)

Flavio Francesco
(b. 1975)

Index of Places

Index of Names